STOP!

This is the back of the book.
You wouldn't want to spoil a great ending!

This book is printed "manga-style," in the authentic Japanese right-to-left format. Since none of the artwork has been flipped or altered, readers get to experience the story just as the creator intended. You've been asking for it, so TOKYOPOP® delivered: authentic, hot-off-the-press, and far more fun!

DIRECTIONS

If this is your first time reading manga-style, here's a quick guide to help you understand how it works.

It's easy... just start in the top right panel and follow the numbers. Have fun, and look for more 100% authentic manga from TOKYOPOP®!

Follow the MAGICAL and MYSTERIOUS adventures of Mikan at the Alice Academy!

Young Mikan runs away to Tokyo after her best friend is transferred to an exclusive and secretive private school for geniuses. But there is more to Alice Academy than meets the eye—it is actually home to children with special powers. If Mikan wants to stay by her friend's side—and stay *alive*— she must discover the Alice that lives within her!

The huge, new series from Japan with more than **3 MILLION BOOKS SOLD!**

FANTASY

T TEEN AGE 13+

© TACHIBANA HIGUCHI / Hakusensha, Inc.

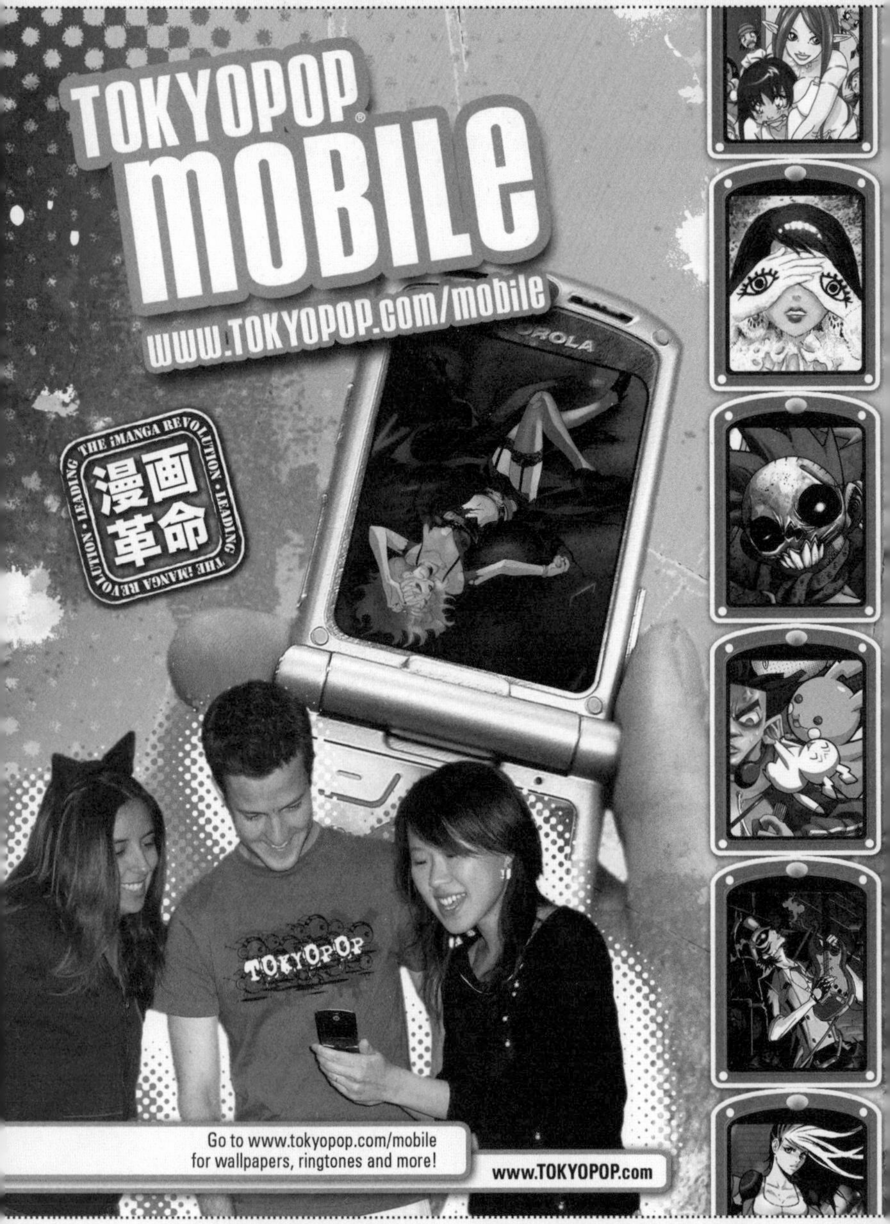
TOKYOPOP® MOBILE
www.TOKYOPOP.com/mobile
THE iMANGA REVOLUTION • LEADING
漫画革命
Go to www.tokyopop.com/mobile
for wallpapers, ringtones and more!
www.TOKYOPOP.com

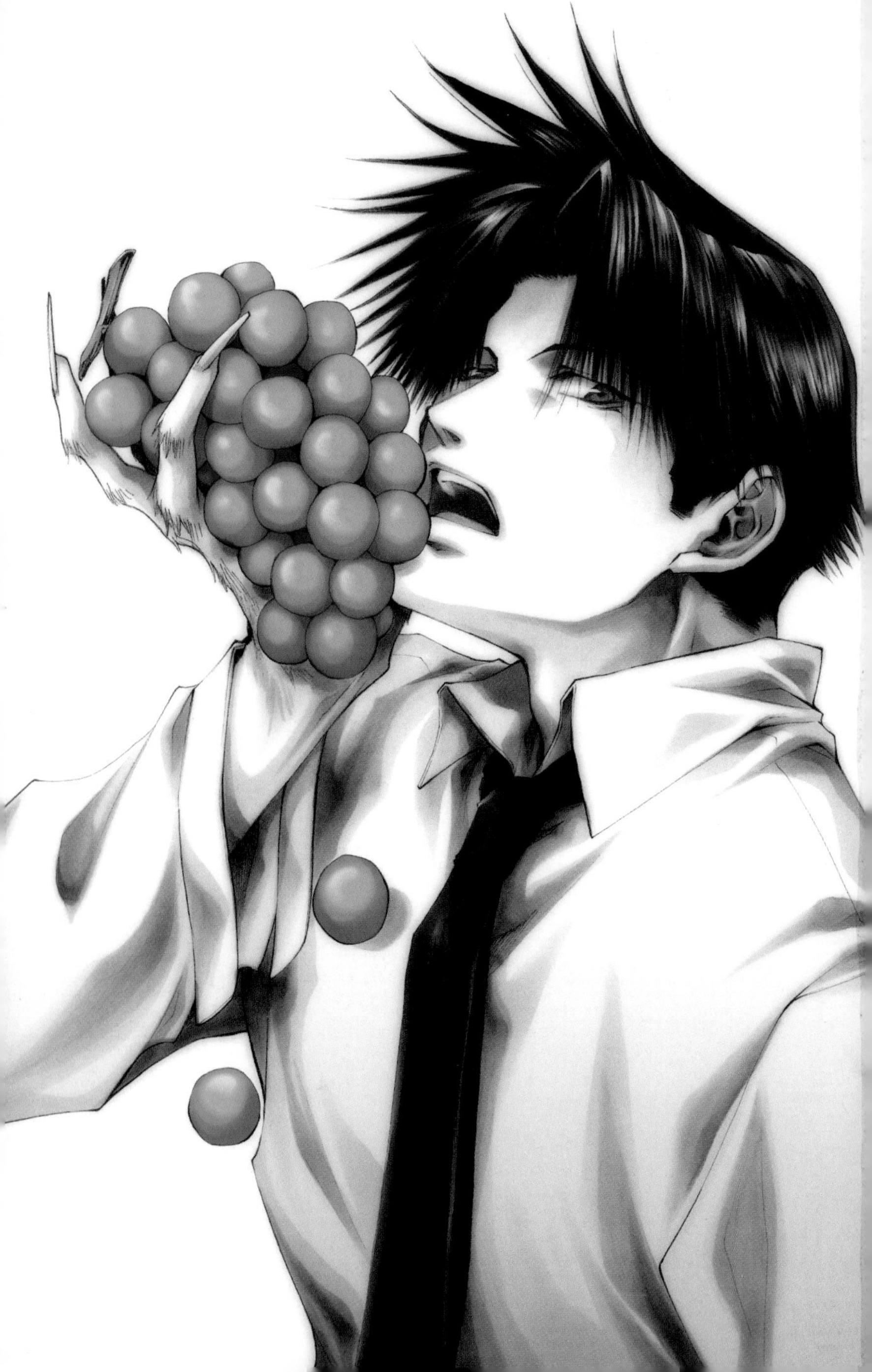

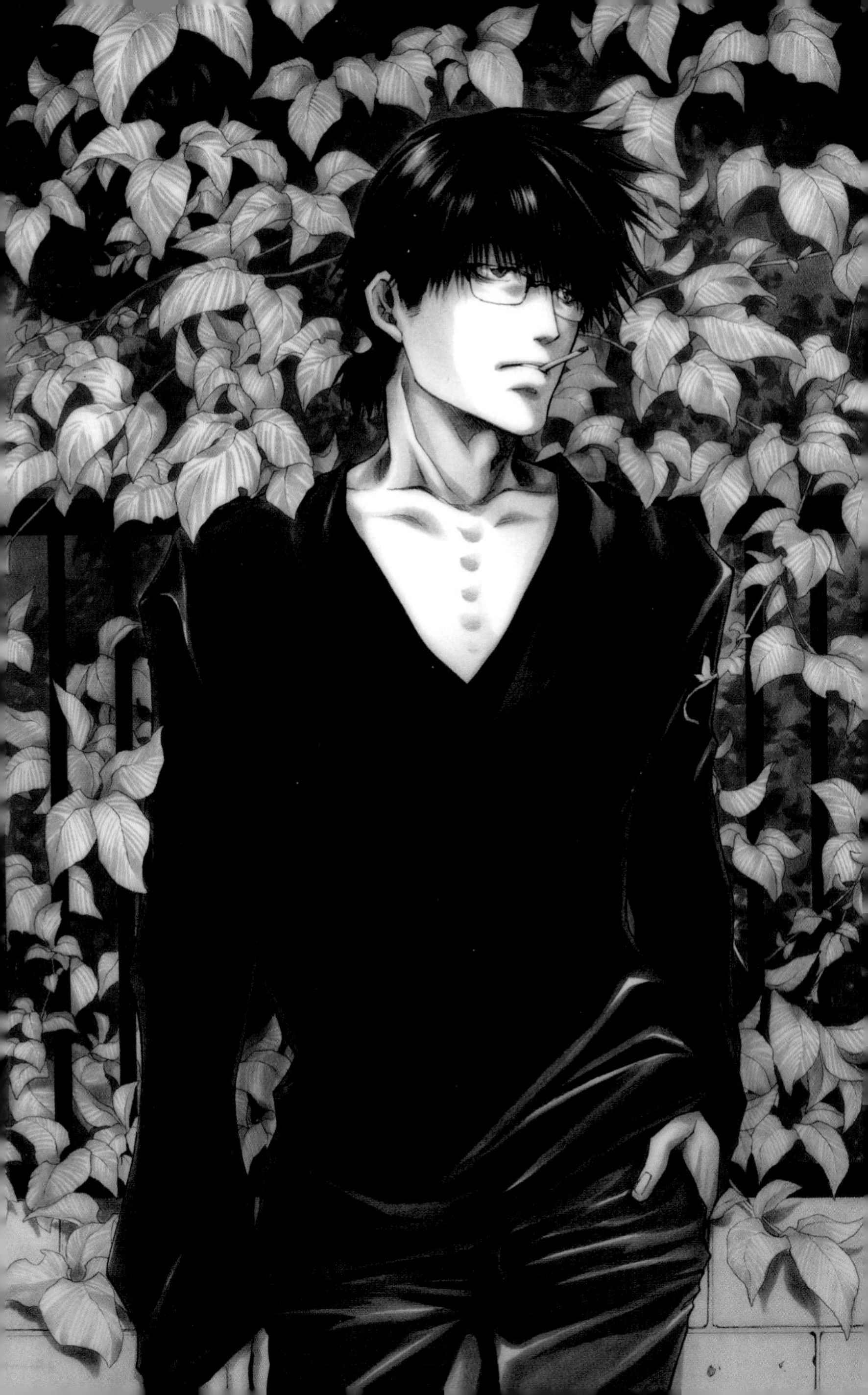

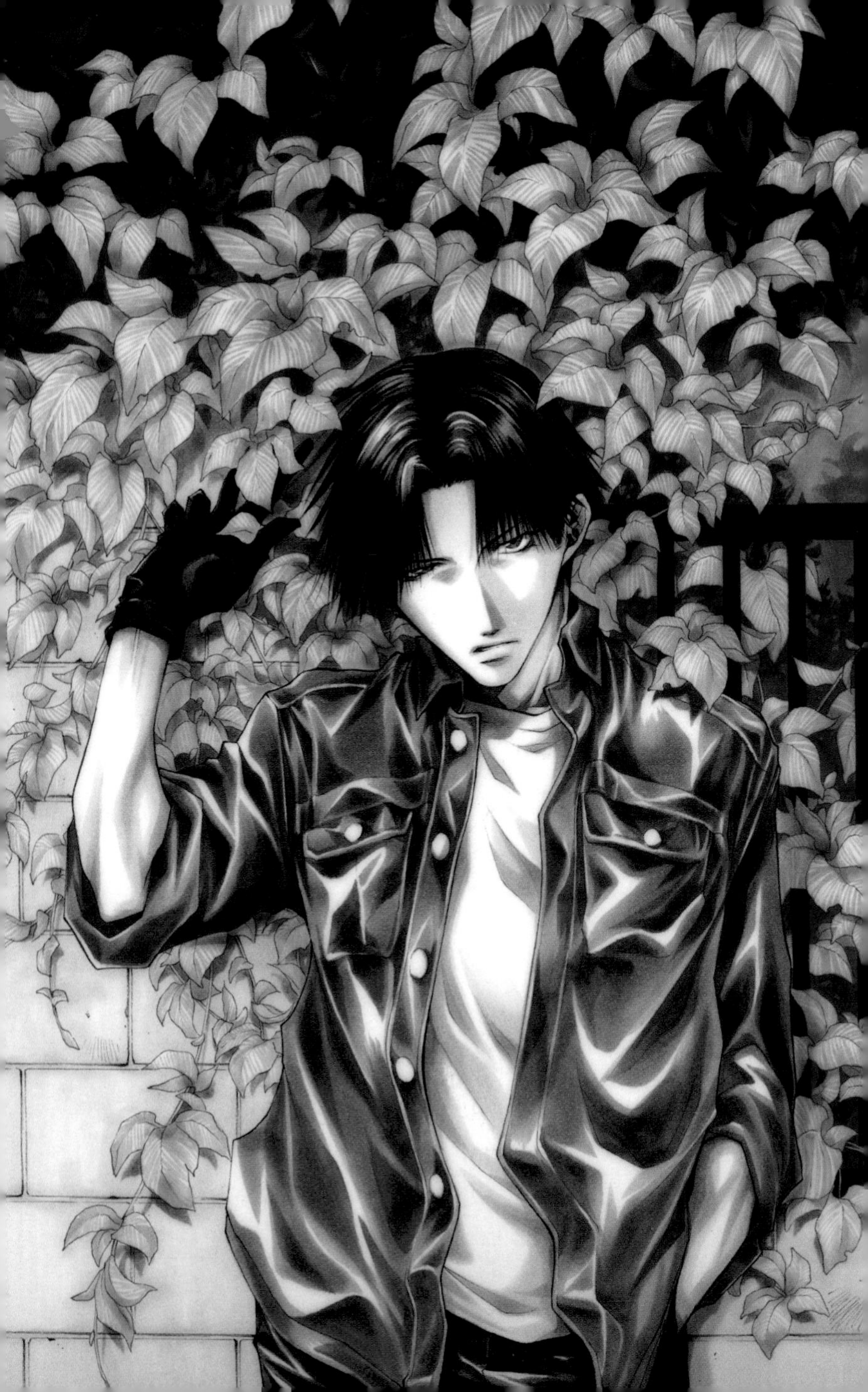

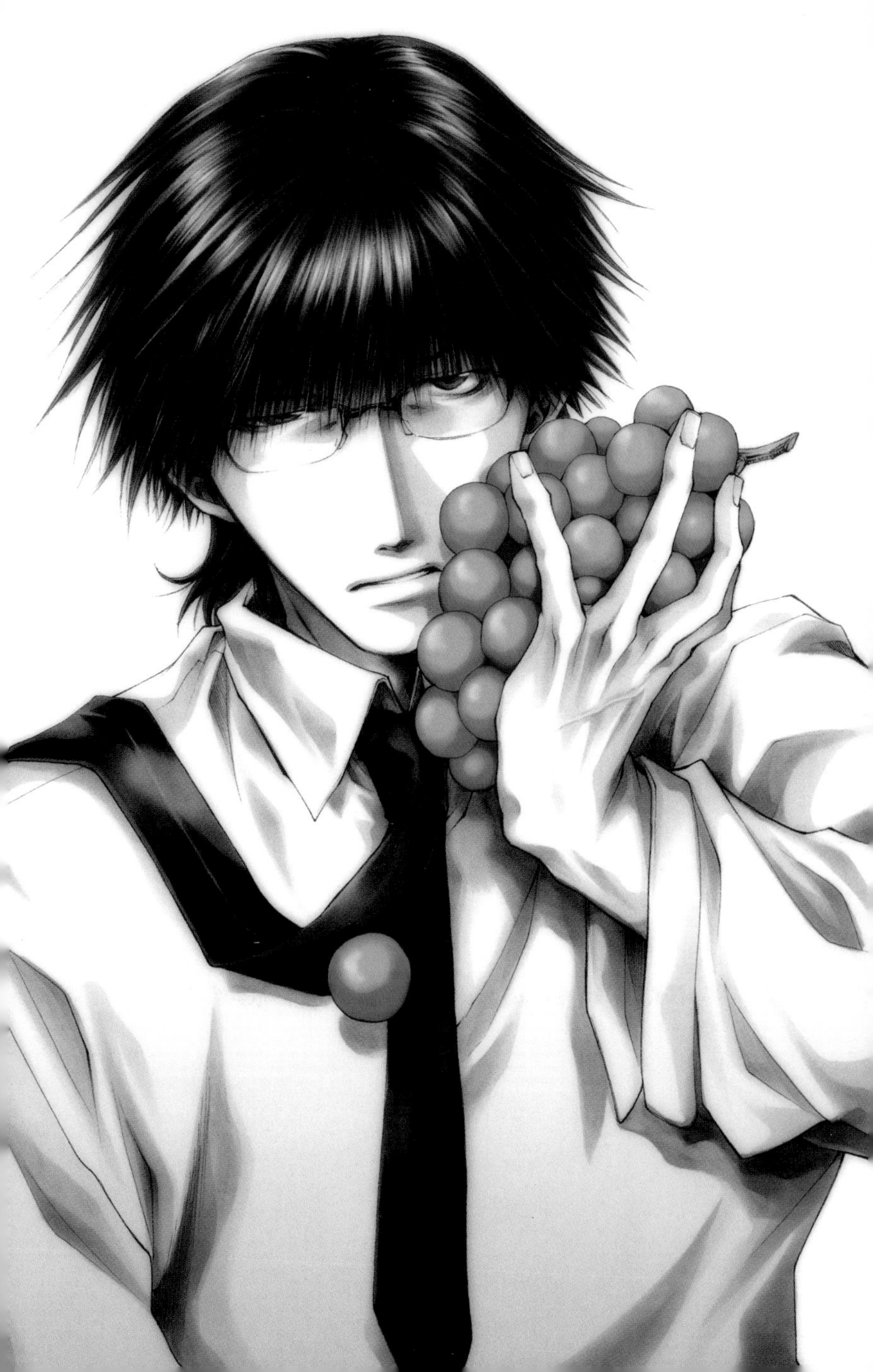

WILD ADAPTER

vol.4

by Kazuya Minekura

HAMBURG // LONDON // LOS ANGELES // TOKYO

Wild Adapter Volume 4
Created by Kazuya Minekura

Translation - Alexis Kirsch
English Adaptation - Christine Boylan
Retouch and Lettering - Star Print Brokers
Graphic Designer - Louis Csontos

Editor - Lillian Diaz-Przybyl
Digital Imaging Manager - Chris Buford
Pre-Production Supervisor - Erika Terriquez
Production Manager - Elisabeth Brizzi
Managing Editor - Vy Nguyen
Creative Director - Anne Marie Horne
Editor-in-Chief - Rob Tokar
Publisher - Mike Kiley
President and C.O.O. - John Parker
C.E.O. and Chief Creative Officer - Stuart Levy

A 🐸 **TOKYOPOP** Manga

TOKYOPOP Inc.
5900 Wilshire Blvd. Suite 2000
Los Angeles, CA 90036

E-mail: info@TOKYOPOP.com
Come visit us online at www.TOKYOPOP.com

ISBN: 978-1-59816-981-2

First TOKYOPOP printing: February 2008
10 9 8 7 6 5 4 3 2 1
Printed in the USA

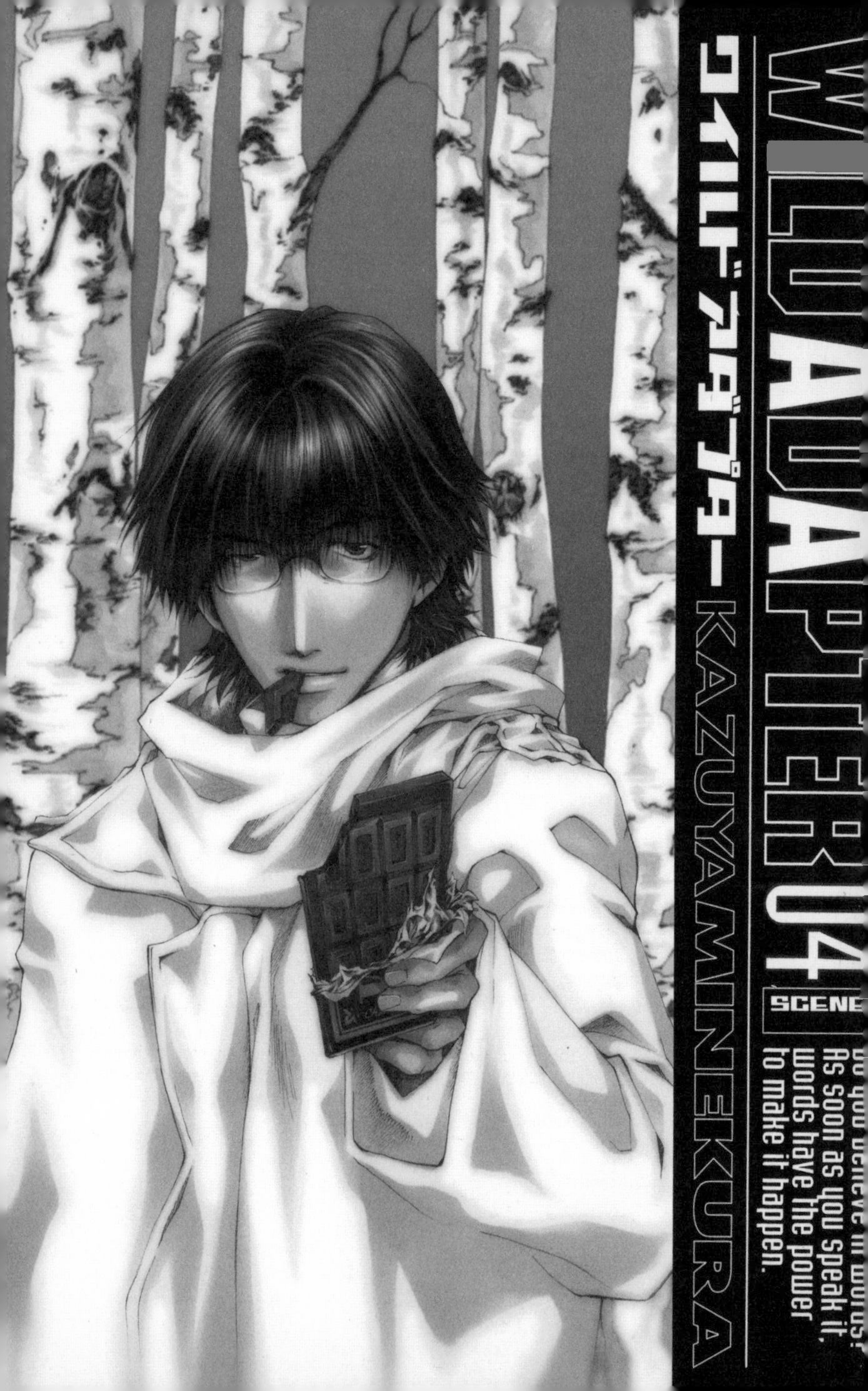
W LD ADAPTER
SCENE 04
ワイルドアダプター
KAZUYA MINEKURA
Do you believe in words?
As soon as you speak it,
words have the power
to make it happen.

WILD ADAPTER 04

ワイルドアダプター

KAZUYA MINEKURA

CONTENTS

SCENE:

Do you believe in words?
As soon as you speak it,
words have the power
to make it happen.

CHARACTERS:

MAKOTO KUBOTA:
ILLEGITIMATE SON OF THE SHADOWY SEIJI MUNAKATA, KUBOTA IS FASCINATED BY EVERYTHING BUT ATTACHED TO NOTHING. AFTER JOINING IZUMO MORE OR LESS ON A WHIM, HIS CALM EXTERIOR LEADS ENEMIES AND FRIENDS ALIKE TO UNDERESTIMATE HIM, UNTIL KUBOTA DESTROYS TOJOU'S HEADQUARTERS ON HIS WAY OUT OF THE YAKUZA WORLD.

MINORU TOKITO:
A YOUNG MAN WITH NO MEMORIES OF THE PAST, AND A CREEPY ANIMAL-LIKE HAND REMINISCENT OF THE DEAD BODIES LEFT BEHIND IN THE WAKE OF THE NEW DRUG WILD ADAPTER. KUBOTA LITERALLY PICKS HIM UP OFF THE STREET, AND THE TWO NOW LIVE TOGETHER. BRASH AND BOISTEROUS, IN CONTRAST TO KUBOTA'S ETERNALLY PLACID FAÇADE, TOKITO SEEMS TO BE THE ONE PERSON WHO KUBOTA REALLY CARES ABOUT.

KASAI:
KUBOTA'S UNCLE AND A LOCAL POLICE DETECTIVE. AN EXCELLENT MAHJONG PLAYER, AND A BIT OF A CROOKED COP, KASAI IS INVESTIGATING WILD ADAPTER WHILE TRYING TO KEEP KUBOTA OUT OF TROUBLE.

SANADA AND SEKIYA:
RIVAL HEADS OF RIVAL YAKUZA ORGANIZATIONS, BOTH HAVE THEIR OWN REASONS FOR PURSUING WILD ADAPTER, AND APPARENTLY KUBOTA, AS WELL.

KOU:
AN UNLICENSED PHYSICIAN AND PHARMACIST WORKING OUT OF YOKOHAMA'S CHINATOWN, KOU SELLS INFORMATION AND ILLEGAL GOODS ALONG WITH HIS MEDICAL SERVICES. HE OCCASIONALLY EMPLOYS KUBOTA ON A PART-TIME BASIS FOR DELIVERIES AND KEEPS A WARY EYE ON TOKITO'S RIGHT HAND.

STORY SO FAR:

MAKOTO KUBOTA'S TIME WITH THE IZUMO CRIME SYNDICATE IS SHORT-LIVED AND BLOODY. AFTER TAKING OVER AS THE HEAD OF THE ORGANIZATION'S YOUTH GANG, HE SPENDS SEVEN MONTHS PLAYING VIDEO GAMES WITH HIS YOUNG COHORTS, BEFRIENDING SMALL ANIMALS AND WRECKING RIVAL YOUTH GANGS UNTIL HIS ONE FRIEND IN IZUMO IS KILLED OVER A MYSTERIOUS DRUG CALLED "WILD ADAPTER." KUBOTA QUITS THE YAKUZA, TAKING OUT THE HEAD OF THE RIVAL TOJOU ORGANIZATION AS A PARTING GIFT. BUT SANADA, THE CURRENT BOSS OF IZUMO, ISN'T QUITE SATISFIED WITH THIS TURN OF EVENTS.

MEANWHILE, GRUESOME CORPSES HAVE BEEN TURNING UP ON THE STREETS OF YOKOHAMA, MONSTROUSLY DEFORMED, AND ALL SEEMINGLY CONNECTED TO THE APPEARANCE OF W.A. IZUMO AND TOJOU BOTH WANT TO GET AHOLD OF THIS NEW DRUG, AND AFTER KUBOTA PICKS UP A STRAY YOUNG MAN WITH A BEAST-LIKE RIGHT HAND, HE MAY BE STUCK IN THE MIDDLE OF A GROWING YAKUZA WAR.

ALMOST TWO YEARS HAVE PASSED, AND WHILE KUBOTA AND HIS NEW ROOMMATE, TOKITO, HAVE GROWN CLOSER TO EACH OTHER, THEY DON'T SEEM TO BE ANY CLOSER TO SOLVING THE MYSTERY BEHIND TOKITO'S FREAKISH HAND... ALTHOUGH AN ENCOUNTER WITH A BIZARRE CULT BRIEFLY SENDS TOKITO INTO A STATE OF SHOCK, DURING WHICH HE CRIES OUT AGAINST A MYSTERIOUS MAN NAMED "AKIRA."

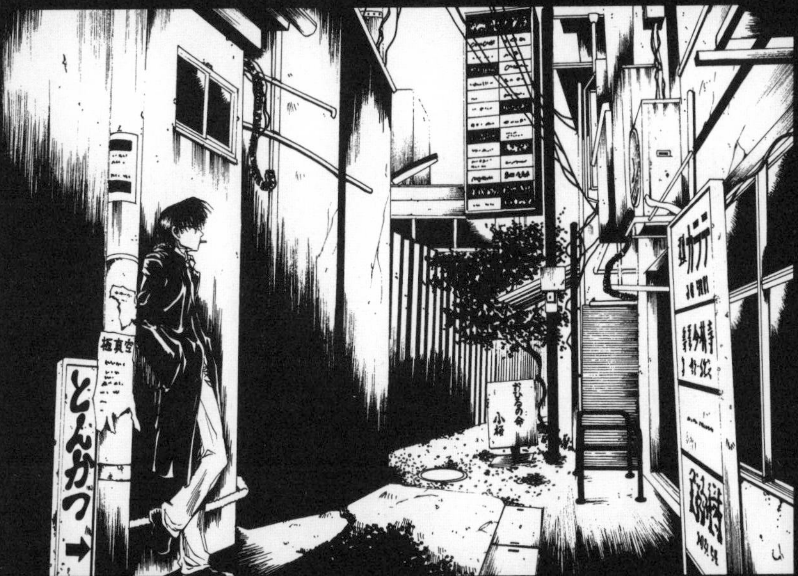
とんかつ

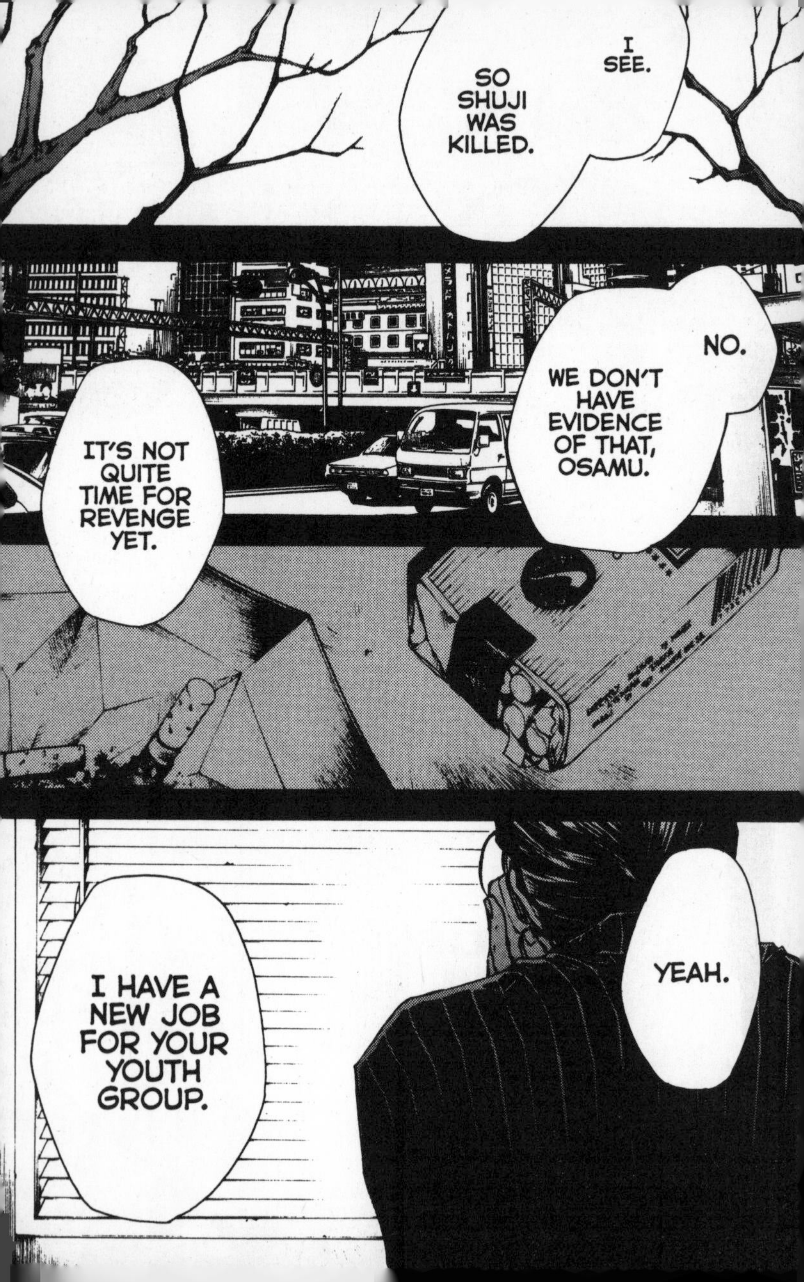
I SEE.
SO SHUJI WAS KILLED.
NO.
WE DON'T HAVE EVIDENCE OF THAT, OSAMU.
IT'S NOT QUITE TIME FOR REVENGE YET.
YEAH.
I HAVE A NEW JOB FOR YOUR YOUTH GROUP.

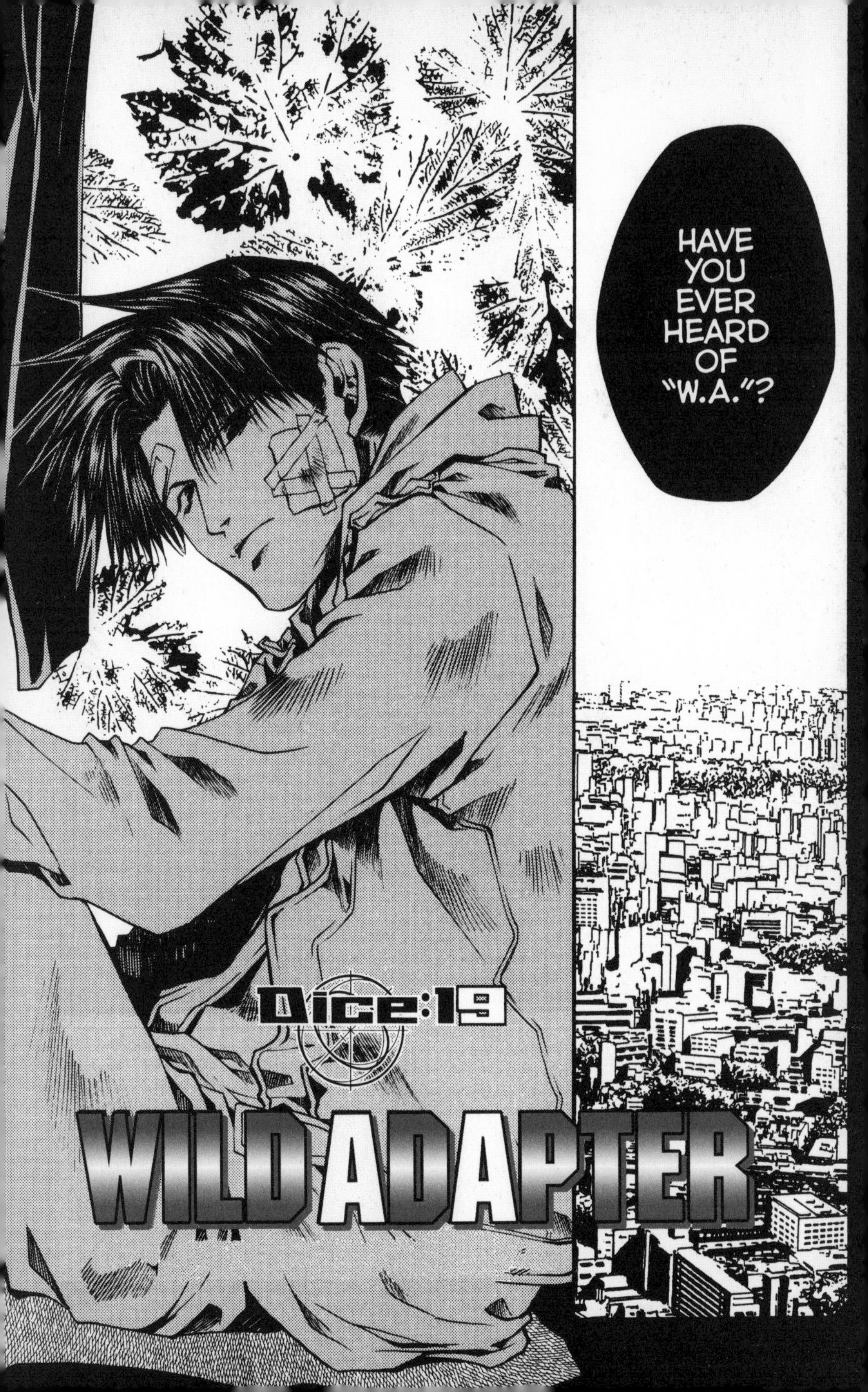
HAVE YOU EVER HEARD OF "W.A."?
Dice:19
WILD ADAPTER

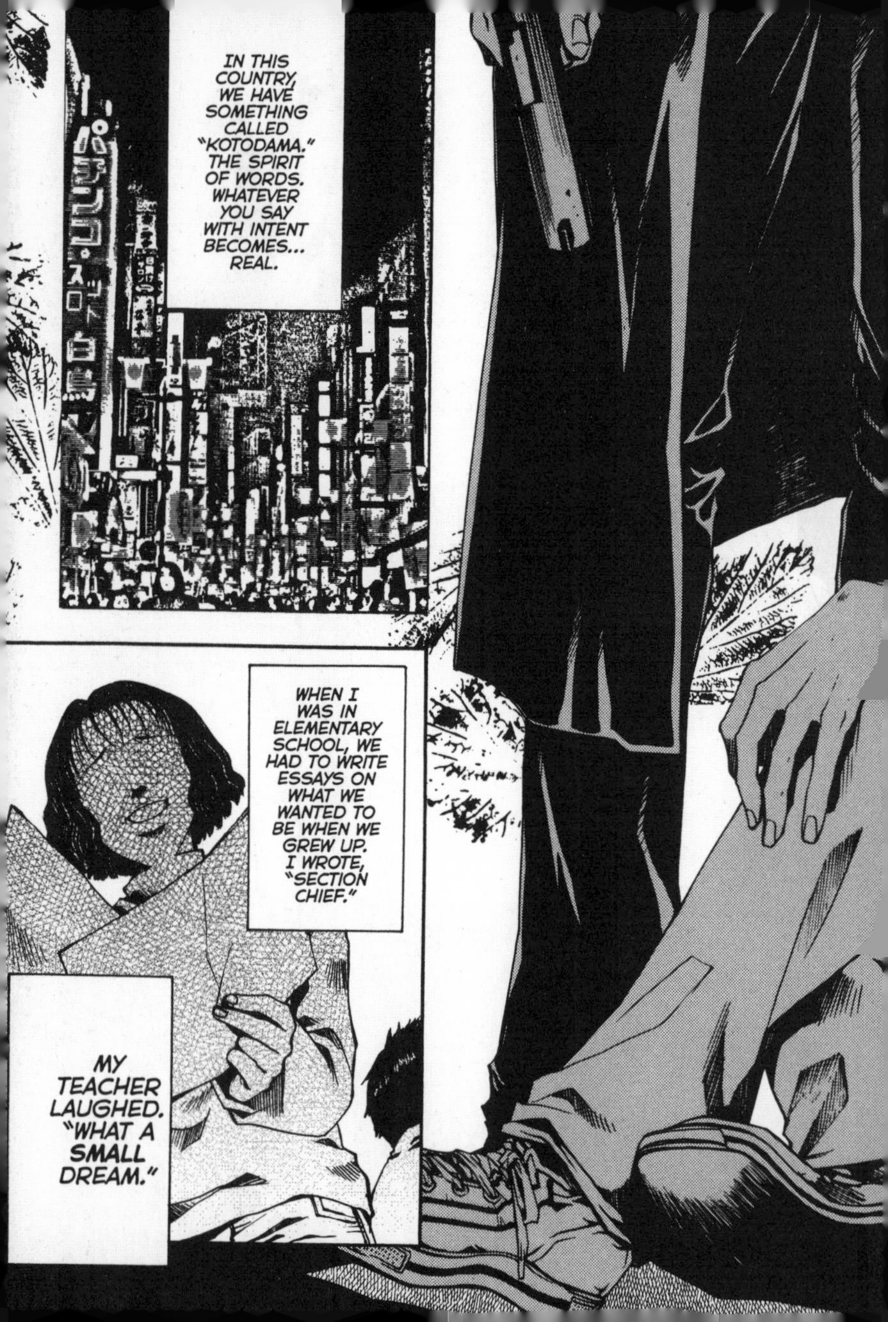
IN THIS COUNTRY, WE HAVE SOMETHING CALLED "KOTODAMA." THE SPIRIT OF WORDS. WHATEVER YOU SAY WITH INTENT BECOMES... REAL.
WHEN I WAS IN ELEMENTARY SCHOOL, WE HAD TO WRITE ESSAYS ON WHAT WE WANTED TO BE WHEN WE GREW UP. I WROTE, "SECTION CHIEF."
MY TEACHER LAUGHED. "WHAT A SMALL DREAM."

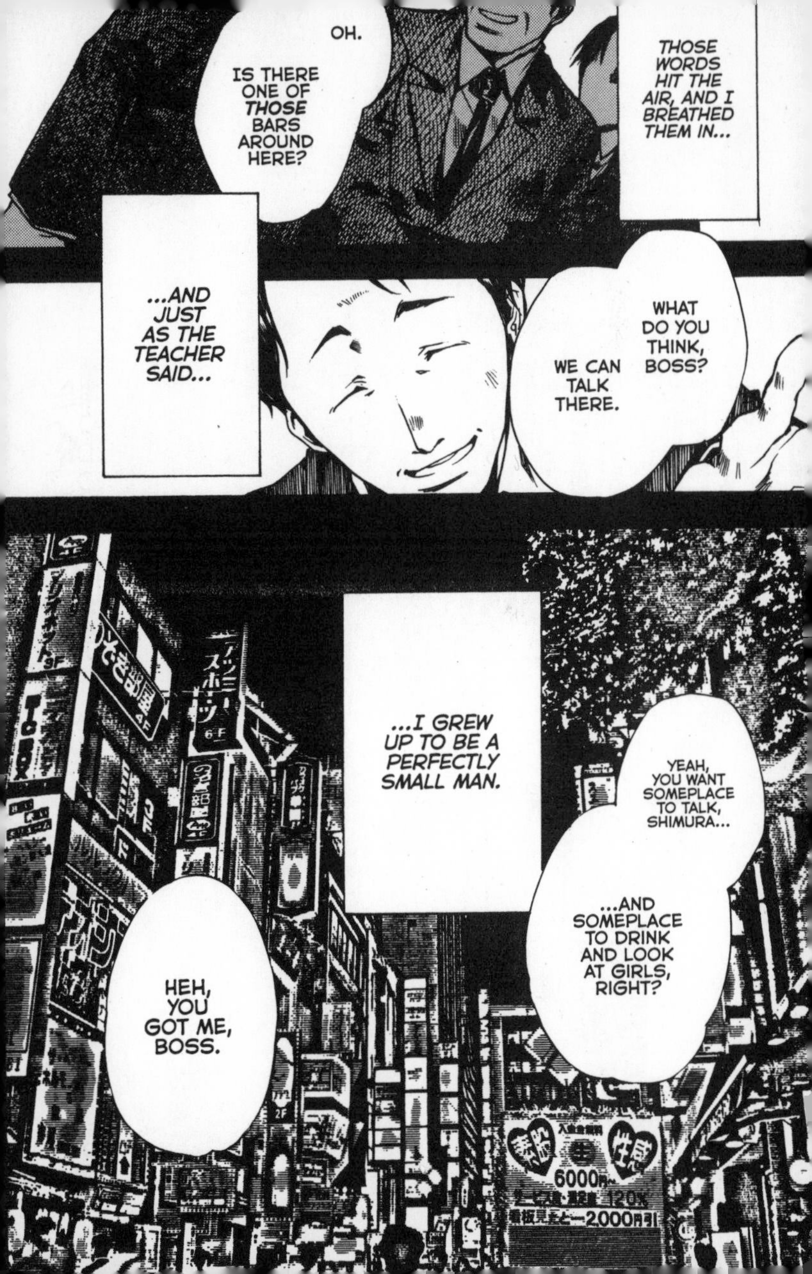
THOSE WORDS HIT THE AIR, AND I BREATHED THEM IN...
OH.
IS THERE ONE OF THOSE BARS AROUND HERE?
WHAT DO YOU THINK, BOSS?
WE CAN TALK THERE.
...AND JUST AS THE TEACHER SAID...
...I GREW UP TO BE A PERFECTLY SMALL MAN.
YEAH, YOU WANT SOMEPLACE TO TALK, SHIMURA...
...AND SOMEPLACE TO DRINK AND LOOK AT GIRLS, RIGHT?
HEH, YOU GOT ME, BOSS.

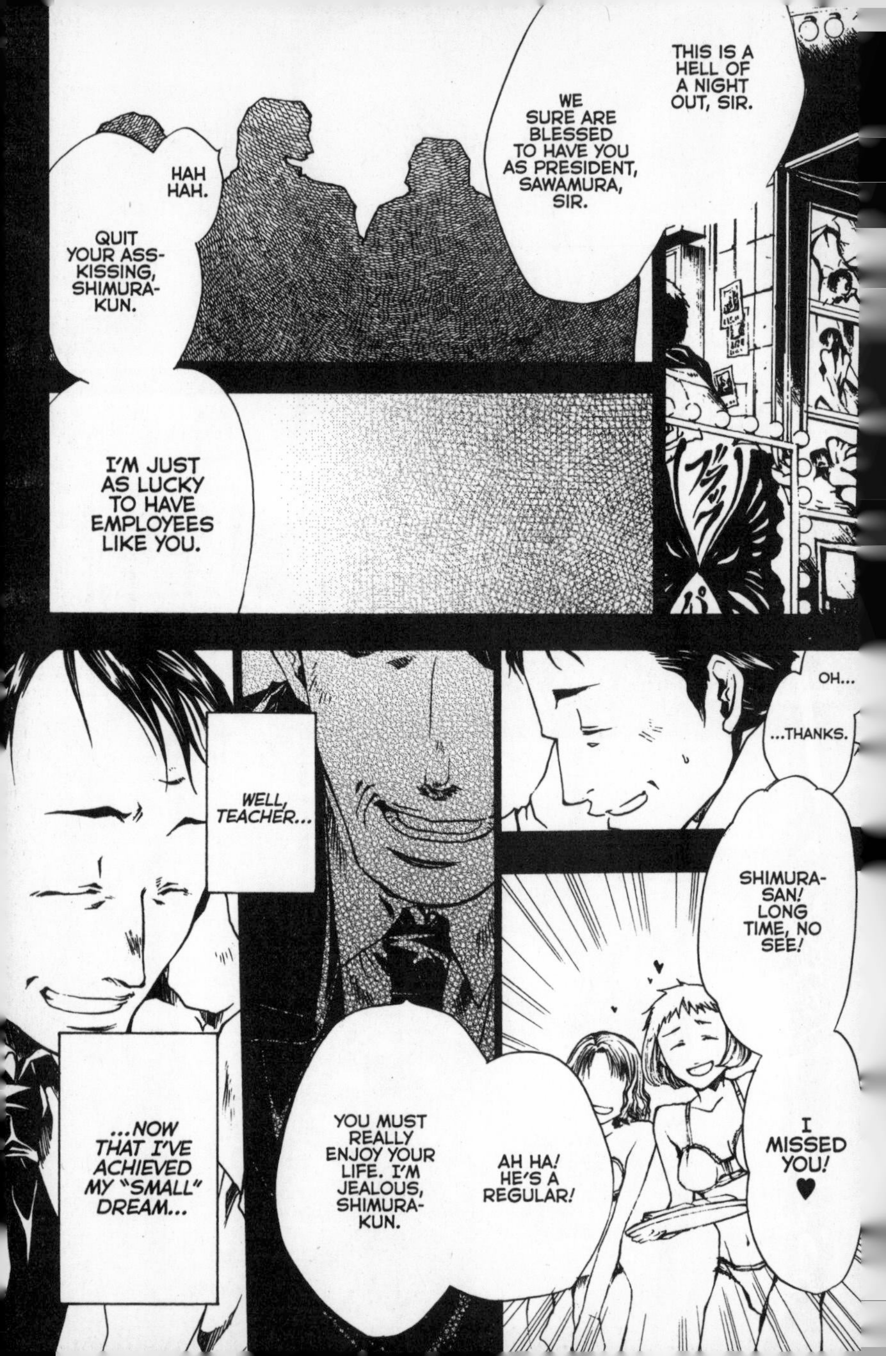
THIS IS A HELL OF A NIGHT OUT, SIR.
WE SURE ARE BLESSED TO HAVE YOU AS PRESIDENT, SAWAMURA, SIR.
HAH HAH.
QUIT YOUR ASS-KISSING, SHIMURA-KUN.
I'M JUST AS LUCKY TO HAVE EMPLOYEES LIKE YOU.
OH...
...THANKS.
SHIMURA-SAN! LONG TIME, NO SEE!
I MISSED YOU! ♥
AH HA! HE'S A REGULAR!
WELL, TEACHER...
YOU MUST REALLY ENJOY YOUR LIFE. I'M JEALOUS, SHIMURA-KUN.
...NOW THAT I'VE ACHIEVED MY "SMALL" DREAM...

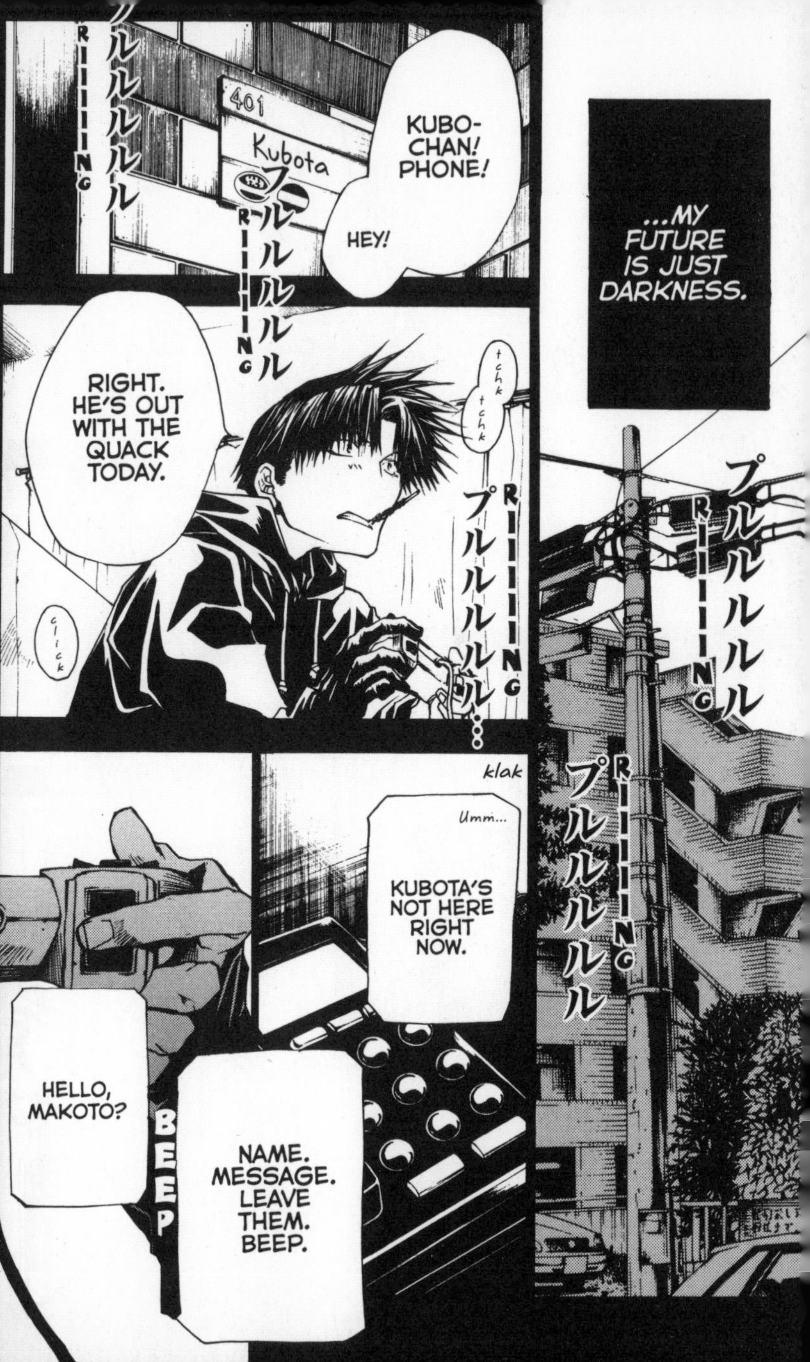
...MY FUTURE IS JUST DARKNESS.
プルルルル
RIIIING
プルルルル
RIIIING
401
Kubota
KUBO-CHAN! PHONE!
HEY!
プルルルル
RIIIING
プルルルル
RIIIING
tchk tchk
プルルルル...
RIIIING
RIGHT. HE'S OUT WITH THE QUACK TODAY.
click
klak
Umm...
KUBOTA'S NOT HERE RIGHT NOW.
NAME. MESSAGE. LEAVE THEM. BEEP.
BEEP
HELLO, MAKOTO?

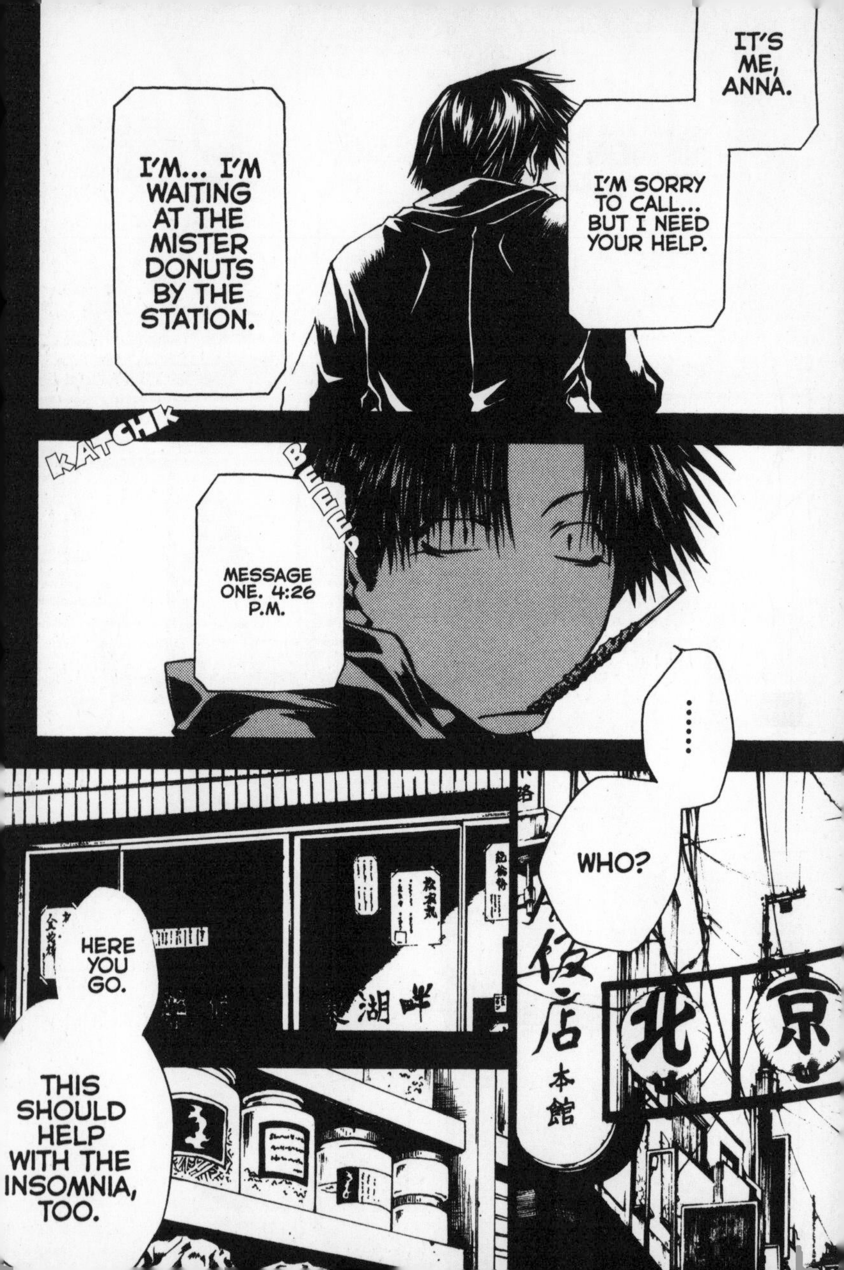
IT'S ME, ANNA.
I'M SORRY TO CALL... BUT I NEED YOUR HELP.
I'M... I'M WAITING AT THE MISTER DONUTS BY THE STATION.
KATCHK
BEEEP
MESSAGE ONE. 4:26 P.M.
......
WHO?
北京
本館
HERE YOU GO.
THIS SHOULD HELP WITH THE INSOMNIA, TOO.

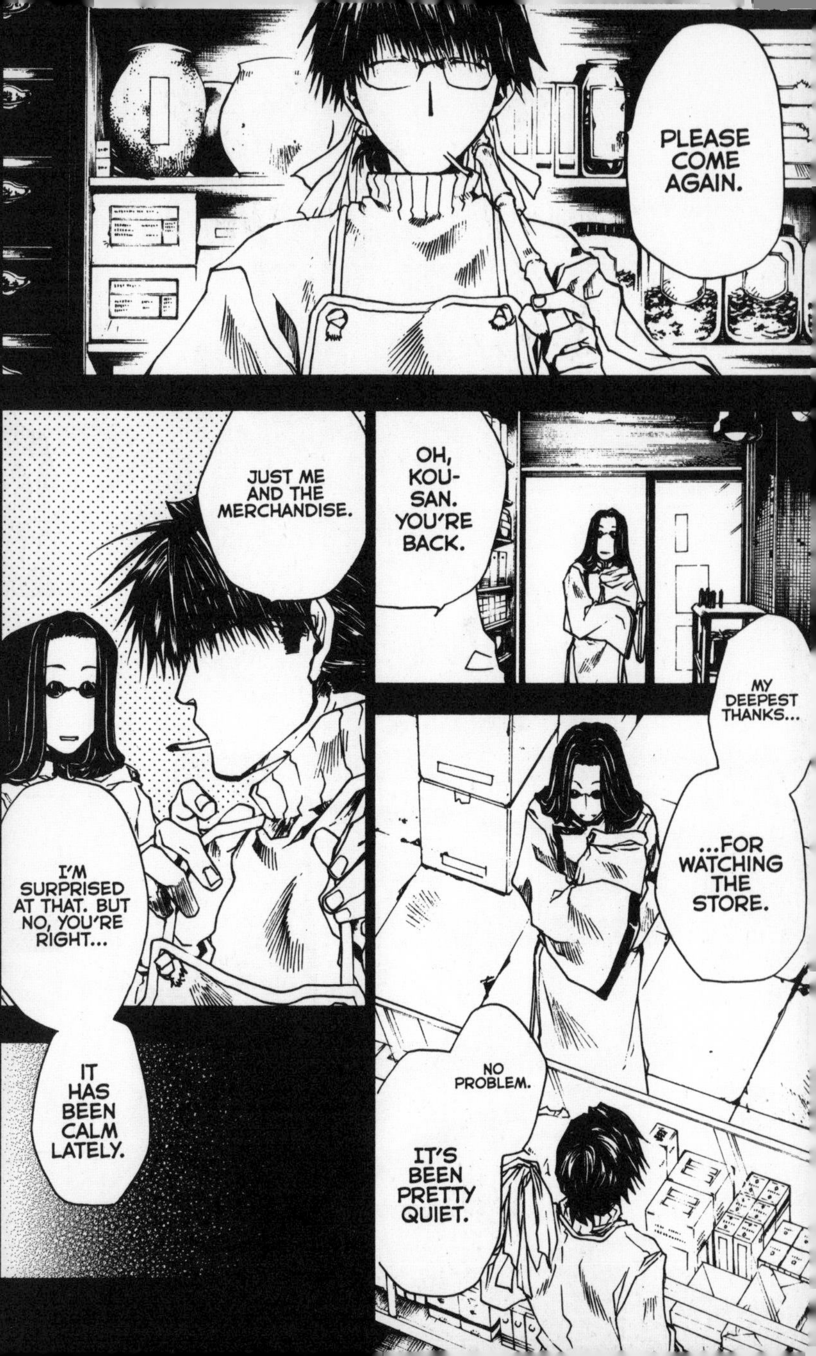
PLEASE COME AGAIN.
OH, KOU-SAN. YOU'RE BACK.
MY DEEPEST THANKS...
...FOR WATCHING THE STORE.
NO PROBLEM.
IT'S BEEN PRETTY QUIET.
JUST ME AND THE MERCHANDISE.
I'M SURPRISED AT THAT. BUT NO, YOU'RE RIGHT...
IT HAS BEEN CALM LATELY.

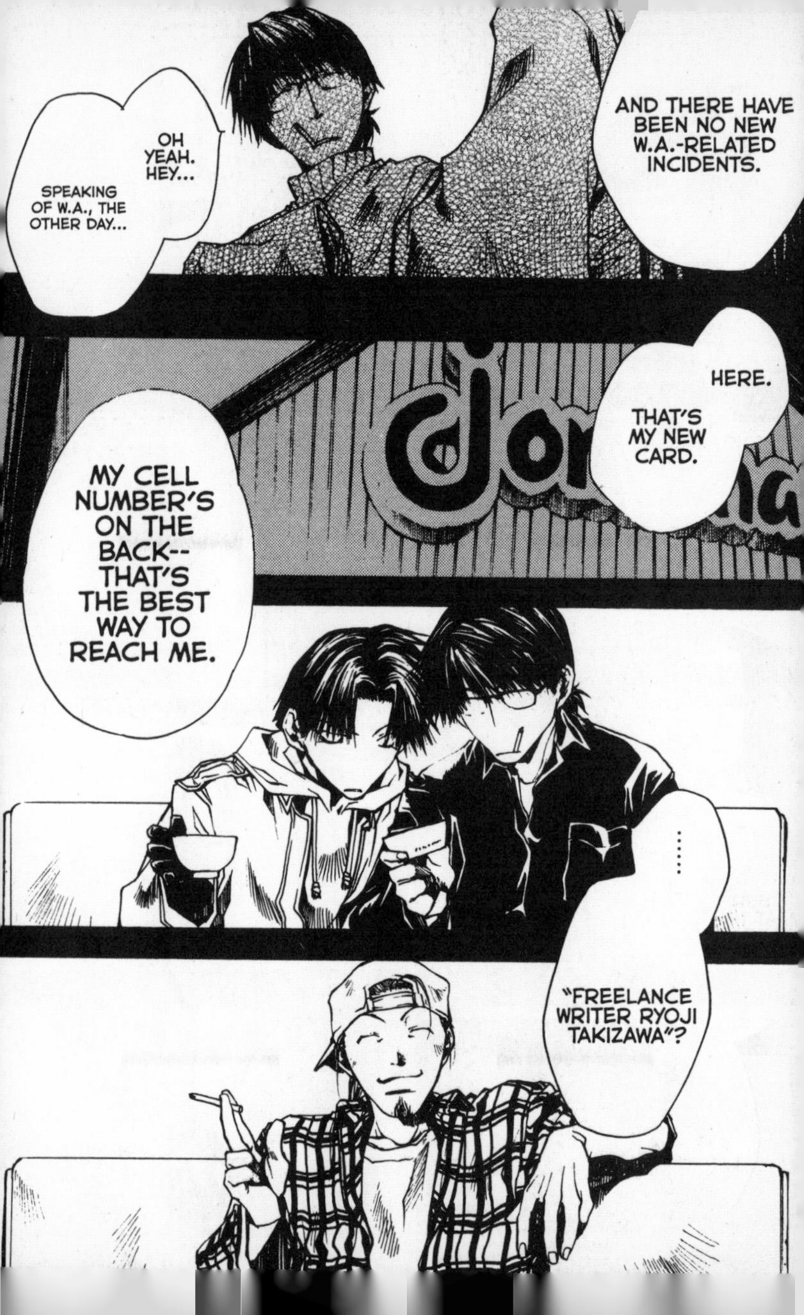
AND THERE HAVE BEEN NO NEW W.A.-RELATED INCIDENTS.
OH YEAH. HEY...
SPEAKING OF W.A., THE OTHER DAY...
HERE.
THAT'S MY NEW CARD.
MY CELL NUMBER'S ON THE BACK--THAT'S THE BEST WAY TO REACH ME.
......
"FREELANCE WRITER RYOJI TAKIZAWA"?

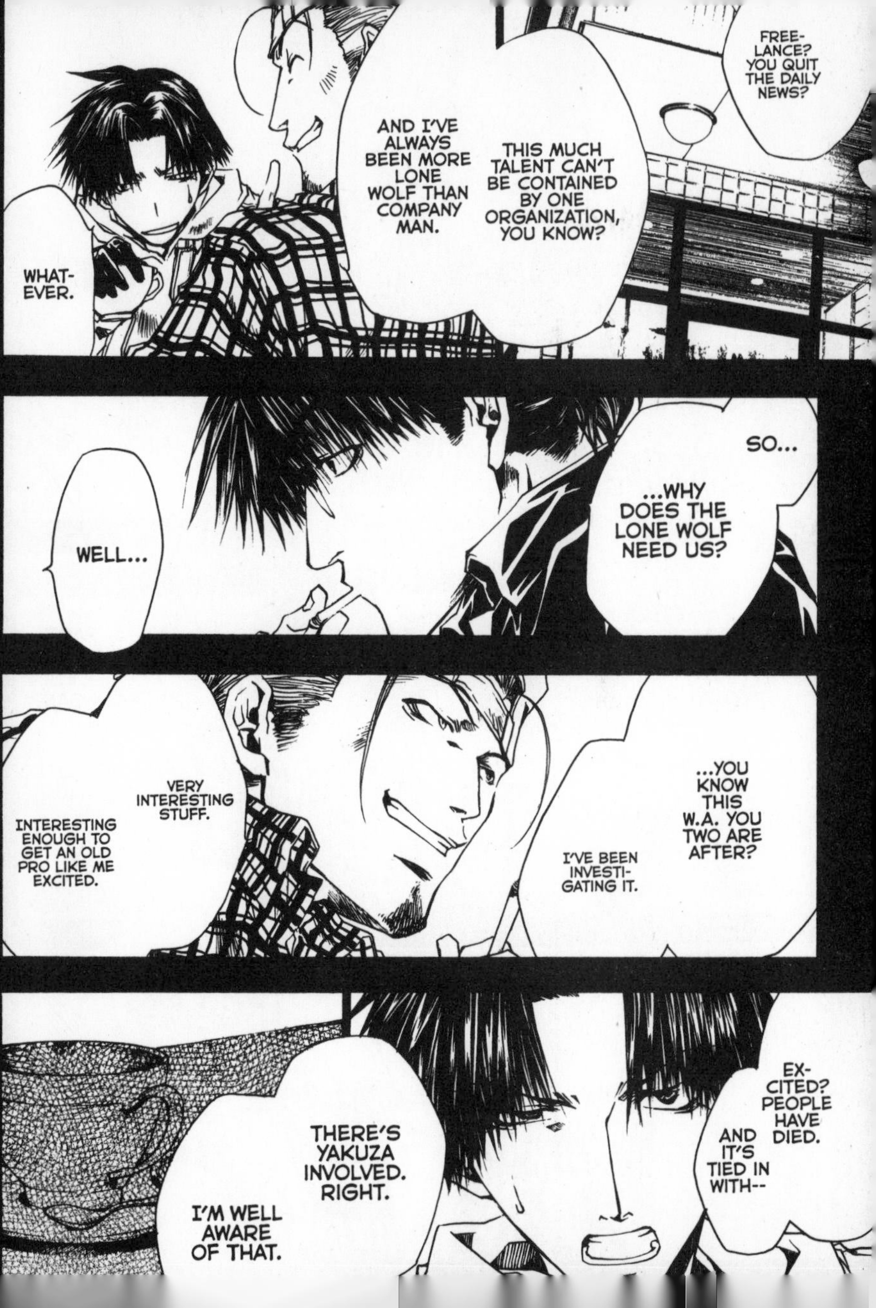
FREE-LANCE? YOU QUIT THE DAILY NEWS?
THIS MUCH TALENT CAN'T BE CONTAINED BY ONE ORGANIZATION, YOU KNOW?
AND I'VE ALWAYS BEEN MORE LONE WOLF THAN COMPANY MAN.
WHAT-EVER.
SO...
...WHY DOES THE LONE WOLF NEED US?
WELL...
...YOU KNOW THIS W.A. YOU TWO ARE AFTER?
I'VE BEEN INVESTI-GATING IT.
VERY INTERESTING STUFF.
INTERESTING ENOUGH TO GET AN OLD PRO LIKE ME EXCITED.
EX-CITED? PEOPLE HAVE DIED.
AND IT'S TIED IN WITH--
THERE'S YAKUZA INVOLVED. RIGHT.
I'M WELL AWARE OF THAT.

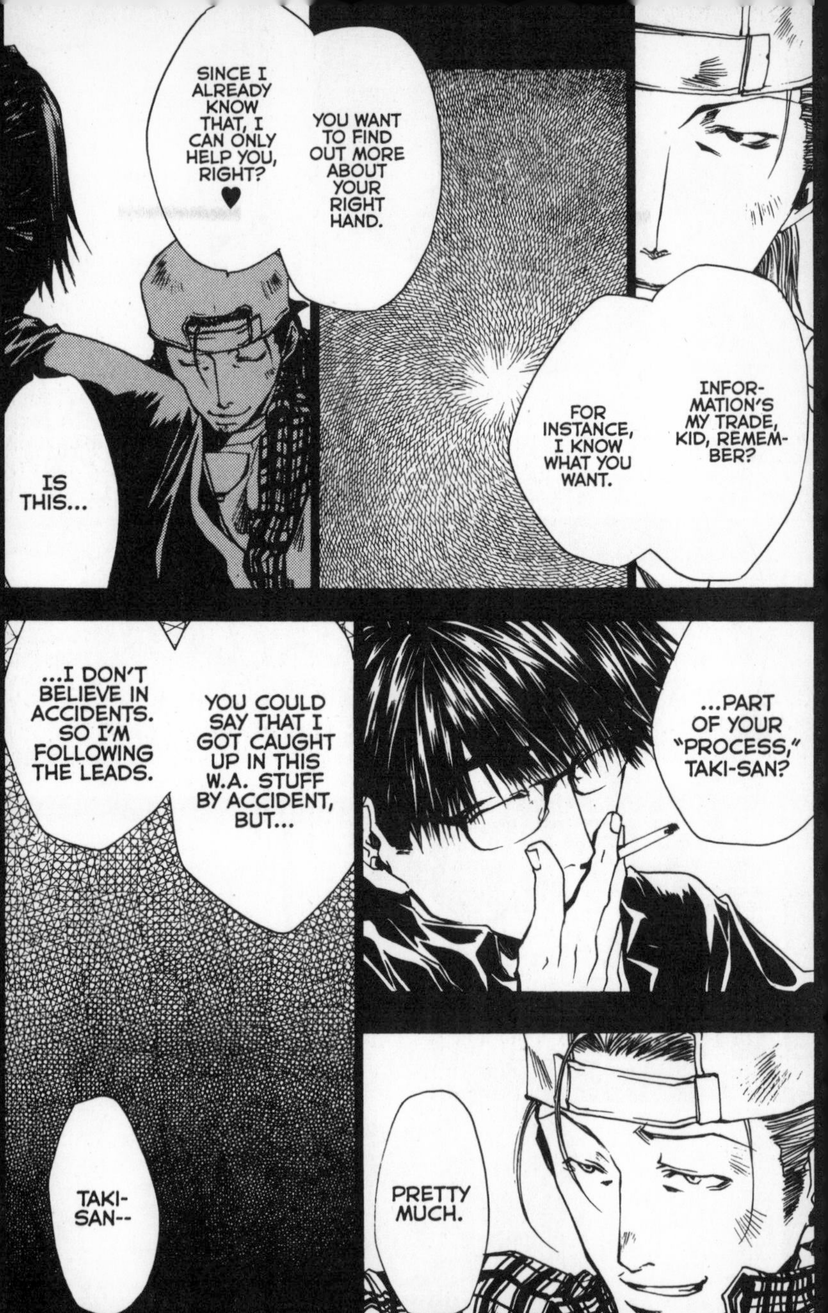

INFORMATION'S MY TRADE, KID, REMEMBER?
FOR INSTANCE, I KNOW WHAT YOU WANT.
YOU WANT TO FIND OUT MORE ABOUT YOUR RIGHT HAND.
SINCE I ALREADY KNOW THAT, I CAN ONLY HELP YOU, RIGHT? ♥
IS THIS...
...PART OF YOUR "PROCESS," TAKI-SAN?
PRETTY MUCH.
YOU COULD SAY THAT I GOT CAUGHT UP IN THIS W.A. STUFF BY ACCIDENT, BUT...
...I DON'T BELIEVE IN ACCIDENTS. SO I'M FOLLOWING THE LEADS.
TAKI-SAN--

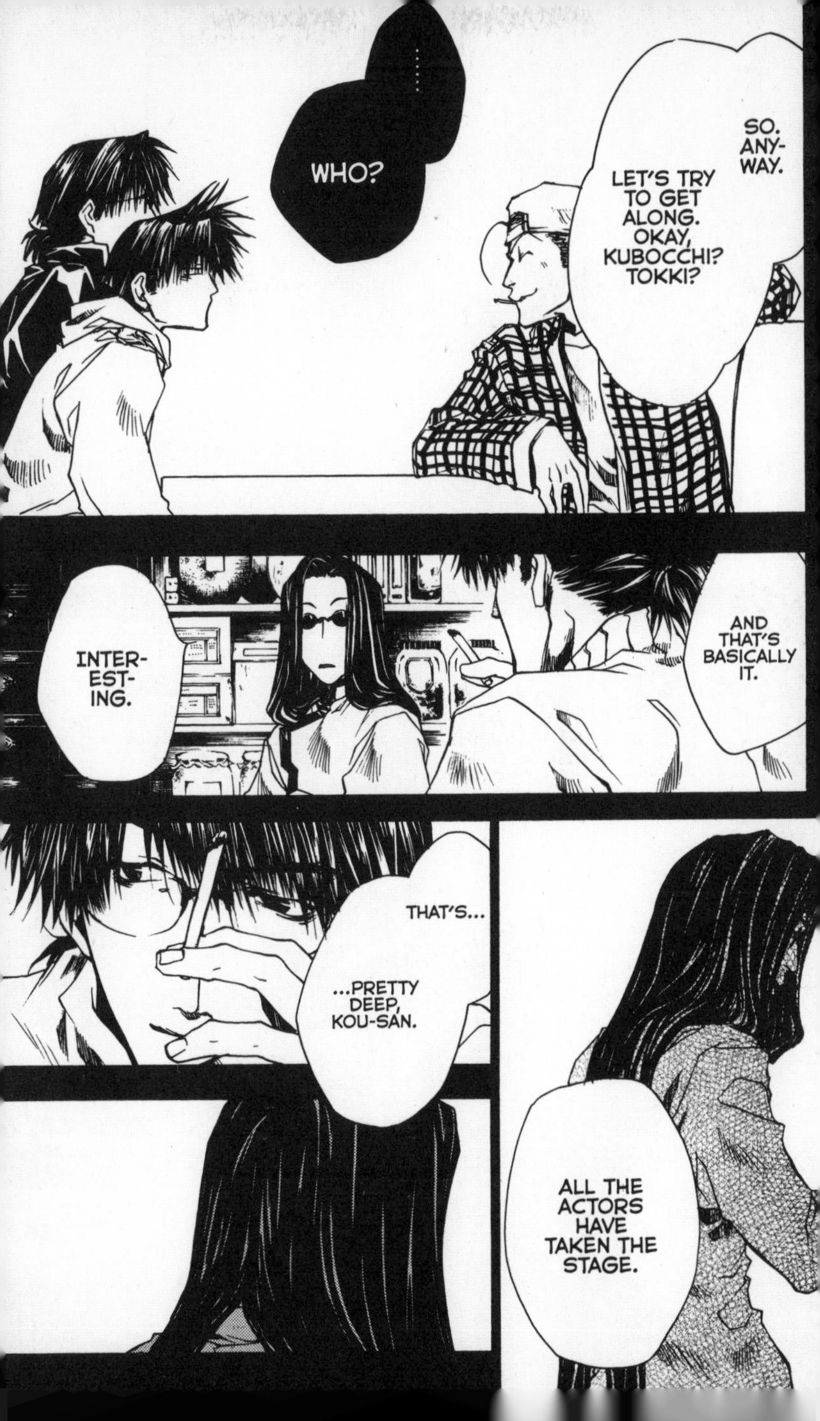
SO. ANYWAY.
LET'S TRY TO GET ALONG. OKAY, KUBOCCHI? TOKKI?
......
WHO?
AND THAT'S BASICALLY IT.
INTERESTING.
ALL THE ACTORS HAVE TAKEN THE STAGE.
THAT'S...
...PRETTY DEEP, KOU-SAN.

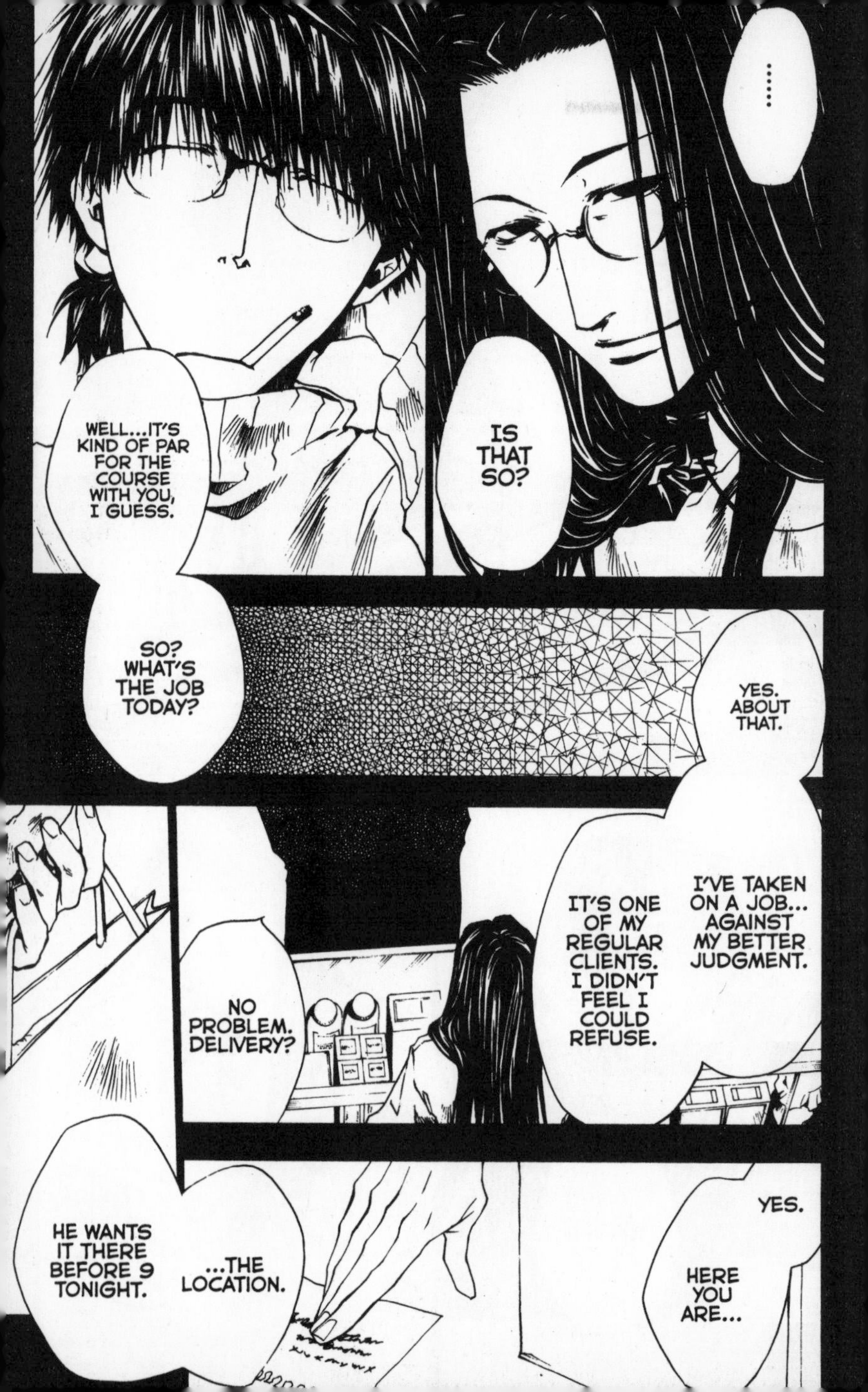
......
IS THAT SO?
WELL...IT'S KIND OF PAR FOR THE COURSE WITH YOU, I GUESS.
SO? WHAT'S THE JOB TODAY?
YES. ABOUT THAT.
I'VE TAKEN ON A JOB... AGAINST MY BETTER JUDGMENT.
IT'S ONE OF MY REGULAR CLIENTS. I DIDN'T FEEL I COULD REFUSE.
NO PROBLEM. DELIVERY?
YES.
HERE YOU ARE...
...THE LOCATION.
HE WANTS IT THERE BEFORE 9 TONIGHT.

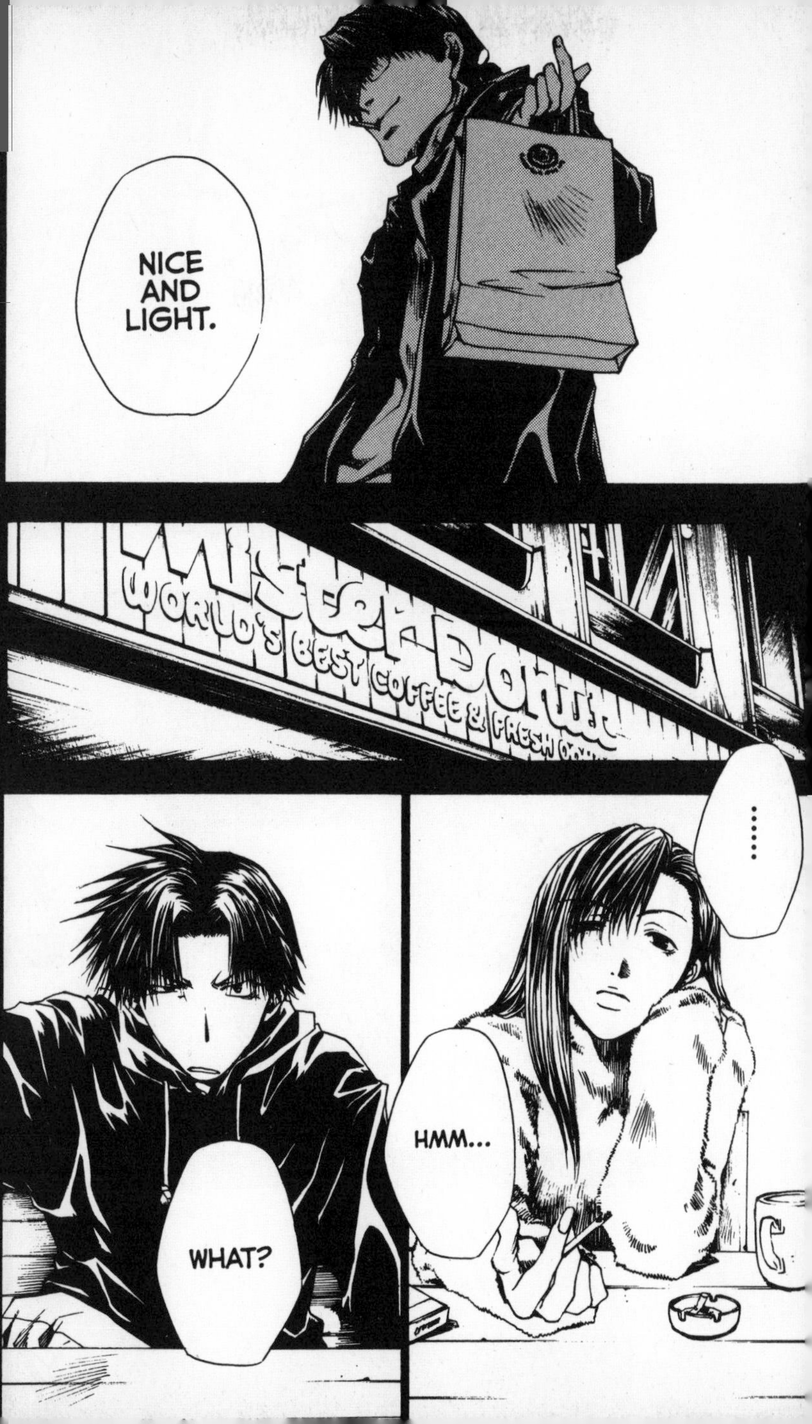
NICE AND LIGHT.
WORLD'S BEST COFFEE & FRESH
......
HMM...
WHAT?

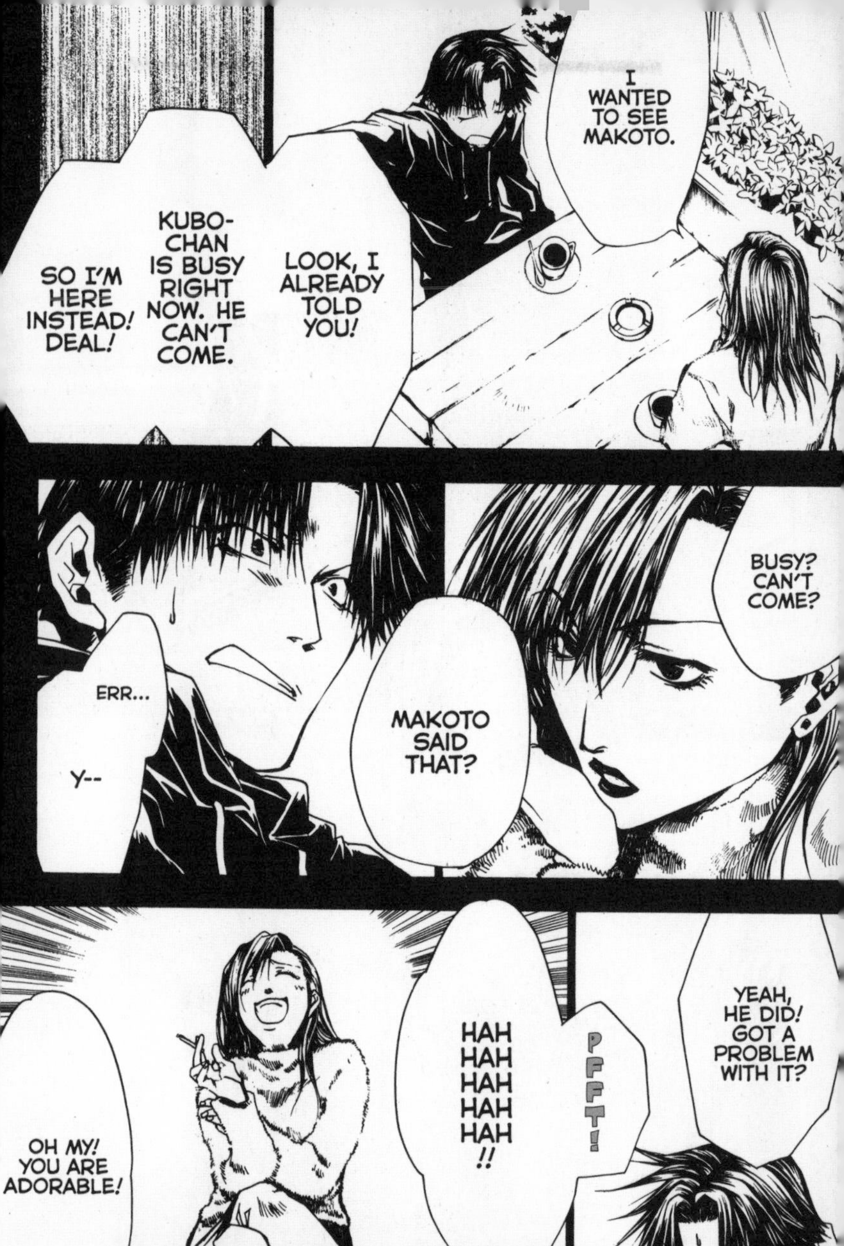
I WANTED TO SEE MAKOTO.
LOOK, I ALREADY TOLD YOU!
KUBO-CHAN IS BUSY RIGHT NOW. HE CAN'T COME.
SO I'M HERE INSTEAD! DEAL!
BUSY? CAN'T COME?
MAKOTO SAID THAT?
ERR...
Y--
YEAH, HE DID! GOT A PROBLEM WITH IT?
PFFT!
HAH HAH HAH HAH HAH!!
OH MY! YOU ARE ADORABLE!

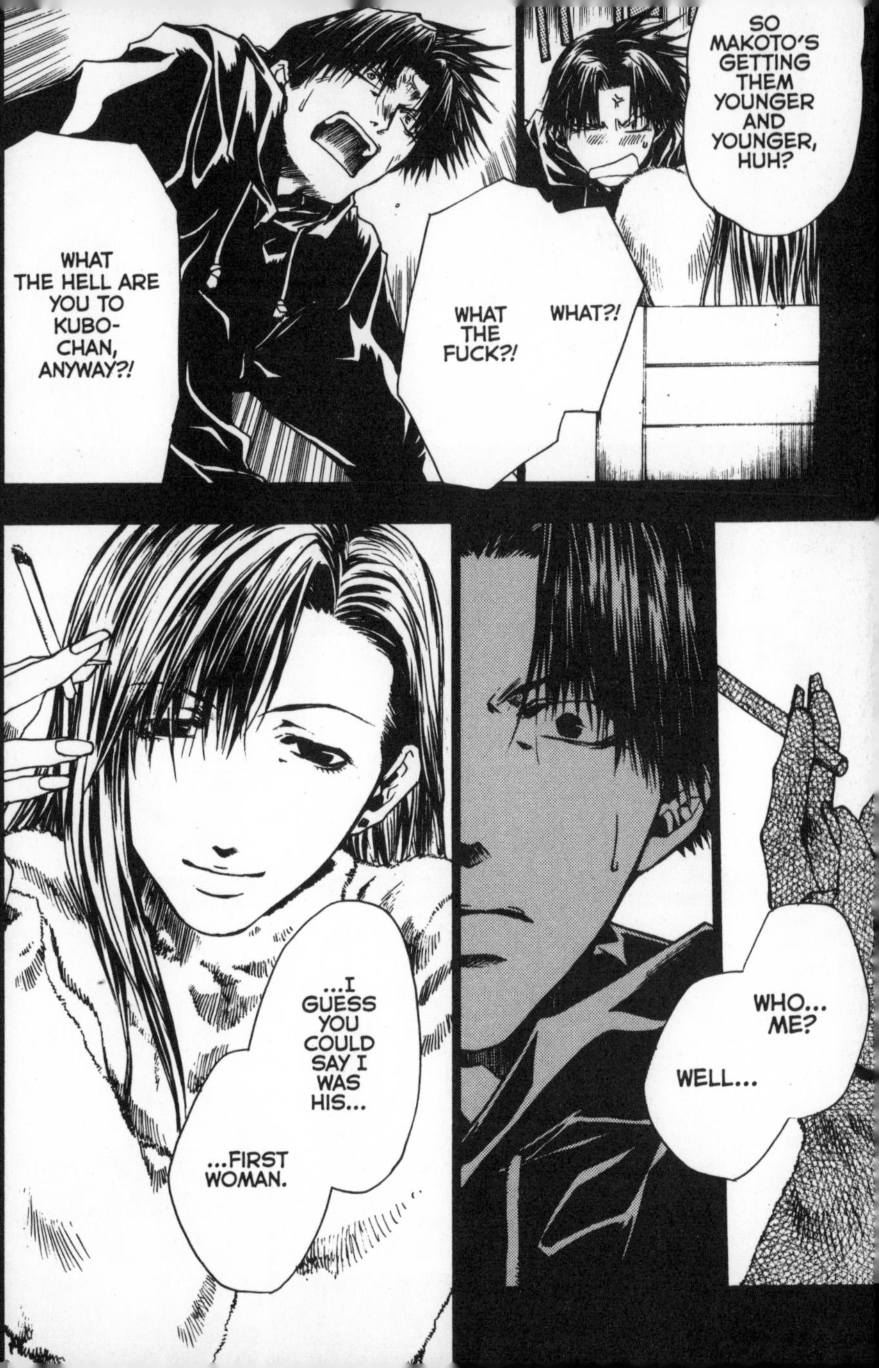
SO MAKOTO'S GETTING THEM YOUNGER AND YOUNGER, HUH?
WHAT?!
WHAT THE FUCK?!
WHAT THE HELL ARE YOU TO KUBO-CHAN, ANYWAY?!
WHO... ME?
WELL...
...I GUESS YOU COULD SAY I WAS HIS...
...FIRST WOMAN.

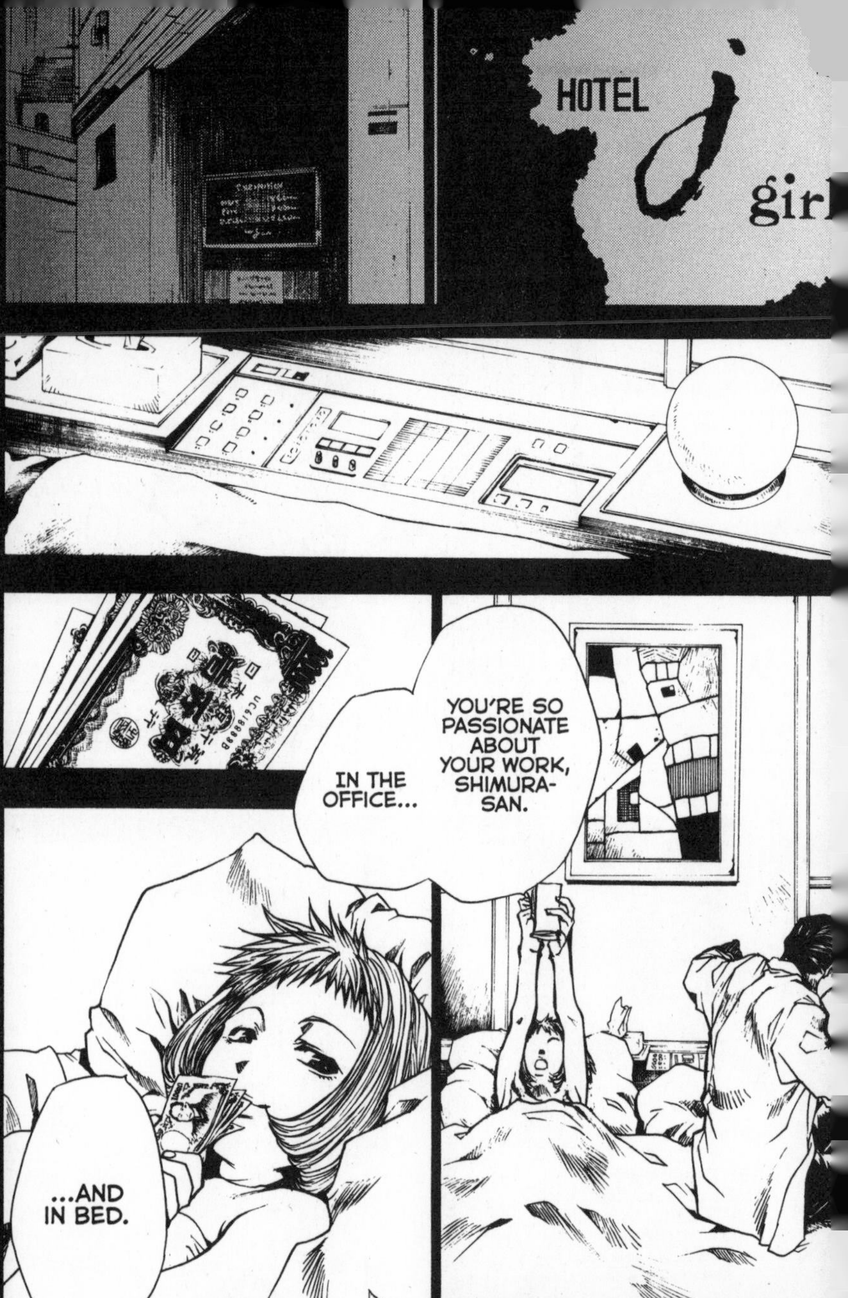
HOTEL
YOU'RE SO PASSIONATE ABOUT YOUR WORK, SHIMURA-SAN.
IN THE OFFICE...
...AND IN BED.

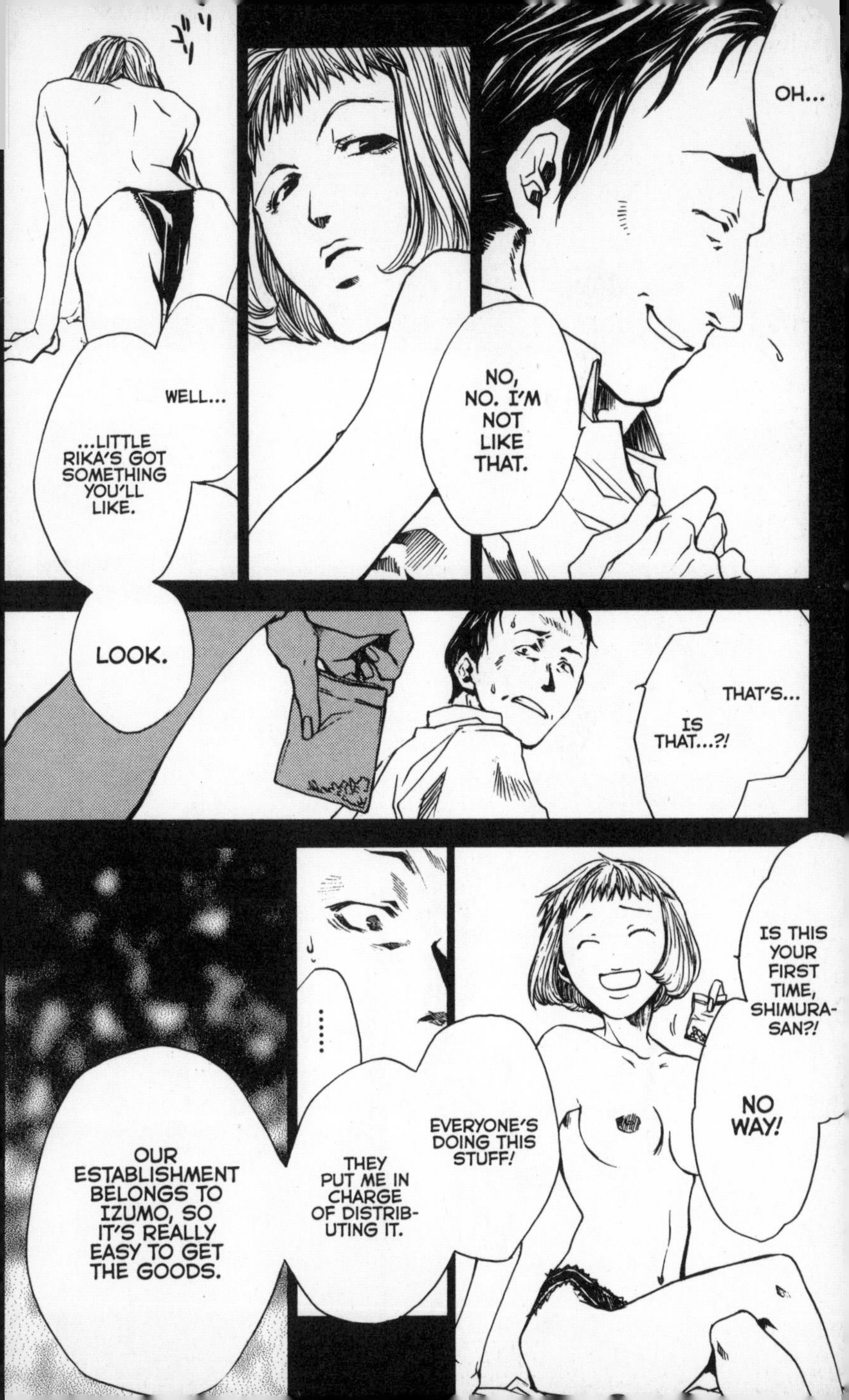
OH...
NO, NO. I'M NOT LIKE THAT.
WELL...
...LITTLE RIKA'S GOT SOMETHING YOU'LL LIKE.
LOOK.
THAT'S...
IS THAT...?!
IS THIS YOUR FIRST TIME, SHIMURA-SAN?!
NO WAY!
EVERYONE'S DOING THIS STUFF!
THEY PUT ME IN CHARGE OF DISTRIB-UTING IT.
......
OUR ESTABLISHMENT BELONGS TO IZUMO, SO IT'S REALLY EASY TO GET THE GOODS.

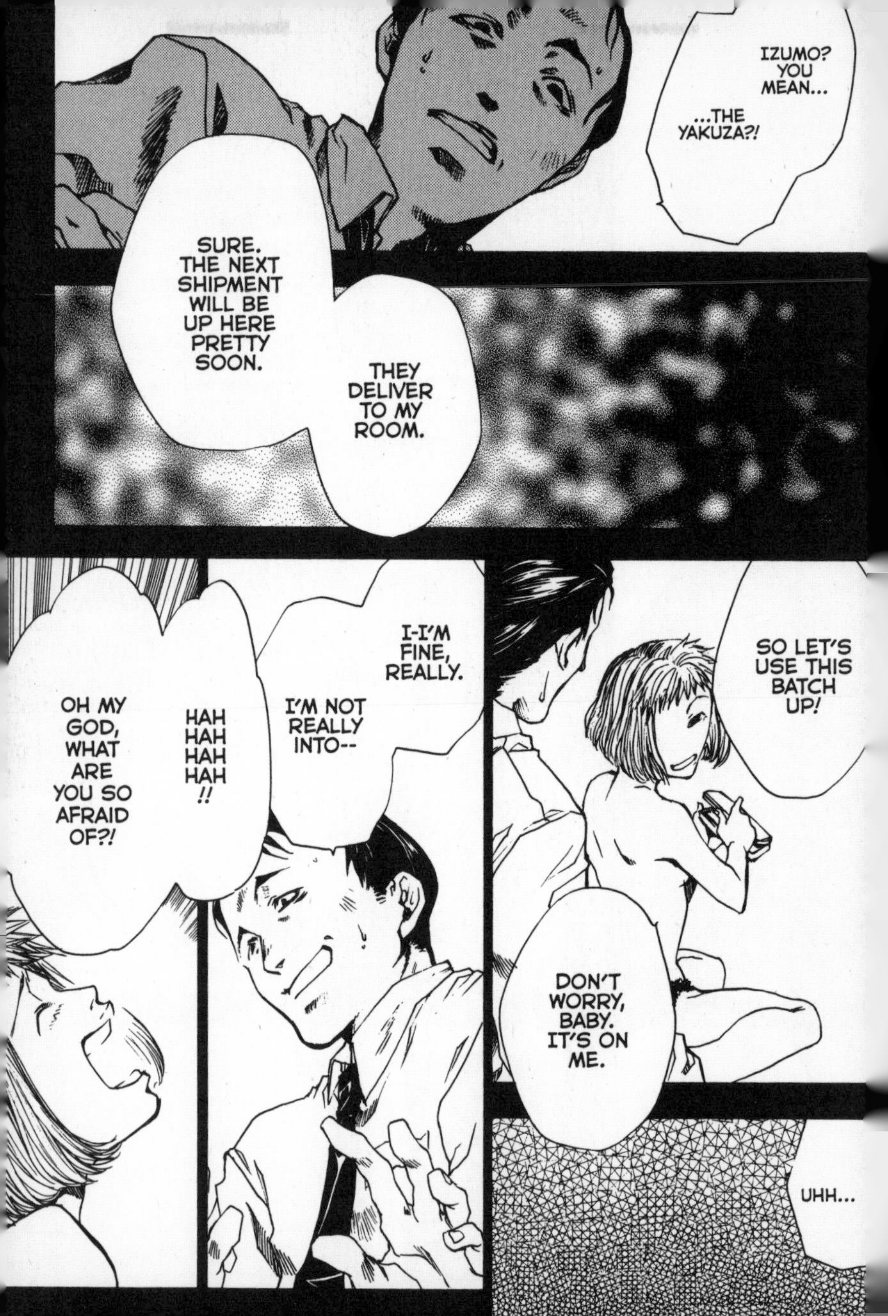
IZUMO? YOU MEAN...
...THE YAKUZA?!
SURE. THE NEXT SHIPMENT WILL BE UP HERE PRETTY SOON.
THEY DELIVER TO MY ROOM.
SO LET'S USE THIS BATCH UP!
DON'T WORRY, BABY. IT'S ON ME.
UHH...
I-I'M FINE, REALLY.
I'M NOT REALLY INTO--
HAH HAH HAH HAH !!
OH MY GOD, WHAT ARE YOU SO AFRAID OF?!

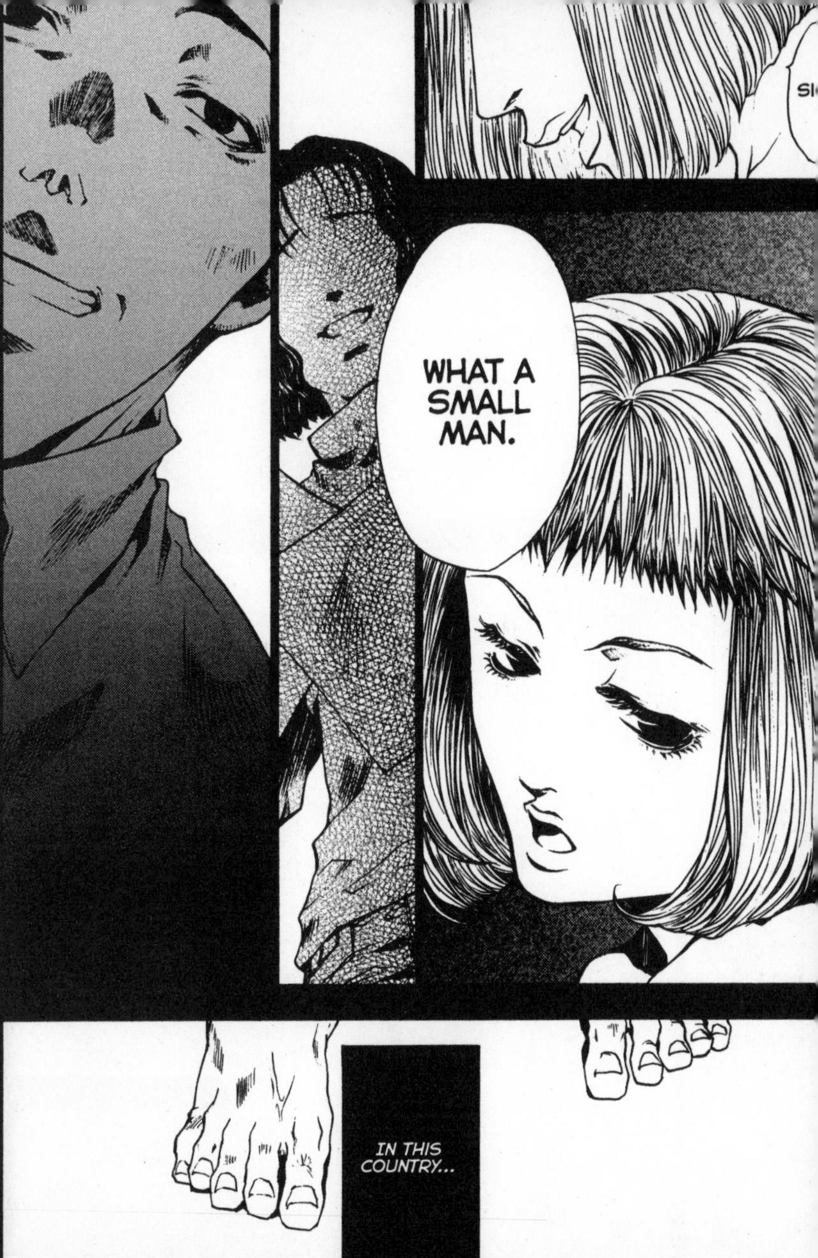
WHAT A SMALL MAN.
IN THIS COUNTRY...

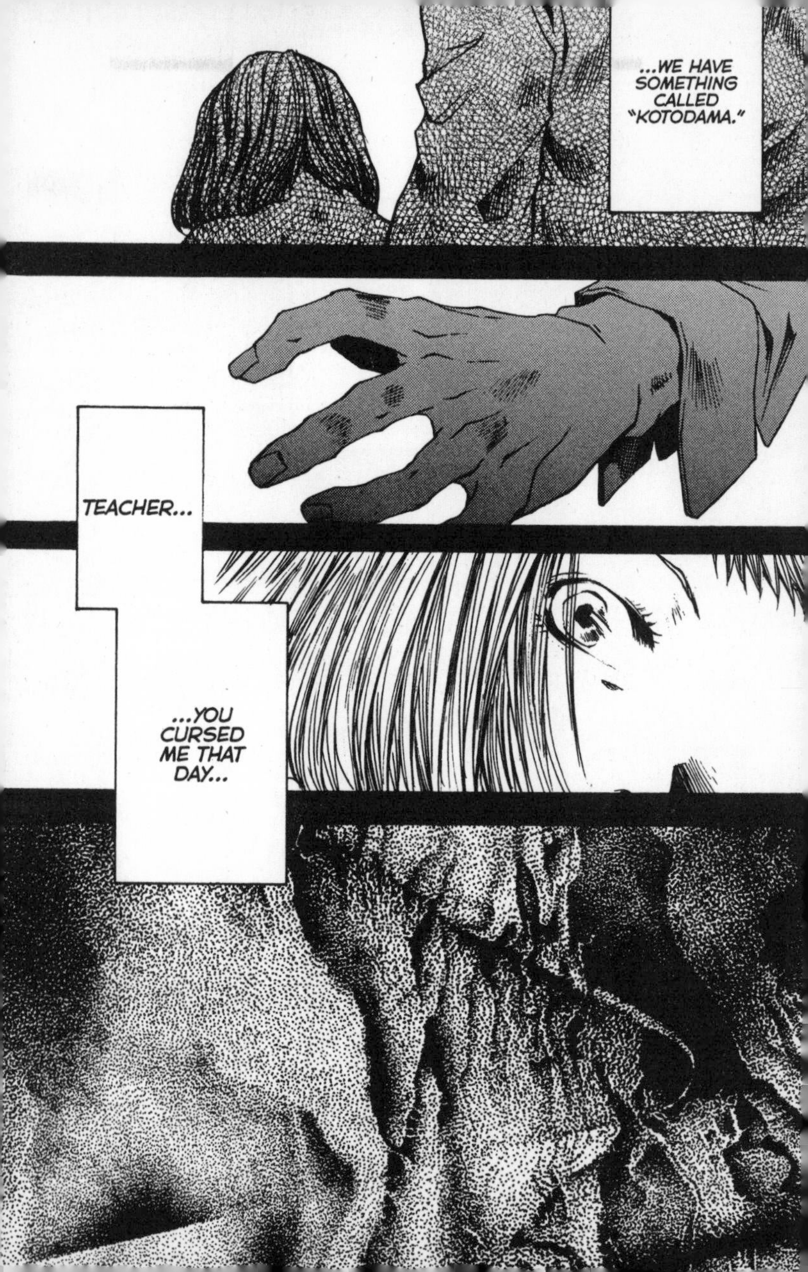
...WE HAVE SOMETHING CALLED "KOTODAMA."
TEACHER...
...YOU CURSED ME THAT DAY...

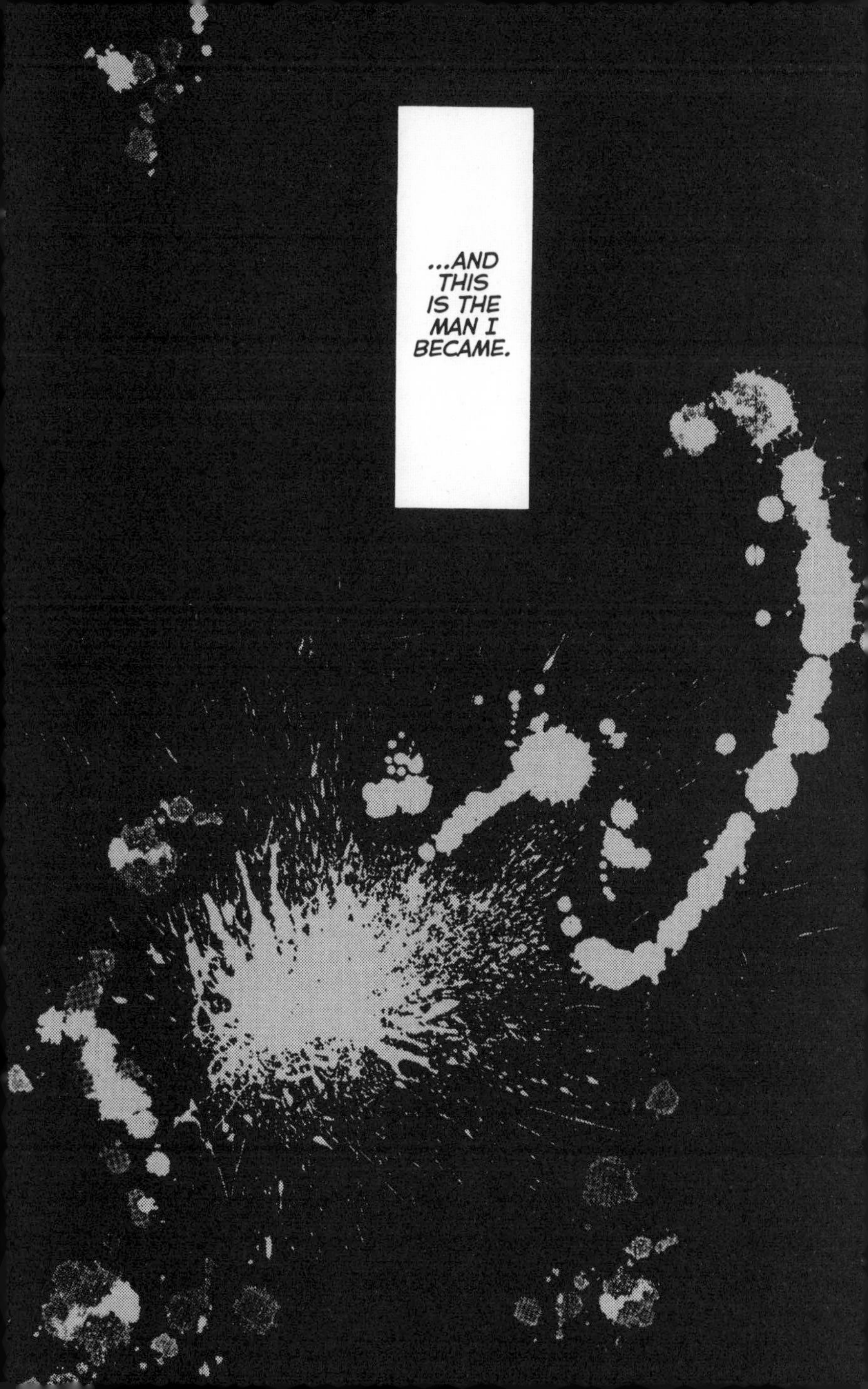
...AND THIS IS THE MAN I BECAME.

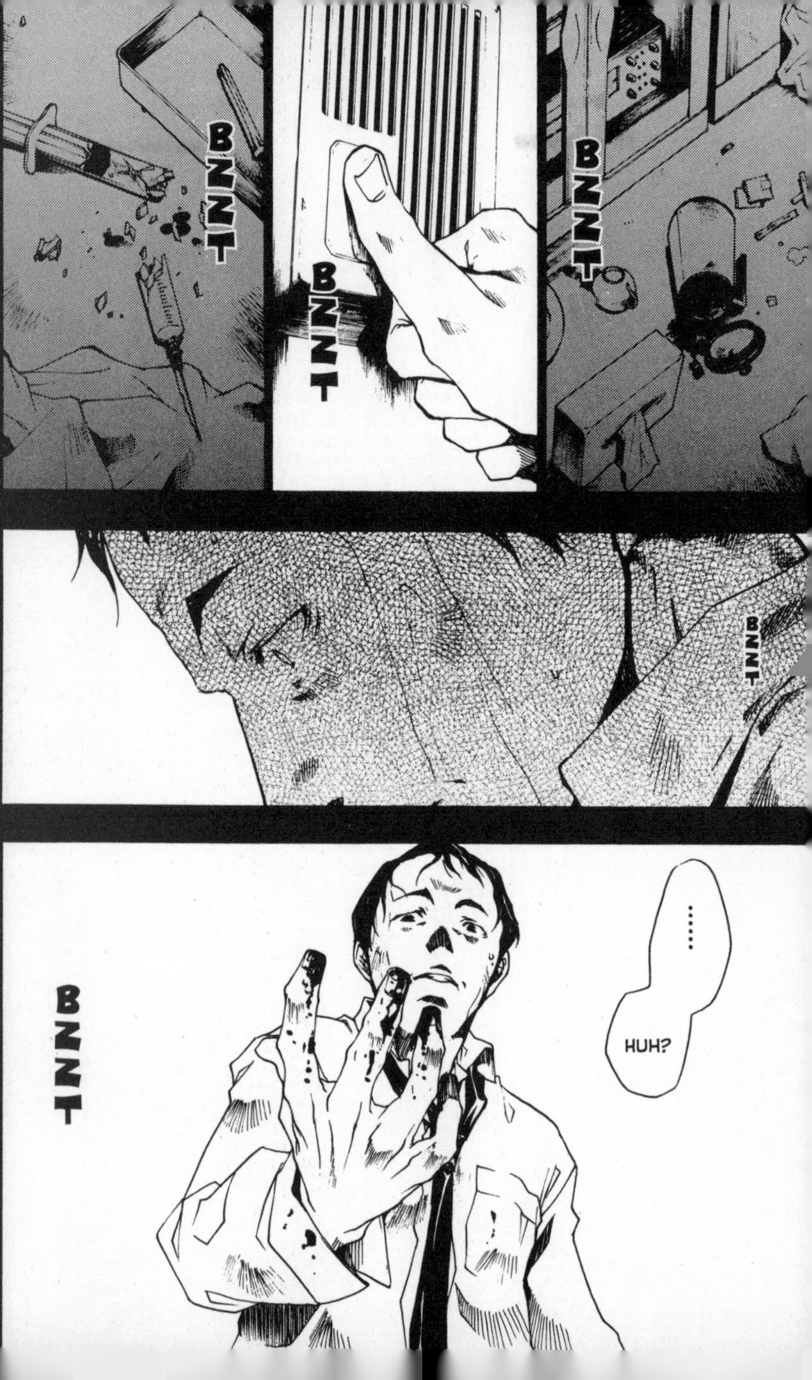
BZZT
BZZT
BZZT
BZZT
……
HUH?
BZZT

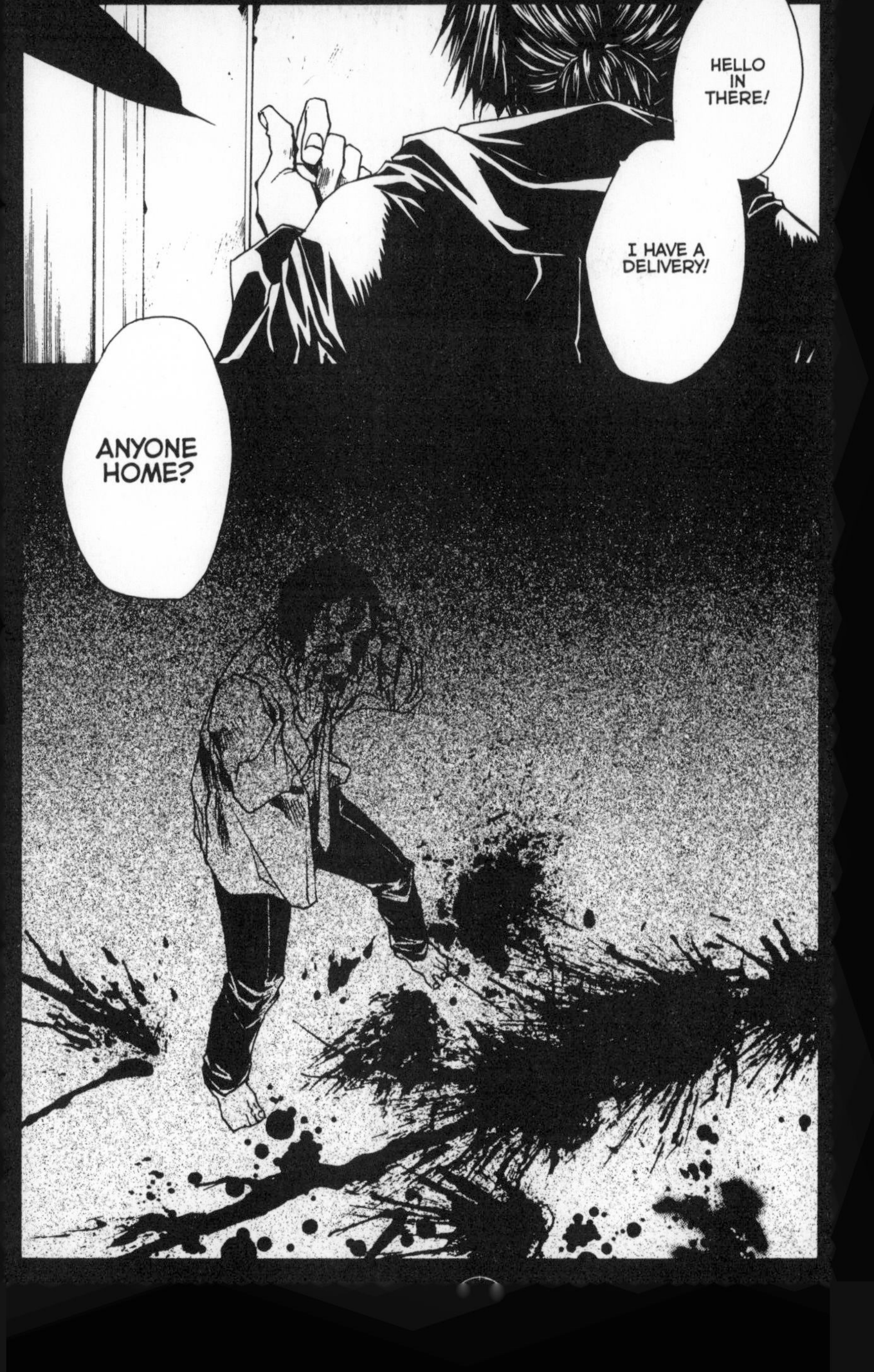
HELLO IN THERE!
I HAVE A DELIVERY!
ANYONE HOME?

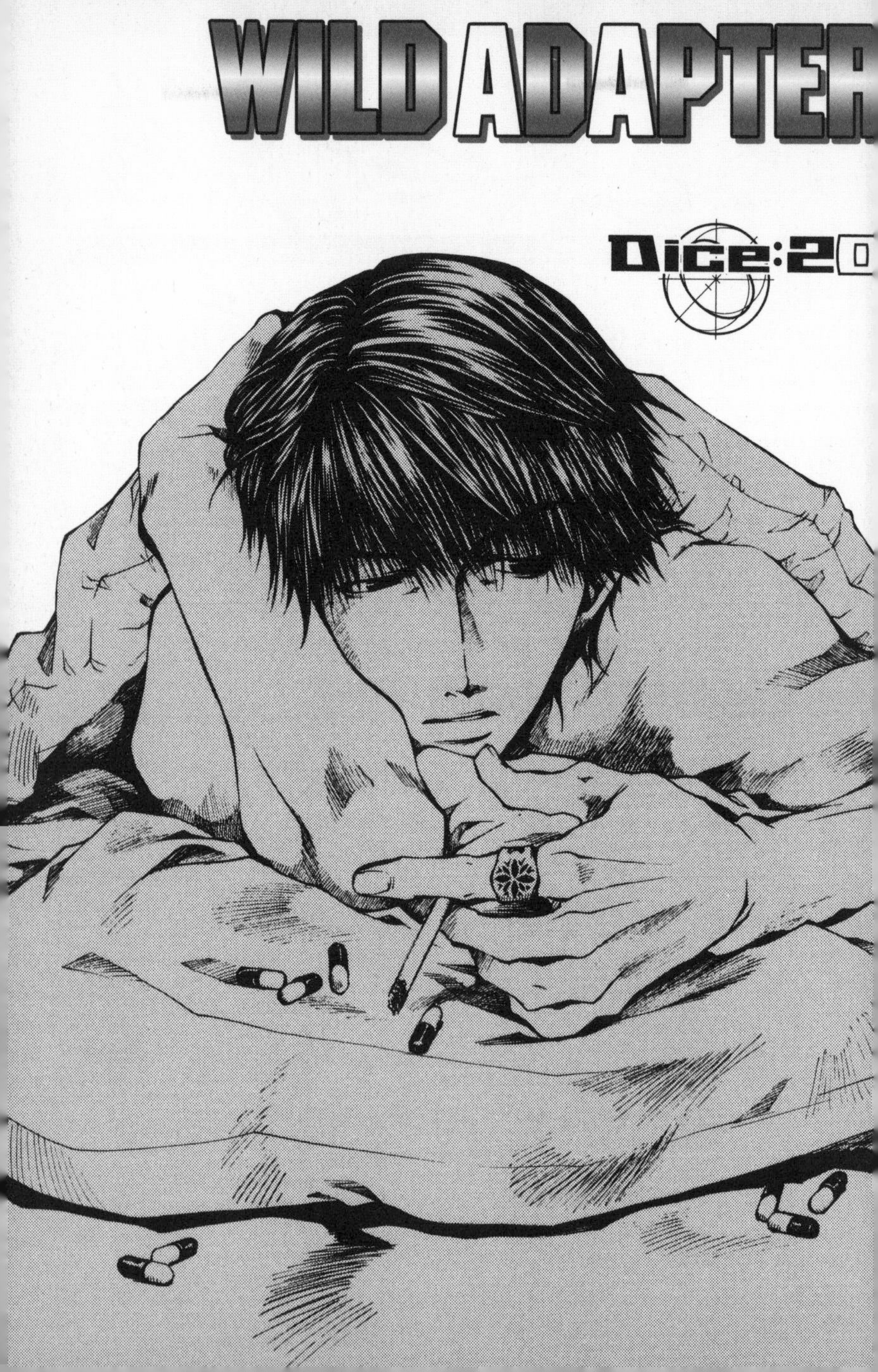
WILD ADAPTER
Dice:20

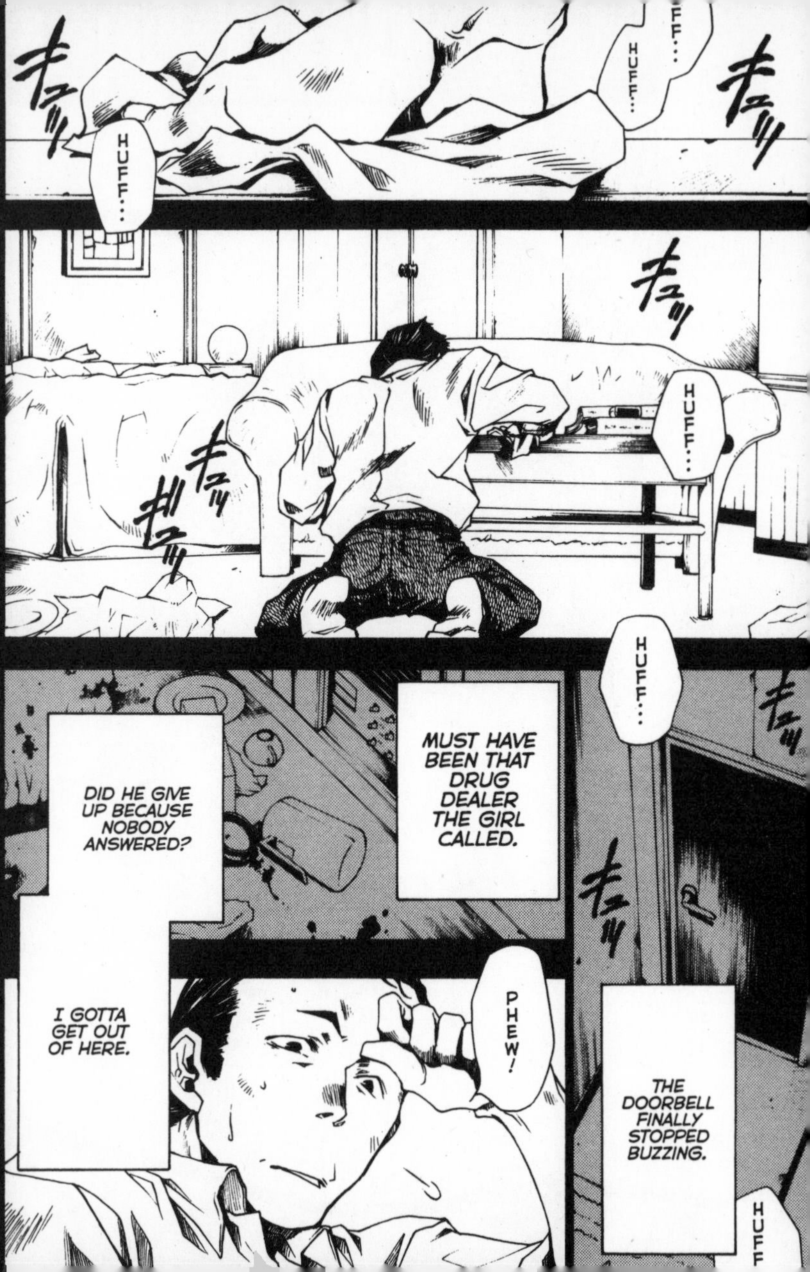
キュッ
HUFF... HUFF...
HUFF...
キュッ
キュッ
HUFF...
キュッ
ギュッ
HUFF...
キュッ
キュッ
THE DOORBELL FINALLY STOPPED BUZZING.
HUFF
MUST HAVE BEEN THAT DRUG DEALER THE GIRL CALLED.
DID HE GIVE UP BECAUSE NOBODY ANSWERED?
PHEW!
I GOTTA GET OUT OF HERE.

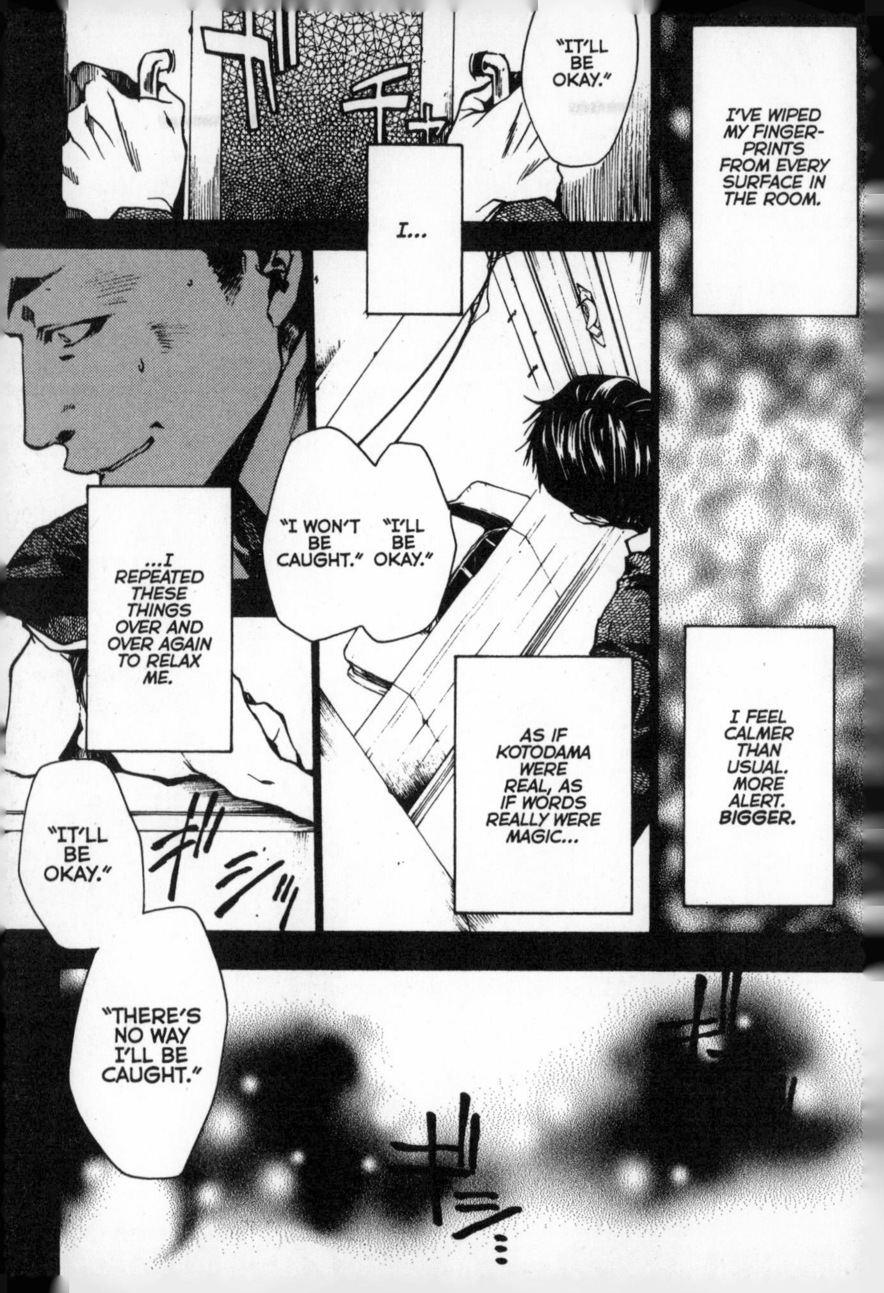
I'VE WIPED MY FINGER-PRINTS FROM EVERY SURFACE IN THE ROOM.
I FEEL CALMER THAN USUAL. MORE ALERT. BIGGER.
"IT'LL BE OKAY."
I...
"I'LL BE OKAY."
"I WON'T BE CAUGHT."
AS IF KOTODAMA WERE REAL, AS IF WORDS REALLY WERE MAGIC...
...I REPEATED THESE THINGS OVER AND OVER AGAIN TO RELAX ME.
"IT'LL BE OKAY."
"THERE'S NO WAY I'LL BE CAUGHT."

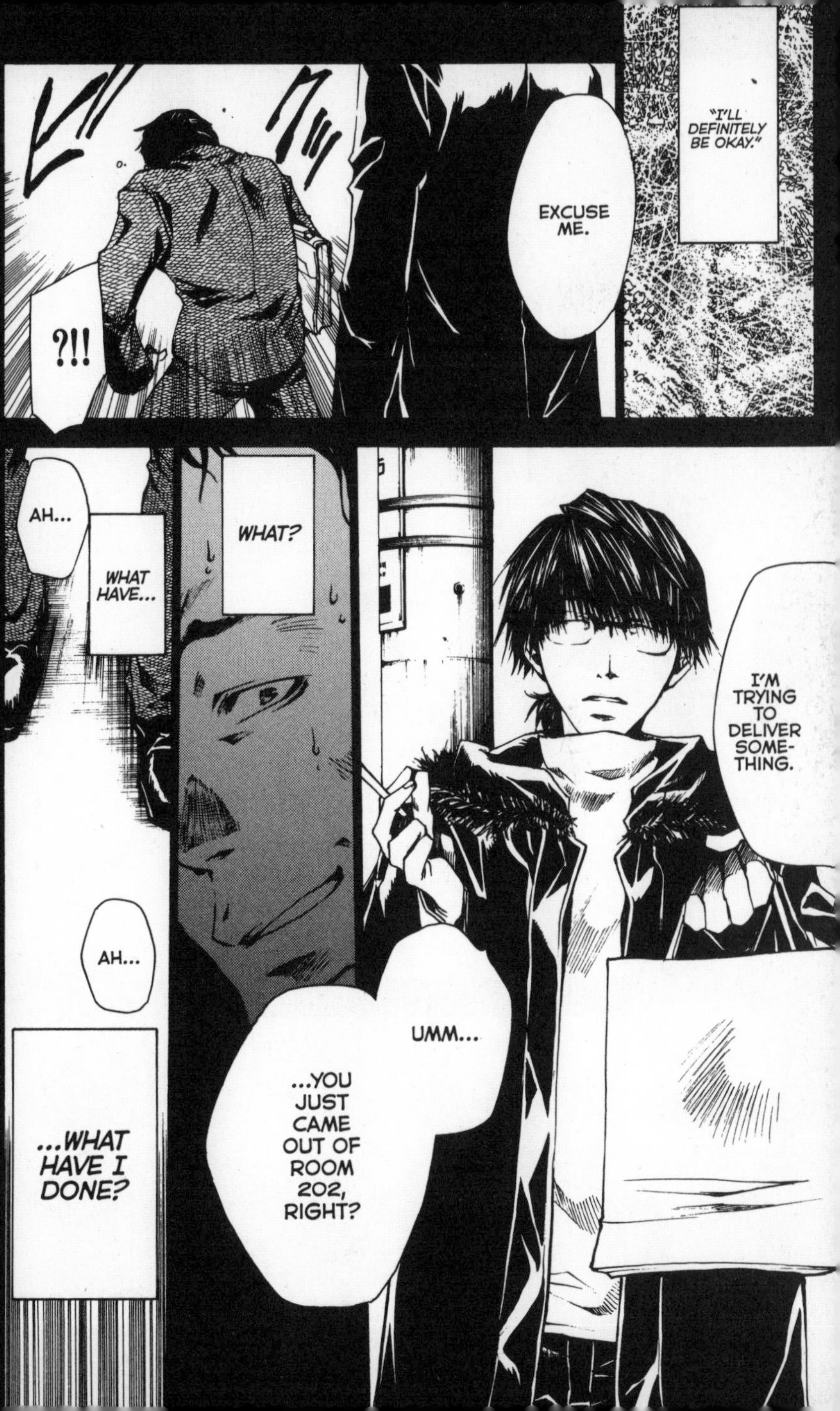
"I'LL DEFINITELY BE OKAY."
EXCUSE ME.
?!!
I'M TRYING TO DELIVER SOMETHING.
UMM...
...YOU JUST CAME OUT OF ROOM 202, RIGHT?
WHAT?
AH...
WHAT HAVE...
AH...
...WHAT HAVE I DONE?

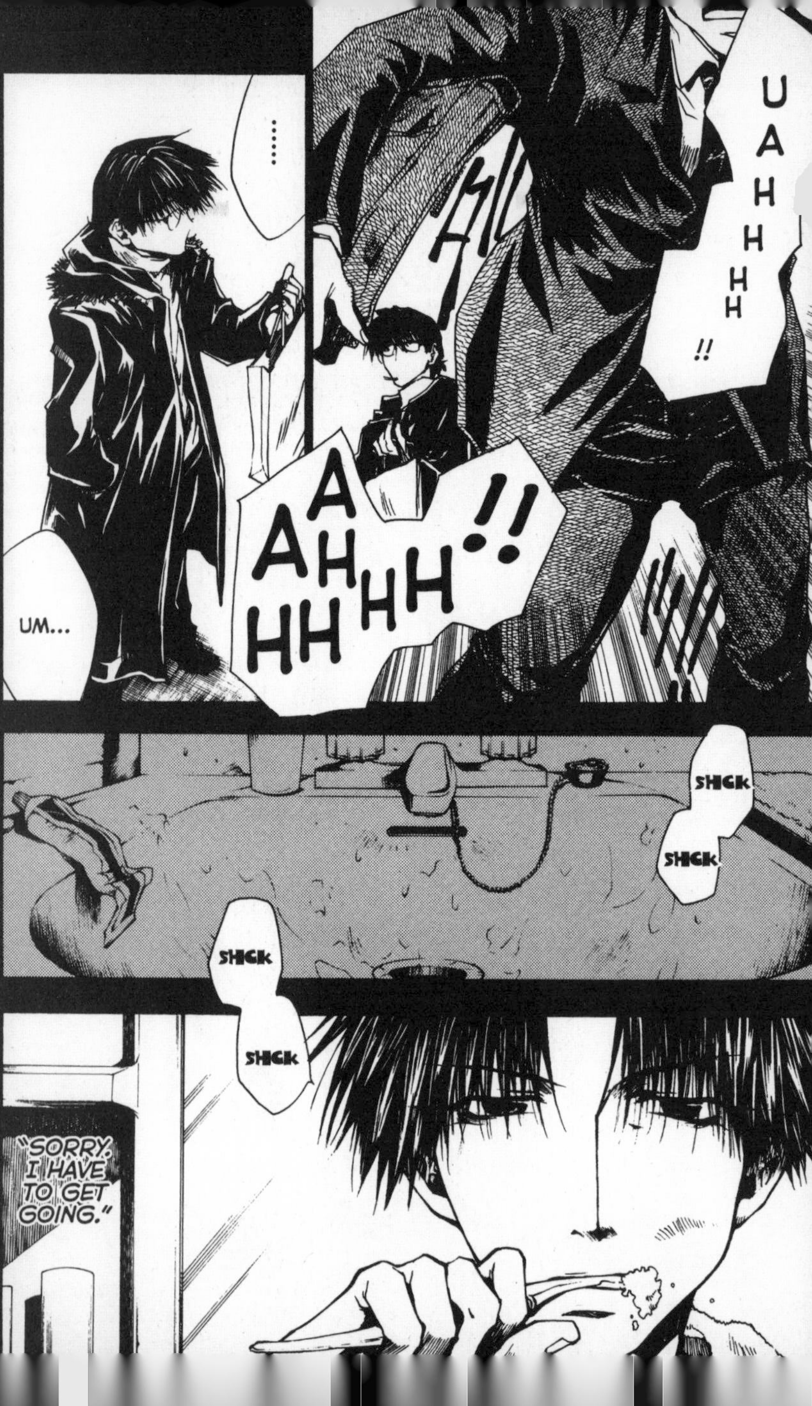
UAHHHH!!
AAHHHHH!!
......
UM...
SHICK
SHICK
SHICK
SHICK
"SORRY. I HAVE TO GET GOING."

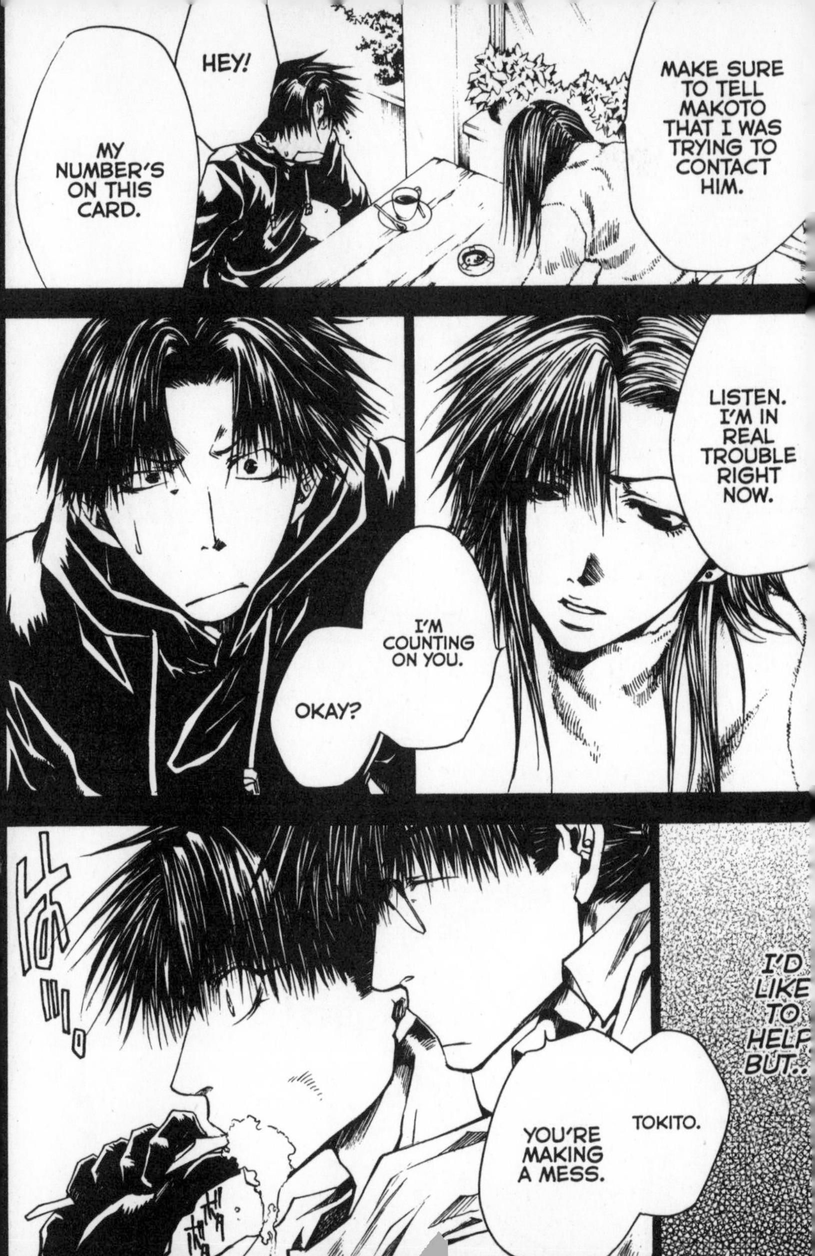
MAKE SURE TO TELL MAKOTO THAT I WAS TRYING TO CONTACT HIM.
HEY!
MY NUMBER'S ON THIS CARD.
LISTEN. I'M IN REAL TROUBLE RIGHT NOW.
I'M COUNTING ON YOU.
OKAY?
I'D LIKE TO HELP BUT...
TOKITO.
YOU'RE MAKING A MESS.

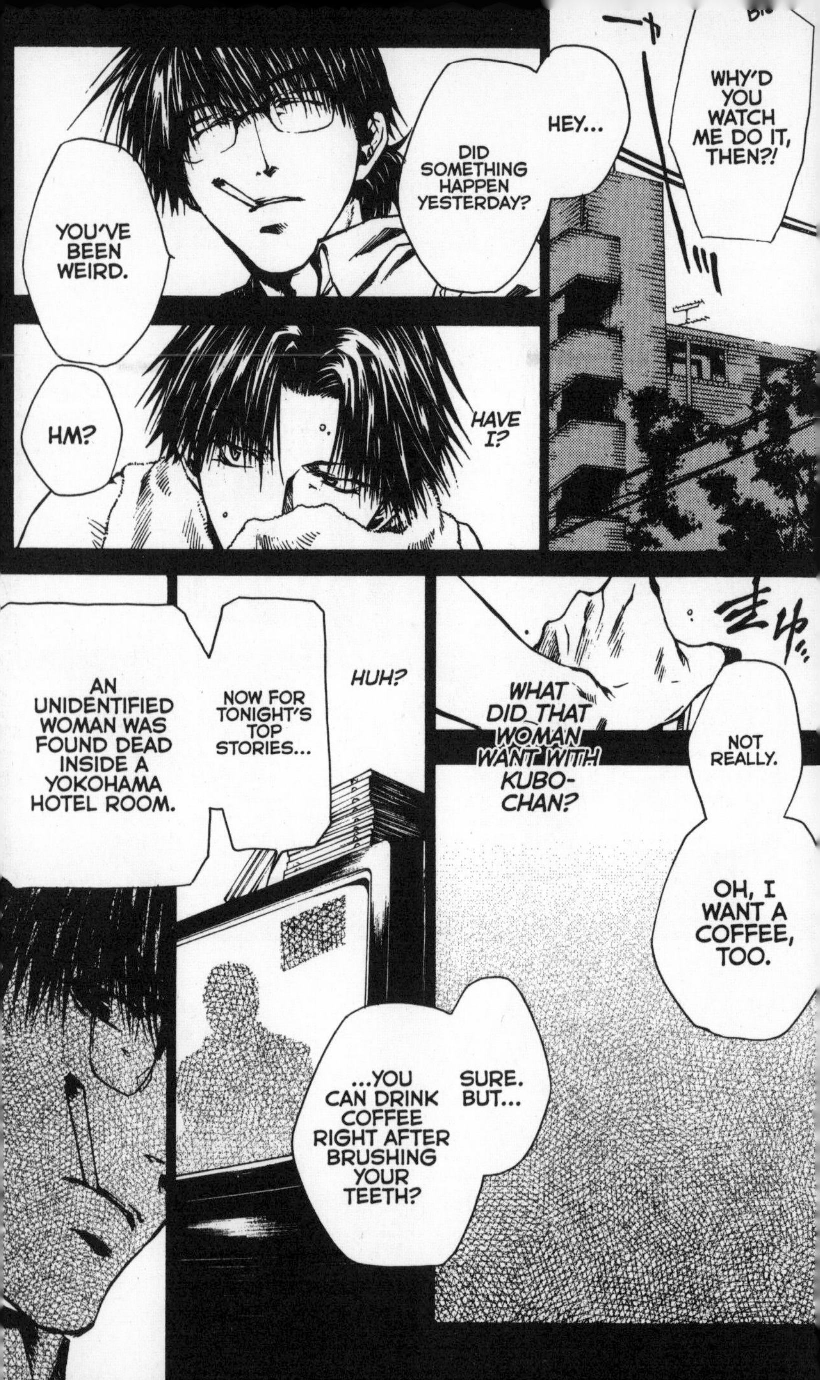
WHY'D YOU WATCH ME DO IT, THEN?!
HEY...
DID SOMETHING HAPPEN YESTERDAY?
YOU'VE BEEN WEIRD.
HAVE I?
HM?
NOT REALLY.
WHAT DID THAT WOMAN WANT WITH KUBO-CHAN?
OH, I WANT A COFFEE, TOO.
SURE. BUT...
...YOU CAN DRINK COFFEE RIGHT AFTER BRUSHING YOUR TEETH?
HUH?
NOW FOR TONIGHT'S TOP STORIES...
AN UNIDENTIFIED WOMAN WAS FOUND DEAD INSIDE A YOKOHAMA HOTEL ROOM.

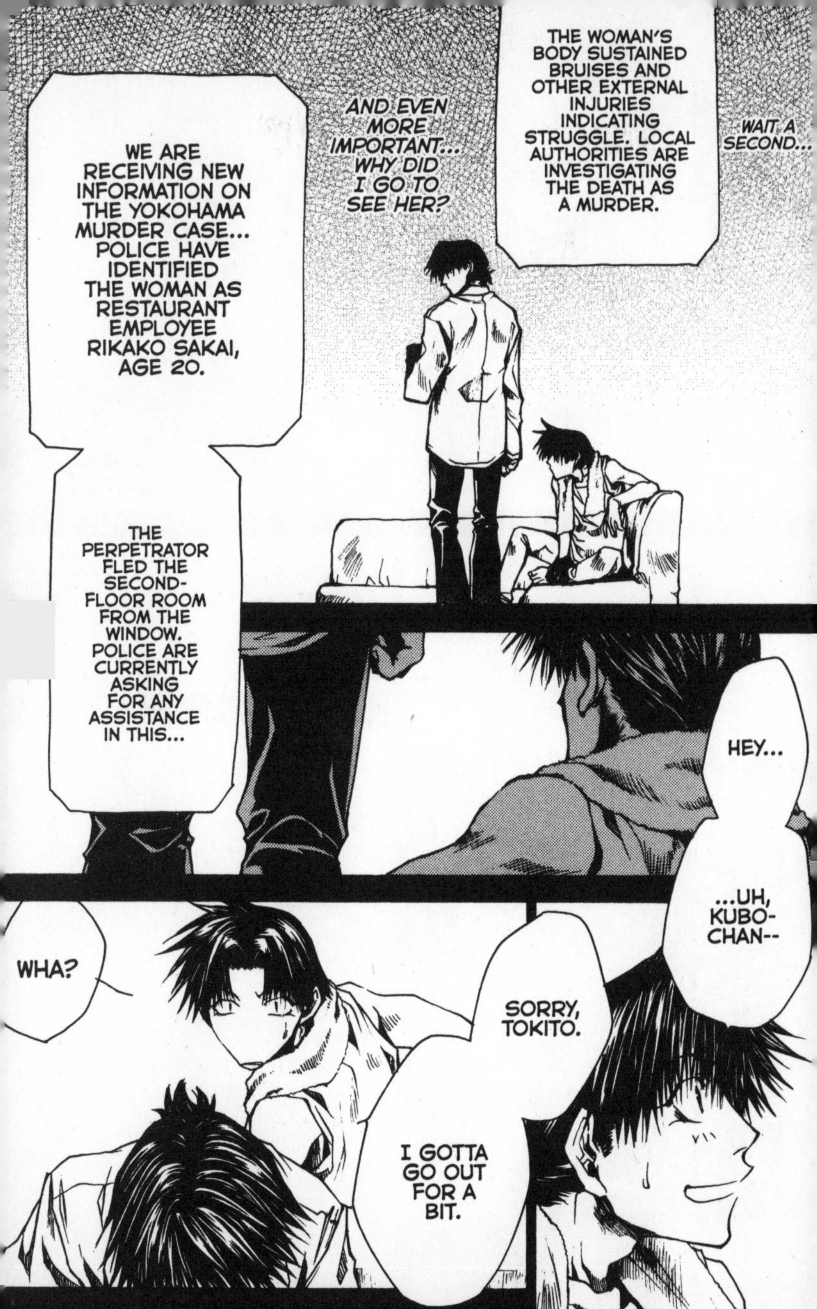

WAIT A SECOND...
THE WOMAN'S BODY SUSTAINED BRUISES AND OTHER EXTERNAL INJURIES INDICATING STRUGGLE. LOCAL AUTHORITIES ARE INVESTIGATING THE DEATH AS A MURDER.
AND EVEN MORE IMPORTANT... WHY DID I GO TO SEE HER?
WE ARE RECEIVING NEW INFORMATION ON THE YOKOHAMA MURDER CASE... POLICE HAVE IDENTIFIED THE WOMAN AS RESTAURANT EMPLOYEE RIKAKO SAKAI, AGE 20.
THE PERPETRATOR FLED THE SECOND-FLOOR ROOM FROM THE WINDOW. POLICE ARE CURRENTLY ASKING FOR ANY ASSISTANCE IN THIS...
HEY...
...UH, KUBO-CHAN--
SORRY, TOKITO.
I GOTTA GO OUT FOR A BIT.
WHA?

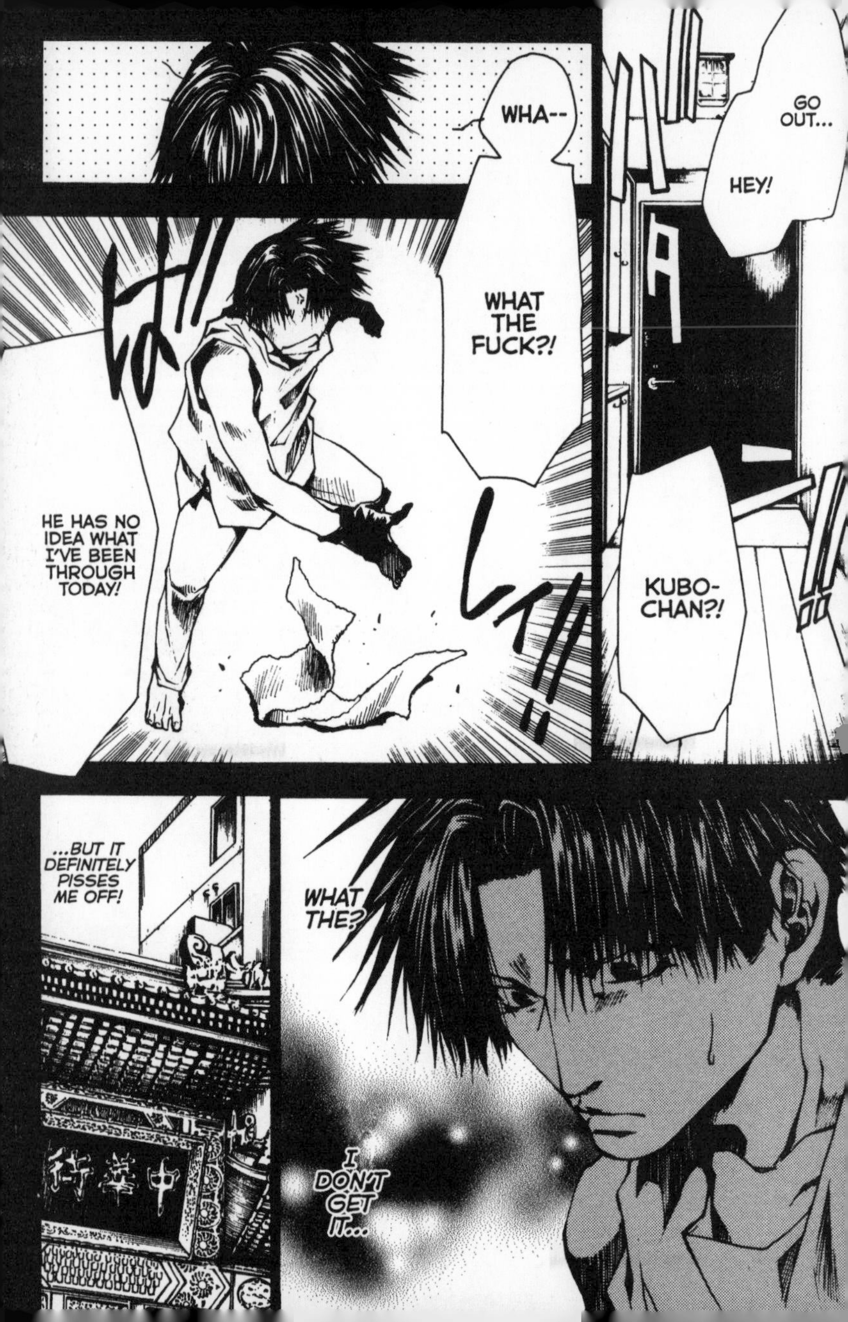
GO OUT...
HEY!
KUBO-CHAN?!
WHA--
WHAT THE FUCK?!
HE HAS NO IDEA WHAT I'VE BEEN THROUGH TODAY!
WHAT THE?
I DON'T GET IT...
...BUT IT DEFINITELY PISSES ME OFF!
中華街

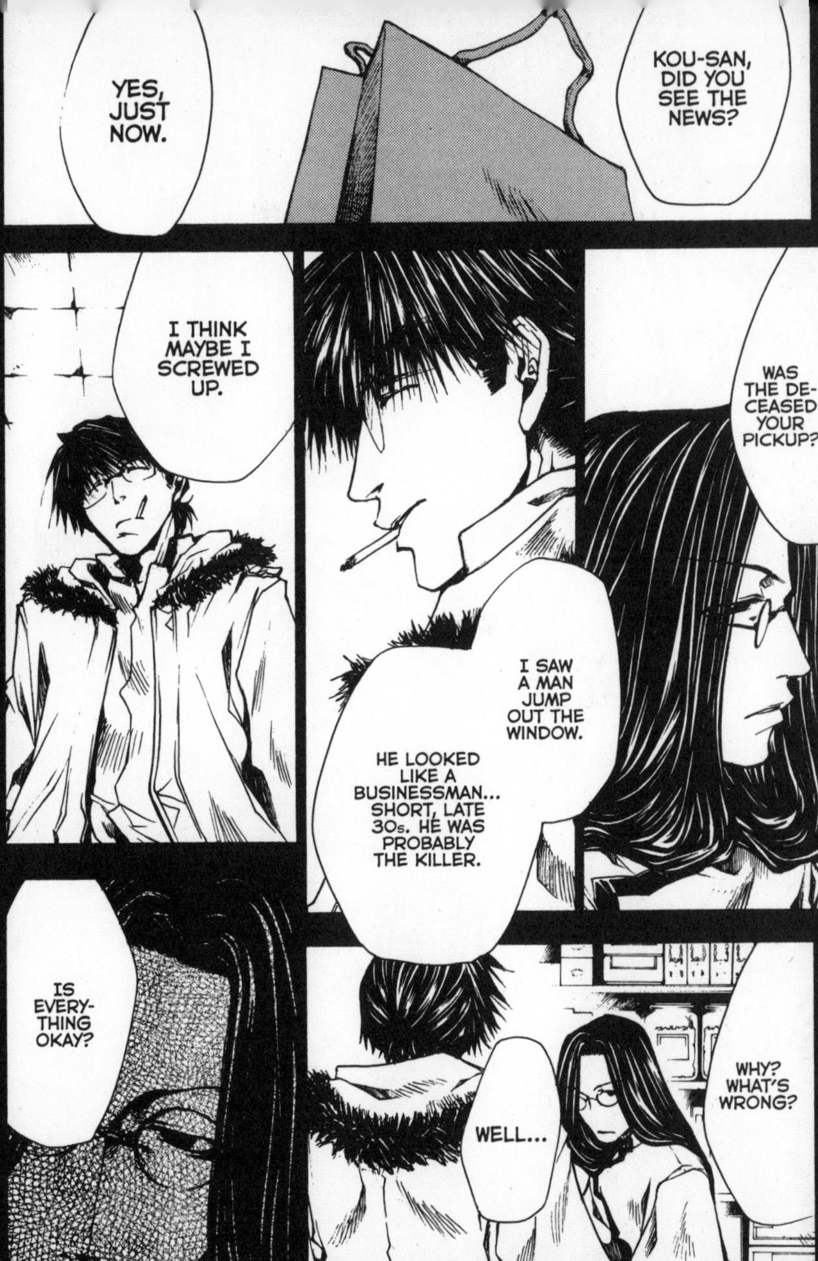
KOU-SAN, DID YOU SEE THE NEWS?
YES, JUST NOW.
WAS THE DE-CEASED YOUR PICKUP?
I THINK MAYBE I SCREWED UP.
I SAW A MAN JUMP OUT THE WINDOW.
HE LOOKED LIKE A BUSINESSMAN... SHORT, LATE 30s. HE WAS PROBABLY THE KILLER.
WHY? WHAT'S WRONG?
WELL...
IS EVERY-THING OKAY?

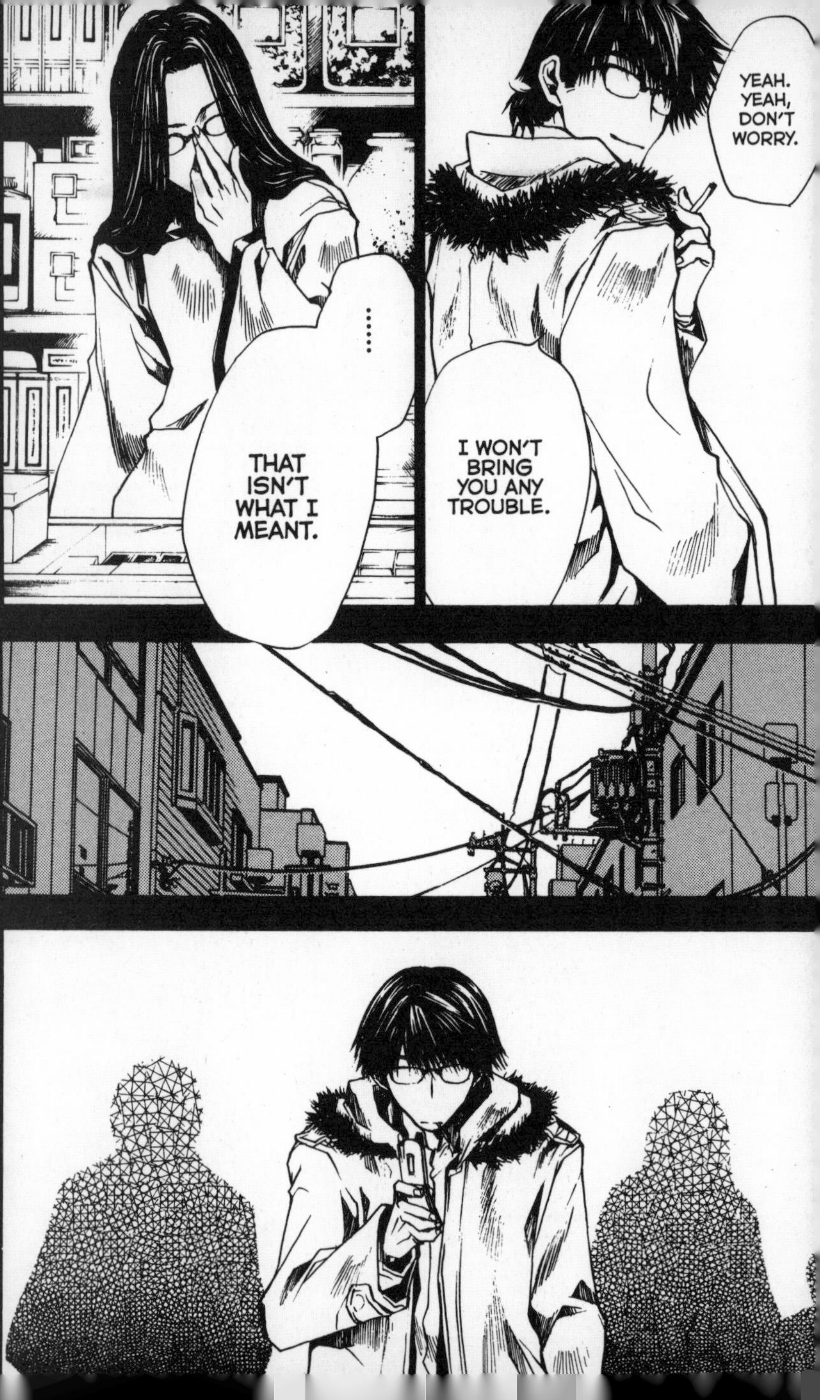
YEAH. YEAH, DON'T WORRY.
I WON'T BRING YOU ANY TROUBLE.
......
THAT ISN'T WHAT I MEANT.

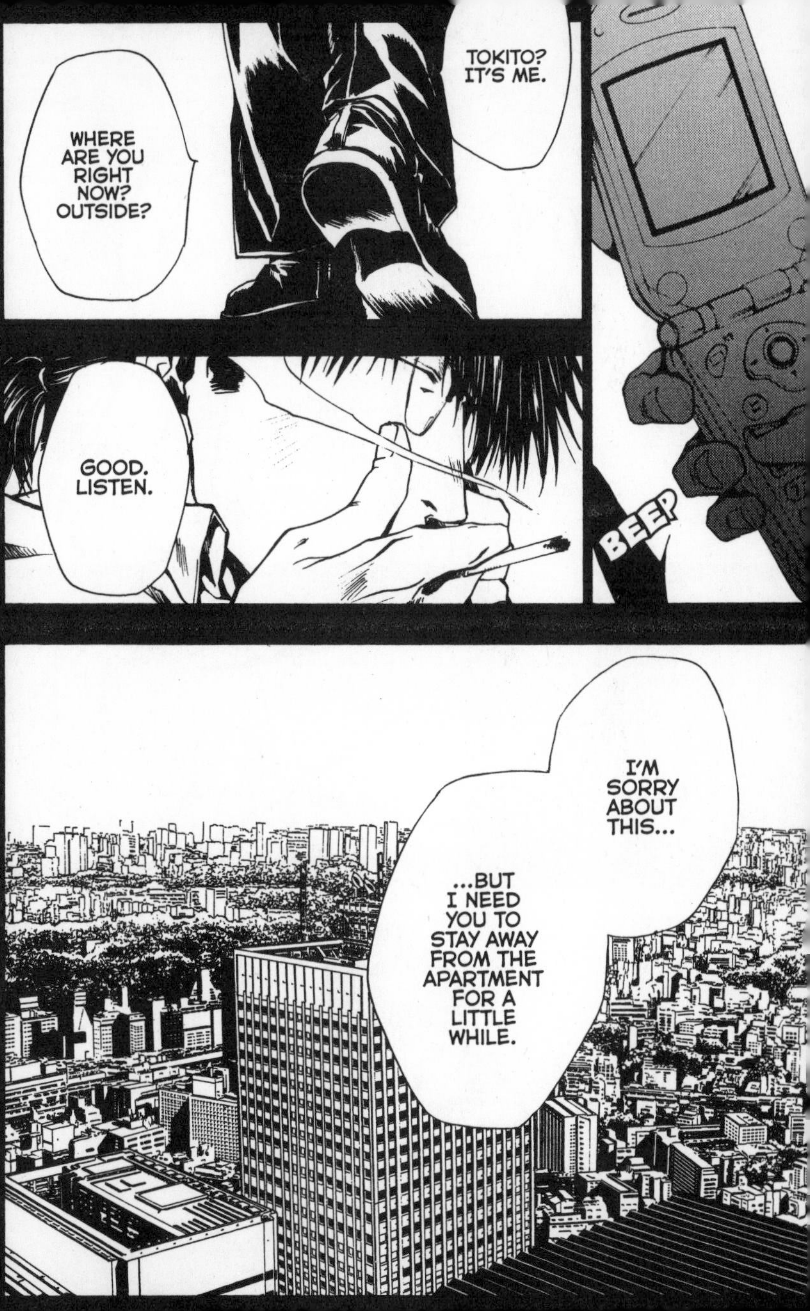
BEEP
TOKITO? IT'S ME.
WHERE ARE YOU RIGHT NOW? OUTSIDE?
GOOD. LISTEN.
I'M SORRY ABOUT THIS...
...BUT I NEED YOU TO STAY AWAY FROM THE APARTMENT FOR A LITTLE WHILE.

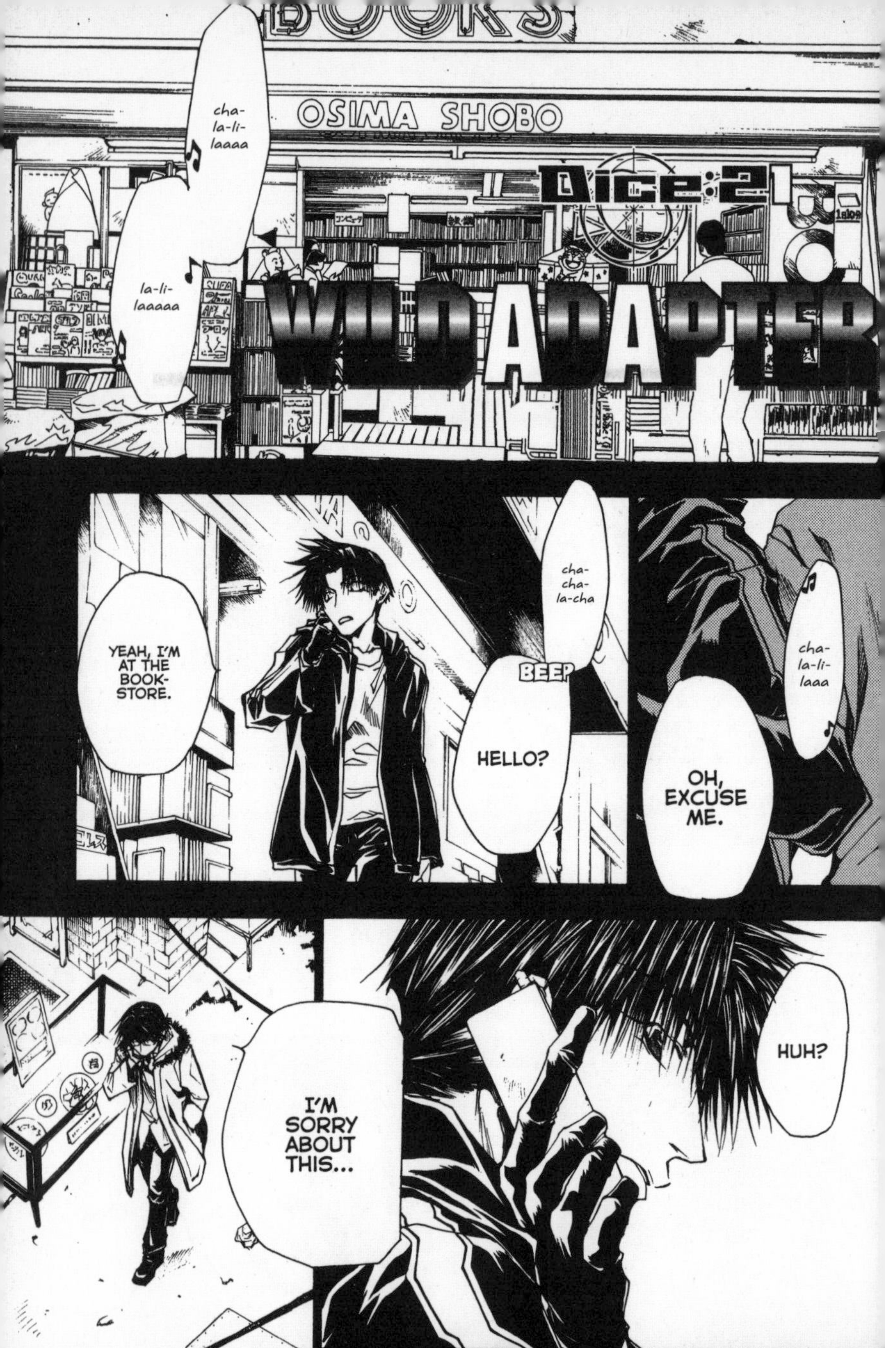
BOOKS
OSIMA SHOBO
Dice:21
WILD ADAPTER
cha-la-li-laaaa
la-li-laaaaa
cha-la-li-laaa
OH, EXCUSE ME.
cha-cha-la-cha
BEEP
HELLO?
YEAH, I'M AT THE BOOK-STORE.
HUH?
I'M SORRY ABOUT THIS...

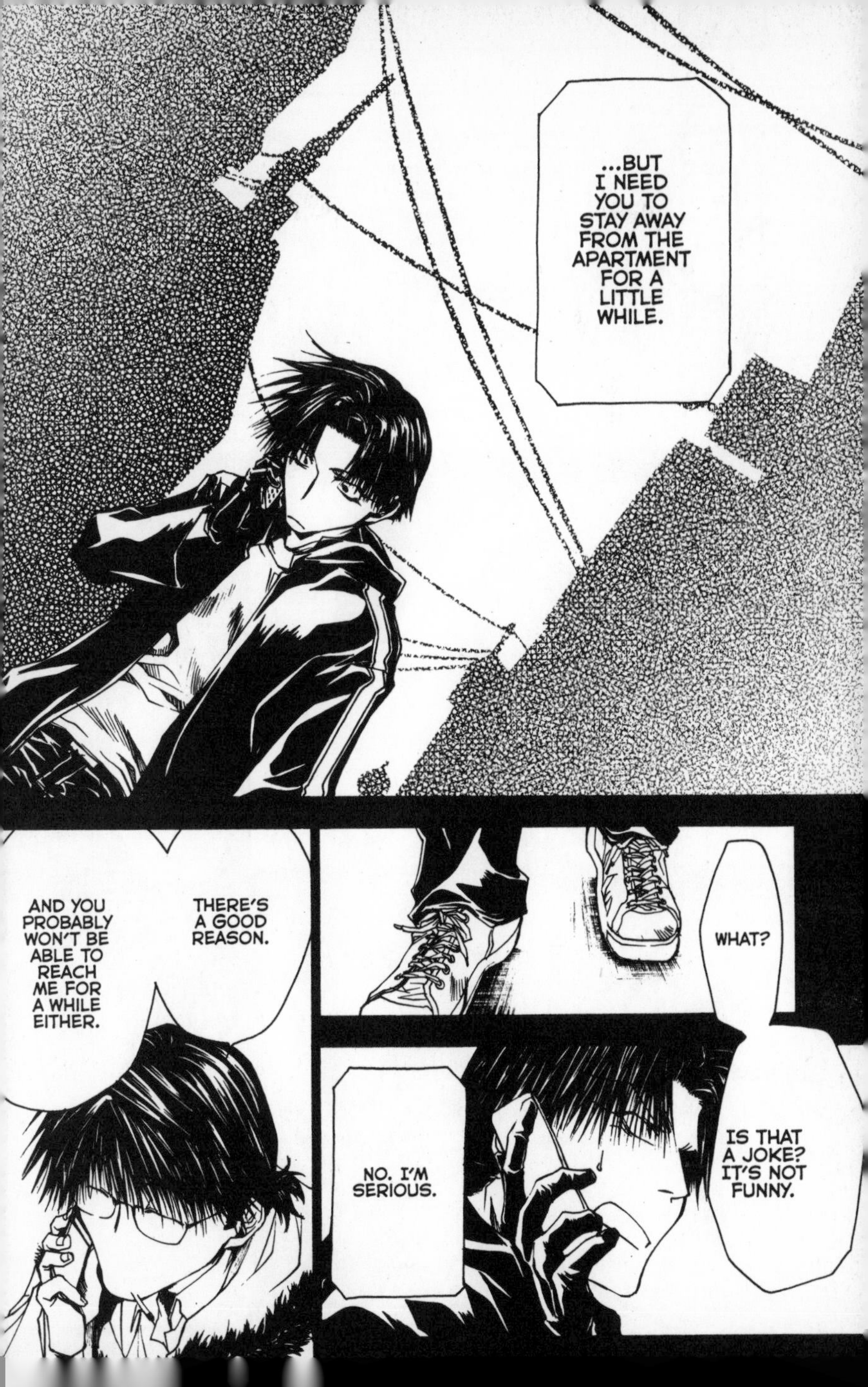
...BUT I NEED YOU TO STAY AWAY FROM THE APARTMENT FOR A LITTLE WHILE.
WHAT?
IS THAT A JOKE? IT'S NOT FUNNY.
NO. I'M SERIOUS.
THERE'S A GOOD REASON.
AND YOU PROBABLY WON'T BE ABLE TO REACH ME FOR A WHILE EITHER.

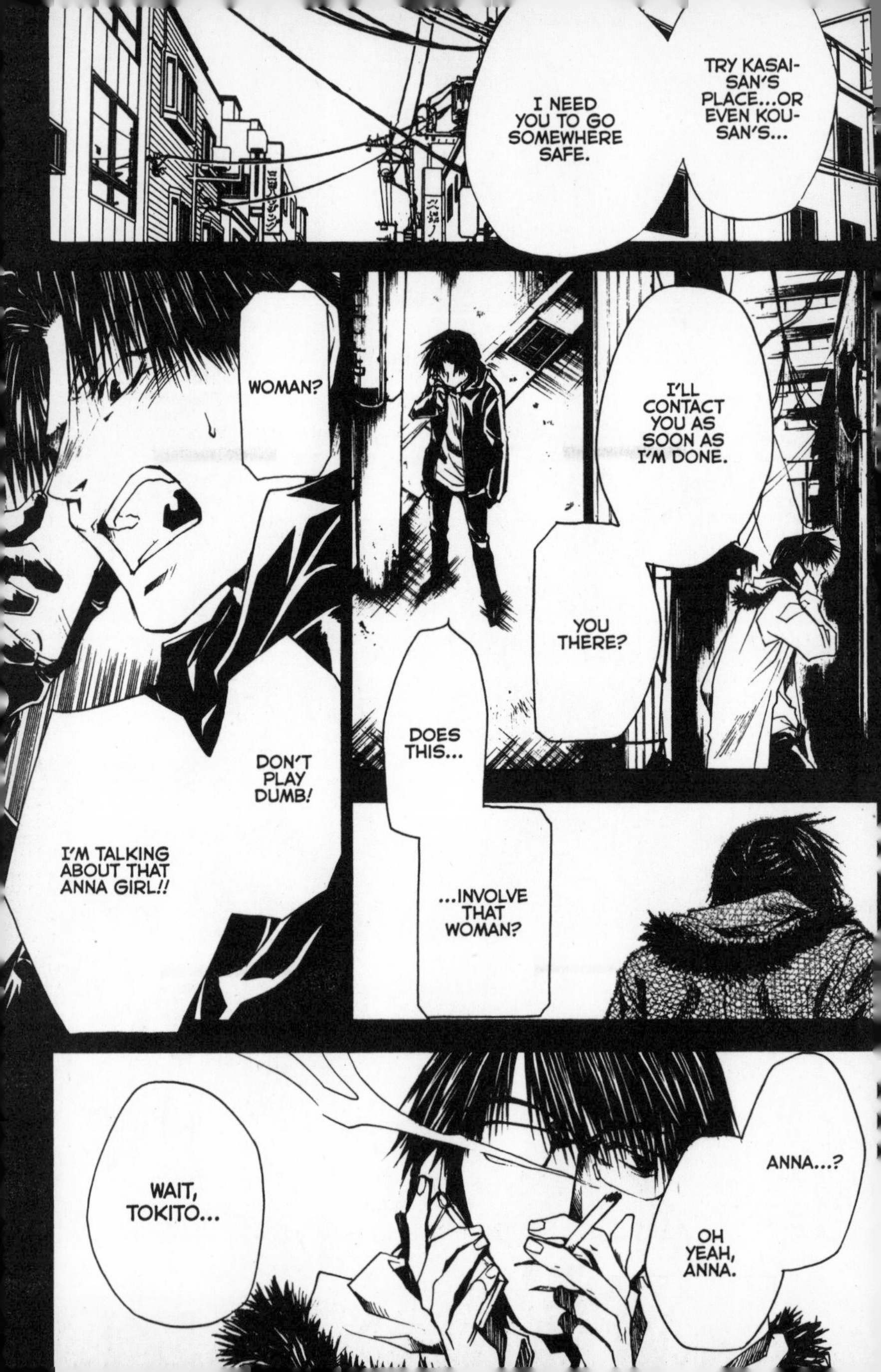

TRY KASAI-SAN'S PLACE...OR EVEN KOU-SAN'S...
I NEED YOU TO GO SOMEWHERE SAFE.
I'LL CONTACT YOU AS SOON AS I'M DONE.
YOU THERE?
DOES THIS...
...INVOLVE THAT WOMAN?
WOMAN?
DON'T PLAY DUMB!
I'M TALKING ABOUT THAT ANNA GIRL!!
ANNA...?
OH YEAH, ANNA.
WAIT, TOKITO...

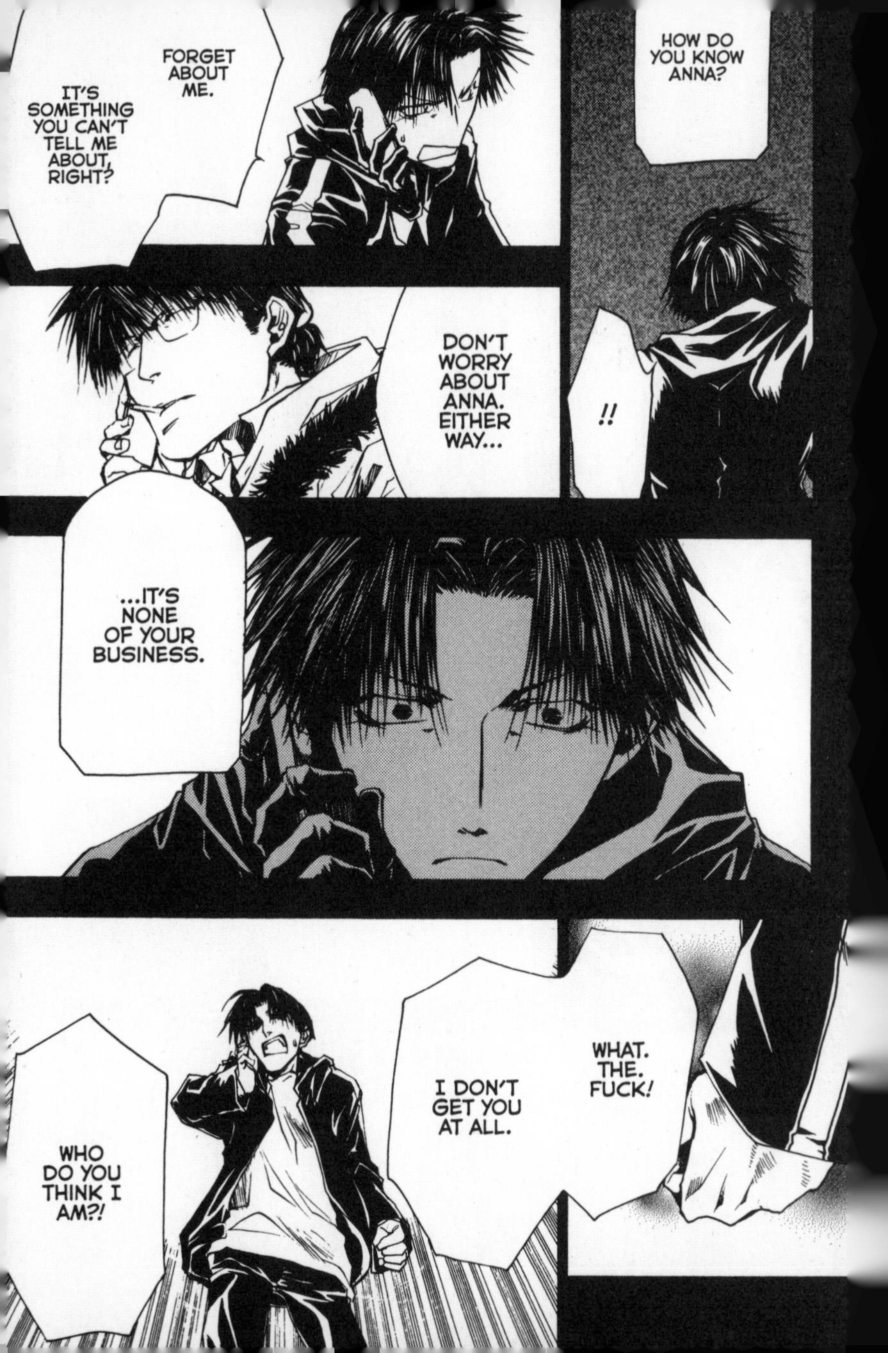
HOW DO YOU KNOW ANNA?
FORGET ABOUT ME.
IT'S SOMETHING YOU CAN'T TELL ME ABOUT, RIGHT?
!!
DON'T WORRY ABOUT ANNA. EITHER WAY...
...IT'S NONE OF YOUR BUSINESS.
WHAT. THE. FUCK!
I DON'T GET YOU AT ALL.
WHO DO YOU THINK I AM?!

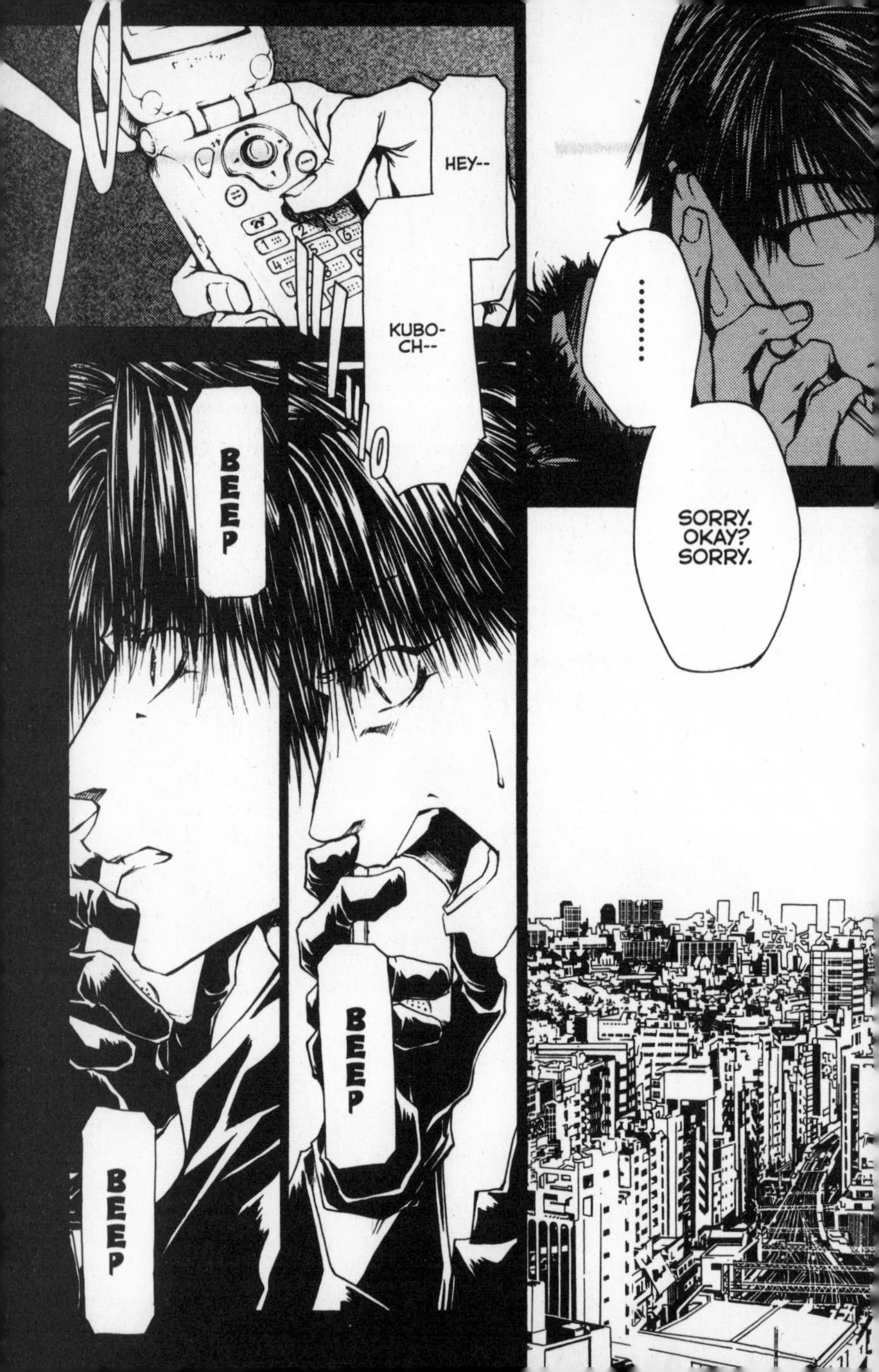

......
SORRY. OKAY? SORRY.
HEY--
KUBO-CH--
BEEP
BEEP
BEEP

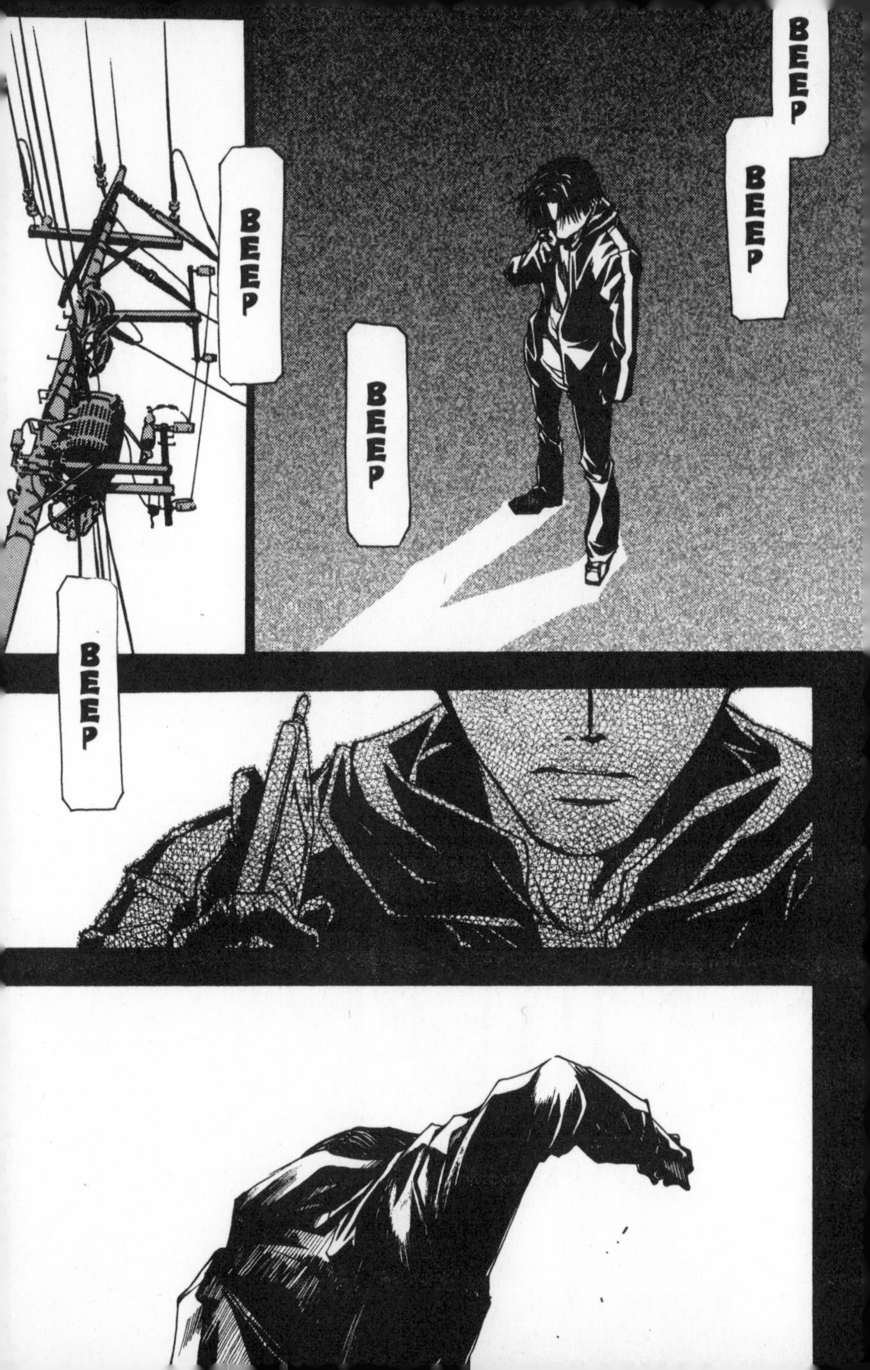
BEEP
BEEP
BEEP
BEEP
BEEP

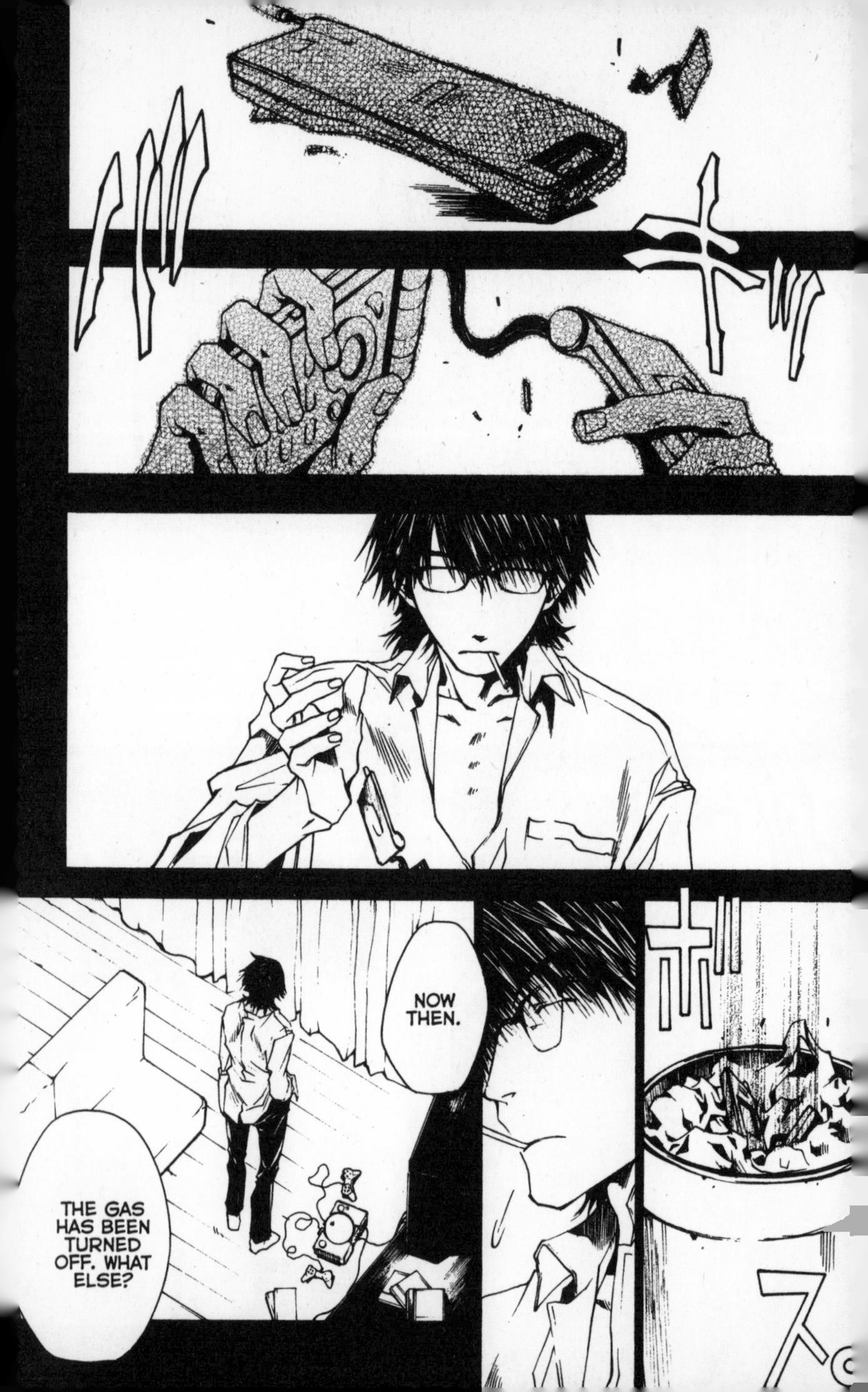
NOW THEN.
THE GAS HAS BEEN TURNED OFF. WHAT ELSE?

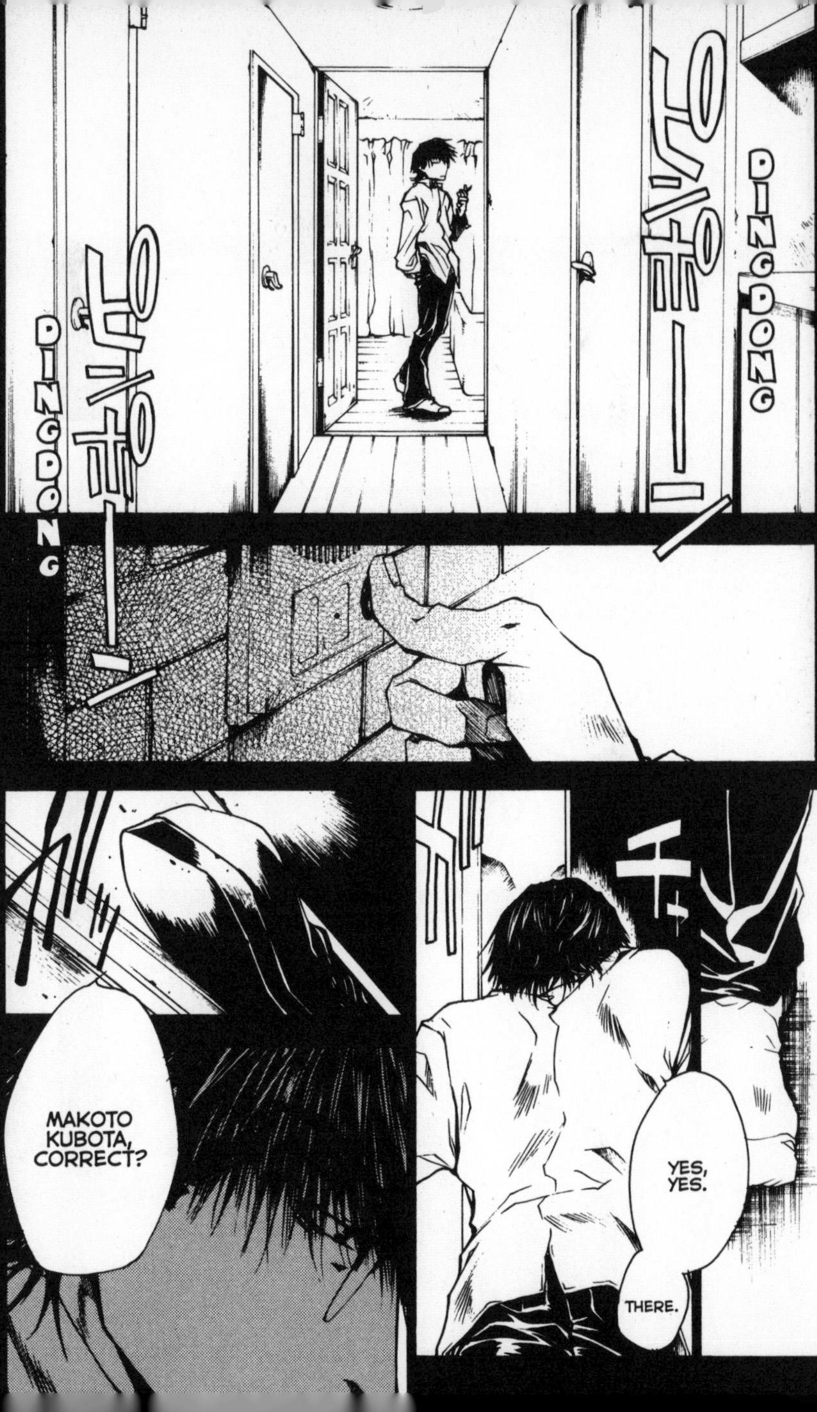
DINGDONG
DINGDONG
MAKOTO KUBOTA, CORRECT?
YES, YES.
THERE.

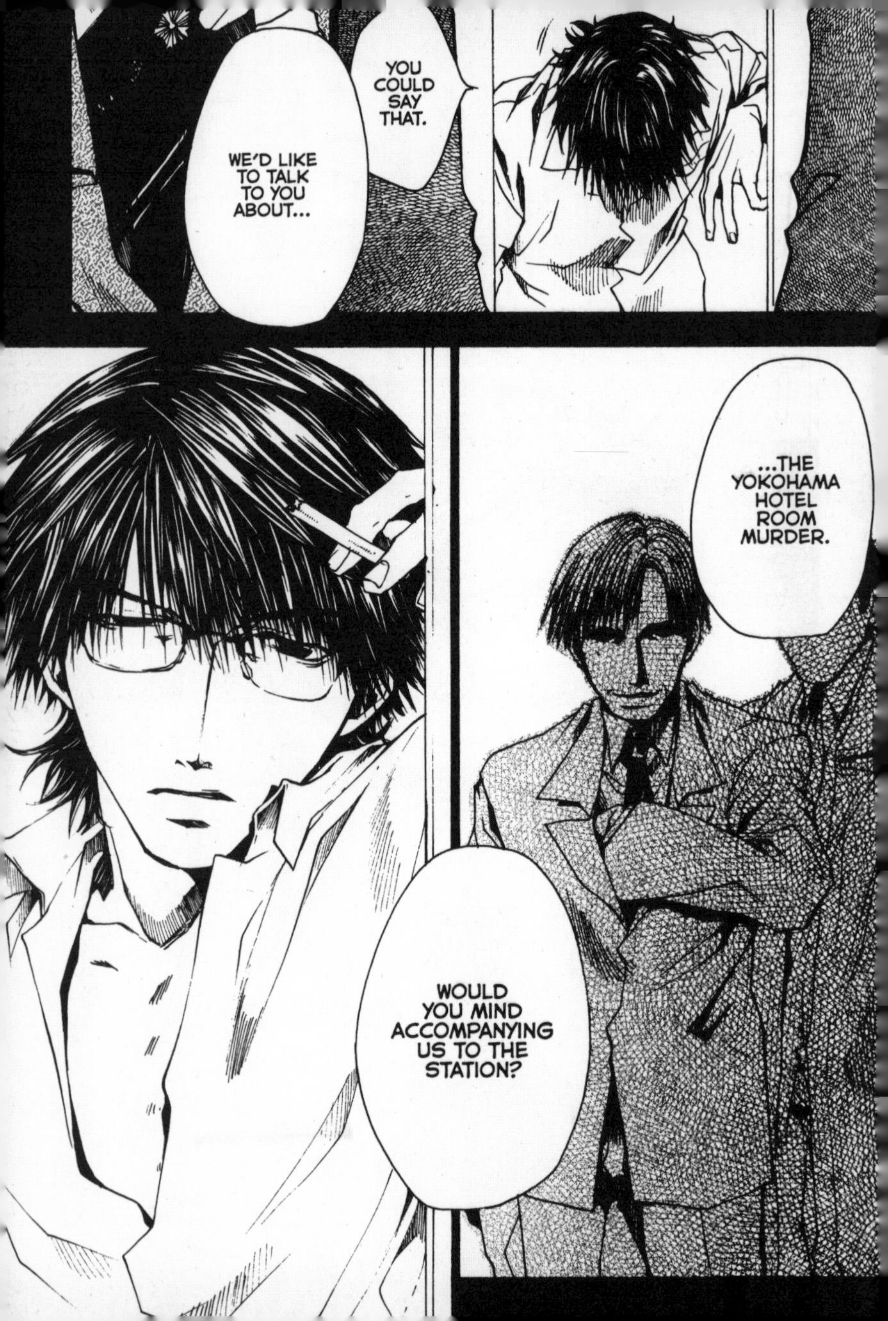
YOU COULD SAY THAT.
WE'D LIKE TO TALK TO YOU ABOUT...
...THE YOKOHAMA HOTEL ROOM MURDER.
WOULD YOU MIND ACCOMPANYING US TO THE STATION?

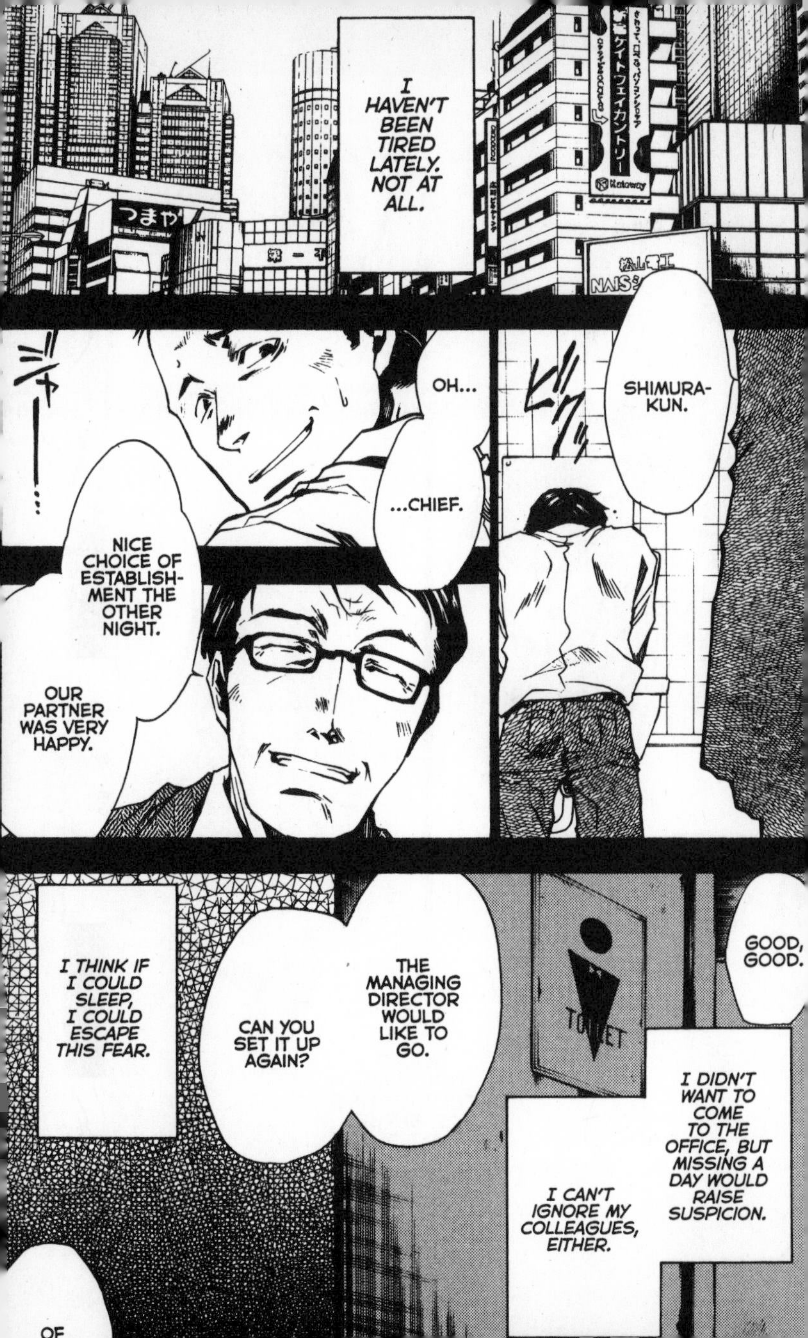
I HAVEN'T BEEN TIRED LATELY. NOT AT ALL.
SHIMURA-KUN.
ビクッ
OH...
...CHIEF.
ジャー…
NICE CHOICE OF ESTABLISHMENT THE OTHER NIGHT.
OUR PARTNER WAS VERY HAPPY.
GOOD, GOOD.
I DIDN'T WANT TO COME TO THE OFFICE, BUT MISSING A DAY WOULD RAISE SUSPICION.
I CAN'T IGNORE MY COLLEAGUES, EITHER.
THE MANAGING DIRECTOR WOULD LIKE TO GO.
CAN YOU SET IT UP AGAIN?
I THINK IF I COULD SLEEP, I COULD ESCAPE THIS FEAR.
OF

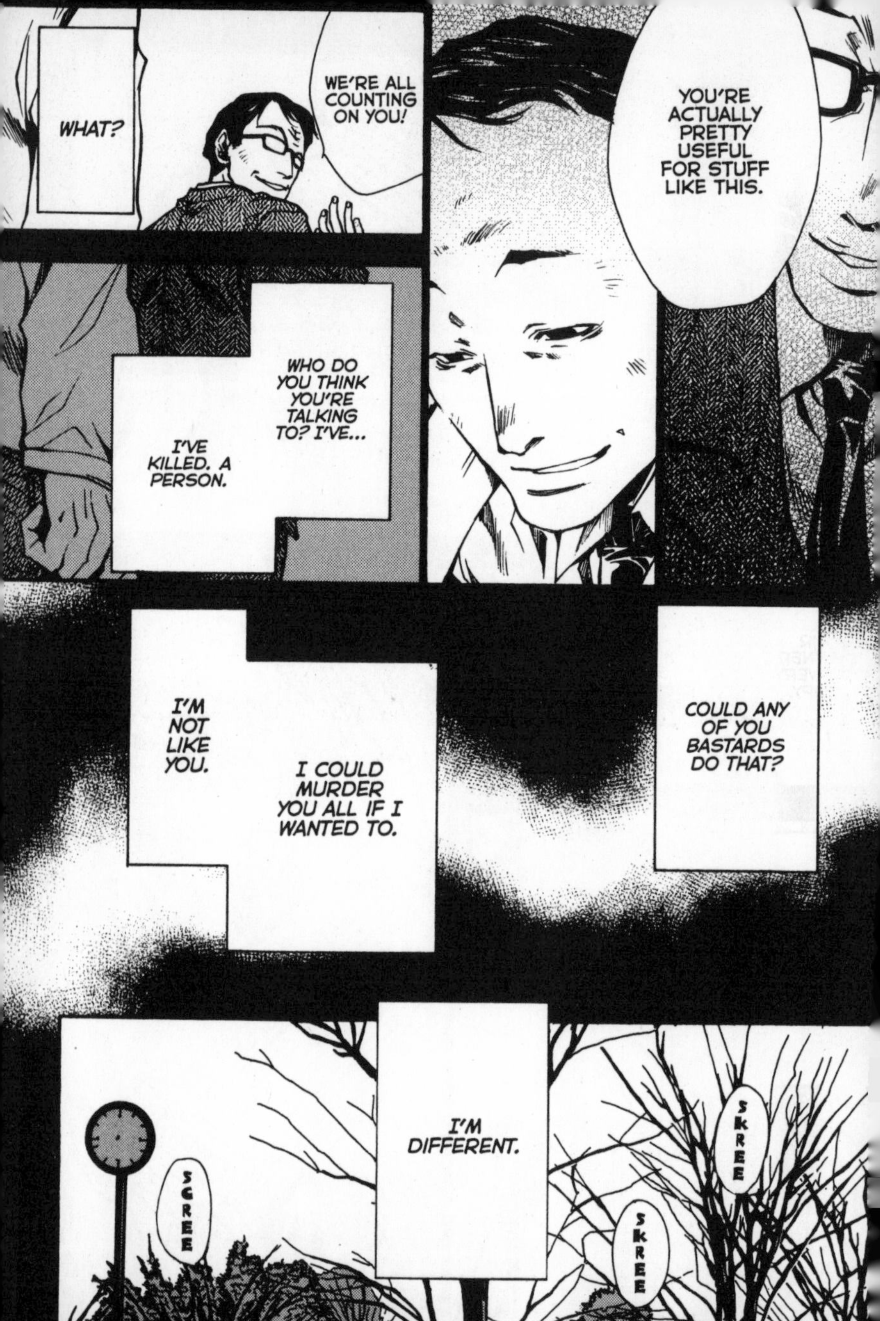
YOU'RE ACTUALLY PRETTY USEFUL FOR STUFF LIKE THIS.
WE'RE ALL COUNTING ON YOU!
WHAT?
WHO DO YOU THINK YOU'RE TALKING TO? I'VE...
I'VE KILLED. A PERSON.
COULD ANY OF YOU BASTARDS DO THAT?
I'M NOT LIKE YOU.
I COULD MURDER YOU ALL IF I WANTED TO.
SKREE
SKREE
I'M DIFFERENT.
SCREE

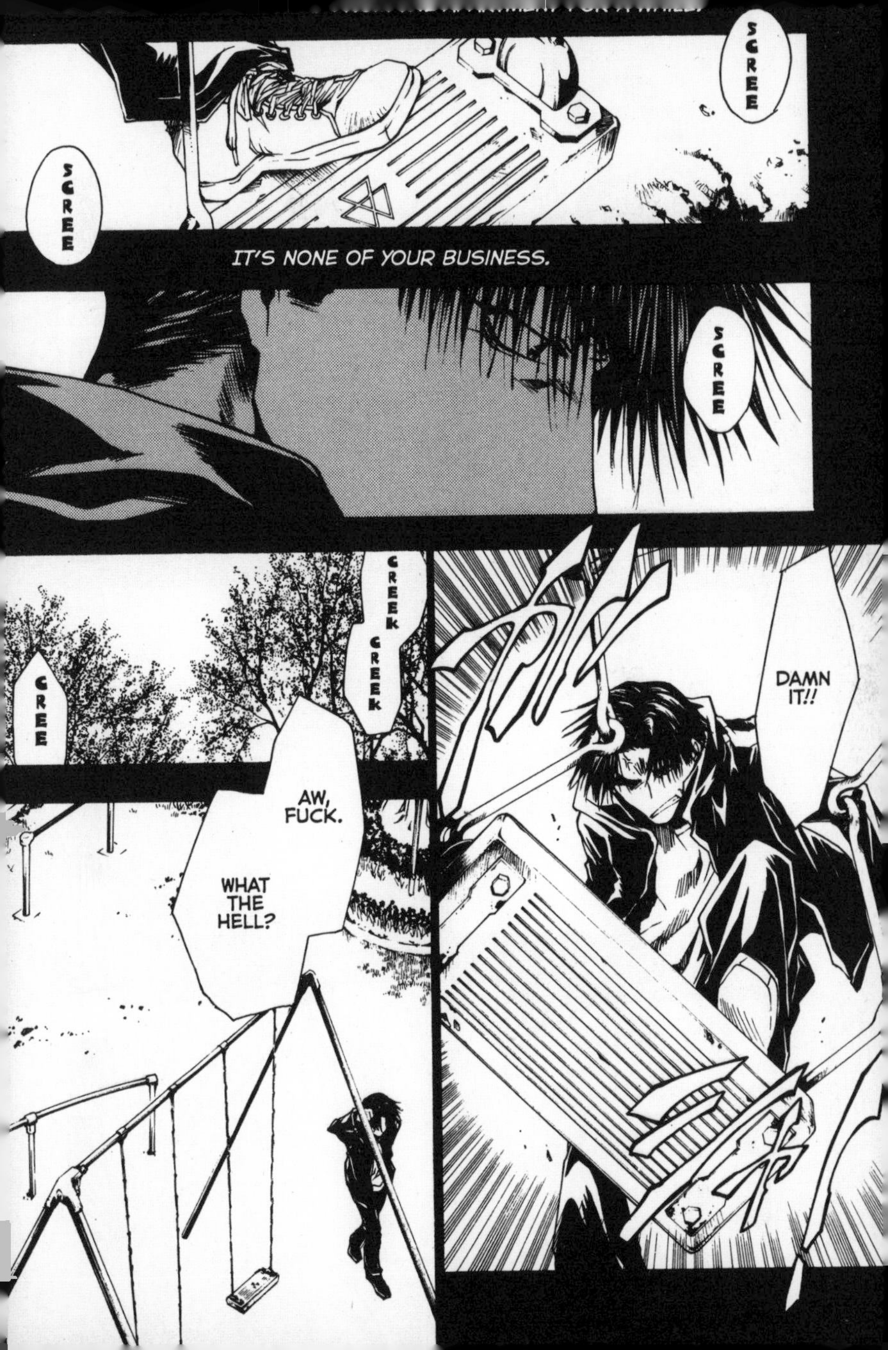
SCREE
SCREE
IT'S NONE OF YOUR BUSINESS.
SCREE
DAMN IT!!
CREEK
CREEK
CREE
AW, FUCK.
WHAT THE HELL?

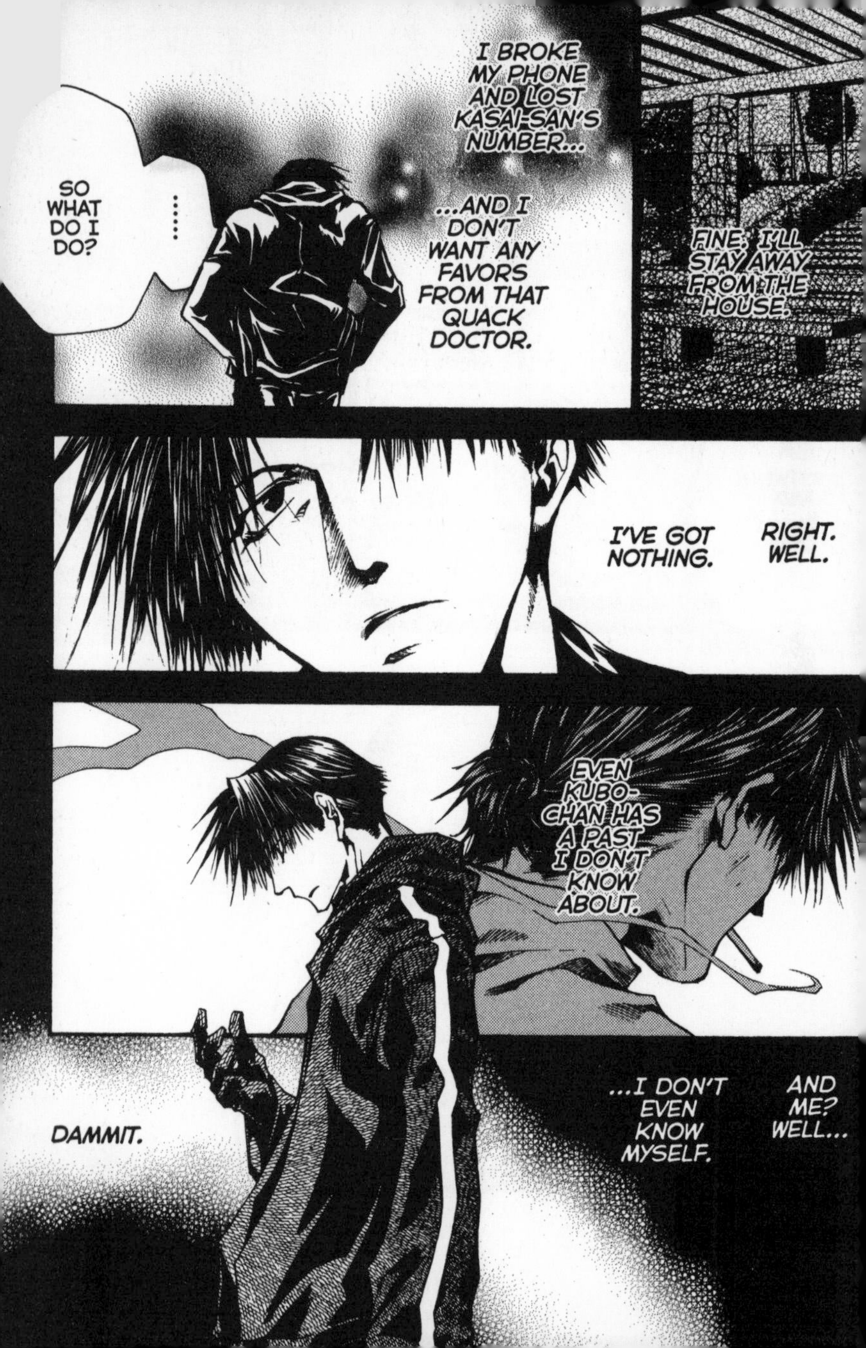
FINE. I'LL STAY AWAY FROM THE HOUSE.
I BROKE MY PHONE AND LOST KASAI-SAN'S NUMBER...
...AND I DON'T WANT ANY FAVORS FROM THAT QUACK DOCTOR.
......
SO WHAT DO I DO?
RIGHT. WELL.
I'VE GOT NOTHING.
EVEN KUBO-CHAN HAS A PAST I DON'T KNOW ABOUT.
AND ME? WELL...
...I DON'T EVEN KNOW MYSELF.
DAMMIT.

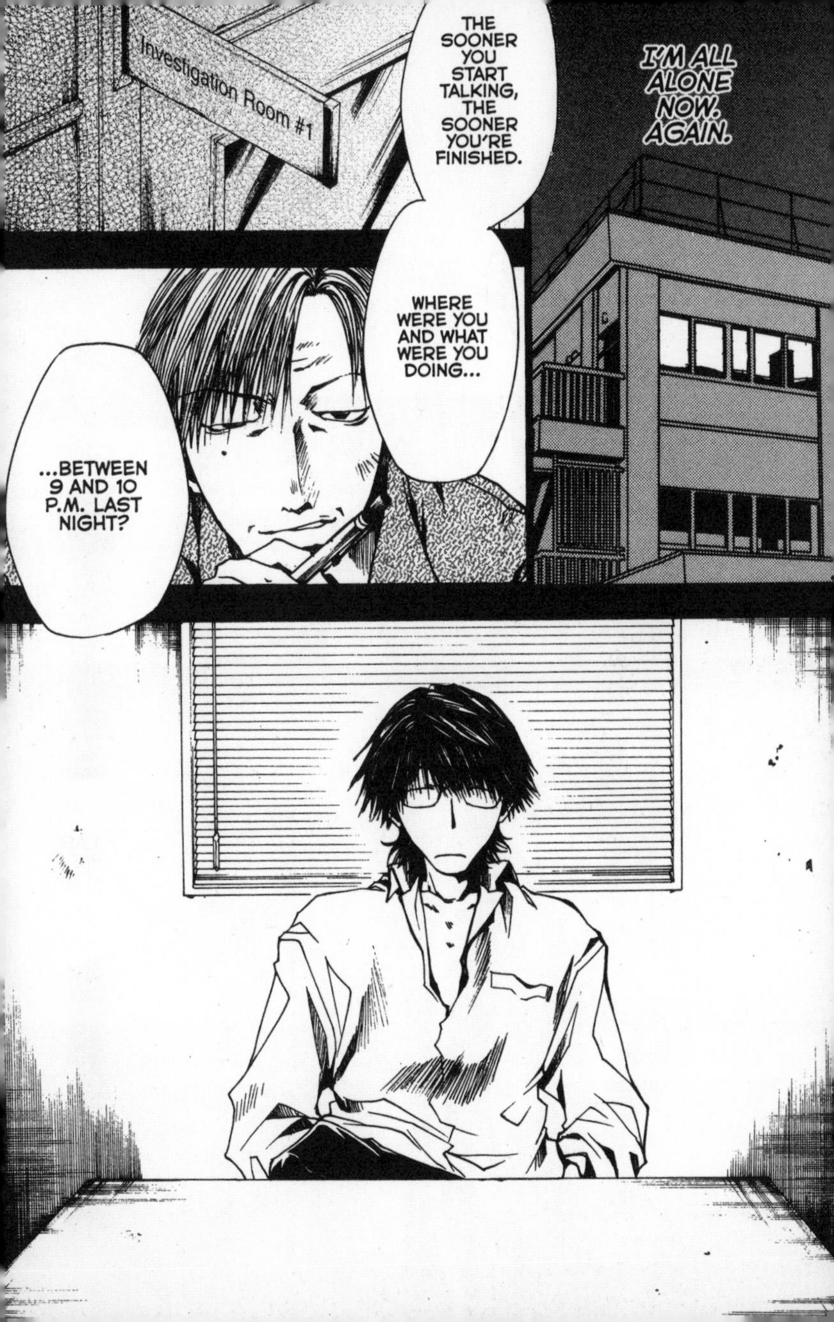
I'M ALL ALONE NOW. AGAIN.
Investigation Room #1
THE SOONER YOU START TALKING, THE SOONER YOU'RE FINISHED.
WHERE WERE YOU AND WHAT WERE YOU DOING...
...BETWEEN 9 AND 10 P.M. LAST NIGHT?

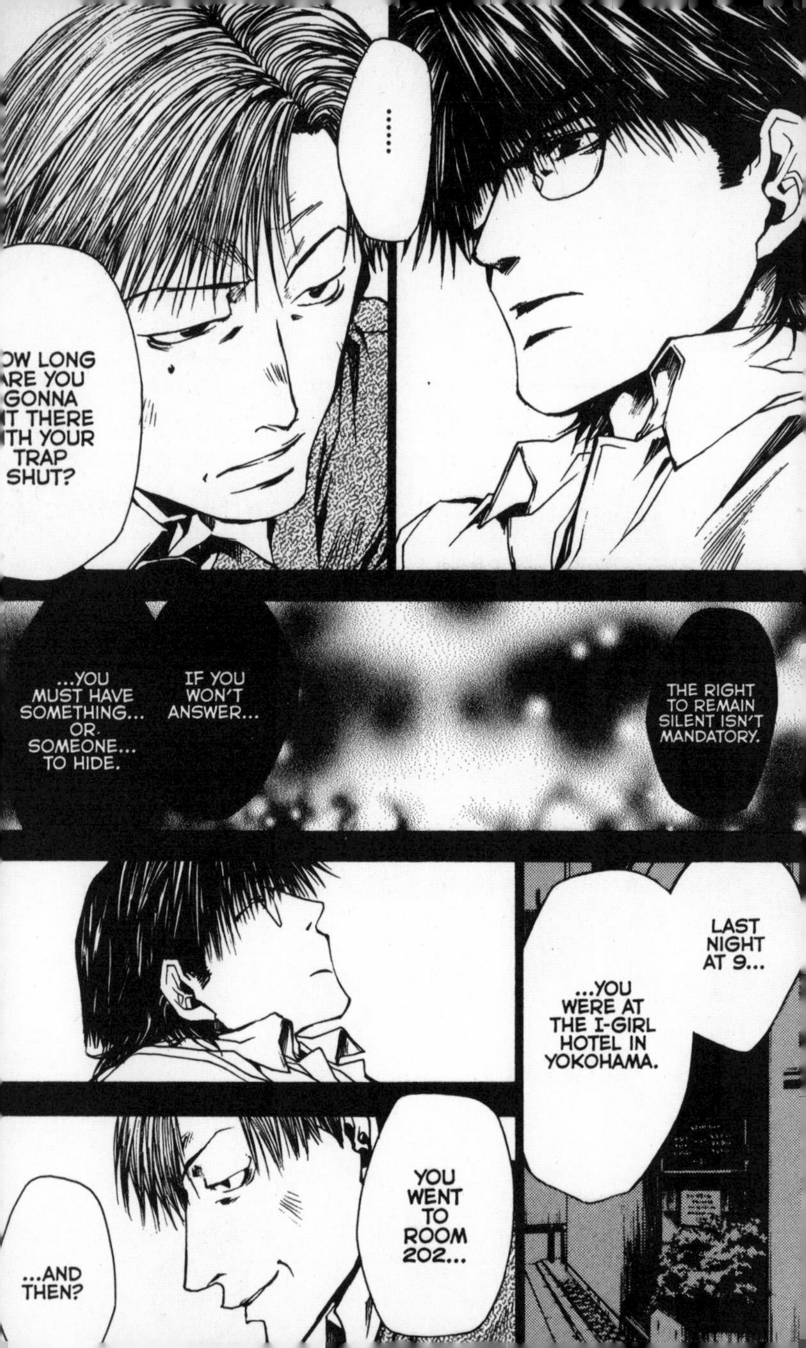
......
OW LONG RE YOU GONNA T THERE TH YOUR TRAP SHUT?
THE RIGHT TO REMAIN SILENT ISN'T MANDATORY.
IF YOU WON'T ANSWER...
...YOU MUST HAVE SOMETHING... OR. SOMEONE... TO HIDE.
LAST NIGHT AT 9...
...YOU WERE AT THE I-GIRL HOTEL IN YOKOHAMA.
YOU WENT TO ROOM 202...
...AND THEN?

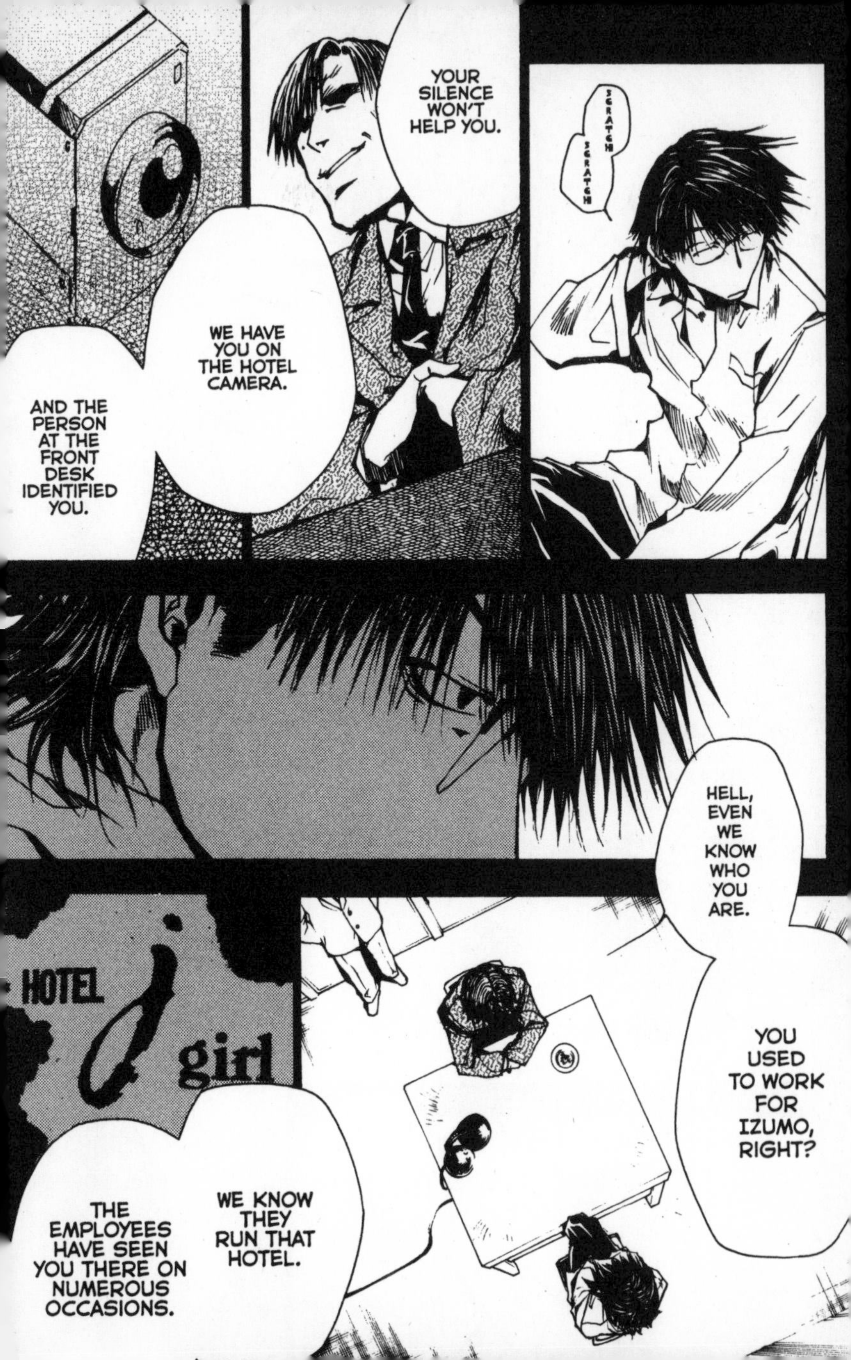
SCRATCH SCRATCH
YOUR SILENCE WON'T HELP YOU.
WE HAVE YOU ON THE HOTEL CAMERA.
AND THE PERSON AT THE FRONT DESK IDENTIFIED YOU.
HELL, EVEN WE KNOW WHO YOU ARE.
YOU USED TO WORK FOR IZUMO, RIGHT?
HOTEL
girl
WE KNOW THEY RUN THAT HOTEL.
THE EMPLOYEES HAVE SEEN YOU THERE ON NUMEROUS OCCASIONS.

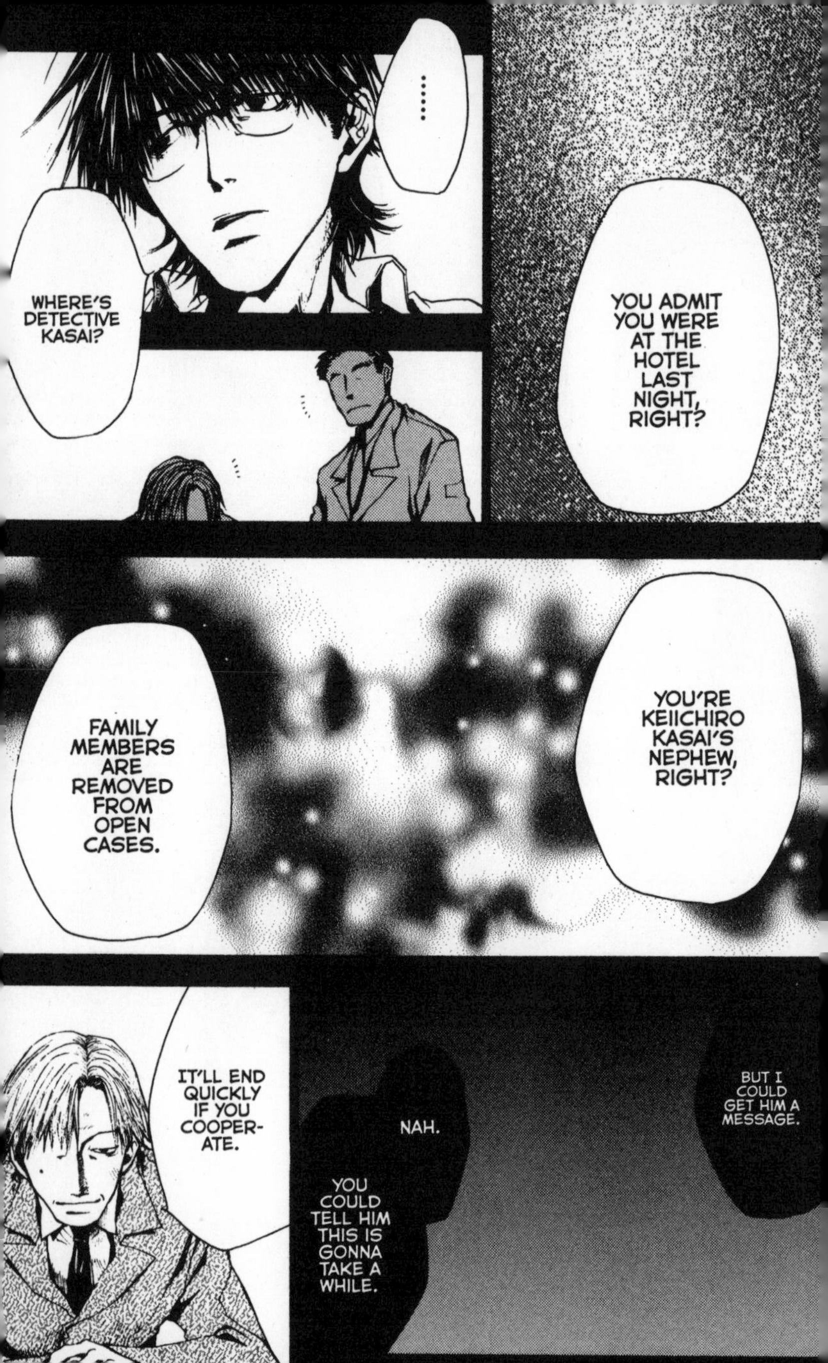
YOU ADMIT YOU WERE AT THE HOTEL LAST NIGHT, RIGHT?
......
WHERE'S DETECTIVE KASAI?
YOU'RE KEIICHIRO KASAI'S NEPHEW, RIGHT?
FAMILY MEMBERS ARE REMOVED FROM OPEN CASES.
BUT I COULD GET HIM A MESSAGE.
NAH.
YOU COULD TELL HIM THIS IS GONNA TAKE A WHILE.
IT'LL END QUICKLY IF YOU COOPER-ATE.

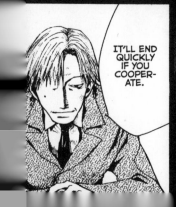

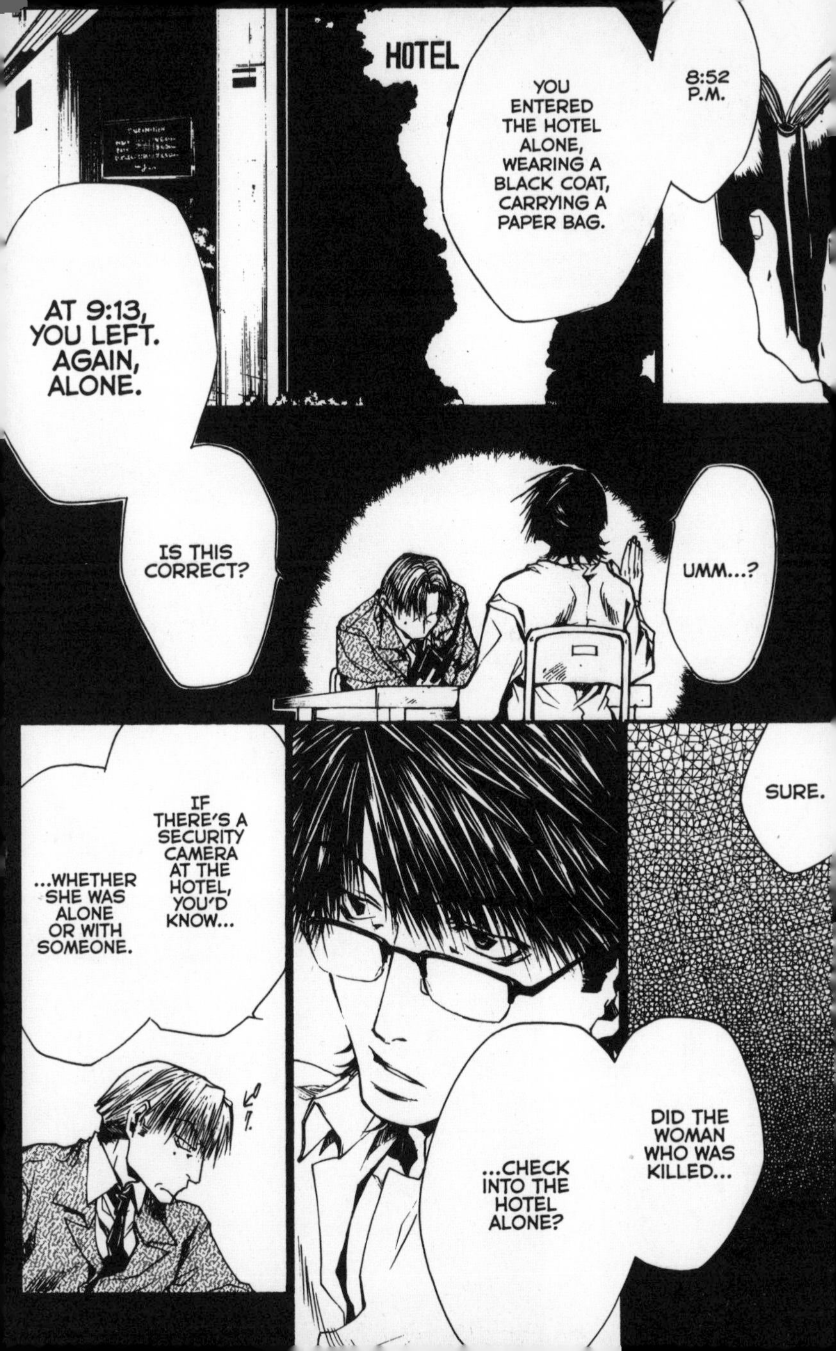
8:52 P.M.
HOTEL
YOU ENTERED THE HOTEL ALONE, WEARING A BLACK COAT, CARRYING A PAPER BAG.
AT 9:13, YOU LEFT. AGAIN, ALONE.
IS THIS CORRECT?
UMM...?
SURE.
DID THE WOMAN WHO WAS KILLED...
...CHECK INTO THE HOTEL ALONE?
IF THERE'S A SECURITY CAMERA AT THE HOTEL, YOU'D KNOW...
...WHETHER SHE WAS ALONE OR WITH SOMEONE.

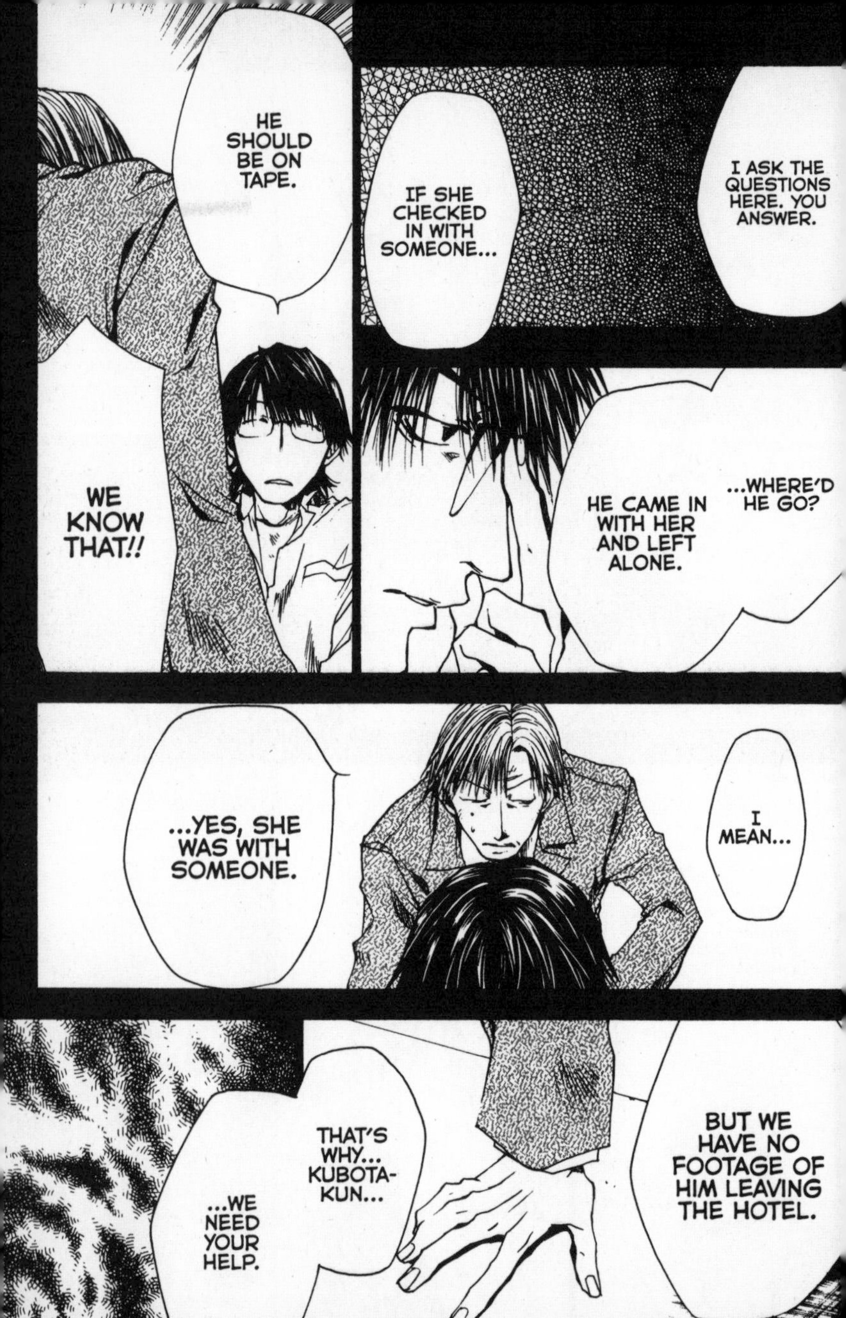
I ASK THE QUESTIONS HERE. YOU ANSWER.
IF SHE CHECKED IN WITH SOMEONE...
...WHERE'D HE GO?
HE CAME IN WITH HER AND LEFT ALONE.
HE SHOULD BE ON TAPE.
WE KNOW THAT!!
I MEAN...
...YES, SHE WAS WITH SOMEONE.
BUT WE HAVE NO FOOTAGE OF HIM LEAVING THE HOTEL.
THAT'S WHY... KUBOTA-KUN...
...WE NEED YOUR HELP.

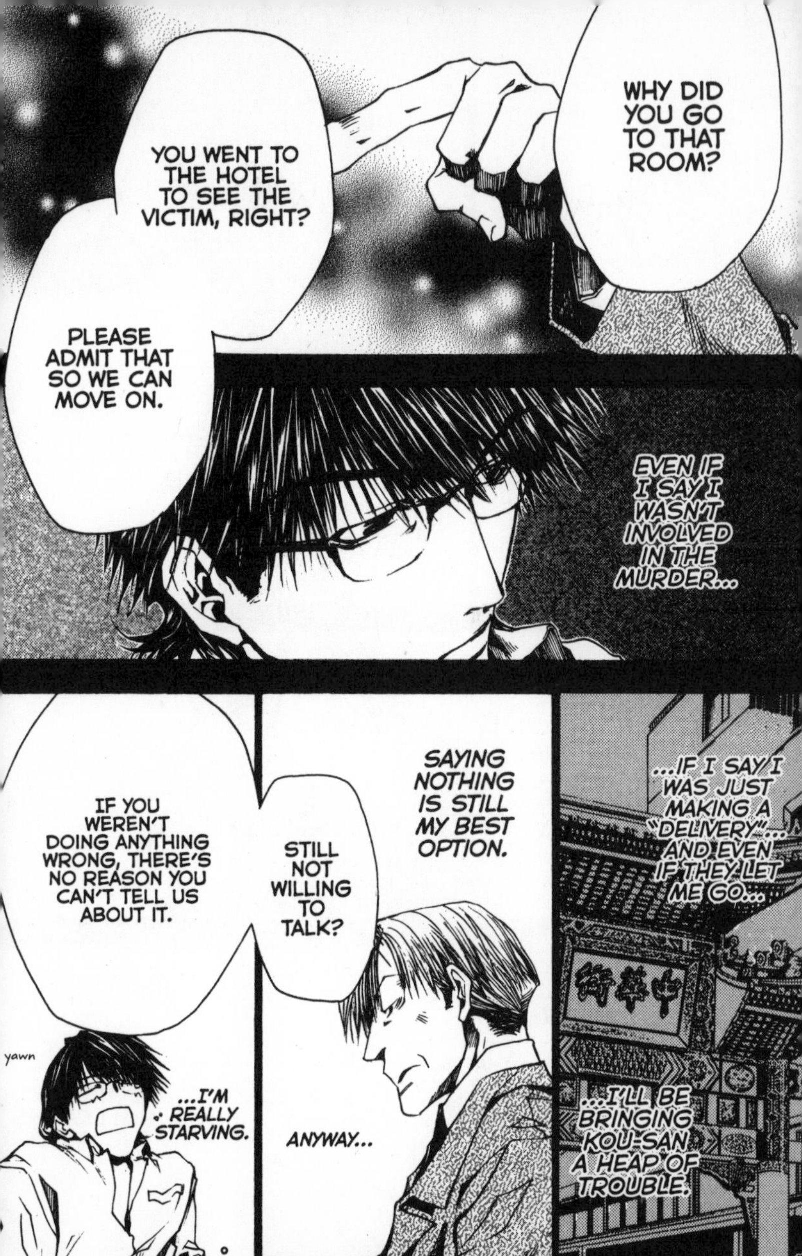
WHY DID YOU GO TO THAT ROOM?
YOU WENT TO THE HOTEL TO SEE THE VICTIM, RIGHT?
PLEASE ADMIT THAT SO WE CAN MOVE ON.
EVEN IF I SAY I WASN'T INVOLVED IN THE MURDER...
...IF I SAY I WAS JUST MAKING A "DELIVERY"... AND EVEN IF THEY LET ME GO...
...I'LL BE BRINGING KOU-SAN A HEAP OF TROUBLE.
SAYING NOTHING IS STILL MY BEST OPTION.
STILL NOT WILLING TO TALK?
ANYWAY...
IF YOU WEREN'T DOING ANYTHING WRONG, THERE'S NO REASON YOU CAN'T TELL US ABOUT IT.
yawn
...I'M REALLY STARVING.

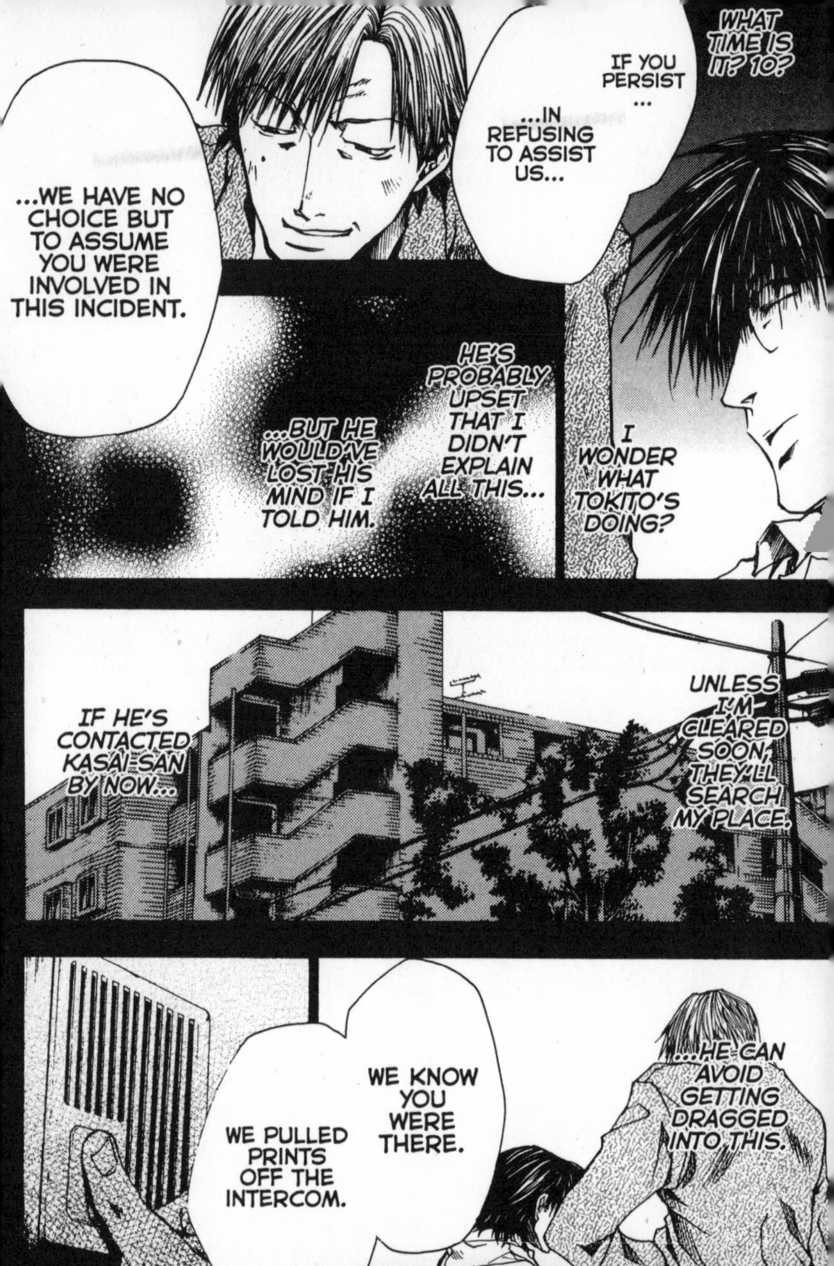
WHAT TIME IS IT? 10?
IF YOU PERSIST ...
...IN REFUSING TO ASSIST US...
...WE HAVE NO CHOICE BUT TO ASSUME YOU WERE INVOLVED IN THIS INCIDENT.
I WONDER WHAT TOKITO'S DOING?
HE'S PROBABLY UPSET THAT I DIDN'T EXPLAIN ALL THIS...
...BUT HE WOULD'VE LOST HIS MIND IF I TOLD HIM.
UNLESS I'M CLEARED SOON, THEY'LL SEARCH MY PLACE.
IF HE'S CONTACTED KASAI-SAN BY NOW...
...HE CAN AVOID GETTING DRAGGED INTO THIS.
WE KNOW YOU WERE THERE.
WE PULLED PRINTS OFF THE INTERCOM.

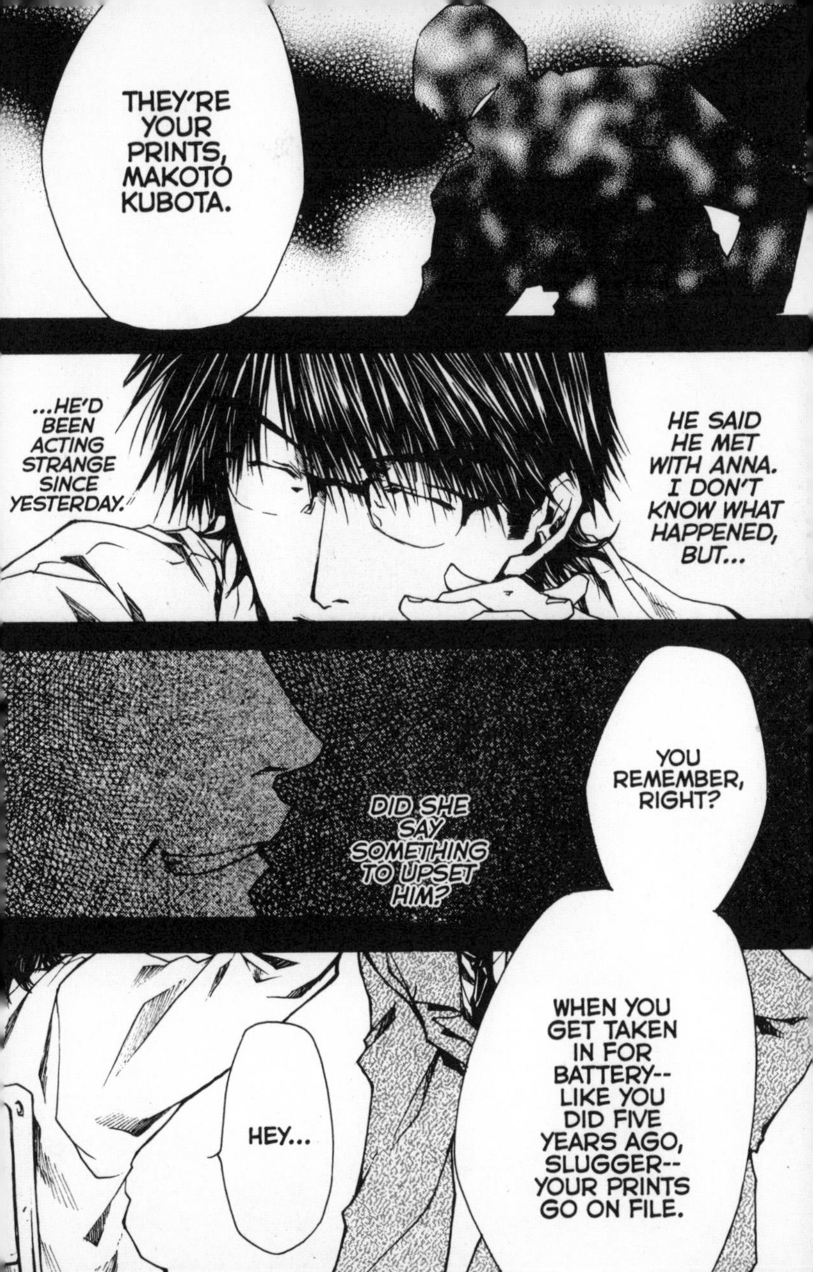
THEY'RE YOUR PRINTS, MAKOTO KUBOTA.
HE SAID HE MET WITH ANNA. I DON'T KNOW WHAT HAPPENED, BUT...
...HE'D BEEN ACTING STRANGE SINCE YESTERDAY.
YOU REMEMBER, RIGHT?
DID SHE SAY SOMETHING TO UPSET HIM?
WHEN YOU GET TAKEN IN FOR BATTERY-- LIKE YOU DID FIVE YEARS AGO, SLUGGER-- YOUR PRINTS GO ON FILE.
HEY...

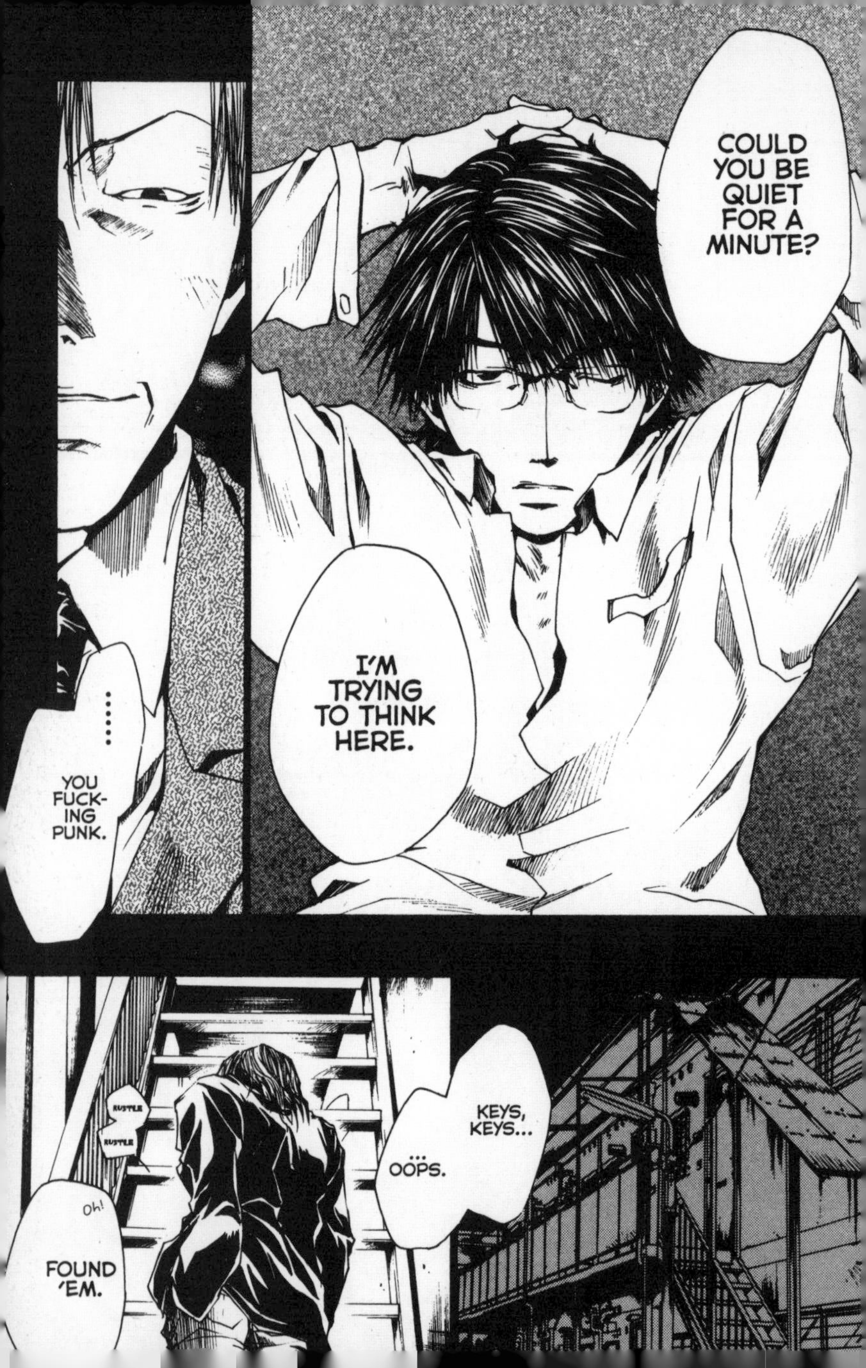
COULD YOU BE QUIET FOR A MINUTE?
I'M TRYING TO THINK HERE.
......
YOU FUCKING PUNK.
KEYS, KEYS...
...OOPS.
RUSTLE
RUSTLE
Oh!
FOUND 'EM.

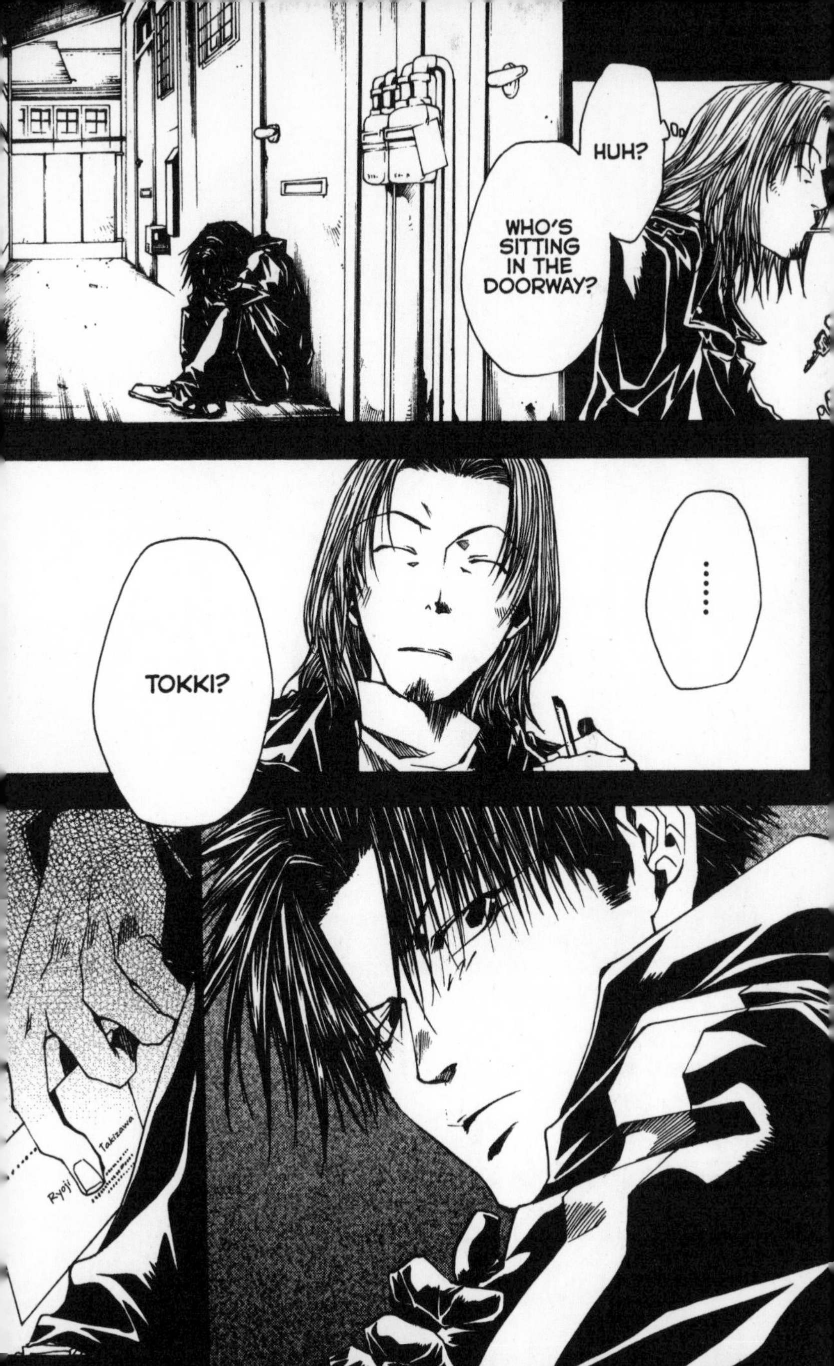
HUH?
WHO'S SITTING IN THE DOORWAY?
......
TOKKI?
Ryoji Takizawa

CONTINUED ON THE Dice:22

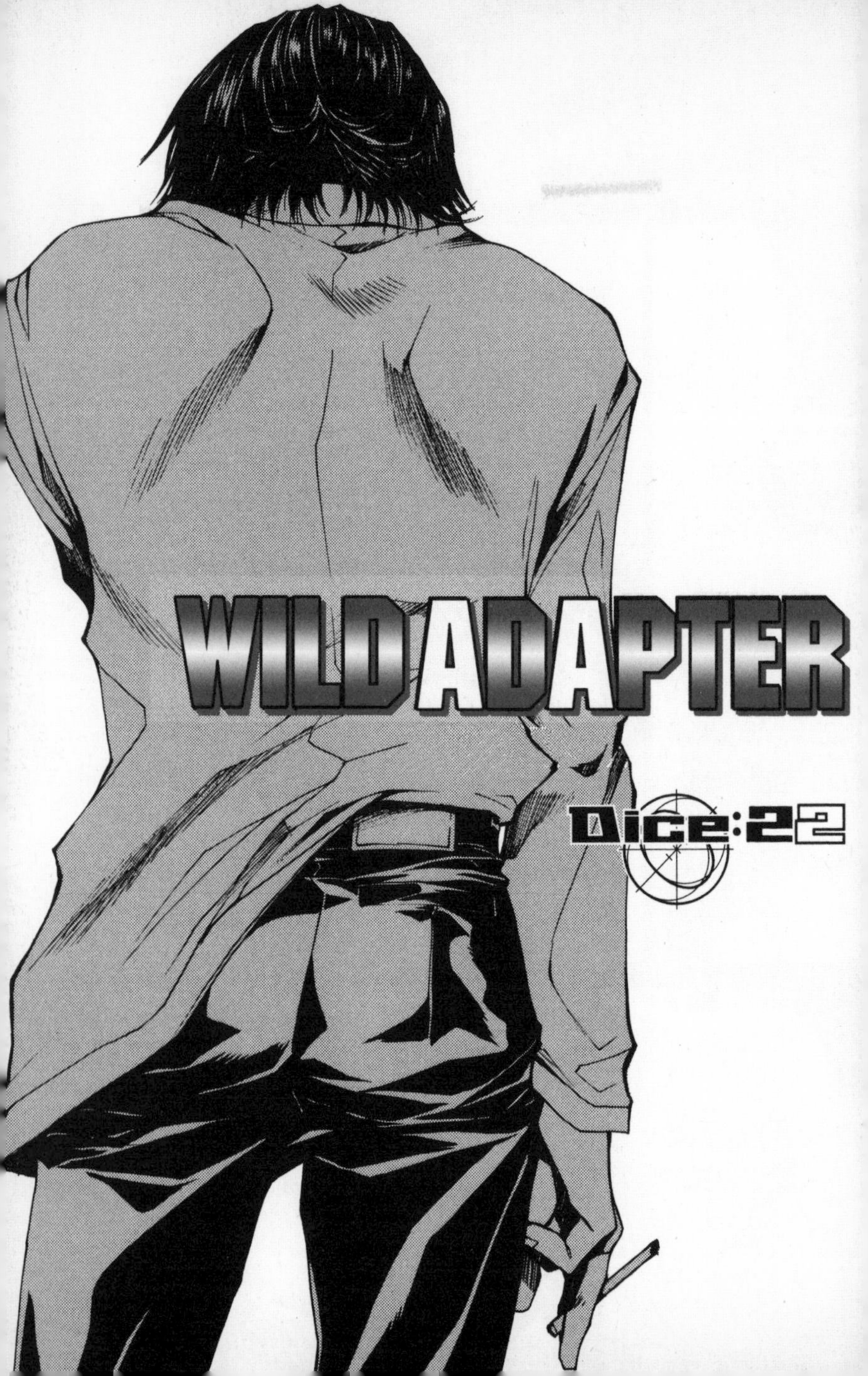

WILD ADAPTER
Dice:22

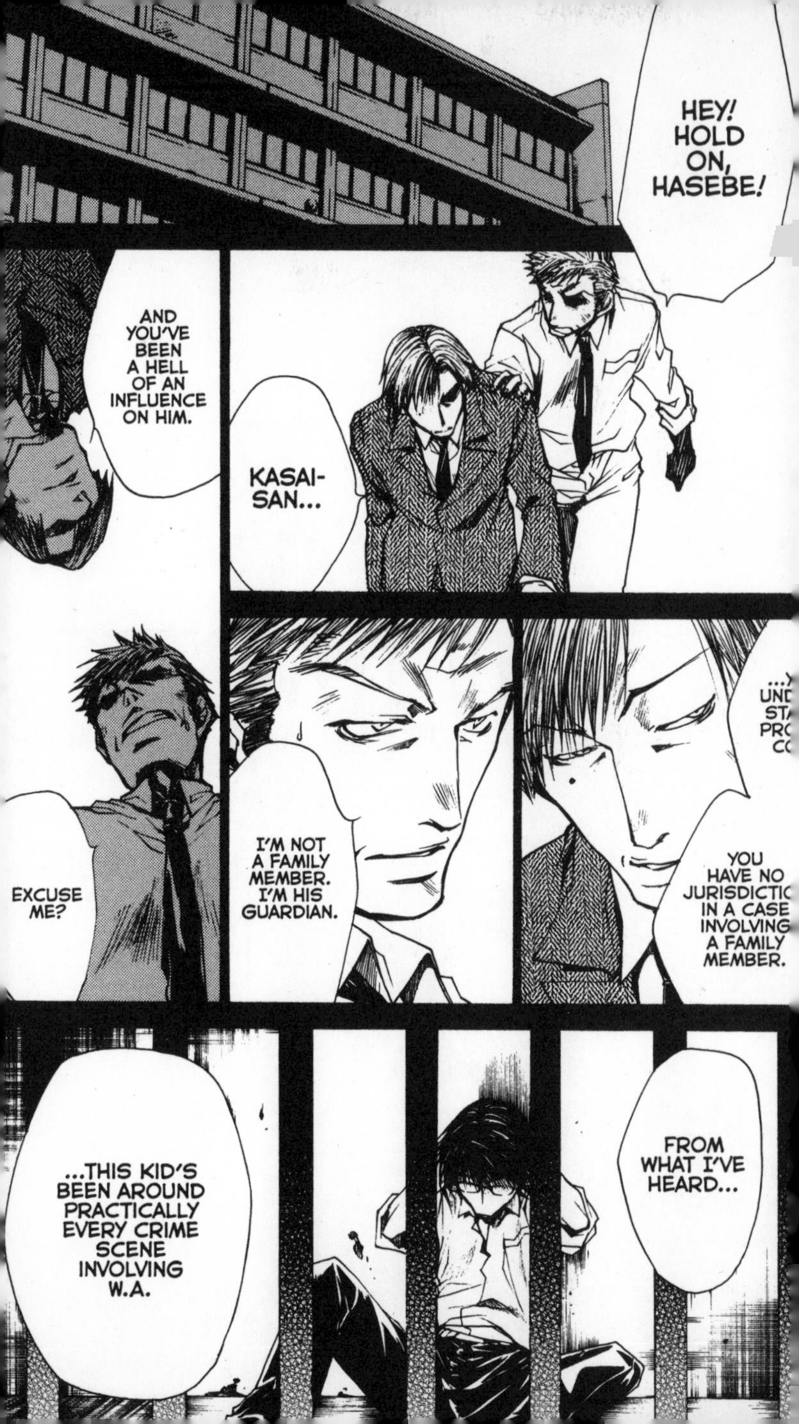
HEY! HOLD ON, HASEBE!
KASAI-SAN...
AND YOU'VE BEEN A HELL OF AN INFLUENCE ON HIM.
YOU HAVE NO JURISDICTIO IN A CASE INVOLVING A FAMILY MEMBER.
I'M NOT A FAMILY MEMBER. I'M HIS GUARDIAN.
EXCUSE ME?
FROM WHAT I'VE HEARD...
...THIS KID'S BEEN AROUND PRACTICALLY EVERY CRIME SCENE INVOLVING W.A.

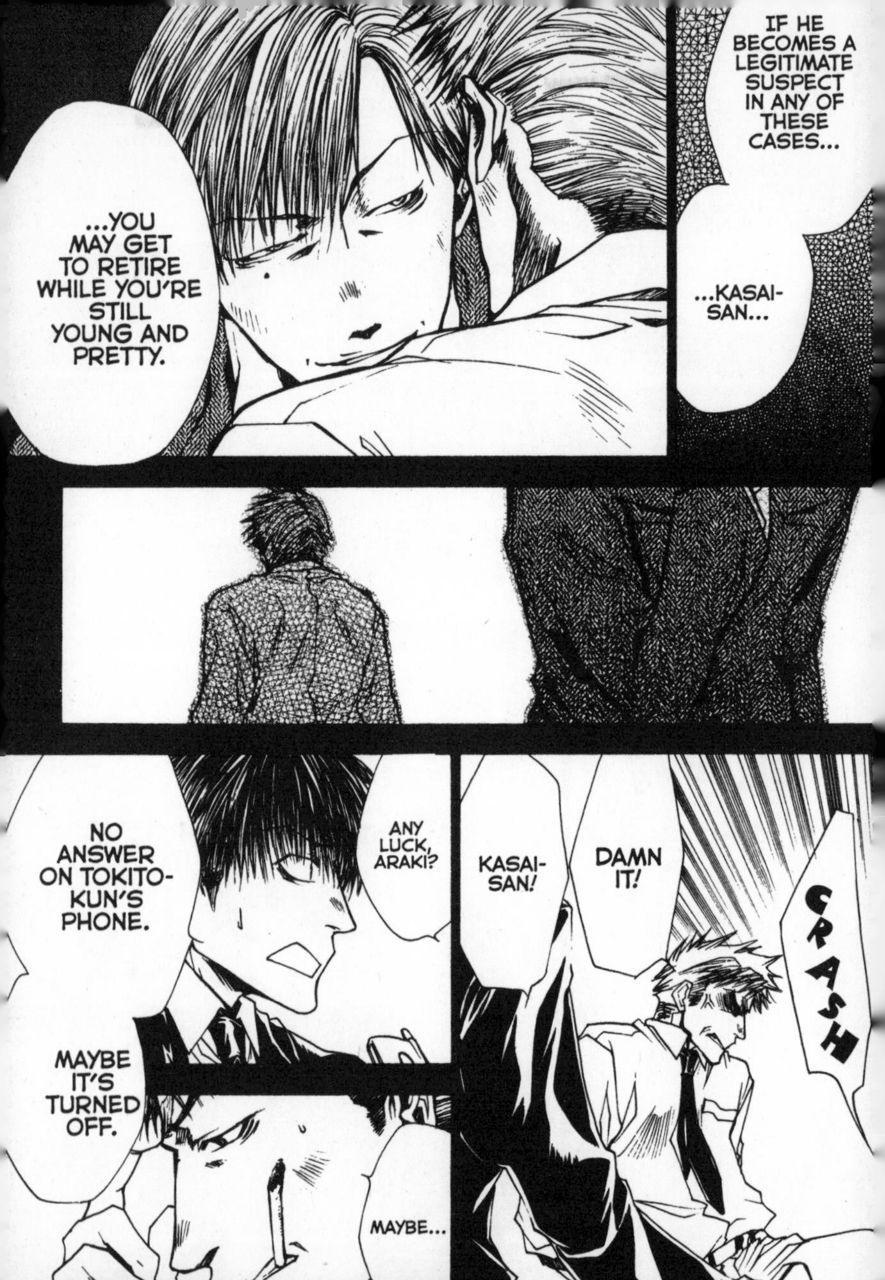
IF HE BECOMES A LEGITIMATE SUSPECT IN ANY OF THESE CASES...
...KASAI-SAN...
...YOU MAY GET TO RETIRE WHILE YOU'RE STILL YOUNG AND PRETTY.
CRASH
DAMN IT!
KASAI-SAN!
ANY LUCK, ARAKI?
NO ANSWER ON TOKITO-KUN'S PHONE.
MAYBE IT'S TURNED OFF.
MAYBE...

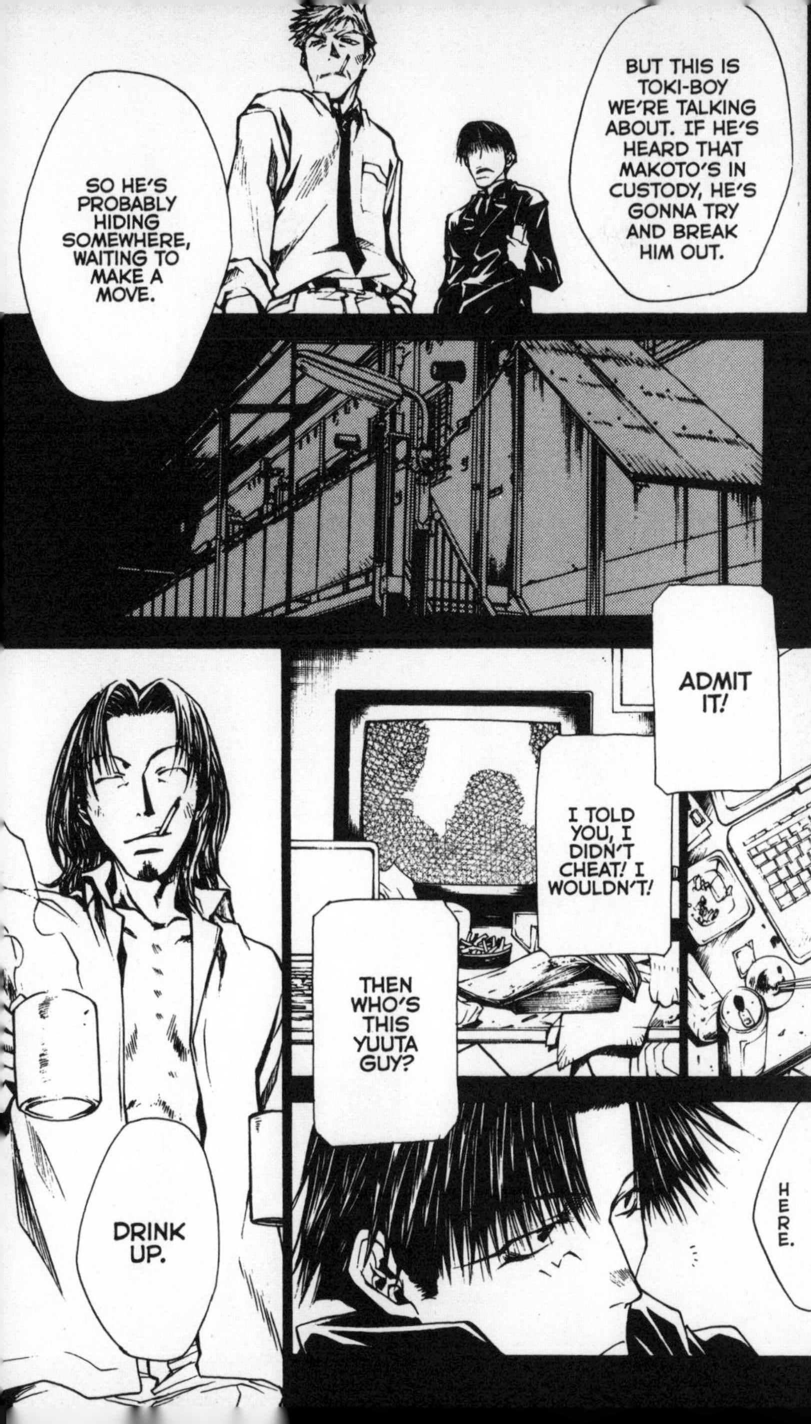
BUT THIS IS TOKI-BOY WE'RE TALKING ABOUT. IF HE'S HEARD THAT MAKOTO'S IN CUSTODY, HE'S GONNA TRY AND BREAK HIM OUT.
SO HE'S PROBABLY HIDING SOMEWHERE, WAITING TO MAKE A MOVE.
ADMIT IT!
I TOLD YOU, I DIDN'T CHEAT! I WOULDN'T!
THEN WHO'S THIS YUUTA GUY?
HERE.
DRINK UP.

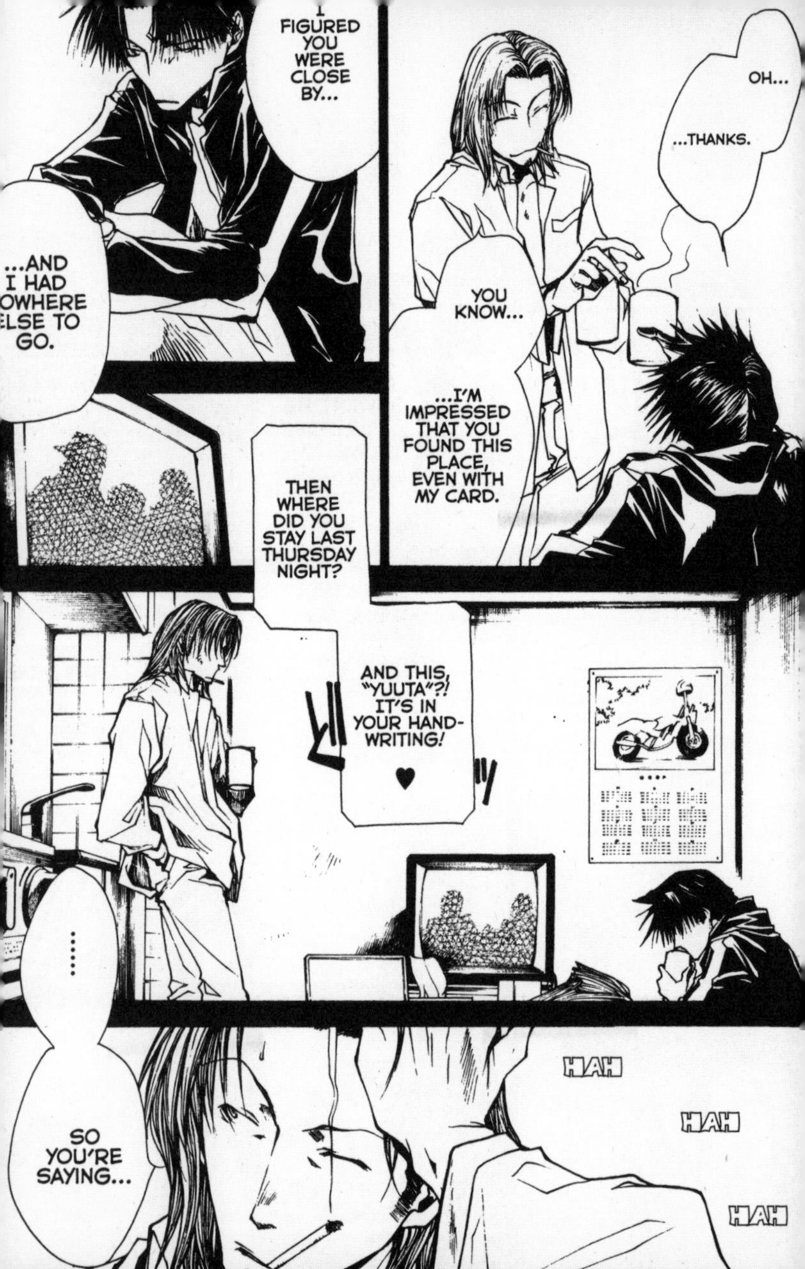
OH...
...THANKS.
YOU KNOW...
...I'M IMPRESSED THAT YOU FOUND THIS PLACE, EVEN WITH MY CARD.
I FIGURED YOU WERE CLOSE BY...
...AND I HAD OWHERE ELSE TO GO.
THEN WHERE DID YOU STAY LAST THURSDAY NIGHT?
AND THIS, "YUUTA"?! IT'S IN YOUR HAND-WRITING! ♥
......
HAH
HAH
HAH
SO YOU'RE SAYING...

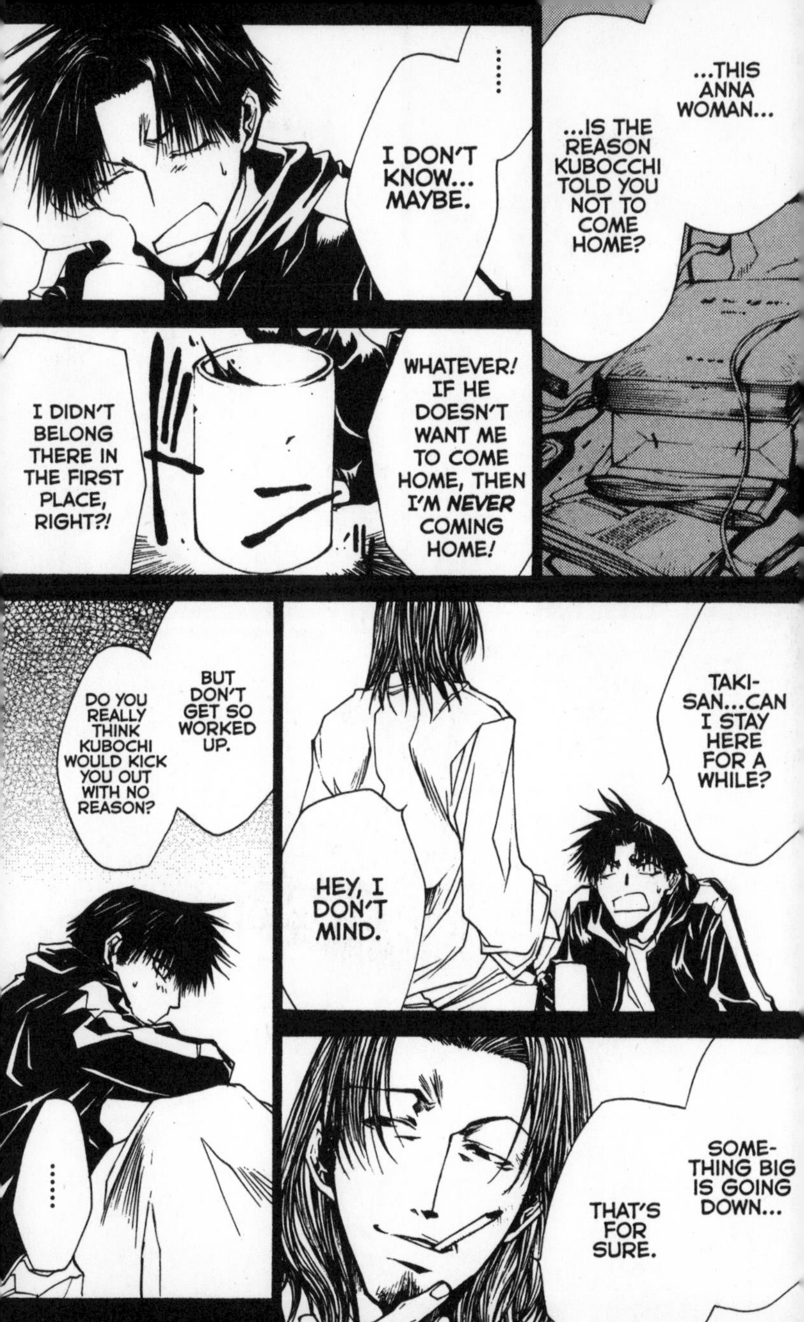
...THIS ANNA WOMAN...
...IS THE REASON KUBOCCHI TOLD YOU NOT TO COME HOME?
......
I DON'T KNOW... MAYBE.
WHATEVER! IF HE DOESN'T WANT ME TO COME HOME, THEN I'M *NEVER* COMING HOME!
I DIDN'T BELONG THERE IN THE FIRST PLACE, RIGHT?!
TAKI-SAN...CAN I STAY HERE FOR A WHILE?
HEY, I DON'T MIND.
SOME-THING BIG IS GOING DOWN...
THAT'S FOR SURE.
BUT DON'T GET SO WORKED UP.
DO YOU REALLY THINK KUBOCHI WOULD KICK YOU OUT WITH NO REASON?
......

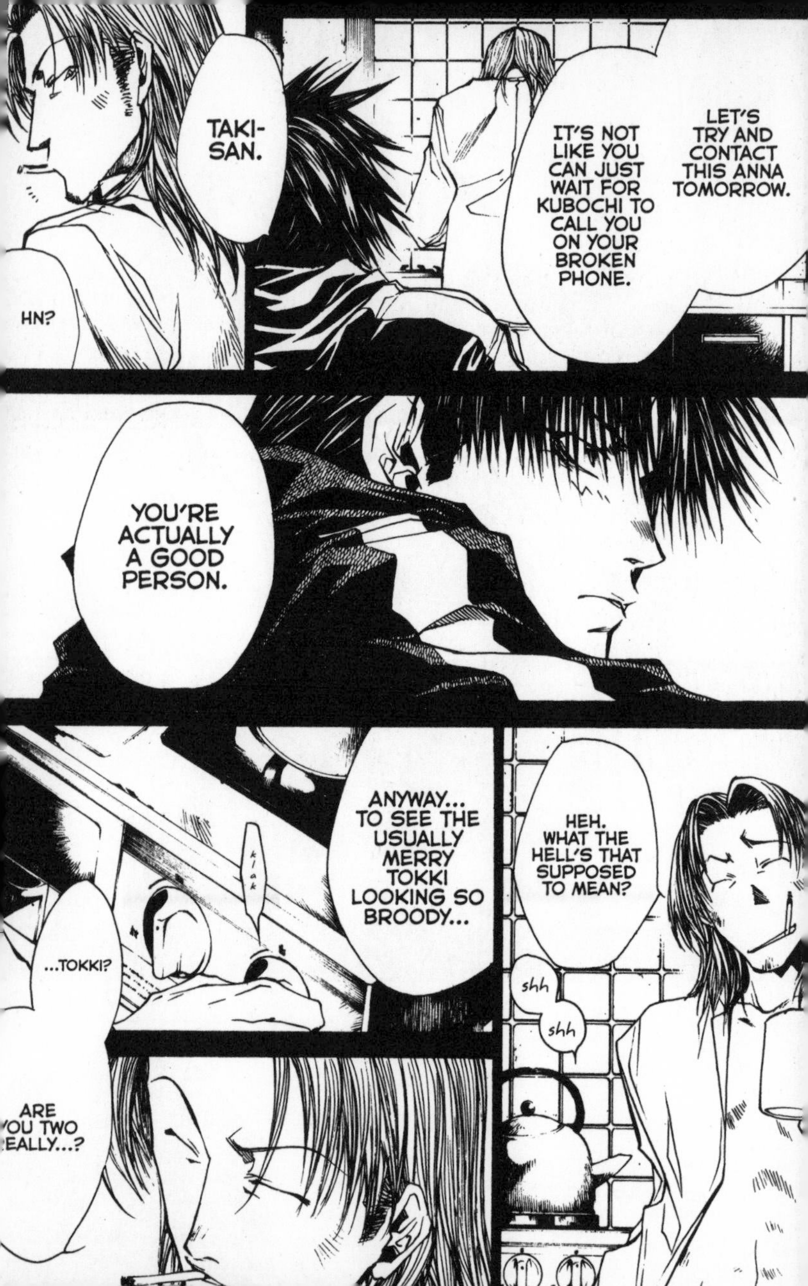
LET'S TRY AND CONTACT THIS ANNA TOMORROW.
IT'S NOT LIKE YOU CAN JUST WAIT FOR KUBOCHI TO CALL YOU ON YOUR BROKEN PHONE.
TAKI-SAN.
HN?
YOU'RE ACTUALLY A GOOD PERSON.
HEH. WHAT THE HELL'S THAT SUPPOSED TO MEAN?
shh
shh
ANYWAY... TO SEE THE USUALLY MERRY TOKKI LOOKING SO BROODY...
klak
...TOKKI?
ARE OU TWO EALLY...?

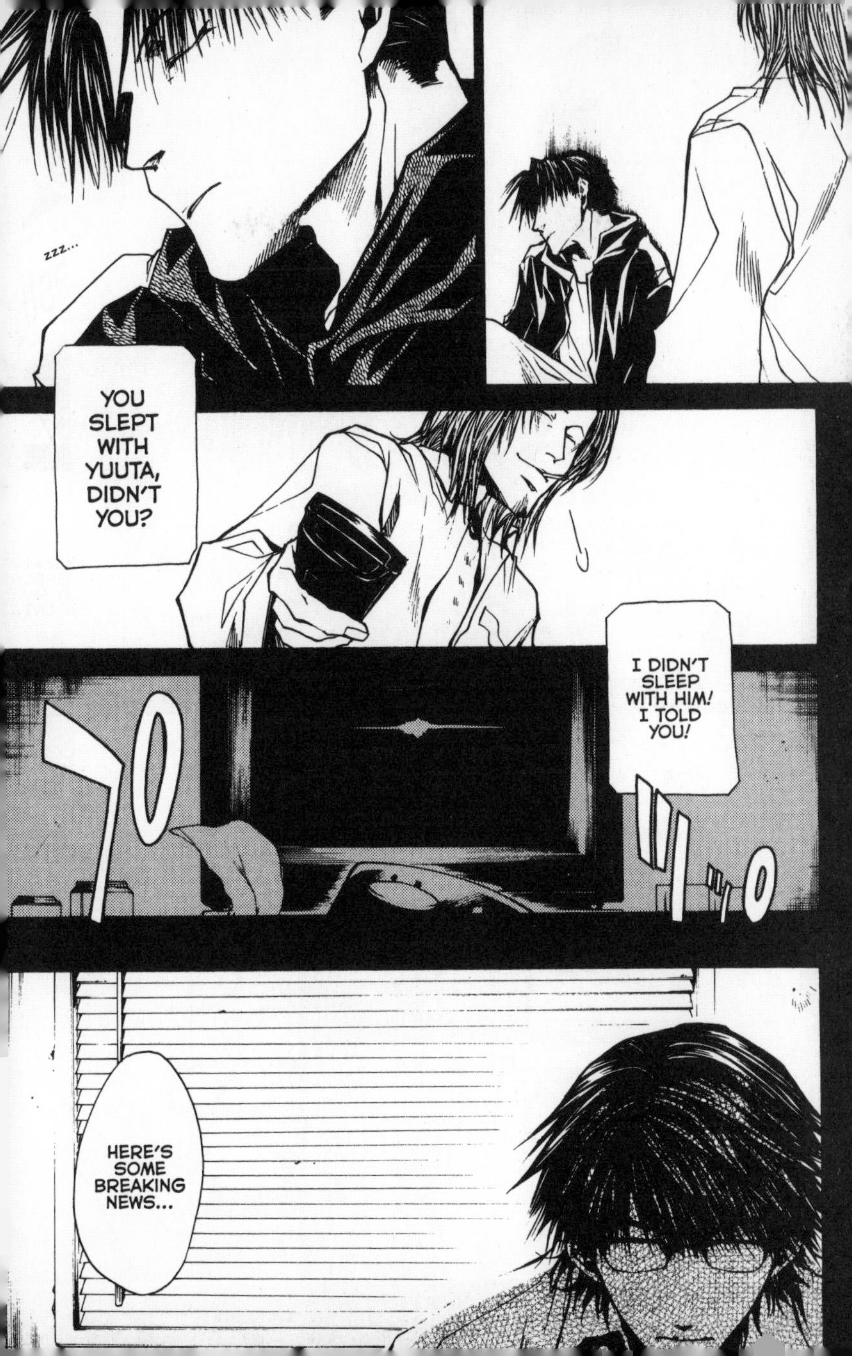
zzz...
YOU SLEPT WITH YUUTA, DIDN'T YOU?
I DIDN'T SLEEP WITH HIM! I TOLD YOU!
HERE'S SOME BREAKING NEWS...

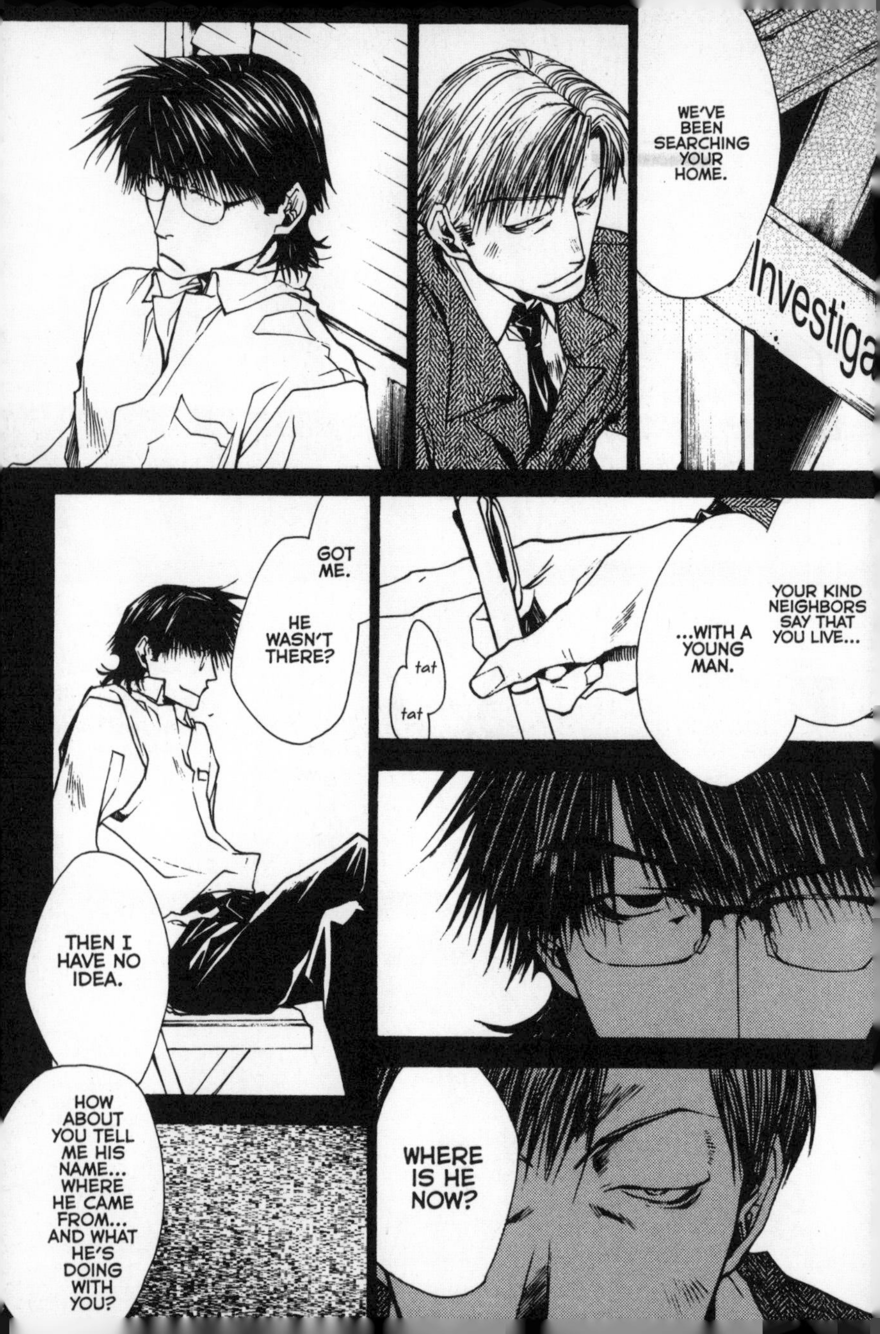
WE'VE BEEN SEARCHING YOUR HOME.
Investiga
YOUR KIND NEIGHBORS SAY THAT YOU LIVE...
...WITH A YOUNG MAN.
tat
tat
GOT ME.
HE WASN'T THERE?
THEN I HAVE NO IDEA.
WHERE IS HE NOW?
HOW ABOUT YOU TELL ME HIS NAME... WHERE HE CAME FROM... AND WHAT HE'S DOING WITH YOU?

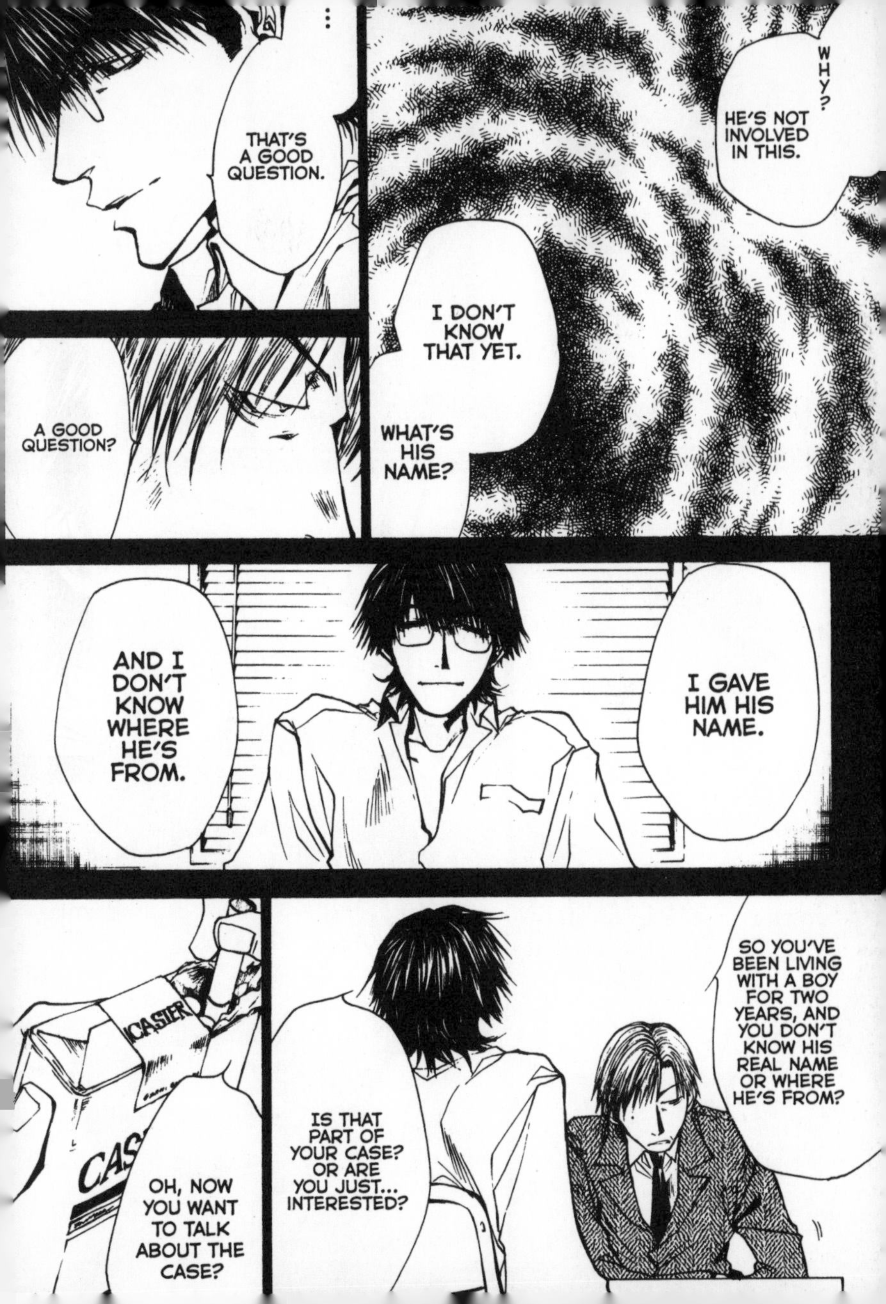
WHY?
HE'S NOT INVOLVED IN THIS.
I DON'T KNOW THAT YET.
WHAT'S HIS NAME?
...
THAT'S A GOOD QUESTION.
A GOOD QUESTION?
I GAVE HIM HIS NAME.
AND I DON'T KNOW WHERE HE'S FROM.
SO YOU'VE BEEN LIVING WITH A BOY FOR TWO YEARS, AND YOU DON'T KNOW HIS REAL NAME OR WHERE HE'S FROM?
IS THAT PART OF YOUR CASE? OR ARE YOU JUST... INTERESTED?
CASTER
OH, NOW YOU WANT TO TALK ABOUT THE CASE?

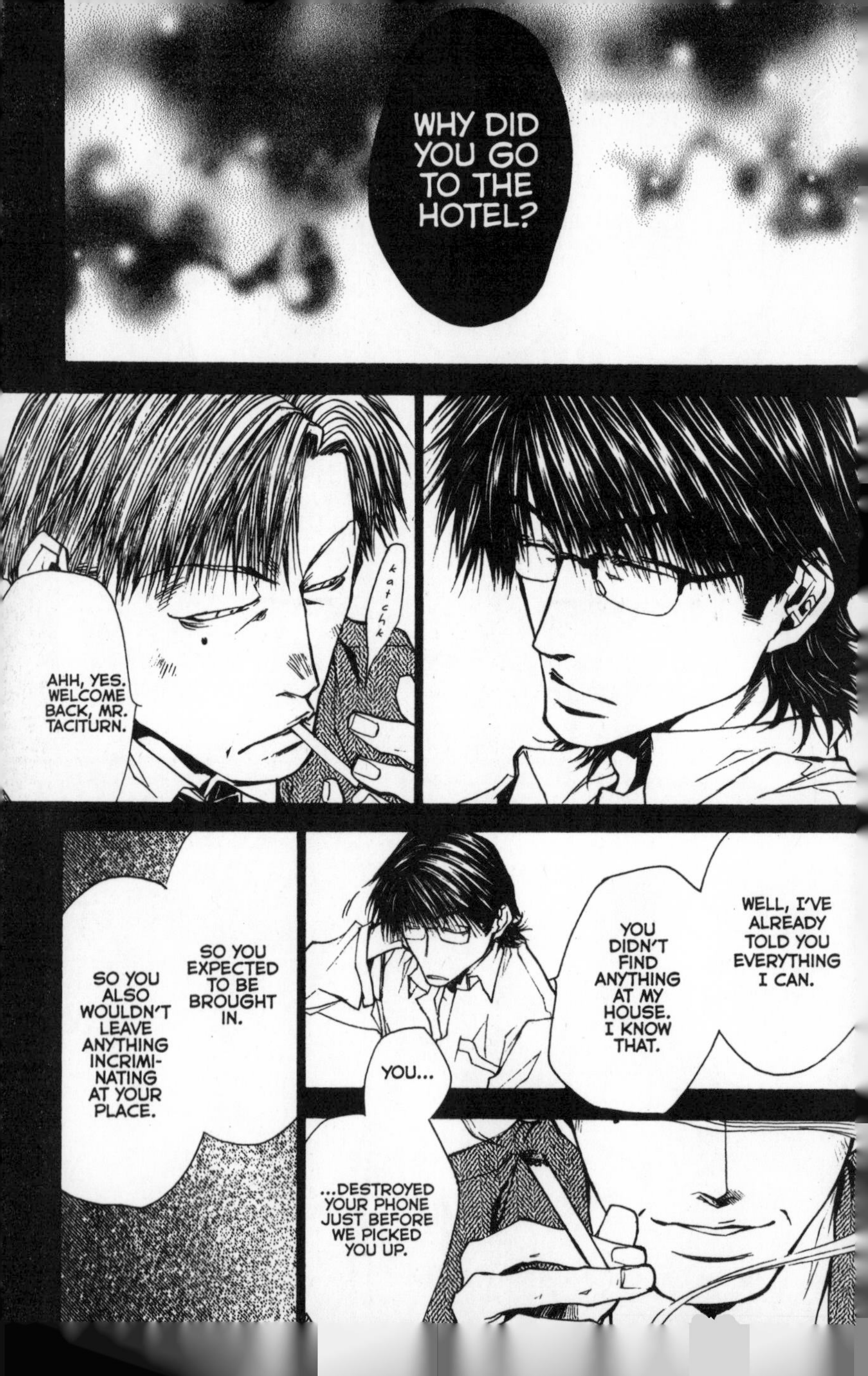
WHY DID YOU GO TO THE HOTEL?
katchk
AHH, YES. WELCOME BACK, MR. TACITURN.
WELL, I'VE ALREADY TOLD YOU EVERYTHING I CAN.
YOU DIDN'T FIND ANYTHING AT MY HOUSE. I KNOW THAT.
YOU...
...DESTROYED YOUR PHONE JUST BEFORE WE PICKED YOU UP.
SO YOU EXPECTED TO BE BROUGHT IN.
SO YOU ALSO WOULDN'T LEAVE ANYTHING INCRIMINATING AT YOUR PLACE.

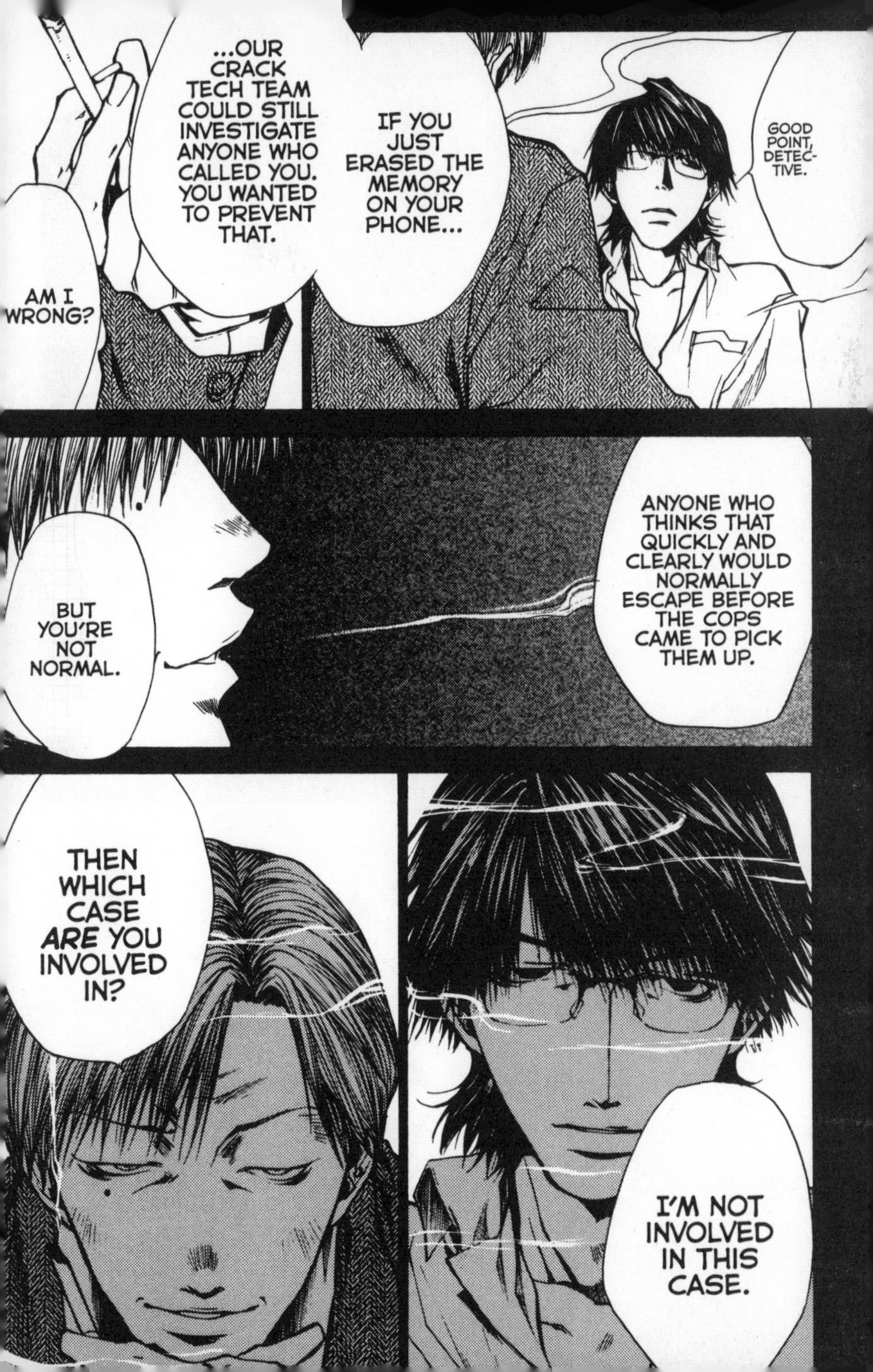
GOOD POINT, DETECTIVE.
IF YOU JUST ERASED THE MEMORY ON YOUR PHONE...
...OUR CRACK TECH TEAM COULD STILL INVESTIGATE ANYONE WHO CALLED YOU. YOU WANTED TO PREVENT THAT.
AM I WRONG?
ANYONE WHO THINKS THAT QUICKLY AND CLEARLY WOULD NORMALLY ESCAPE BEFORE THE COPS CAME TO PICK THEM UP.
BUT YOU'RE NOT NORMAL.
I'M NOT INVOLVED IN THIS CASE.
THEN WHICH CASE *ARE* YOU INVOLVED IN?

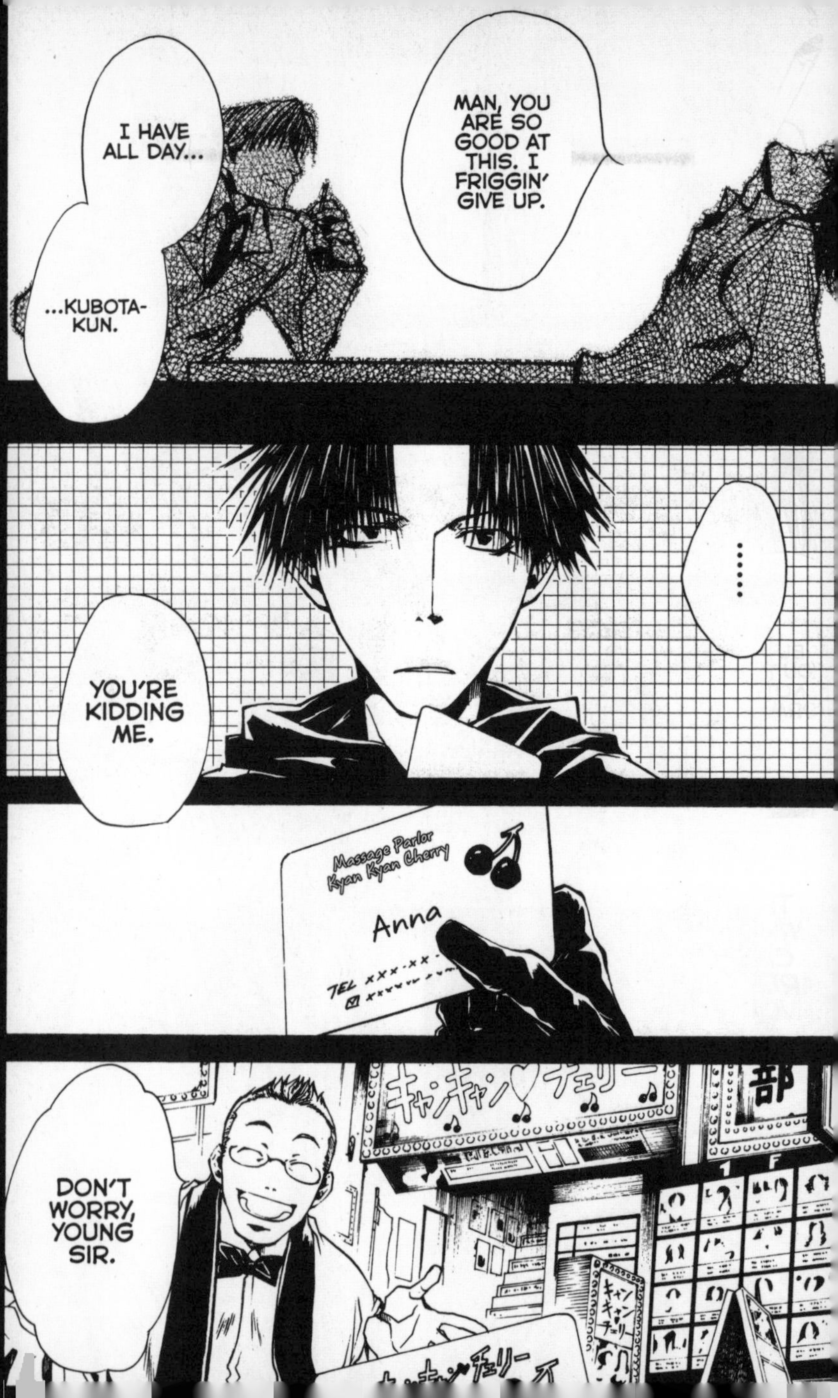
MAN, YOU ARE SO GOOD AT THIS. I FRIGGIN' GIVE UP.
I HAVE ALL DAY...
...KUBOTA-KUN.
......
YOU'RE KIDDING ME.
Massage Parlor Kyan Kyan Cherry
Anna
TEL
部
キャンキャン♡チェリー
1F
キャンキャンチェリー
DON'T WORRY, YOUNG SIR.

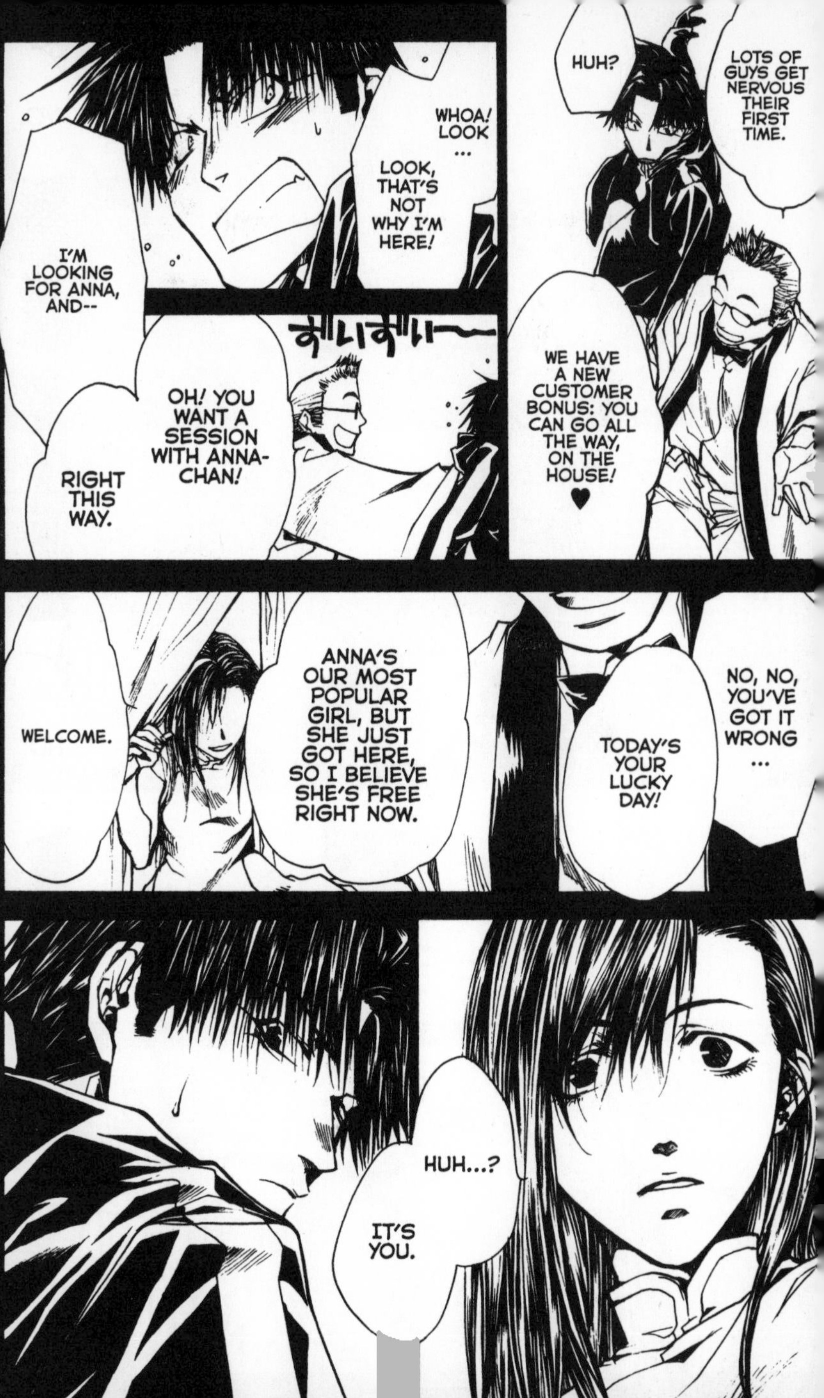
LOTS OF GUYS GET NERVOUS THEIR FIRST TIME.
HUH?
WE HAVE A NEW CUSTOMER BONUS: YOU CAN GO ALL THE WAY, ON THE HOUSE! ♥
WHOA! LOOK ...
LOOK, THAT'S NOT WHY I'M HERE!
I'M LOOKING FOR ANNA, AND--
ずいずい～～
OH! YOU WANT A SESSION WITH ANNA-CHAN!
RIGHT THIS WAY.
NO, NO, YOU'VE GOT IT WRONG ...
TODAY'S YOUR LUCKY DAY!
ANNA'S OUR MOST POPULAR GIRL, BUT SHE JUST GOT HERE, SO I BELIEVE SHE'S FREE RIGHT NOW.
WELCOME.
HUH...?
IT'S YOU.

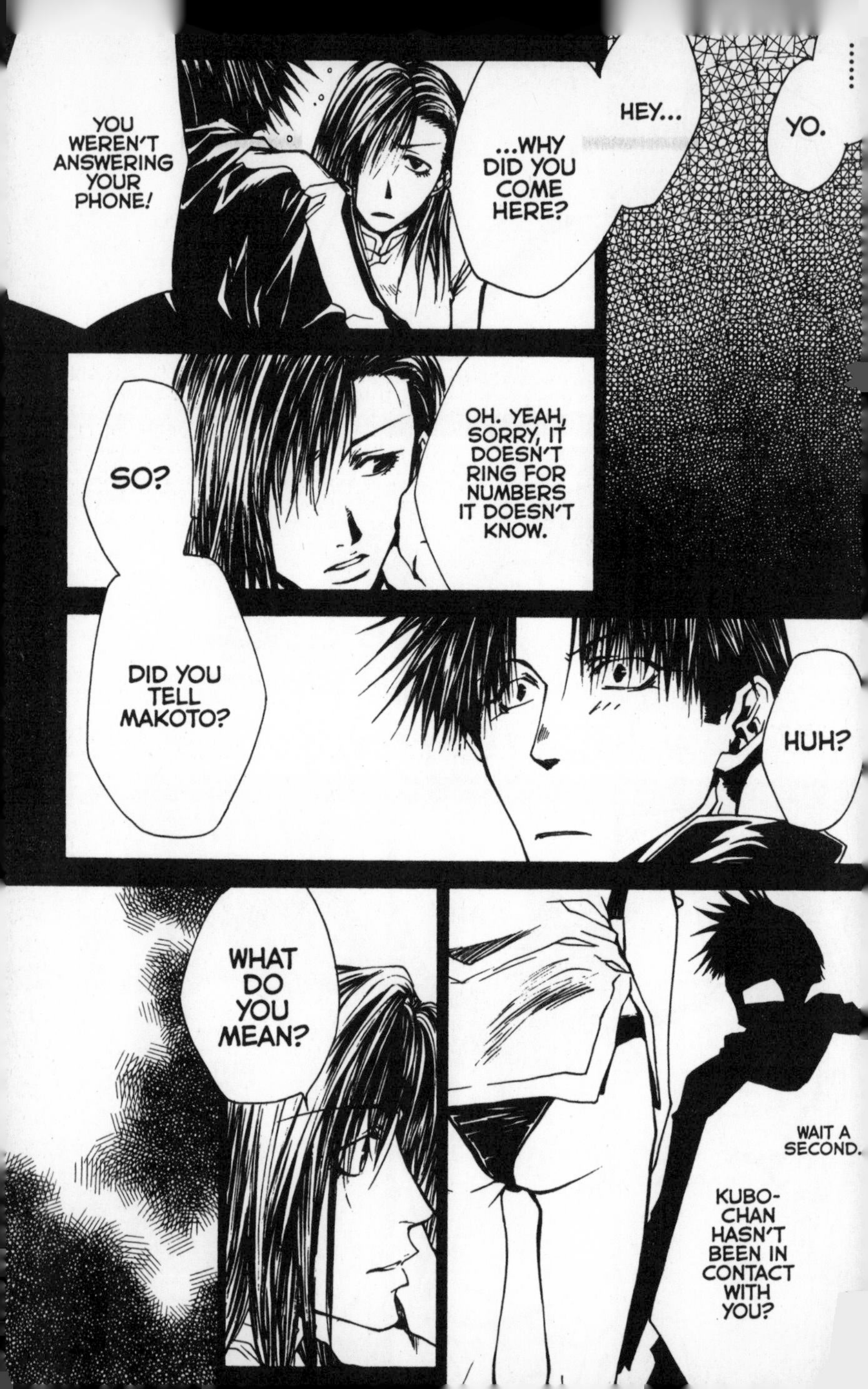
YO.
HEY...
...WHY DID YOU COME HERE?
YOU WEREN'T ANSWERING YOUR PHONE!
OH. YEAH, SORRY, IT DOESN'T RING FOR NUMBERS IT DOESN'T KNOW.
SO?
DID YOU TELL MAKOTO?
HUH?
WAIT A SECOND.
KUBO-CHAN HASN'T BEEN IN CONTACT WITH YOU?
WHAT DO YOU MEAN?

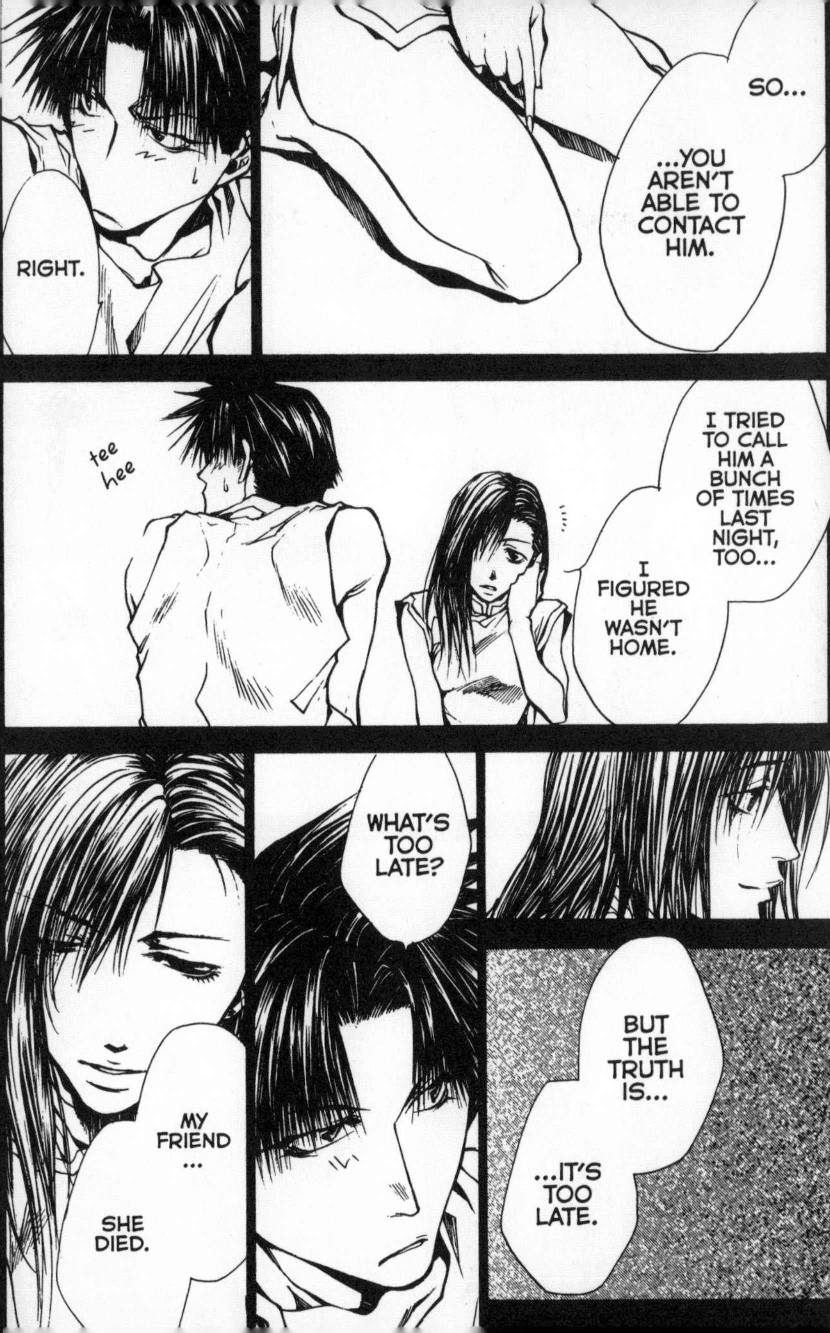
SO...
...YOU AREN'T ABLE TO CONTACT HIM.
RIGHT.
I TRIED TO CALL HIM A BUNCH OF TIMES LAST NIGHT, TOO...
I FIGURED HE WASN'T HOME.
tee hee
くす
BUT THE TRUTH IS...
...IT'S TOO LATE.
WHAT'S TOO LATE?
MY FRIEND...
SHE DIED.

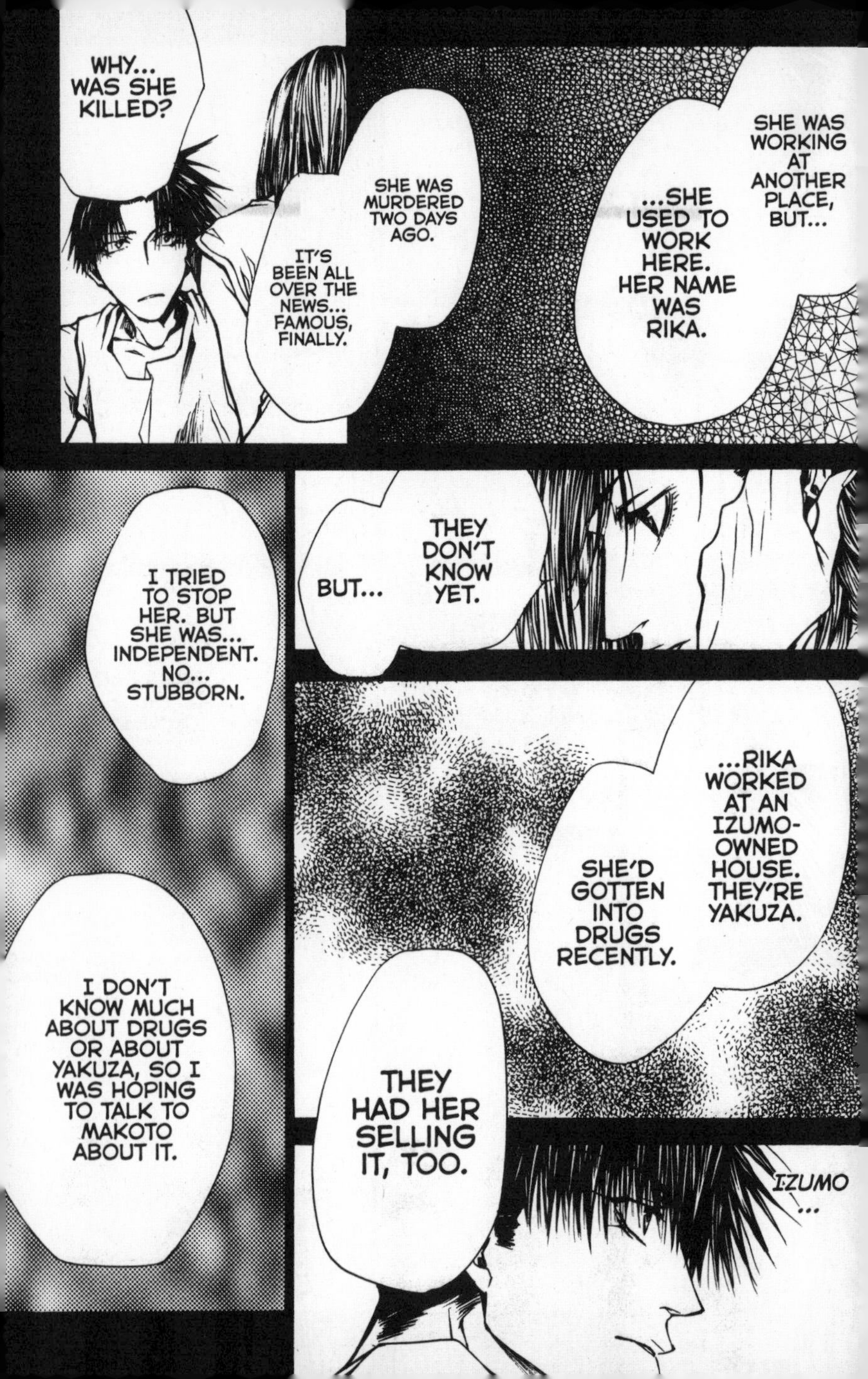
SHE WAS WORKING AT ANOTHER PLACE, BUT...
...SHE USED TO WORK HERE. HER NAME WAS RIKA.
SHE WAS MURDERED TWO DAYS AGO.
IT'S BEEN ALL OVER THE NEWS... FAMOUS, FINALLY.
WHY... WAS SHE KILLED?
THEY DON'T KNOW YET.
BUT...
...RIKA WORKED AT AN IZUMO-OWNED HOUSE. THEY'RE YAKUZA.
SHE'D GOTTEN INTO DRUGS RECENTLY.
THEY HAD HER SELLING IT, TOO.
IZUMO...
I TRIED TO STOP HER. BUT SHE WAS... INDEPENDENT. NO... STUBBORN.
I DON'T KNOW MUCH ABOUT DRUGS OR ABOUT YAKUZA, SO I WAS HOPING TO TALK TO MAKOTO ABOUT IT.

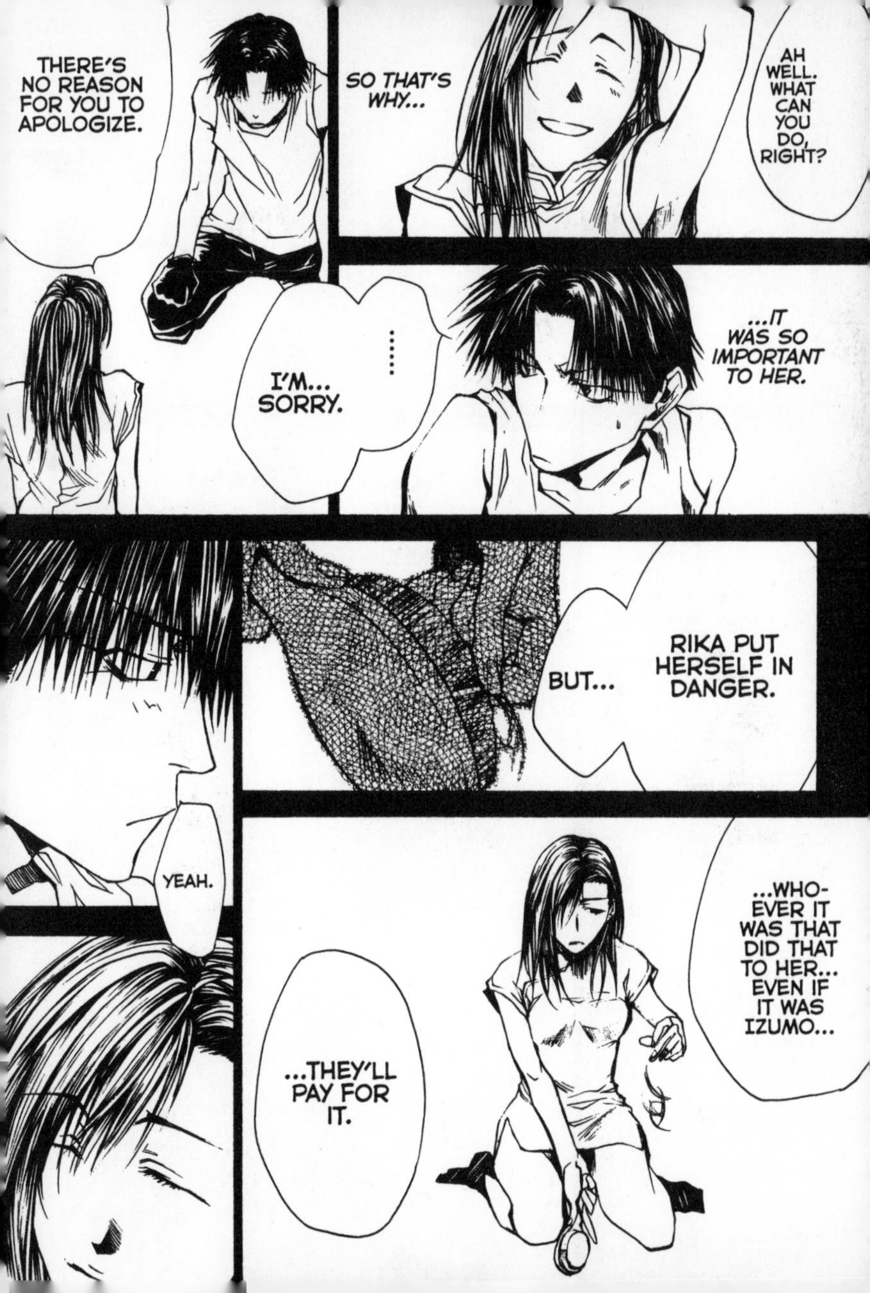
AH WELL. WHAT CAN YOU DO, RIGHT?
SO THAT'S WHY...
...IT WAS SO IMPORTANT TO HER.
......
I'M... SORRY.
THERE'S NO REASON FOR YOU TO APOLOGIZE.
RIKA PUT HERSELF IN DANGER.
BUT...
YEAH.
...WHO-EVER IT WAS THAT DID THAT TO HER... EVEN IF IT WAS IZUMO...
...THEY'LL PAY FOR IT.

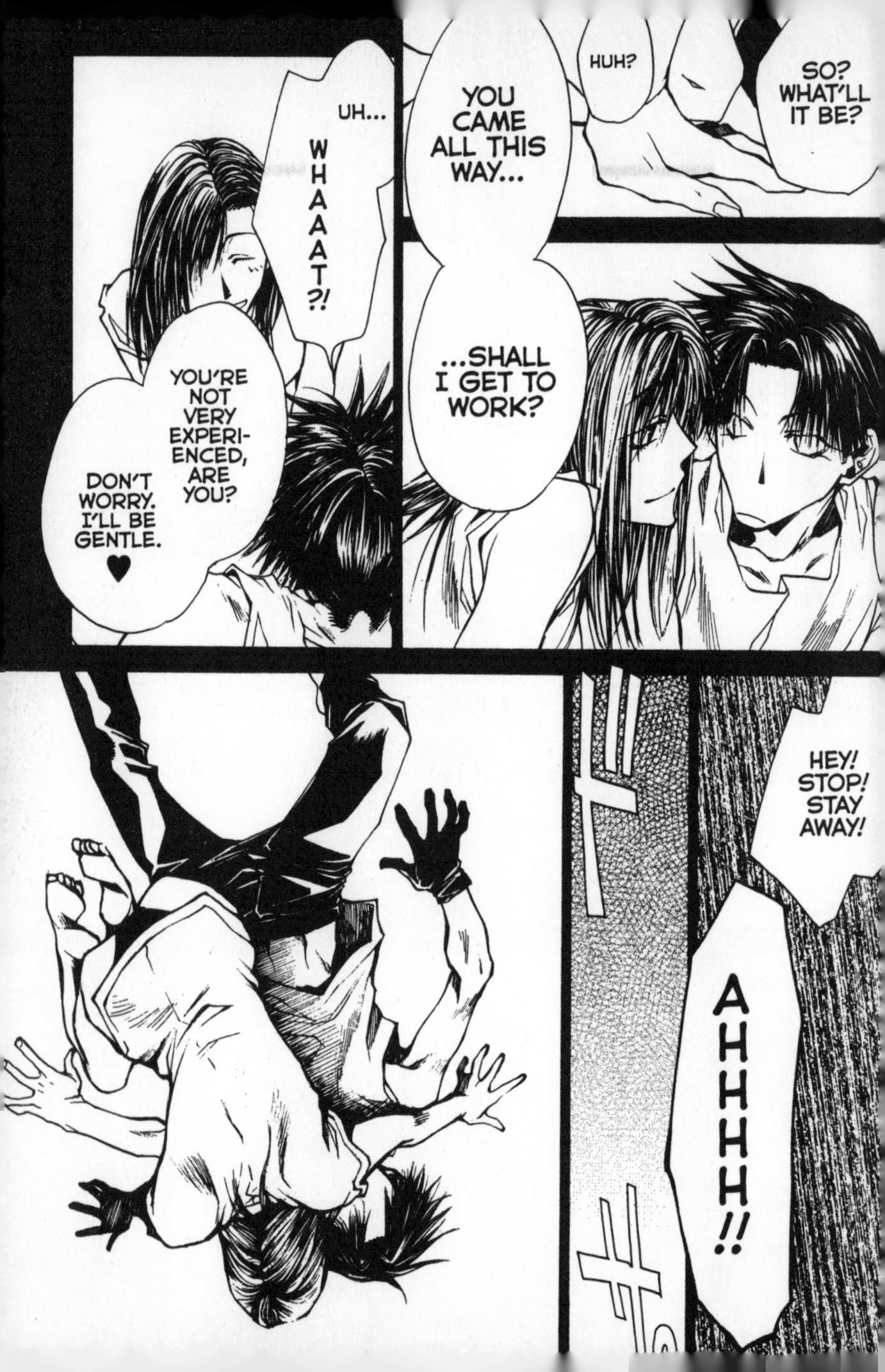
SO? WHAT'LL IT BE?
HUH?
YOU CAME ALL THIS WAY...
...SHALL I GET TO WORK?
UH...
WHAAAAT?!
YOU'RE NOT VERY EXPERIENCED, ARE YOU?
DON'T WORRY. I'LL BE GENTLE. ♥
HEY! STOP! STAY AWAY!
AHHHH!!

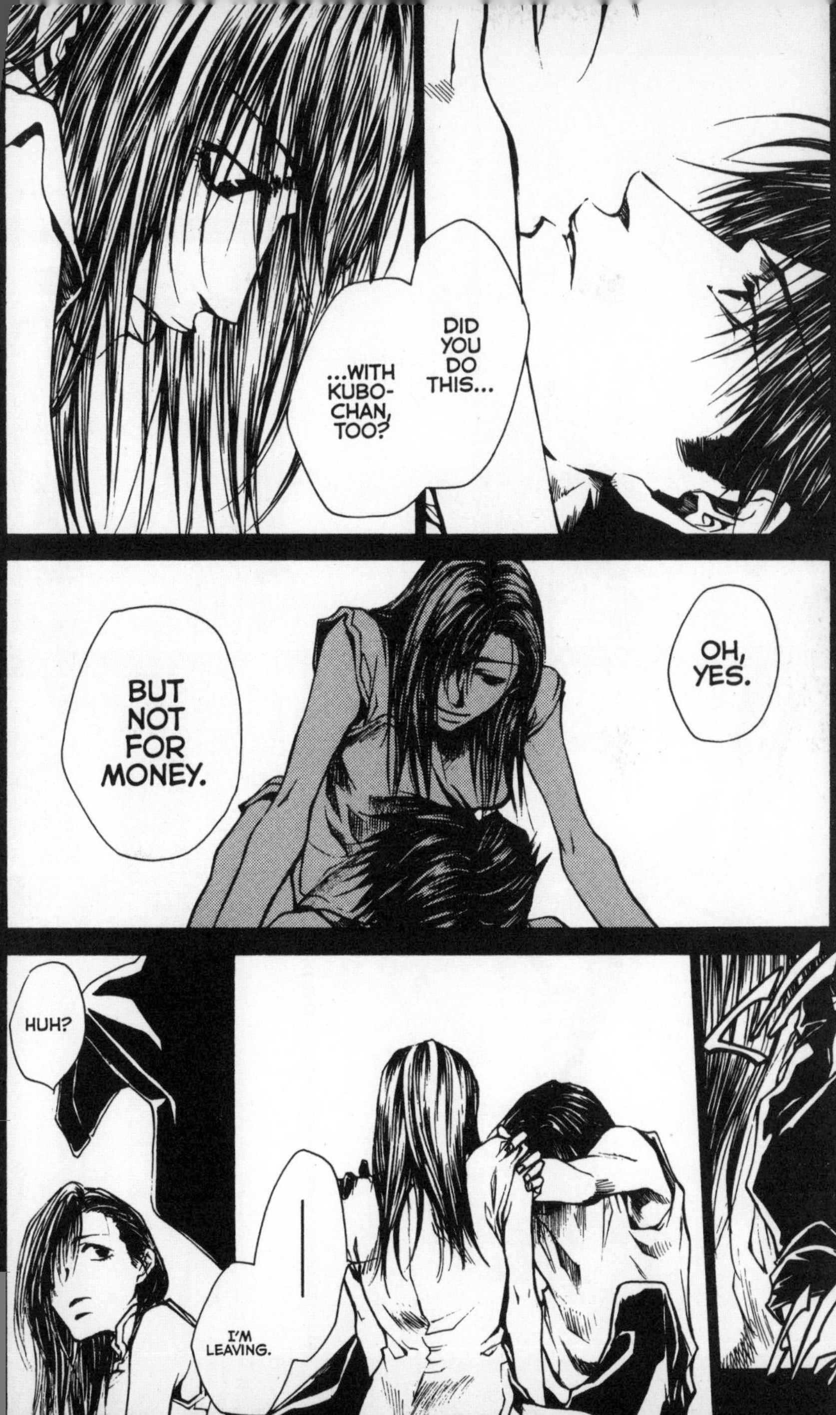
DID YOU DO THIS...
...WITH KUBO-CHAN, TOO?
OH, YES.
BUT NOT FOR MONEY.
I'M LEAVING.
HUH?

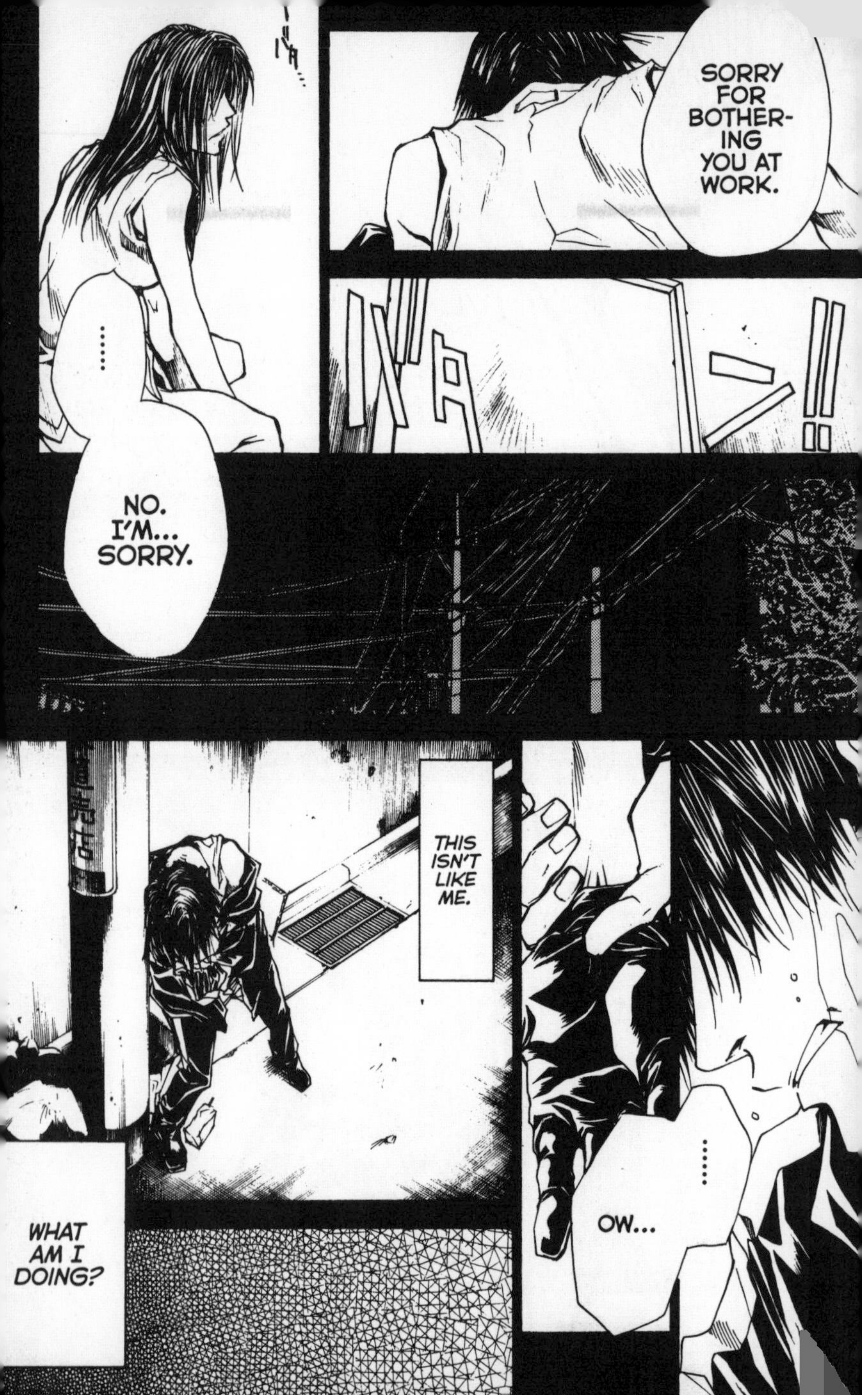
SORRY FOR BOTHERING YOU AT WORK.
......
NO. I'M... SORRY.
......
OW...
THIS ISN'T LIKE ME.
WHAT AM I DOING?

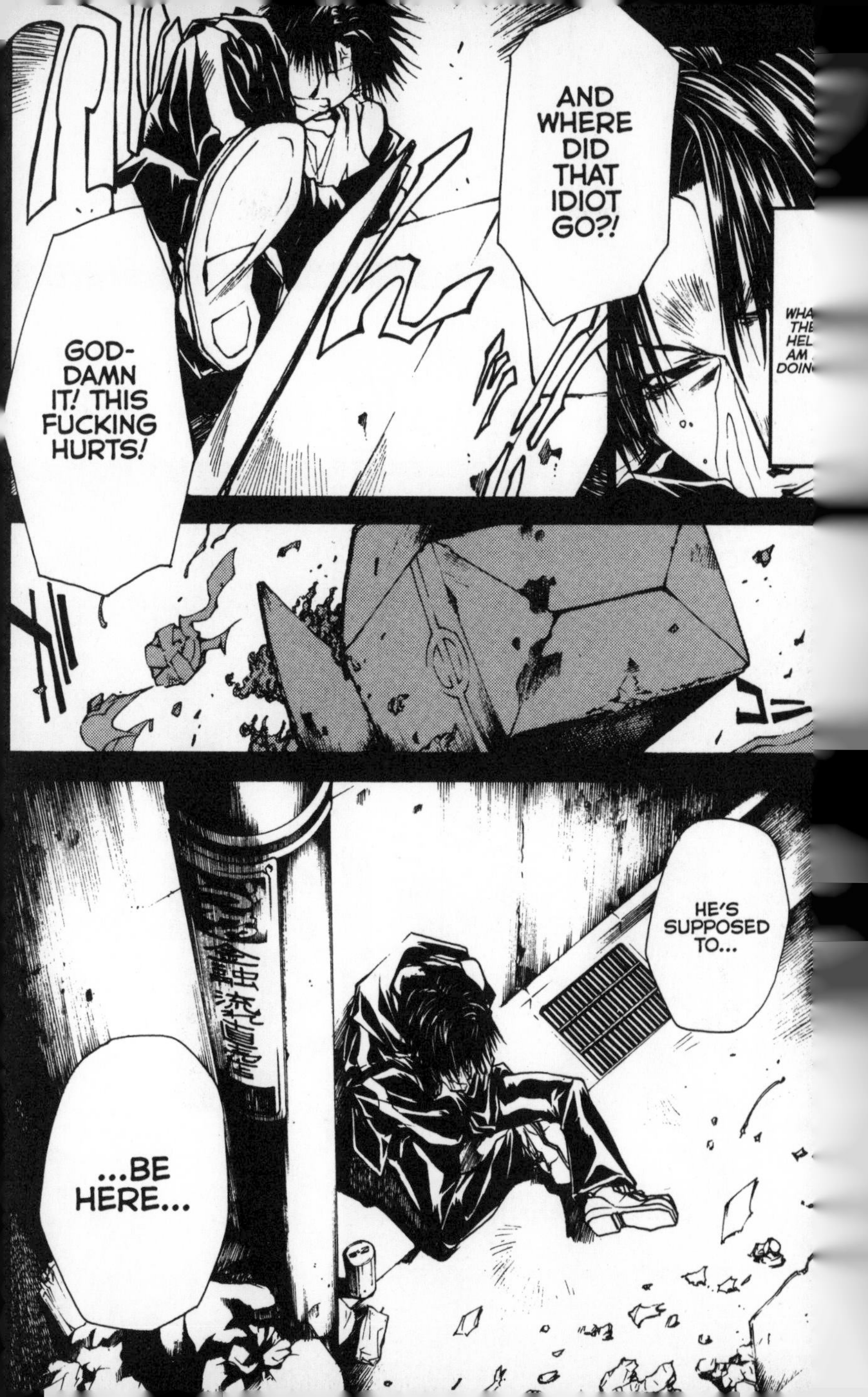
WHA THE HEL AM DOIN
AND WHERE DID THAT IDIOT GO?!
GOD-DAMN IT! THIS FUCKING HURTS!
HE'S SUPPOSED TO...
...BE HERE...

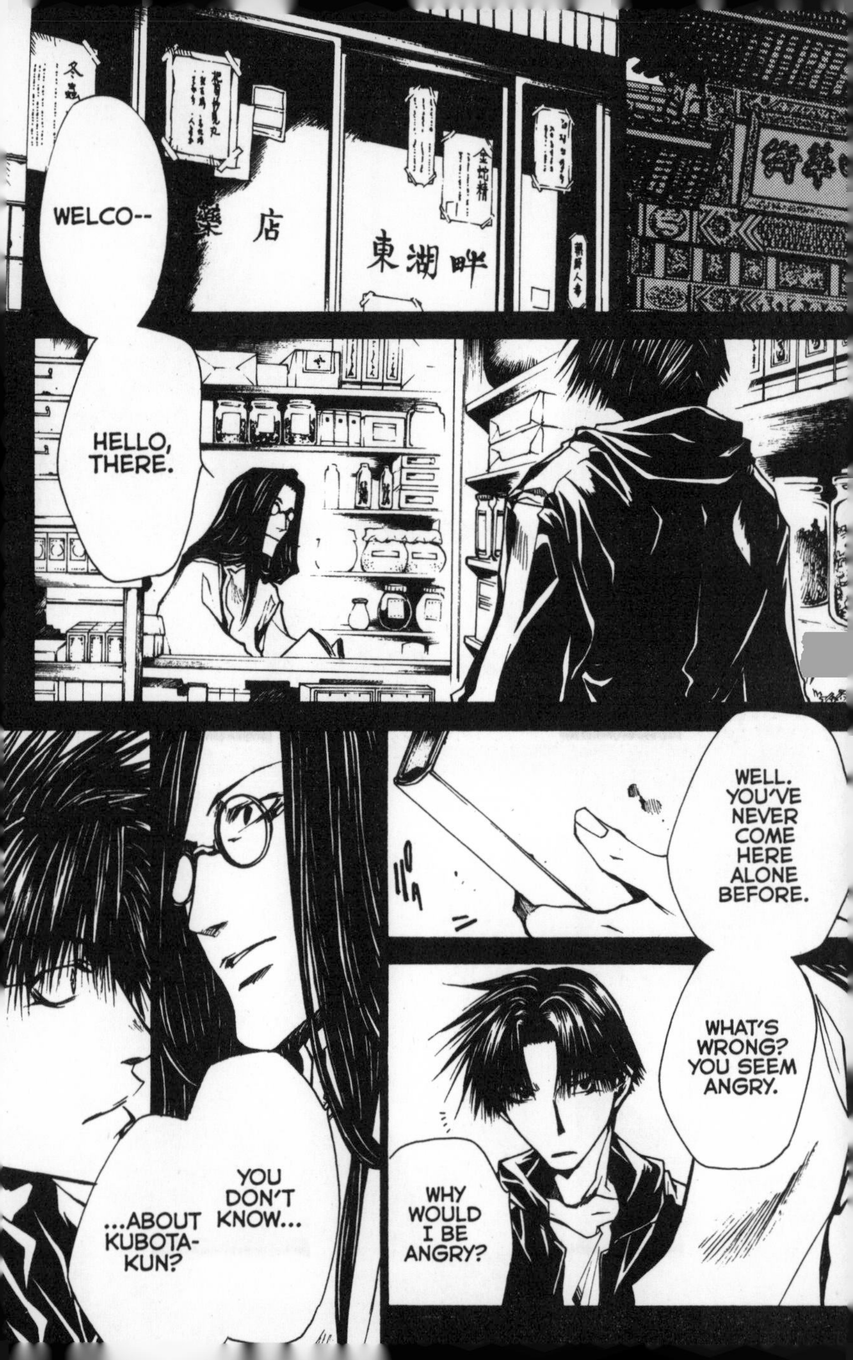
WELCO--
HELLO, THERE.
WELL. YOU'VE NEVER COME HERE ALONE BEFORE.
WHAT'S WRONG? YOU SEEM ANGRY.
WHY WOULD I BE ANGRY?
YOU DON'T KNOW...
...ABOUT KUBOTA-KUN?

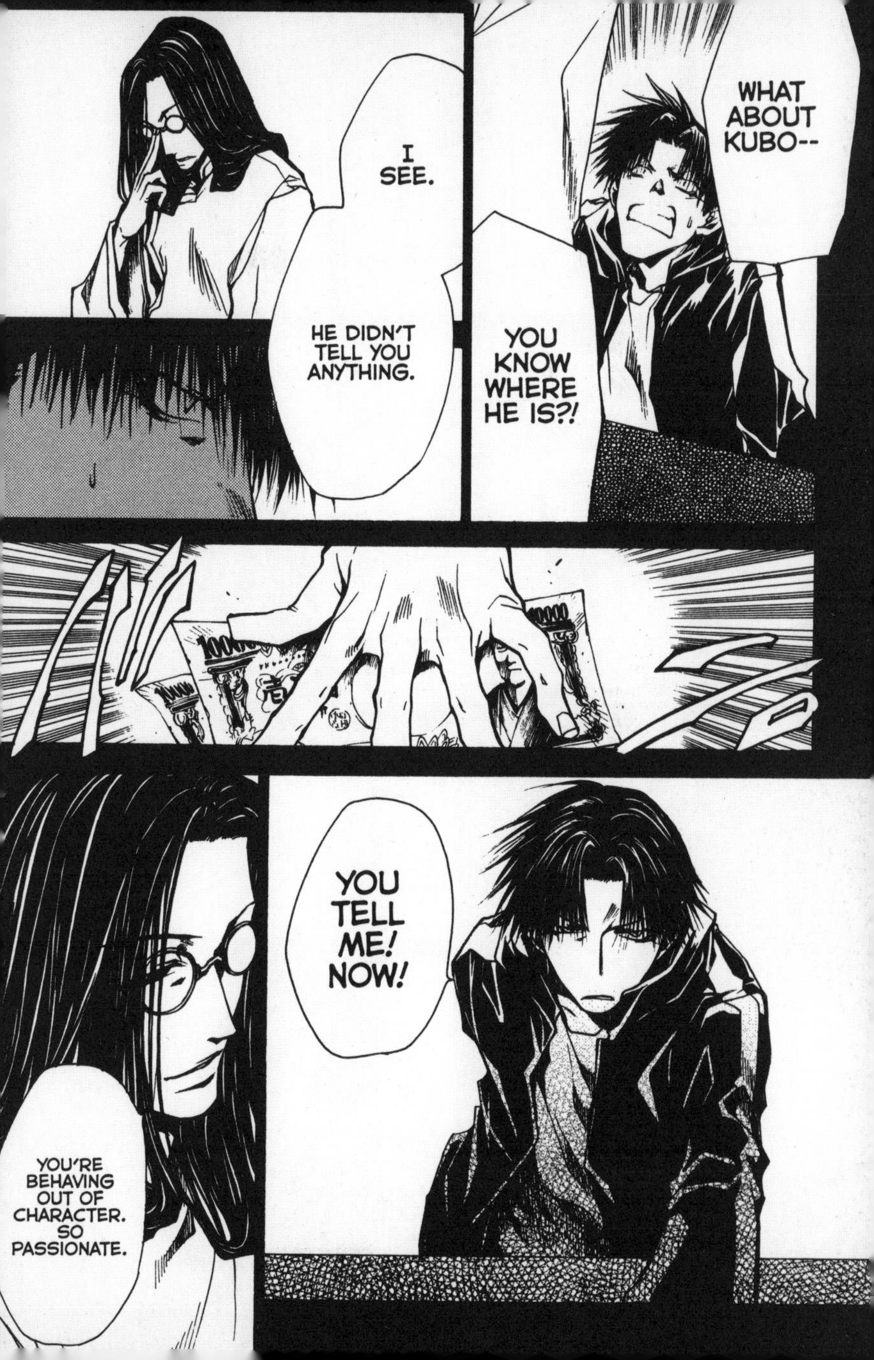
WHAT ABOUT KUBO--
YOU KNOW WHERE HE IS?!
I SEE.
HE DIDN'T TELL YOU ANYTHING.
YOU TELL ME! NOW!
YOU'RE BEHAVING OUT OF CHARACTER. SO PASSIONATE.

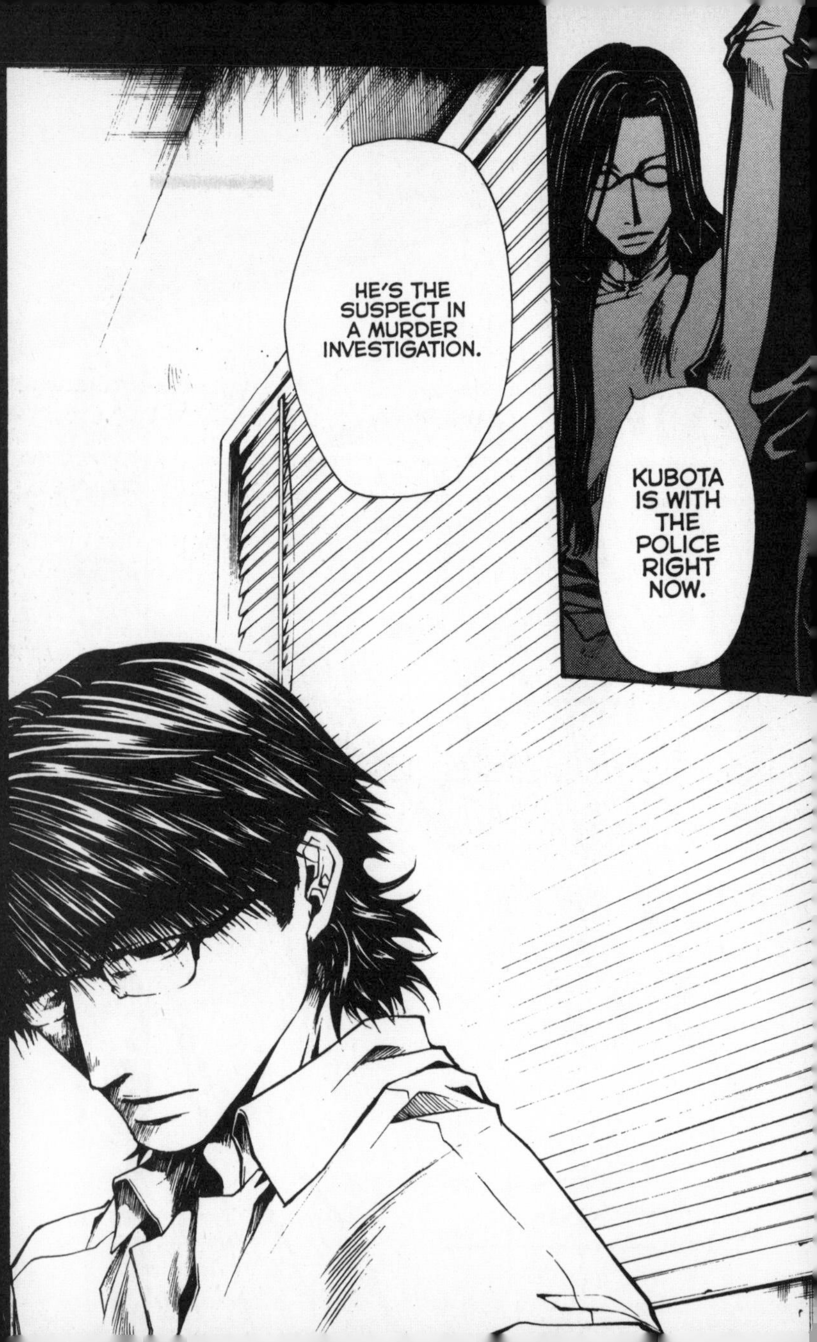
KUBOTA IS WITH THE POLICE RIGHT NOW.
HE'S THE SUSPECT IN A MURDER INVESTIGATION.

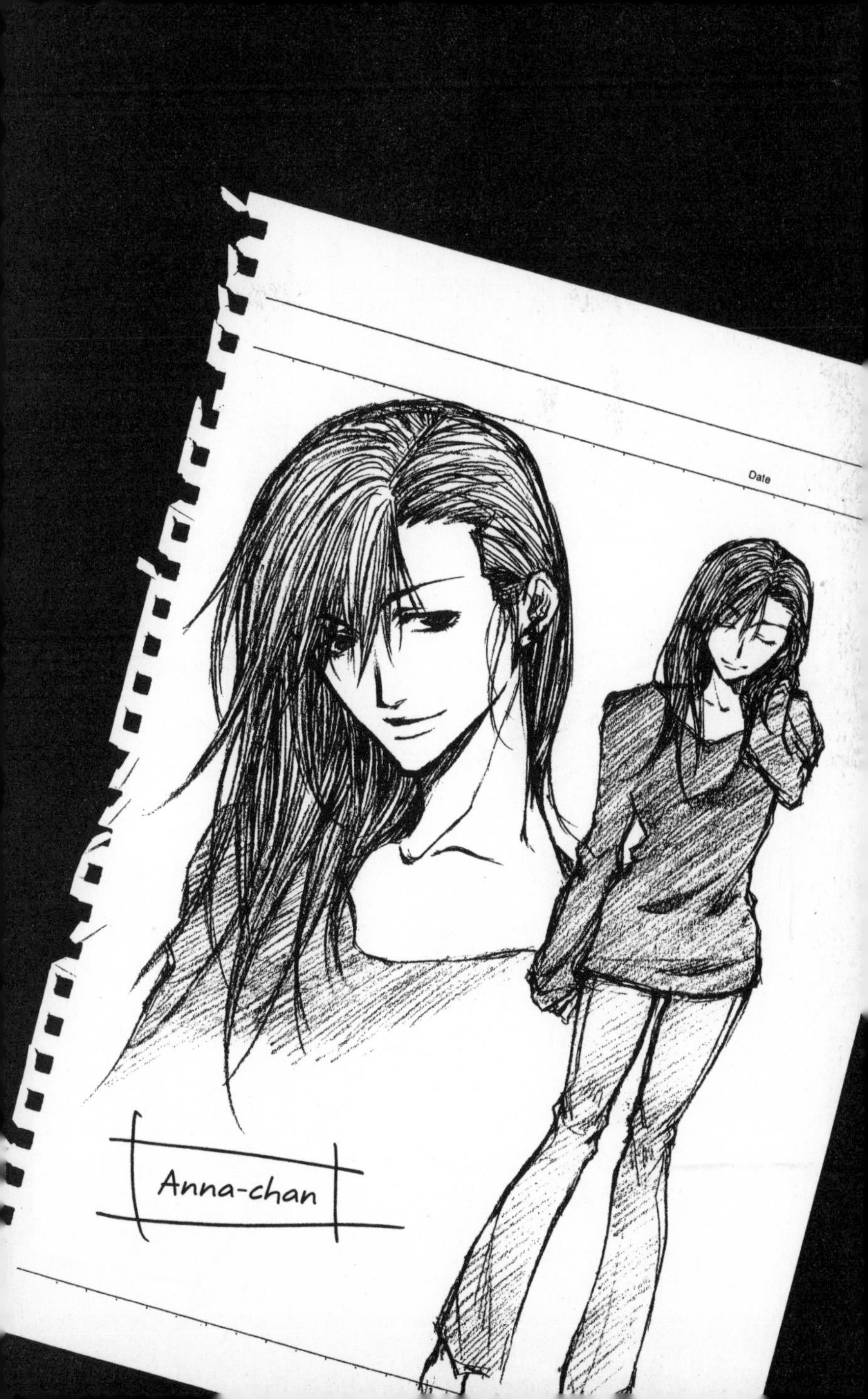
Date
Anna-chan

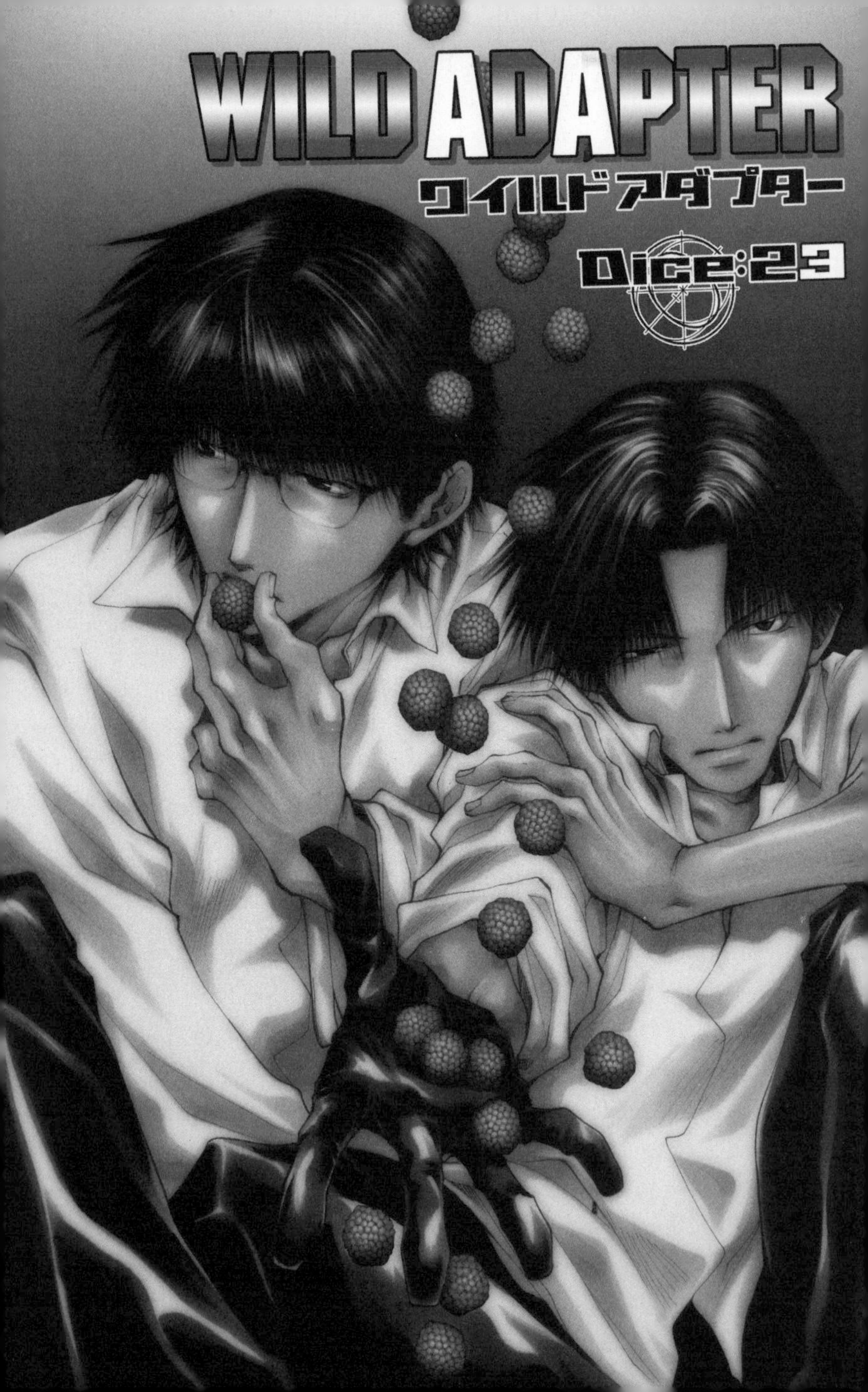
WILD ADAPTER
ワイルドアダプター
Dice:23

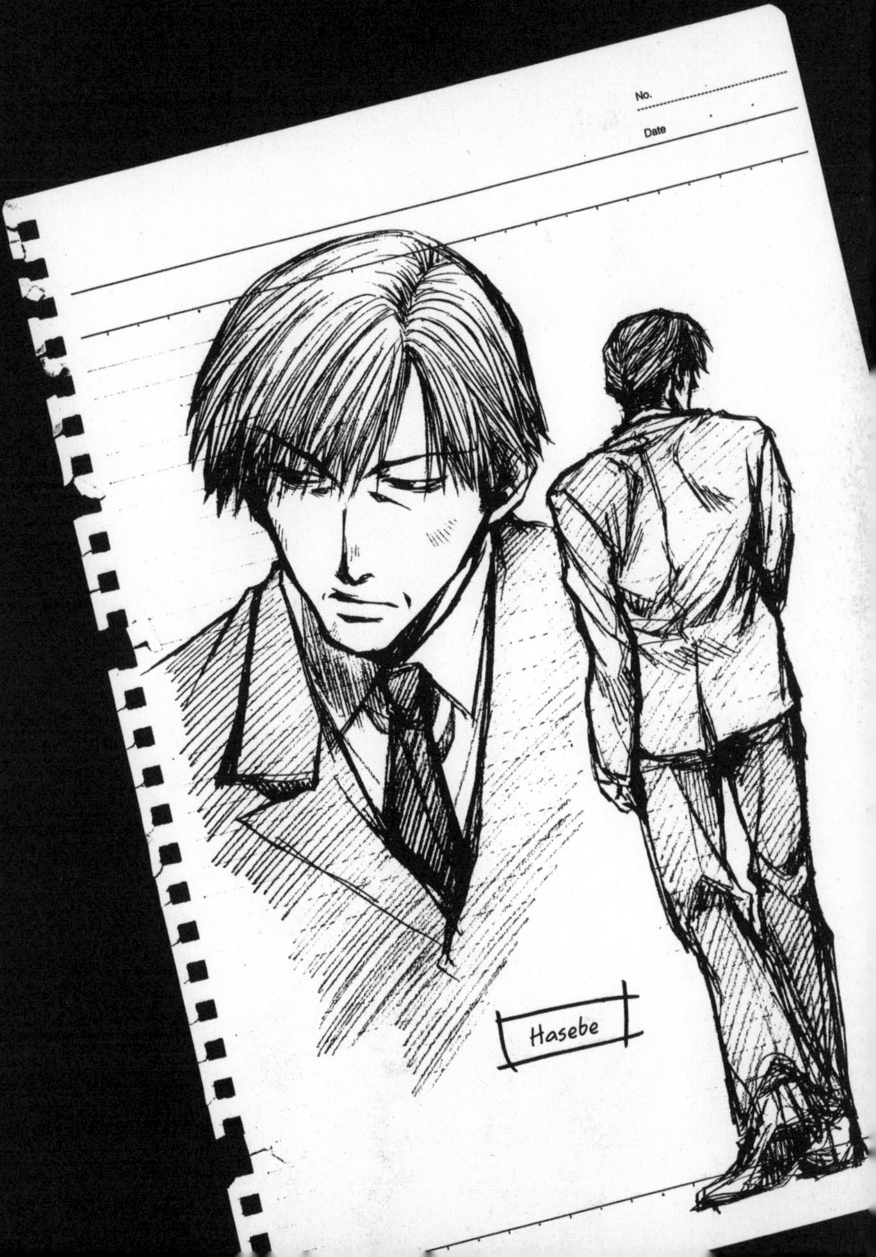
No.
Date
Hasebe

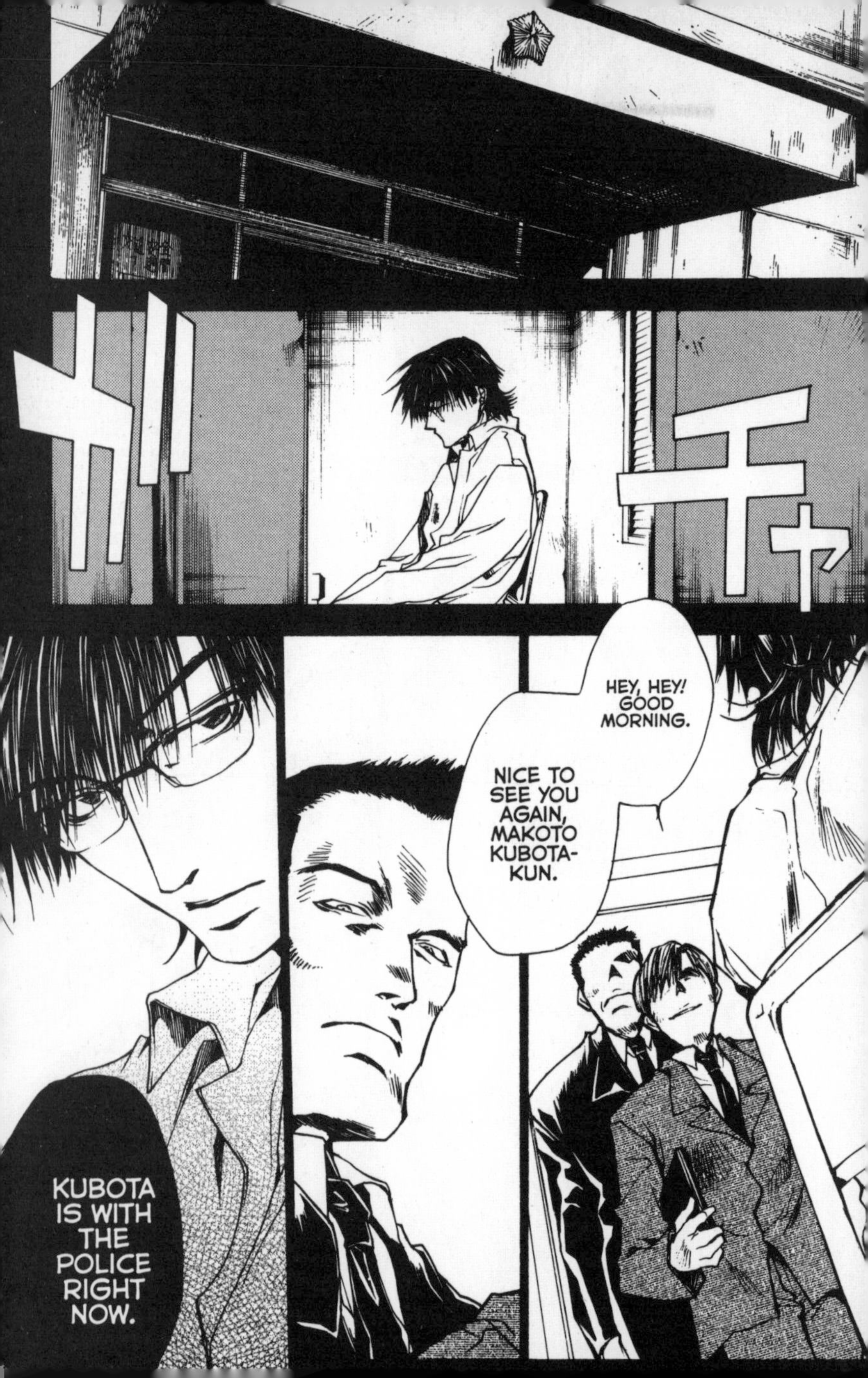
ガチャ
HEY, HEY! GOOD MORNING.
NICE TO SEE YOU AGAIN, MAKOTO KUBOTA-KUN.
KUBOTA IS WITH THE POLICE RIGHT NOW.

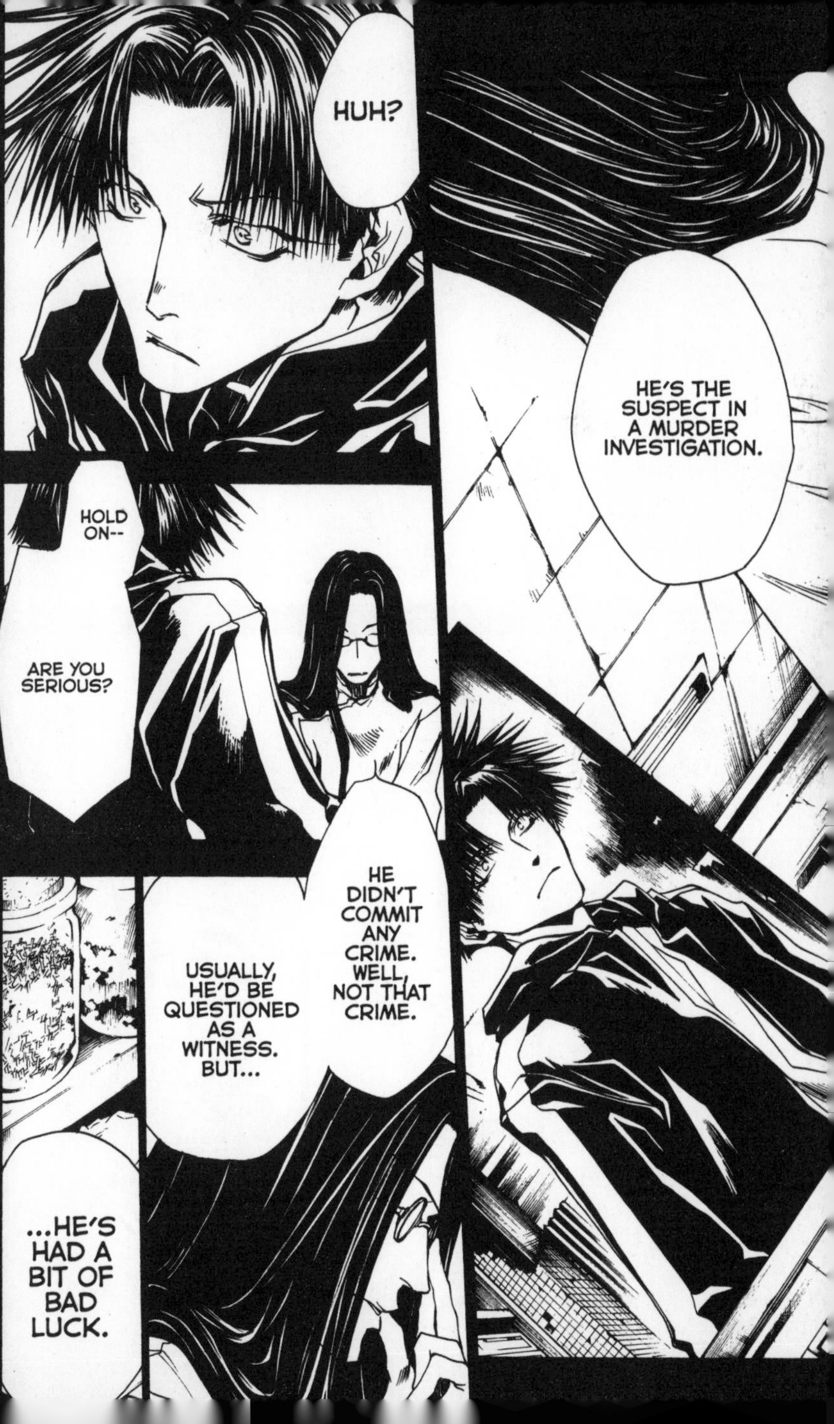
HE'S THE SUSPECT IN A MURDER INVESTIGATION.
HUH?
HOLD ON--
ARE YOU SERIOUS?
HE DIDN'T COMMIT ANY CRIME. WELL, NOT THAT CRIME.
USUALLY, HE'D BE QUESTIONED AS A WITNESS. BUT...
...HE'S HAD A BIT OF BAD LUCK.

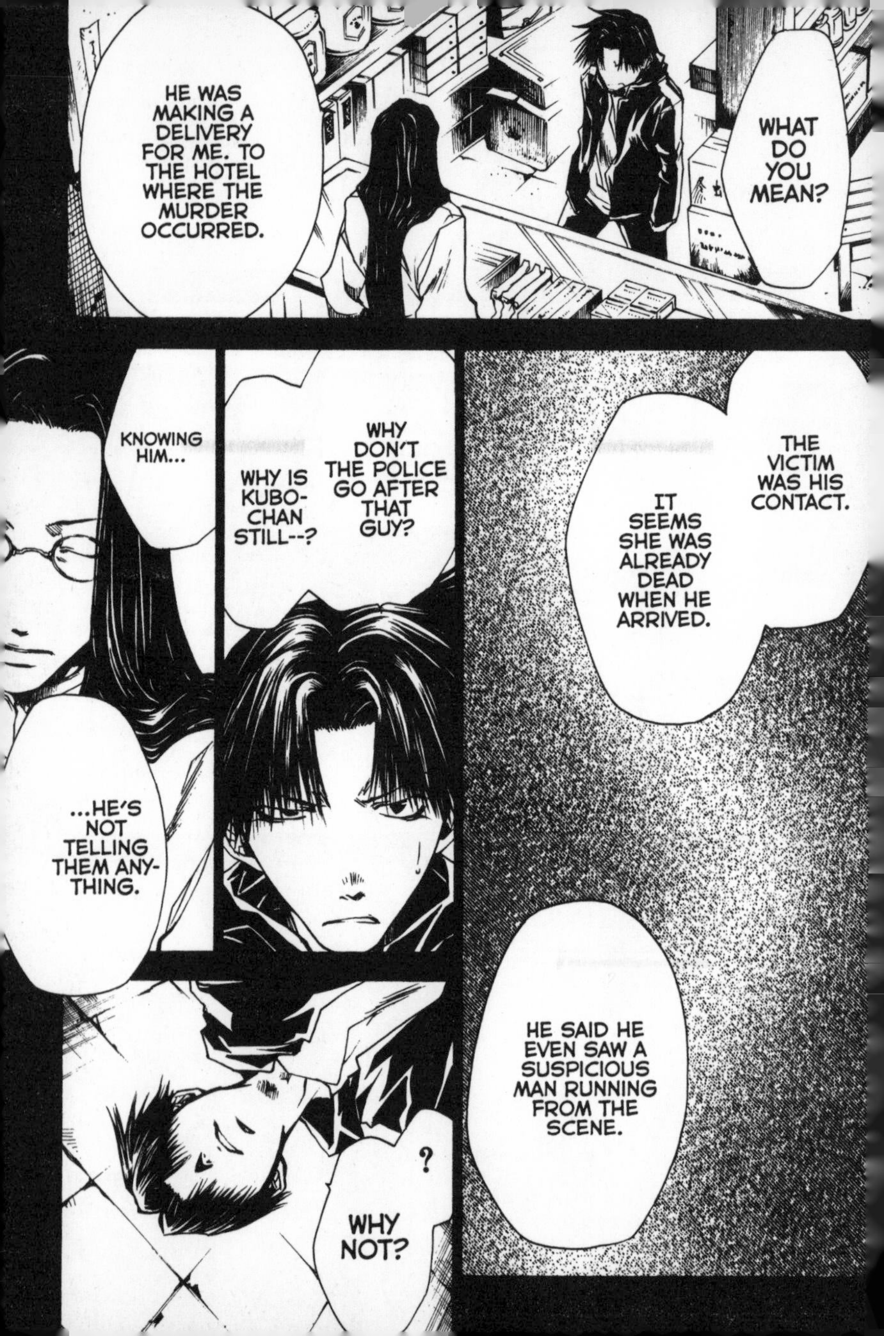
WHAT DO YOU MEAN?
HE WAS MAKING A DELIVERY FOR ME. TO THE HOTEL WHERE THE MURDER OCCURRED.
THE VICTIM WAS HIS CONTACT.
IT SEEMS SHE WAS ALREADY DEAD WHEN HE ARRIVED.
HE SAID HE EVEN SAW A SUSPICIOUS MAN RUNNING FROM THE SCENE.
WHY DON'T THE POLICE GO AFTER THAT GUY?
WHY IS KUBO-CHAN STILL--?
KNOWING HIM...
...HE'S NOT TELLING THEM ANY-THING.
?
WHY NOT?

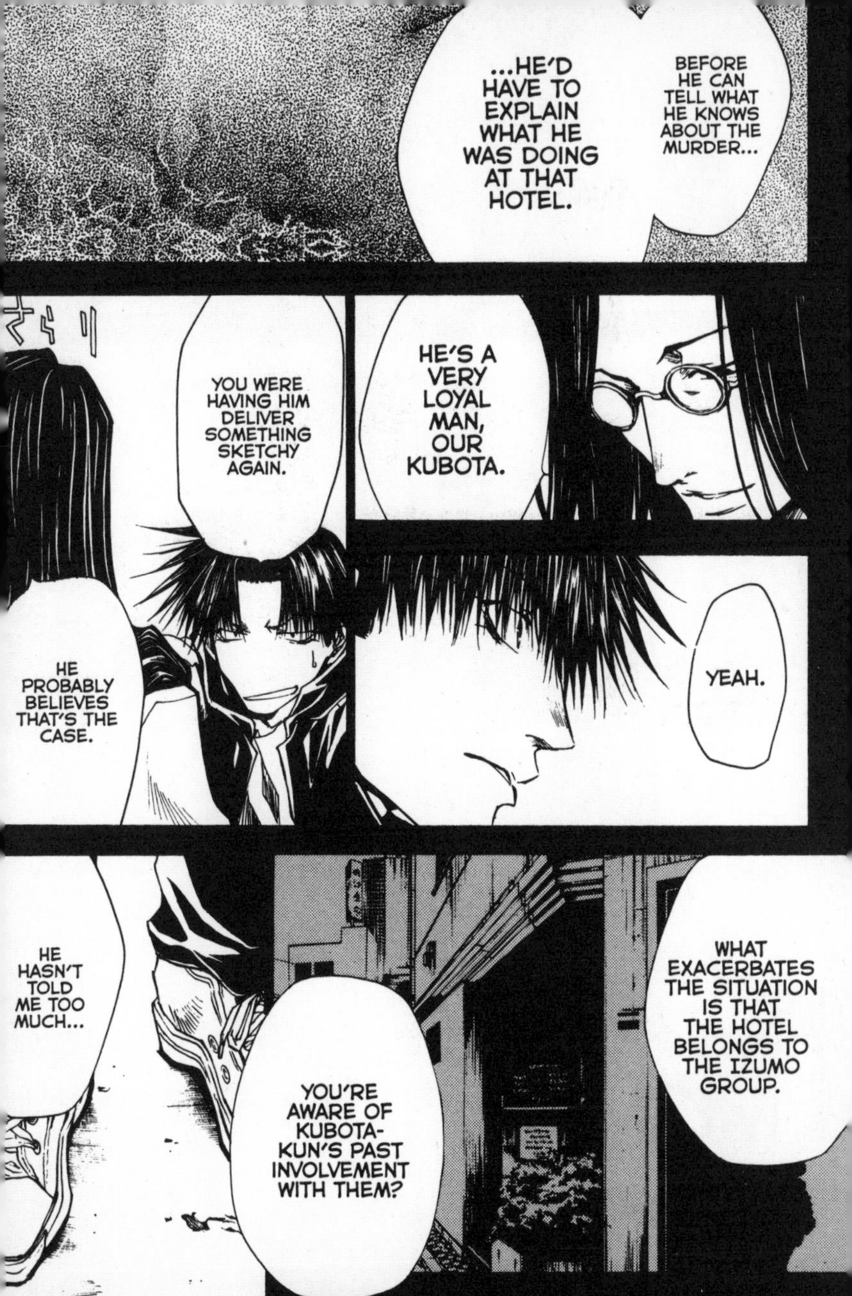
BEFORE HE CAN TELL WHAT HE KNOWS ABOUT THE MURDER...
...HE'D HAVE TO EXPLAIN WHAT HE WAS DOING AT THAT HOTEL.
HE'S A VERY LOYAL MAN, OUR KUBOTA.
YEAH.
さらり
YOU WERE HAVING HIM DELIVER SOMETHING SKETCHY AGAIN.
HE PROBABLY BELIEVES THAT'S THE CASE.
WHAT EXACERBATES THE SITUATION IS THAT THE HOTEL BELONGS TO THE IZUMO GROUP.
YOU'RE AWARE OF KUBOTA-KUN'S PAST INVOLVEMENT WITH THEM?
HE HASN'T TOLD ME TOO MUCH...

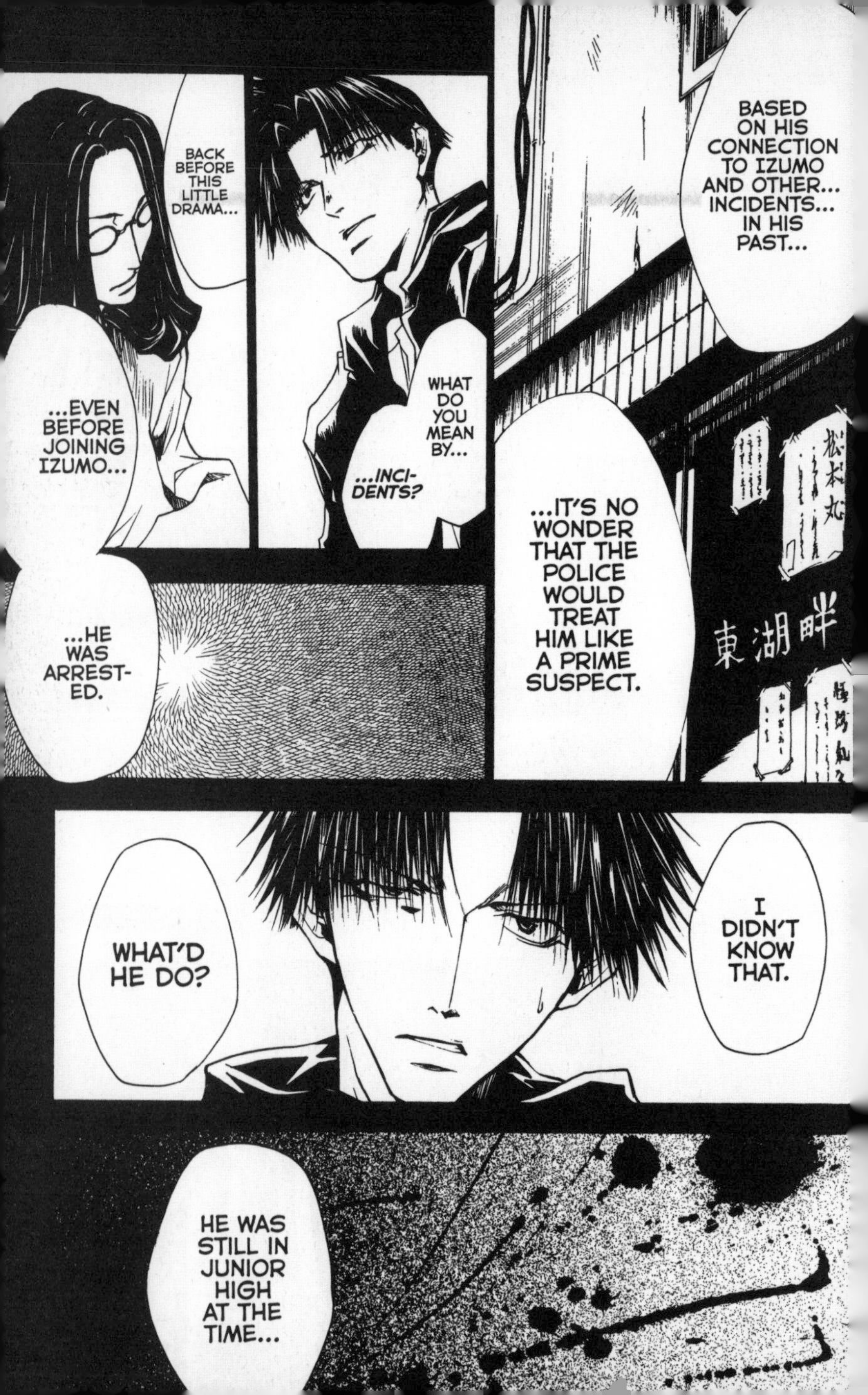
BASED ON HIS CONNECTION TO IZUMO AND OTHER... INCIDENTS... IN HIS PAST...
...IT'S NO WONDER THAT THE POLICE WOULD TREAT HIM LIKE A PRIME SUSPECT.
松本丸
東湖畔
WHAT DO YOU MEAN BY...
...INCI-DENTS?
BACK BEFORE THIS LITTLE DRAMA...
...EVEN BEFORE JOINING IZUMO...
...HE WAS ARREST-ED.
I DIDN'T KNOW THAT.
WHAT'D HE DO?
HE WAS STILL IN JUNIOR HIGH AT THE TIME...

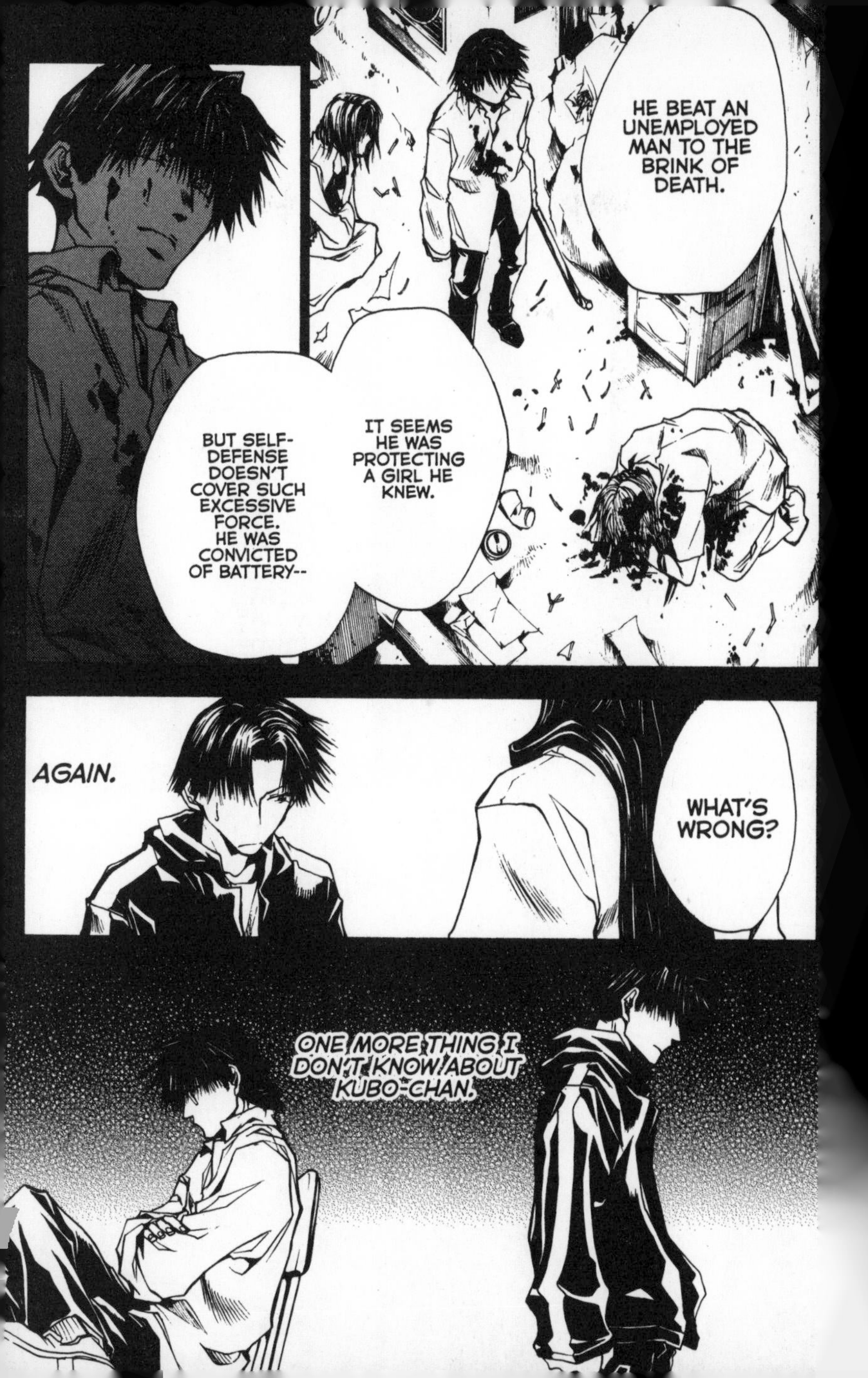
HE BEAT AN UNEMPLOYED MAN TO THE BRINK OF DEATH.
IT SEEMS HE WAS PROTECTING A GIRL HE KNEW.
BUT SELF-DEFENSE DOESN'T COVER SUCH EXCESSIVE FORCE. HE WAS CONVICTED OF BATTERY--
WHAT'S WRONG?
AGAIN.
ONE MORE THING I DON'T KNOW ABOUT KUBO-CHAN.

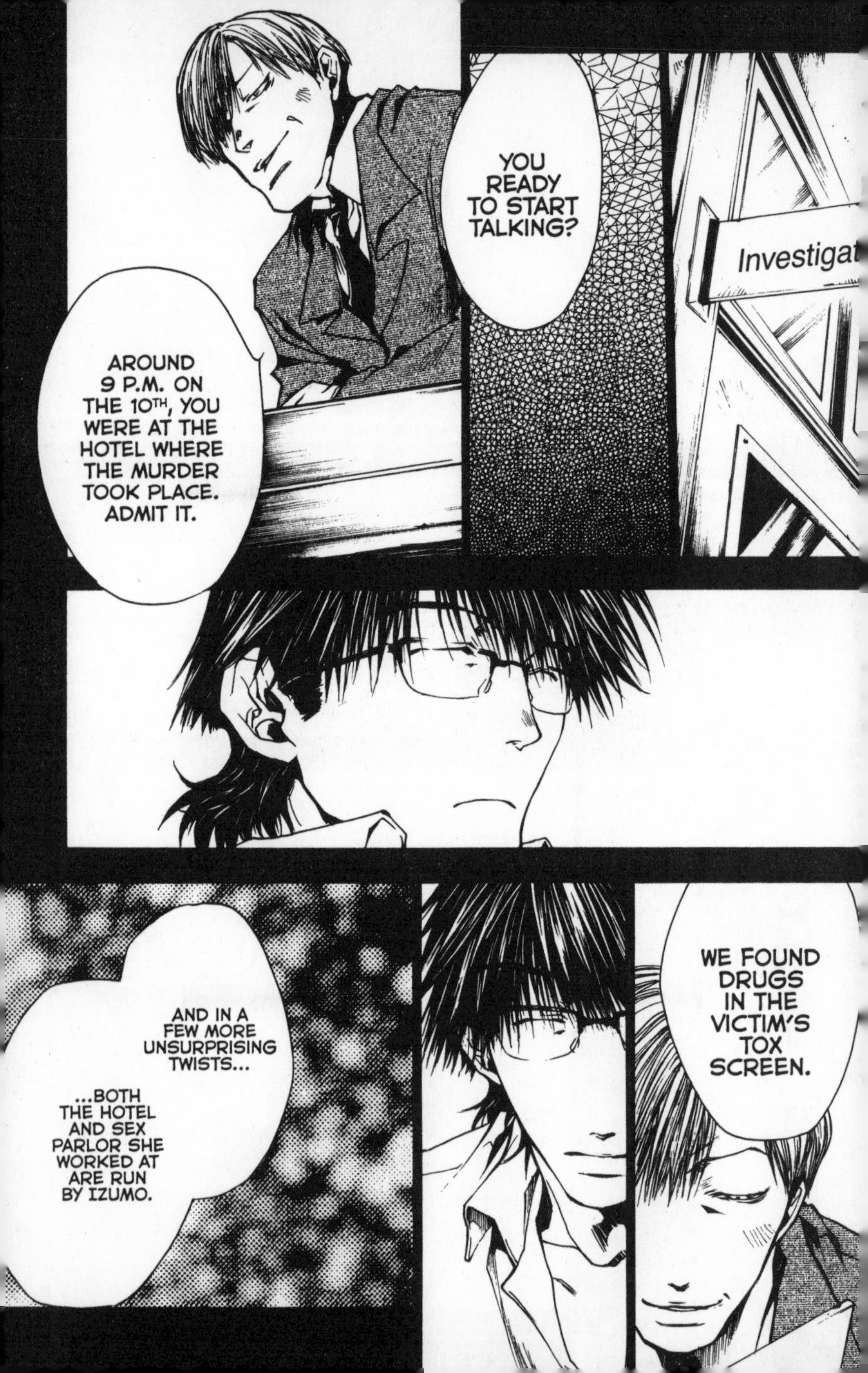

Investigat
YOU READY TO START TALKING?
AROUND 9 P.M. ON THE 10TH, YOU WERE AT THE HOTEL WHERE THE MURDER TOOK PLACE. ADMIT IT.
WE FOUND DRUGS IN THE VICTIM'S TOX SCREEN.
AND IN A FEW MORE UNSURPRISING TWISTS...
...BOTH THE HOTEL AND SEX PARLOR SHE WORKED AT ARE RUN BY IZUMO.

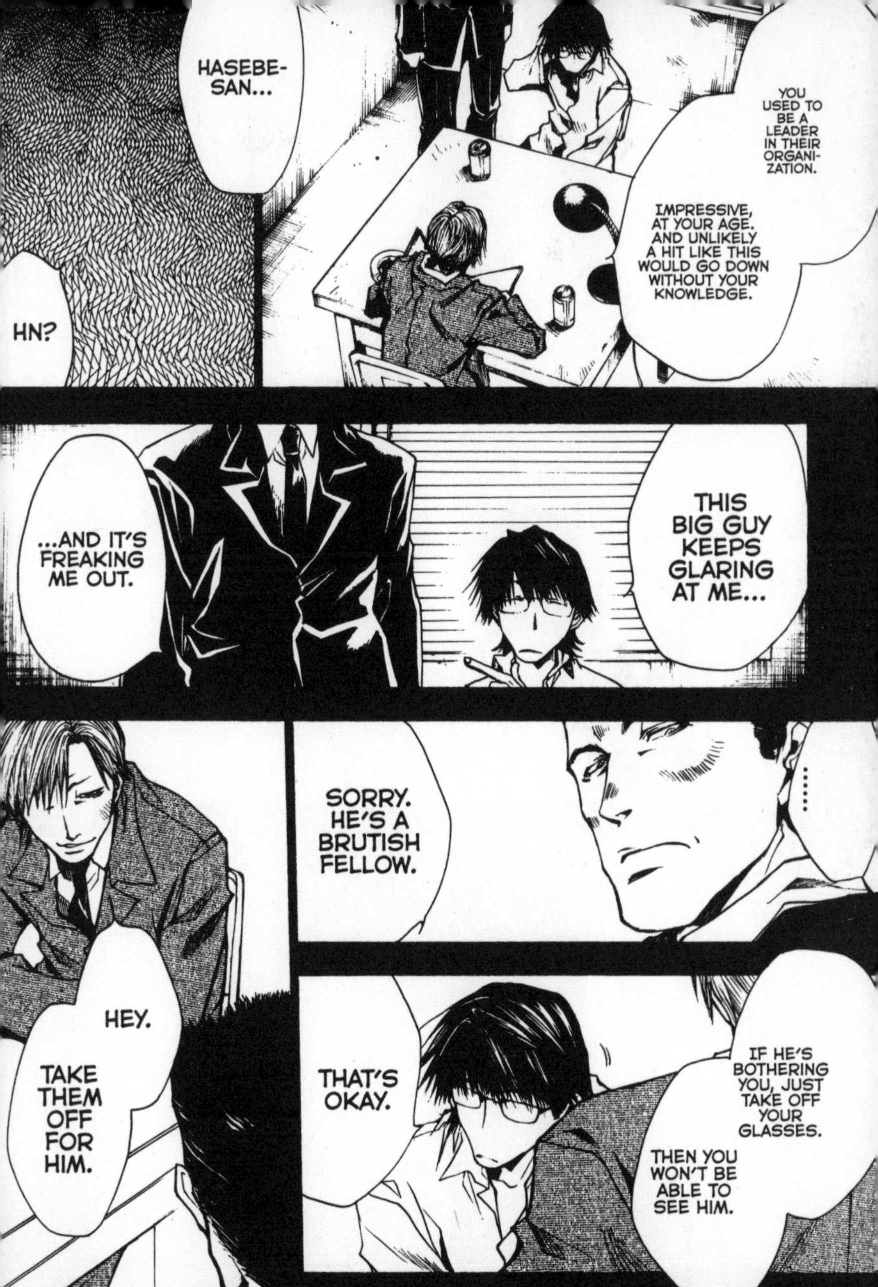

YOU USED TO BE A LEADER IN THEIR ORGANI-ZATION.
IMPRESSIVE, AT YOUR AGE. AND UNLIKELY A HIT LIKE THIS WOULD GO DOWN WITHOUT YOUR KNOWLEDGE.
HASEBE-SAN...
HN?
THIS BIG GUY KEEPS GLARING AT ME...
...AND IT'S FREAKING ME OUT.
......
SORRY. HE'S A BRUTISH FELLOW.
IF HE'S BOTHERING YOU, JUST TAKE OFF YOUR GLASSES.
THEN YOU WON'T BE ABLE TO SEE HIM.
THAT'S OKAY.
HEY.
TAKE THEM OFF FOR HIM.

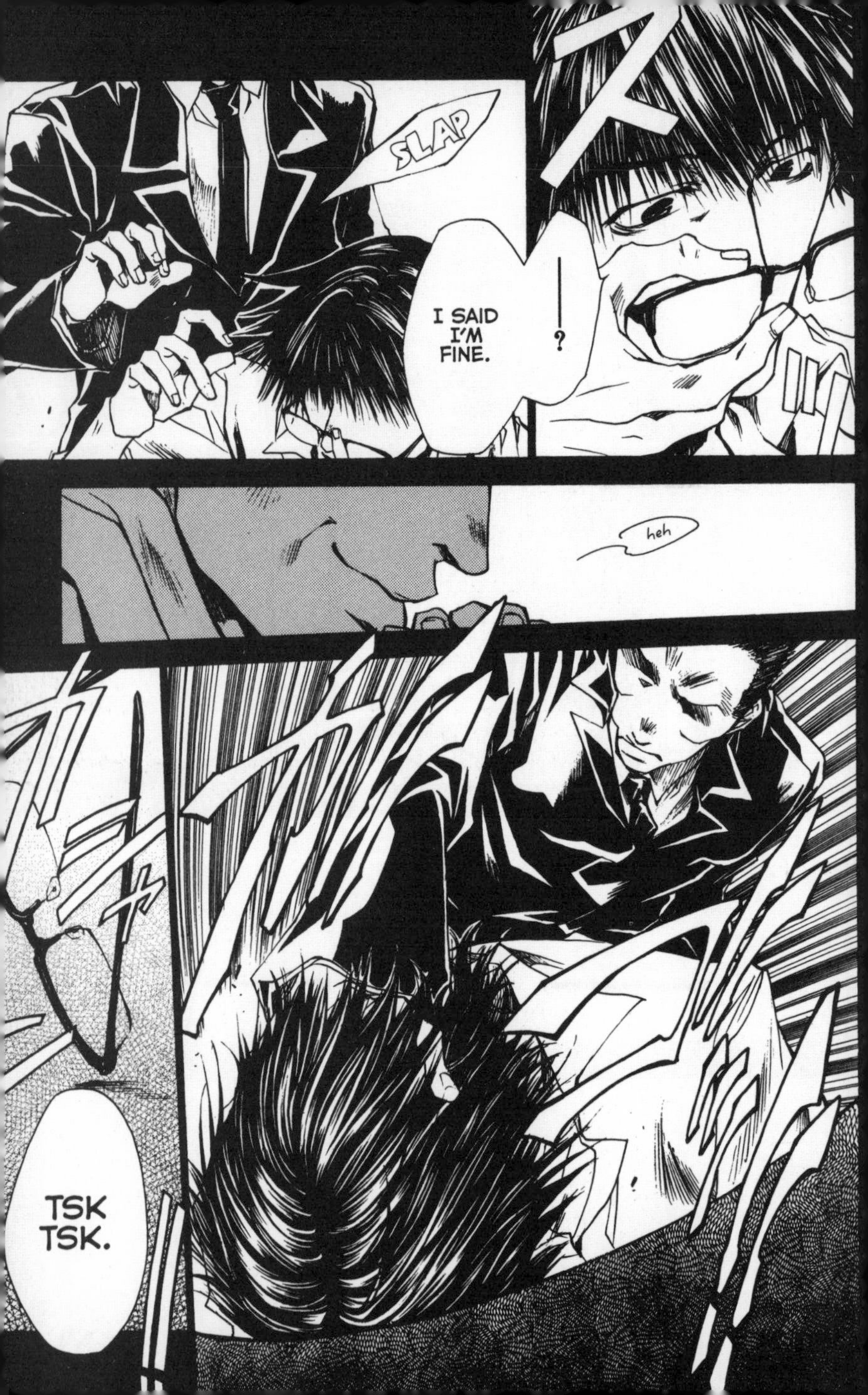
SLAP
--?
I SAID I'M FINE.
heh
TSK TSK.

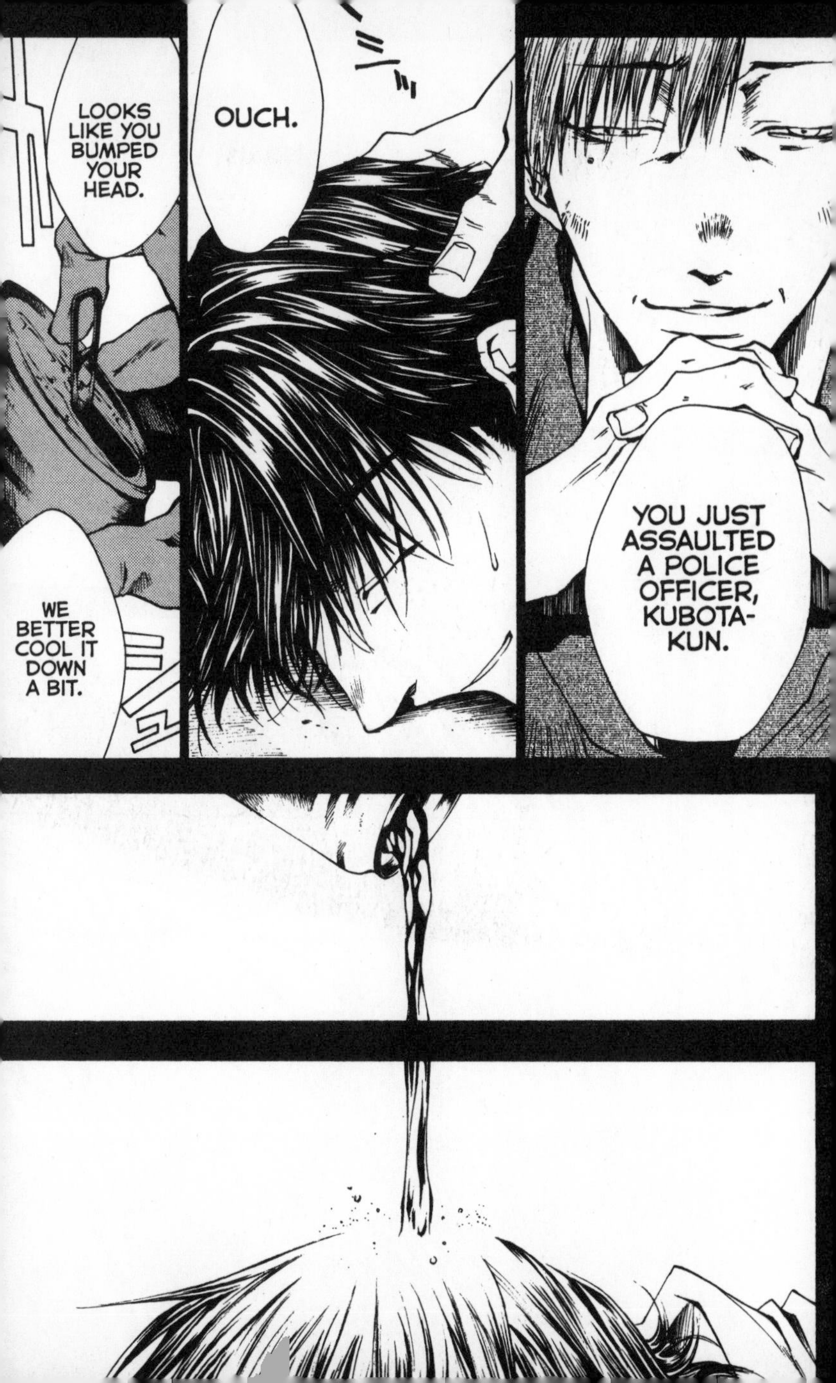
YOU JUST ASSAULTED A POLICE OFFICER, KUBOTA-KUN.
OUCH.
LOOKS LIKE YOU BUMPED YOUR HEAD.
WE BETTER COOL IT DOWN A BIT.

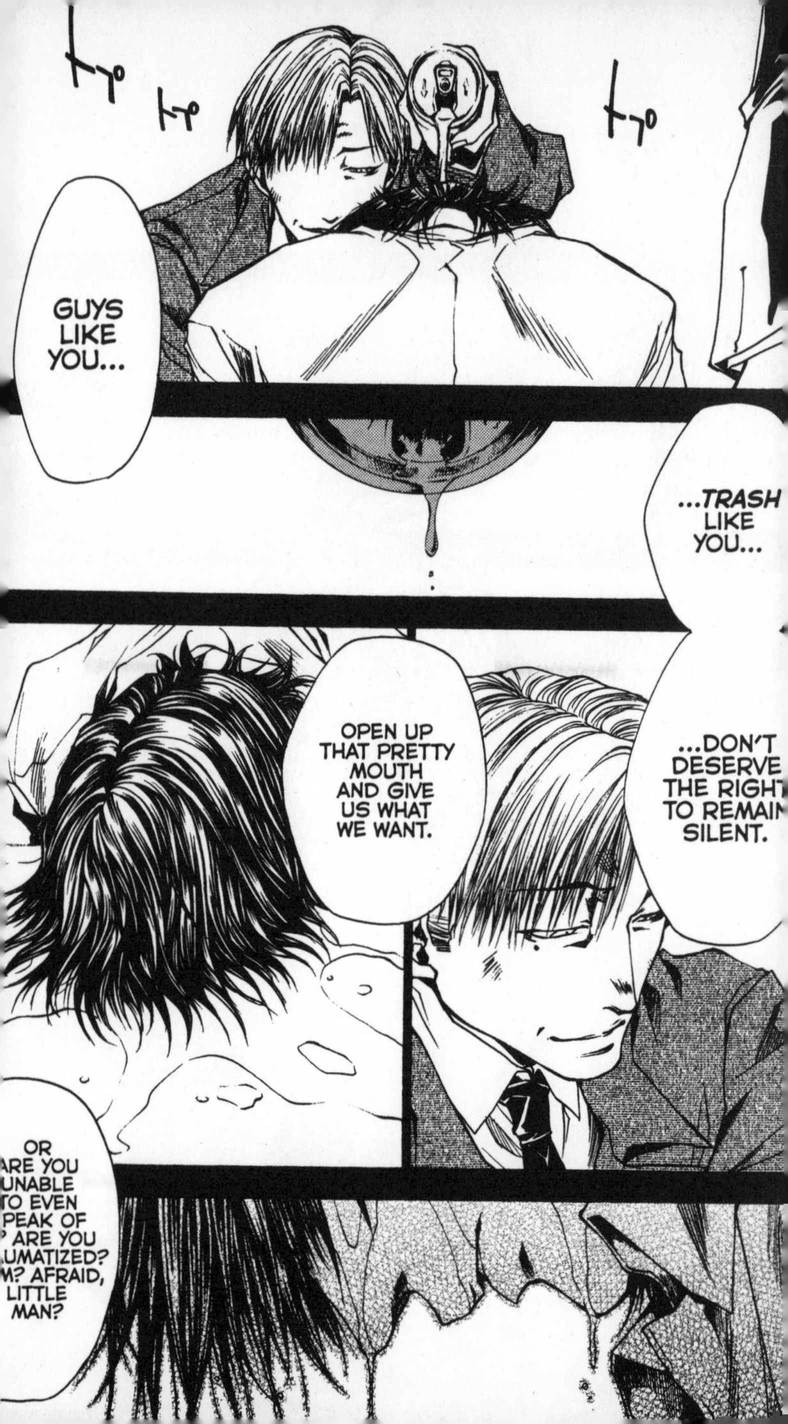
GUYS LIKE YOU...
...TRASH LIKE YOU...
...DON'T DESERVE THE RIGHT TO REMAIN SILENT.
OPEN UP THAT PRETTY MOUTH AND GIVE US WHAT WE WANT.
OR ARE YOU UNABLE TO EVEN PEAK OF ? ARE YOU UMATIZED? M? AFRAID, LITTLE MAN?

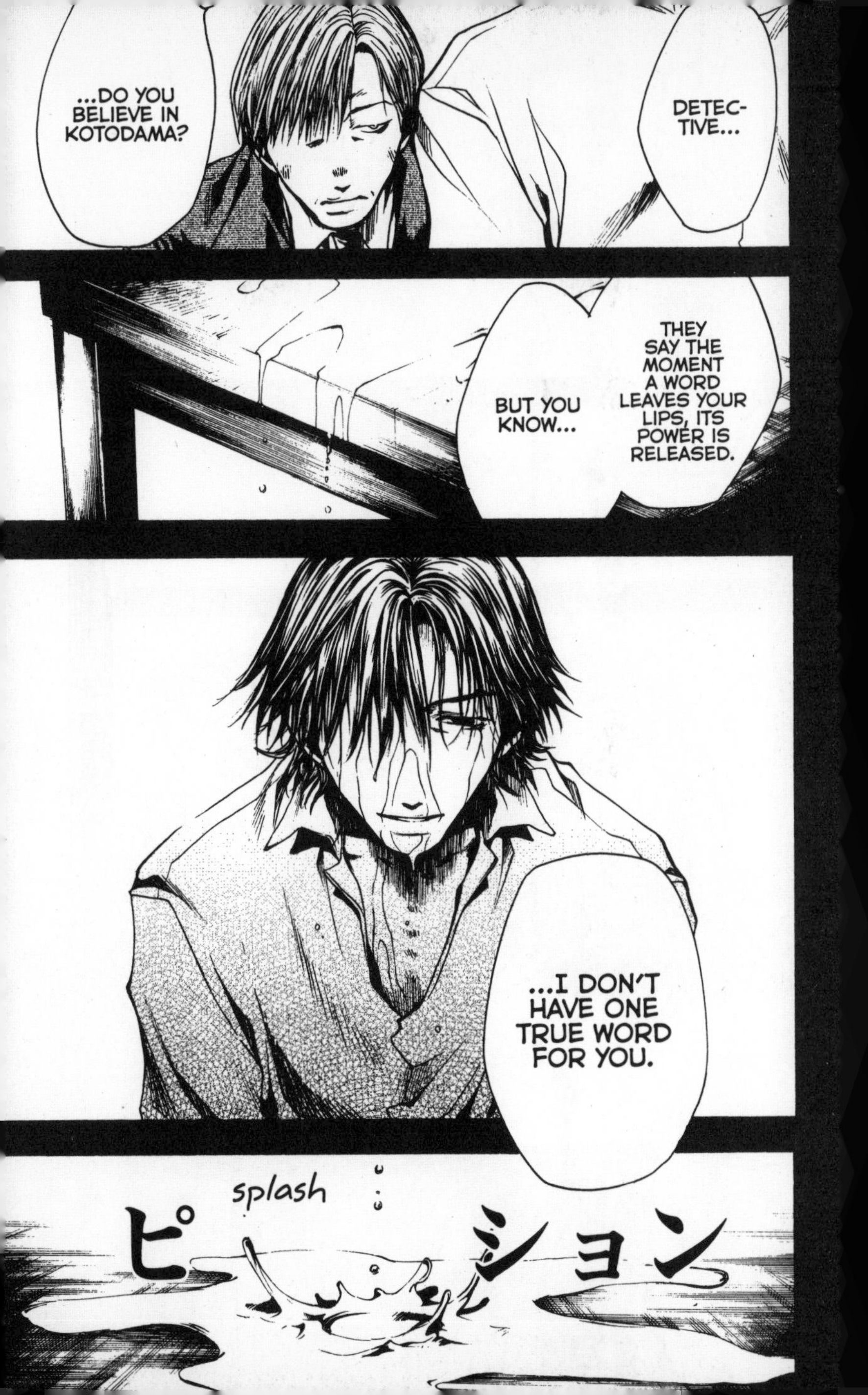
DETEC-
TIVE...
...DO YOU BELIEVE IN KOTODAMA?
THEY SAY THE MOMENT A WORD LEAVES YOUR LIPS, ITS POWER IS RELEASED.
BUT YOU KNOW...
...I DON'T HAVE ONE TRUE WORD FOR YOU.
splash
ピ ション

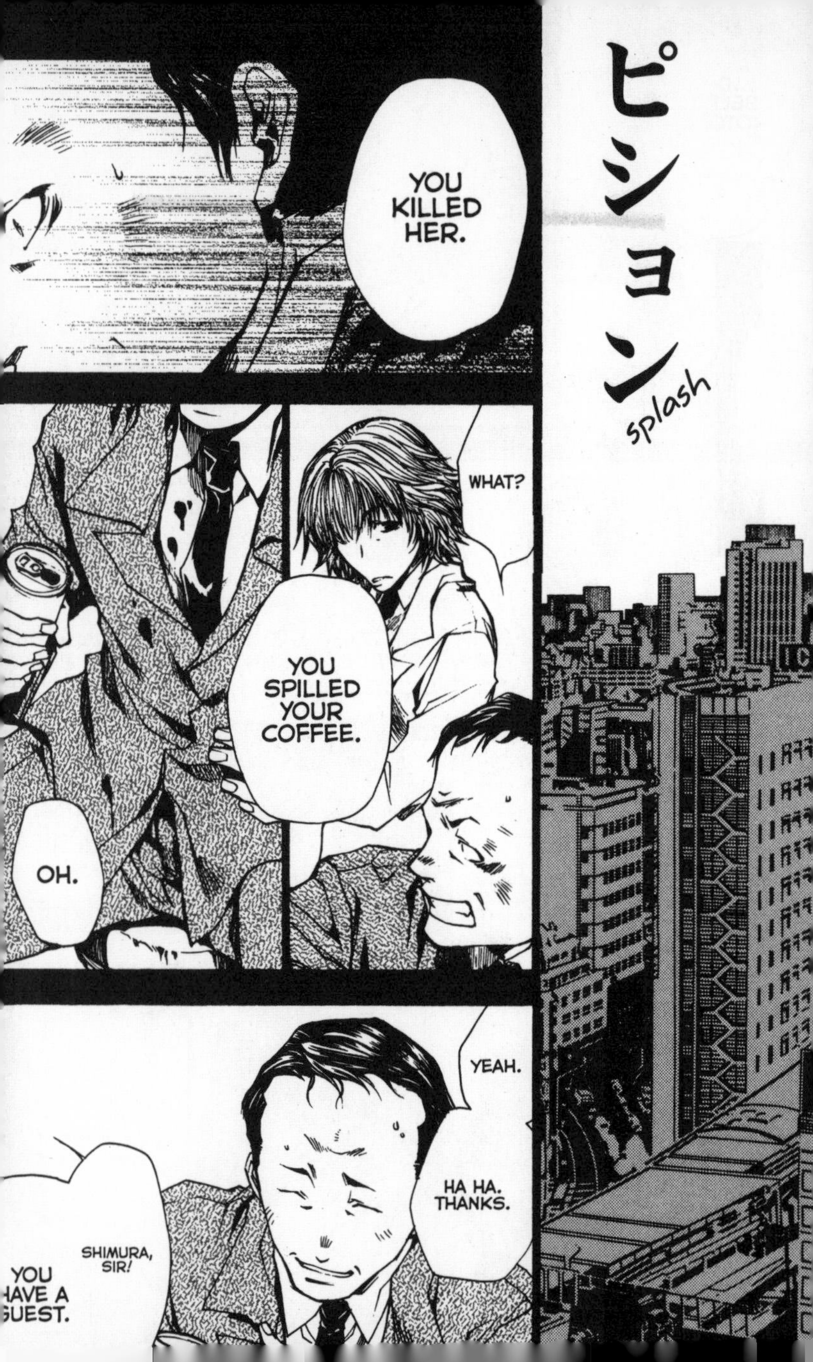
ピション
splash
YOU KILLED HER.
WHAT?
YOU SPILLED YOUR COFFEE.
OH.
YEAH.
HA HA. THANKS.
SHIMURA, SIR!
YOU HAVE A GUEST.

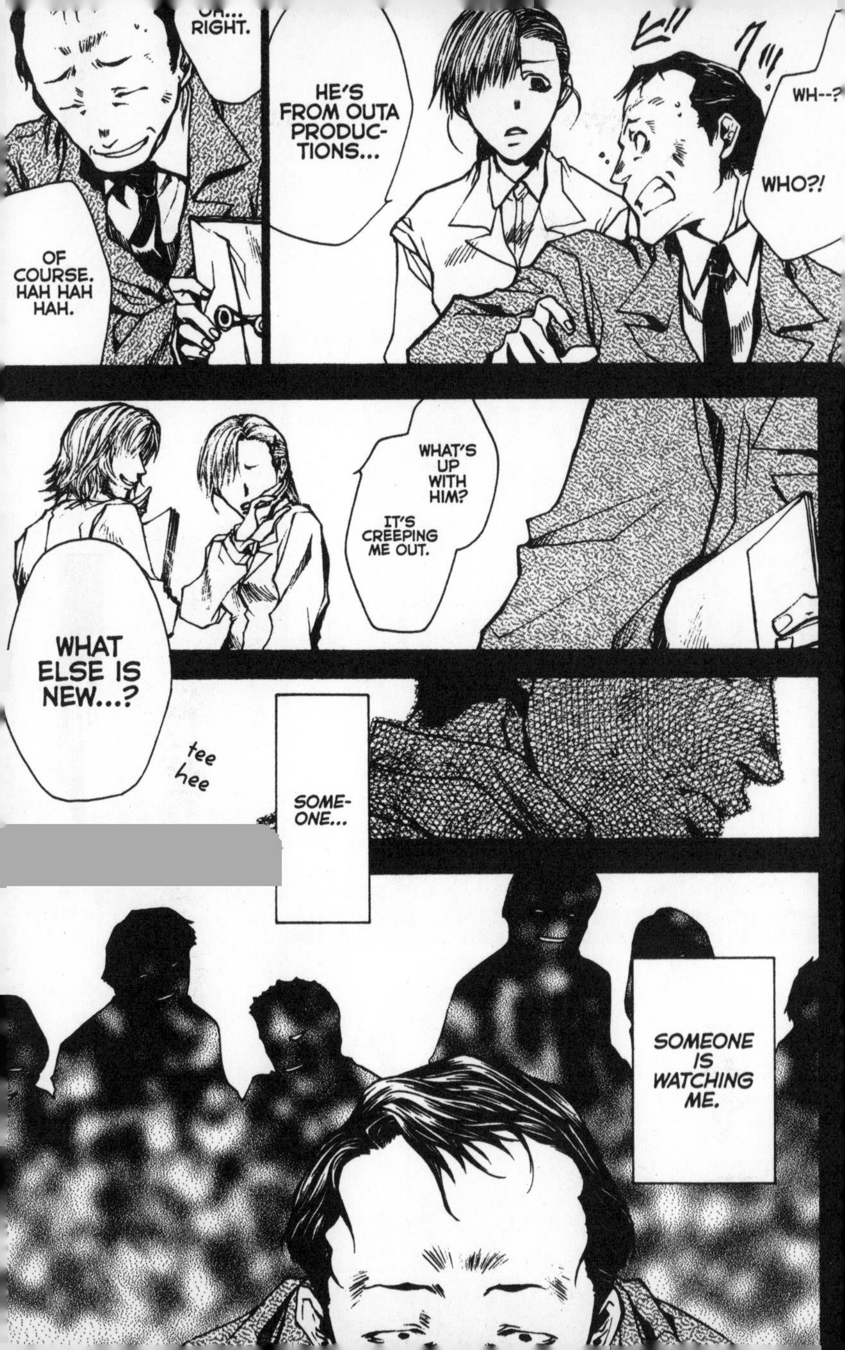
WH--?
WHO?!
HE'S FROM OUTA PRODUC-TIONS...
RIGHT.
OF COURSE. HAH HAH HAH.
WHAT'S UP WITH HIM?
IT'S CREEPING ME OUT.
WHAT ELSE IS NEW...?
tee hee
SOME-ONE...
SOMEONE IS WATCHING ME.

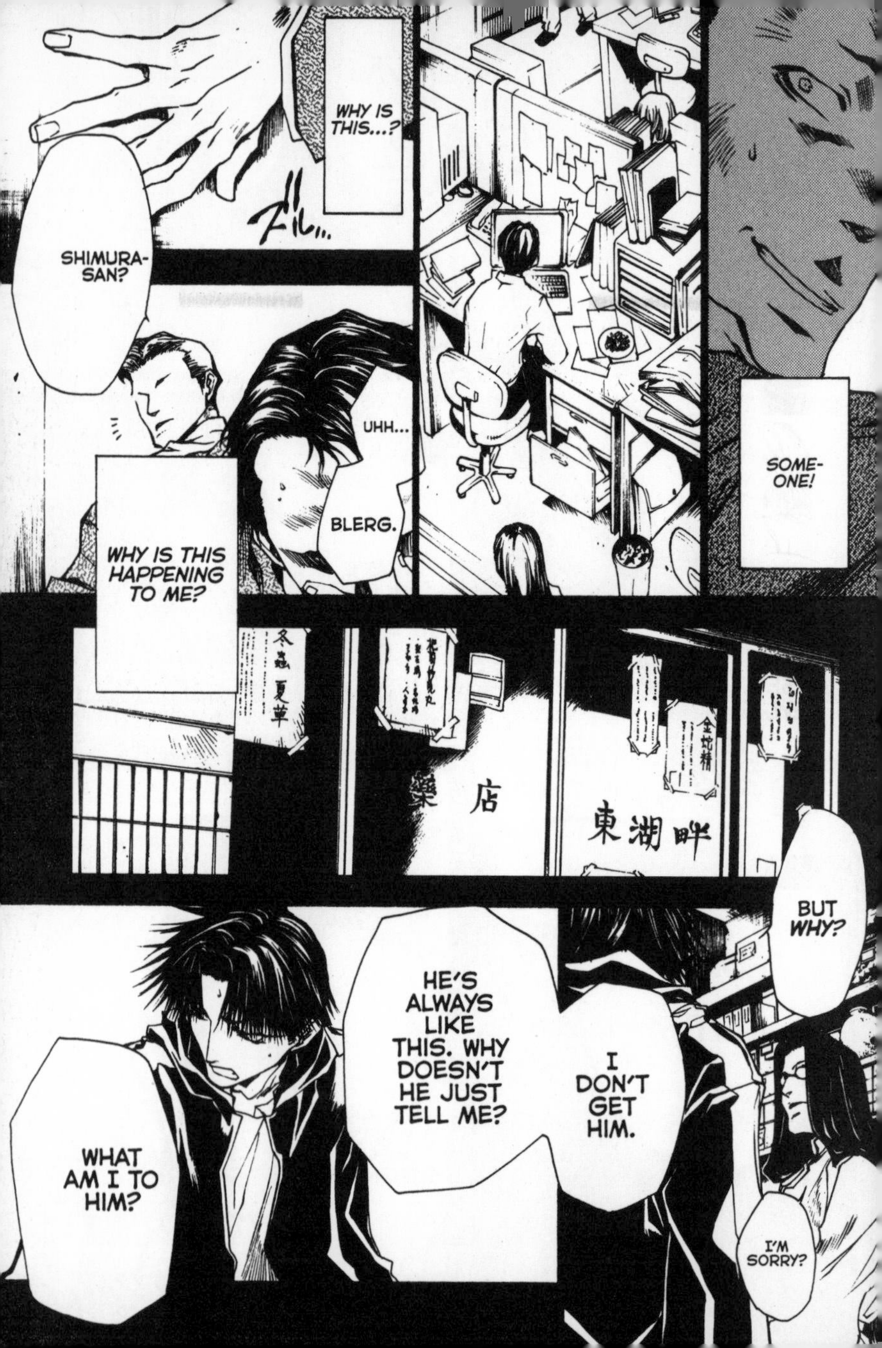
SOME-ONE!
WHY IS THIS...?
SHIMURA-SAN?
UHH...
BLERG.
WHY IS THIS HAPPENING TO ME?
東湖畔
店
BUT WHY?
I'M SORRY?
I DON'T GET HIM.
HE'S ALWAYS LIKE THIS. WHY DOESN'T HE JUST TELL ME?
WHAT AM I TO HIM?

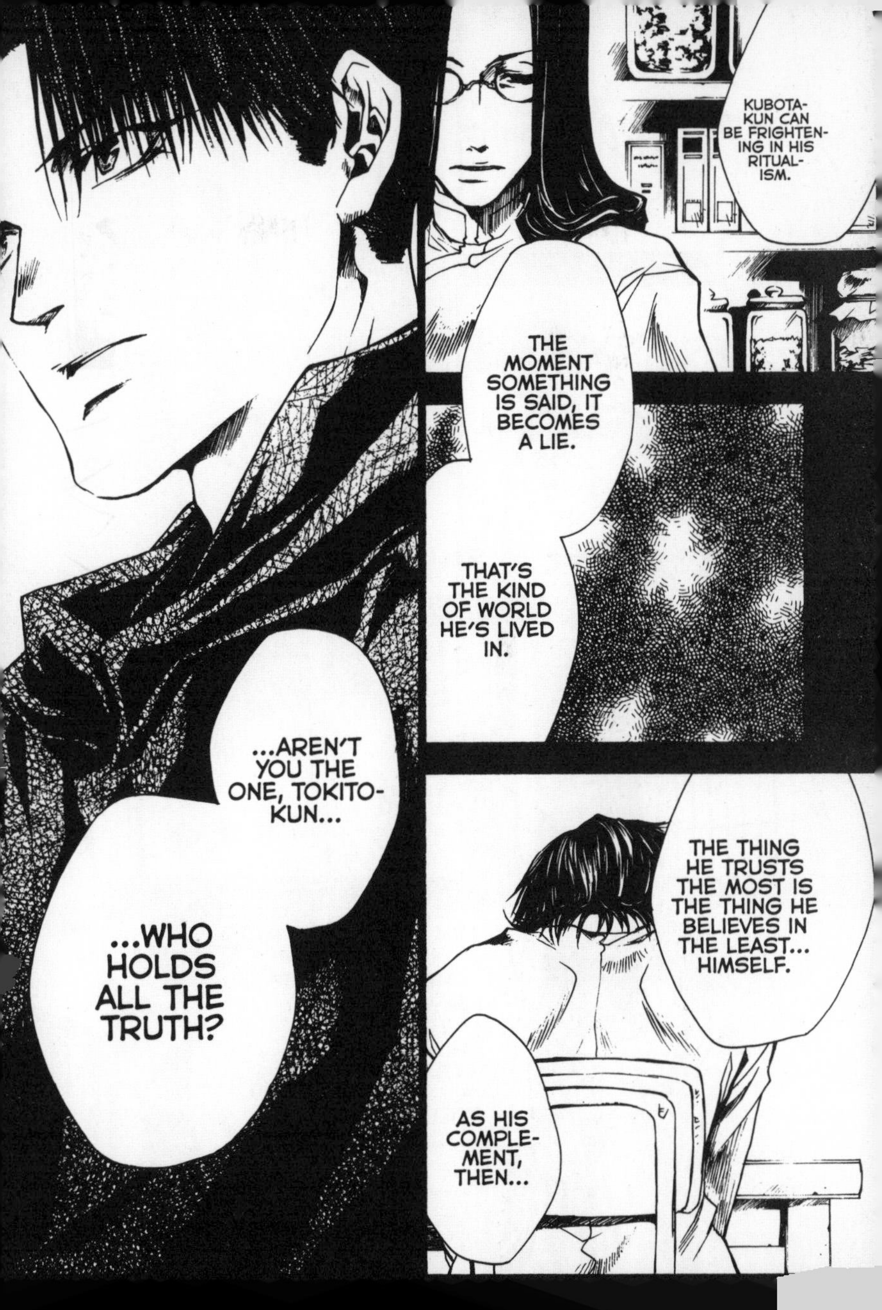
KUBOTA-KUN CAN BE FRIGHTENING IN HIS RITUALISM.
THE MOMENT SOMETHING IS SAID, IT BECOMES A LIE.
THAT'S THE KIND OF WORLD HE'S LIVED IN.
THE THING HE TRUSTS THE MOST IS THE THING HE BELIEVES IN THE LEAST... HIMSELF.
AS HIS COMPLEMENT, THEN...
...AREN'T YOU THE ONE, TOKITO-KUN...
...WHO HOLDS ALL THE TRUTH?

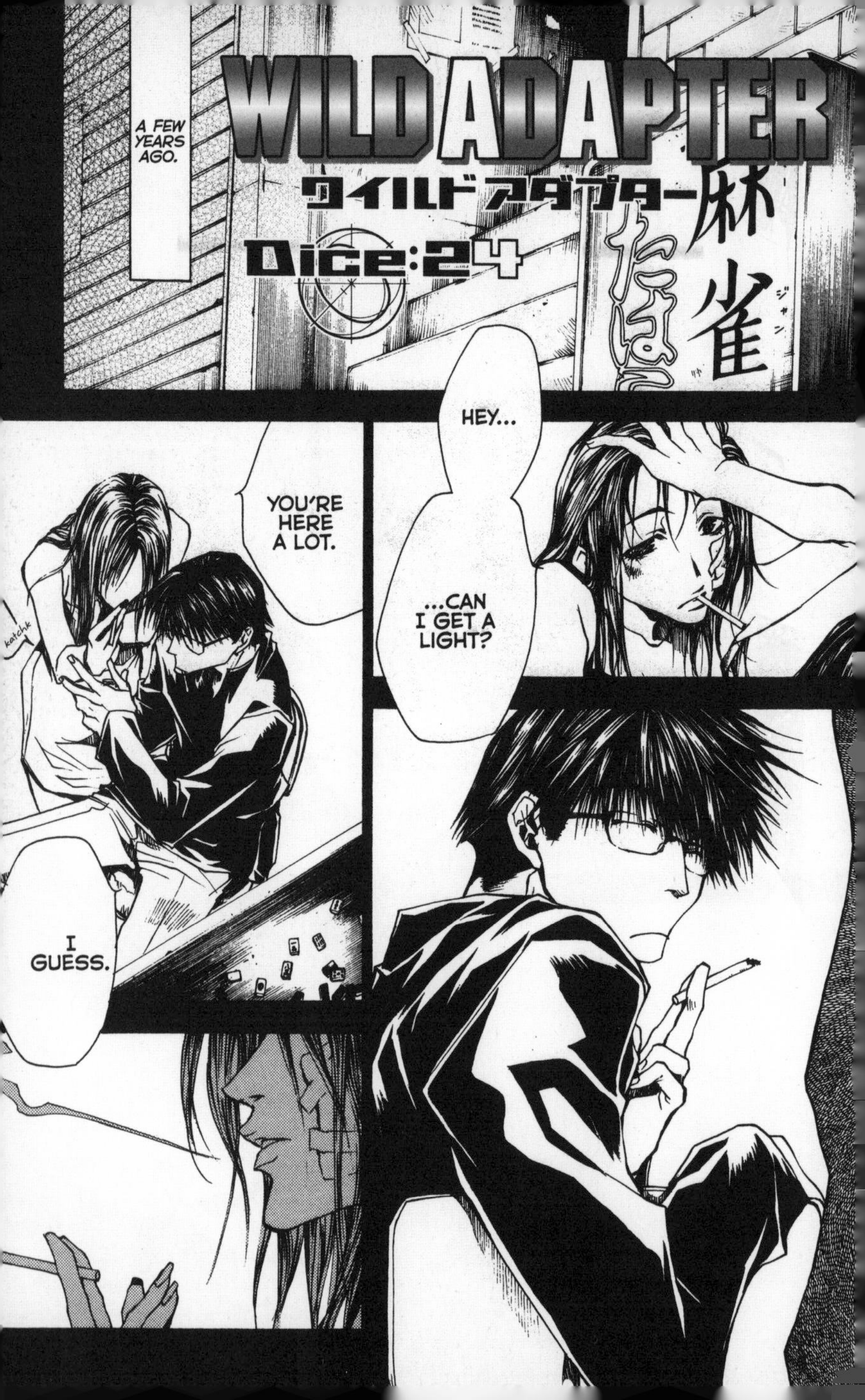
WILD ADAPTER
ワイルドアダプター
Dice:24
A FEW YEARS AGO.
麻雀
HEY...
...CAN I GET A LIGHT?
katchk
YOU'RE HERE A LOT.
I GUESS.

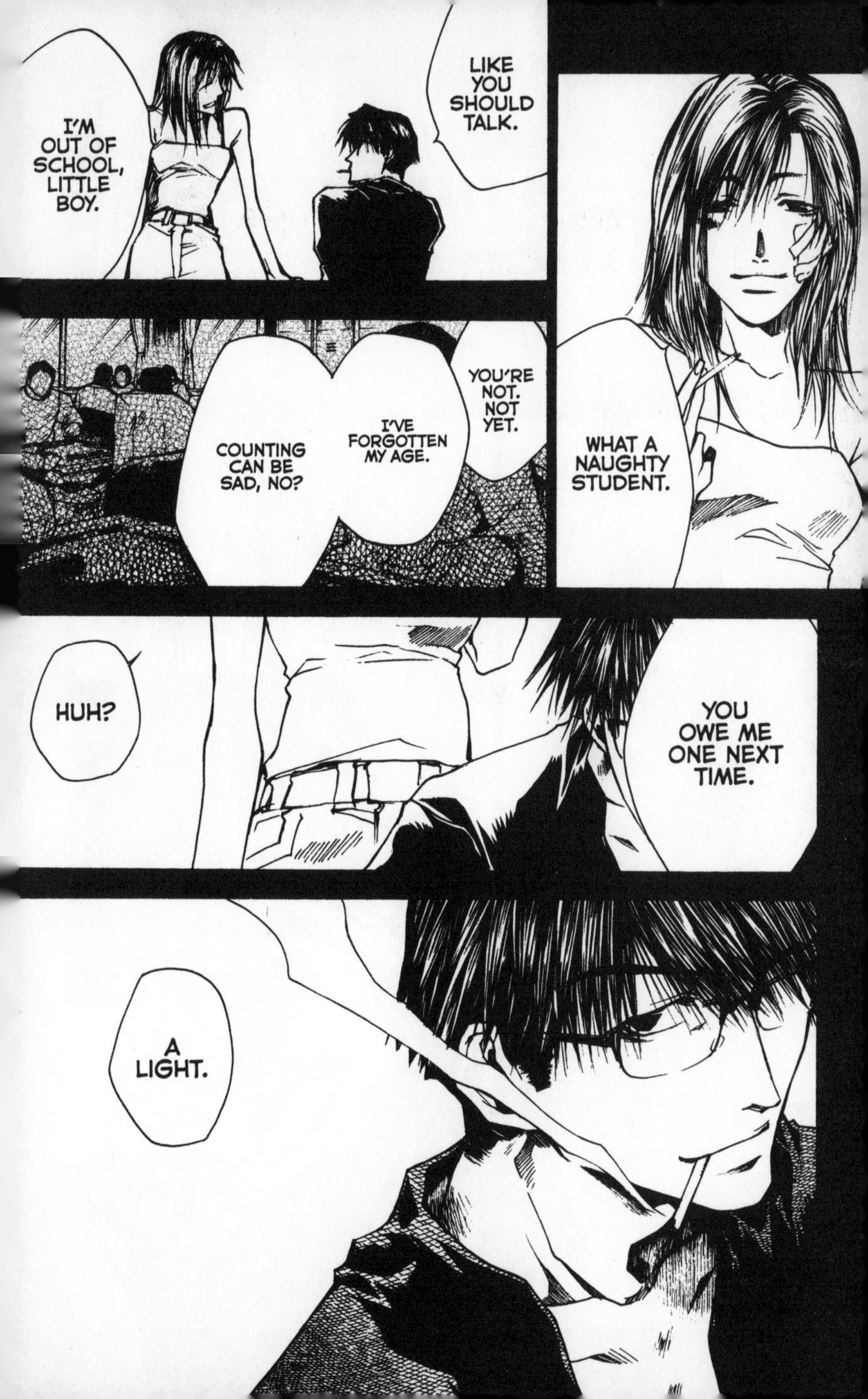
WHAT A NAUGHTY STUDENT.
LIKE YOU SHOULD TALK.
I'M OUT OF SCHOOL, LITTLE BOY.
YOU'RE NOT. NOT YET.
I'VE FORGOTTEN MY AGE.
COUNTING CAN BE SAD, NO?
YOU OWE ME ONE NEXT TIME.
HUH?
A LIGHT.

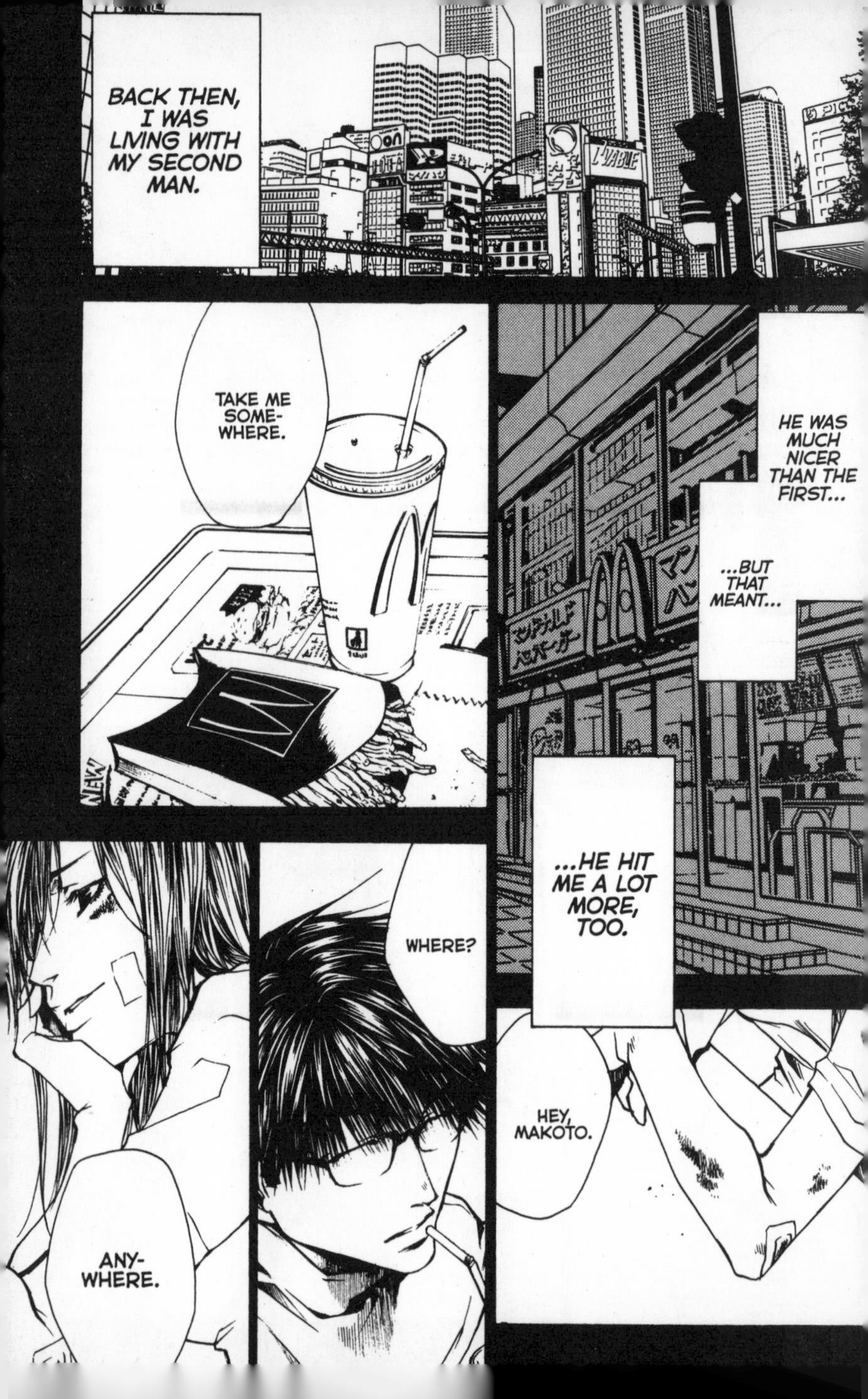
BACK THEN, I WAS LIVING WITH MY SECOND MAN.
HE WAS MUCH NICER THAN THE FIRST...
...BUT THAT MEANT...
...HE HIT ME A LOT MORE, TOO.
HEY, MAKOTO.
TAKE ME SOME-WHERE.
WHERE?
ANY-WHERE.

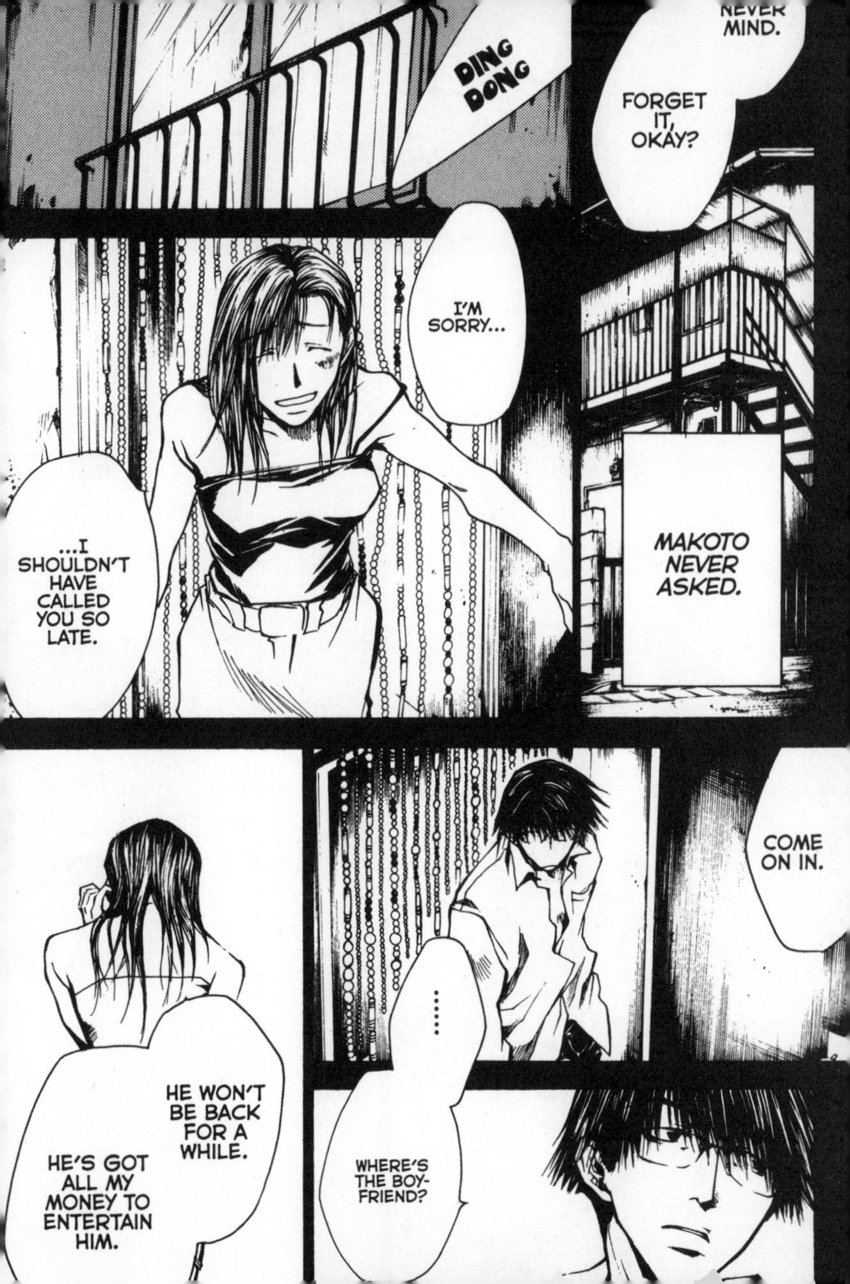
NEVER MIND.
FORGET IT, OKAY?
DING DONG
MAKOTO NEVER ASKED.
I'M SORRY...
...I SHOULDN'T HAVE CALLED YOU SO LATE.
COME ON IN.
......
WHERE'S THE BOY-FRIEND?
HE WON'T BE BACK FOR A WHILE.
HE'S GOT ALL MY MONEY TO ENTERTAIN HIM.

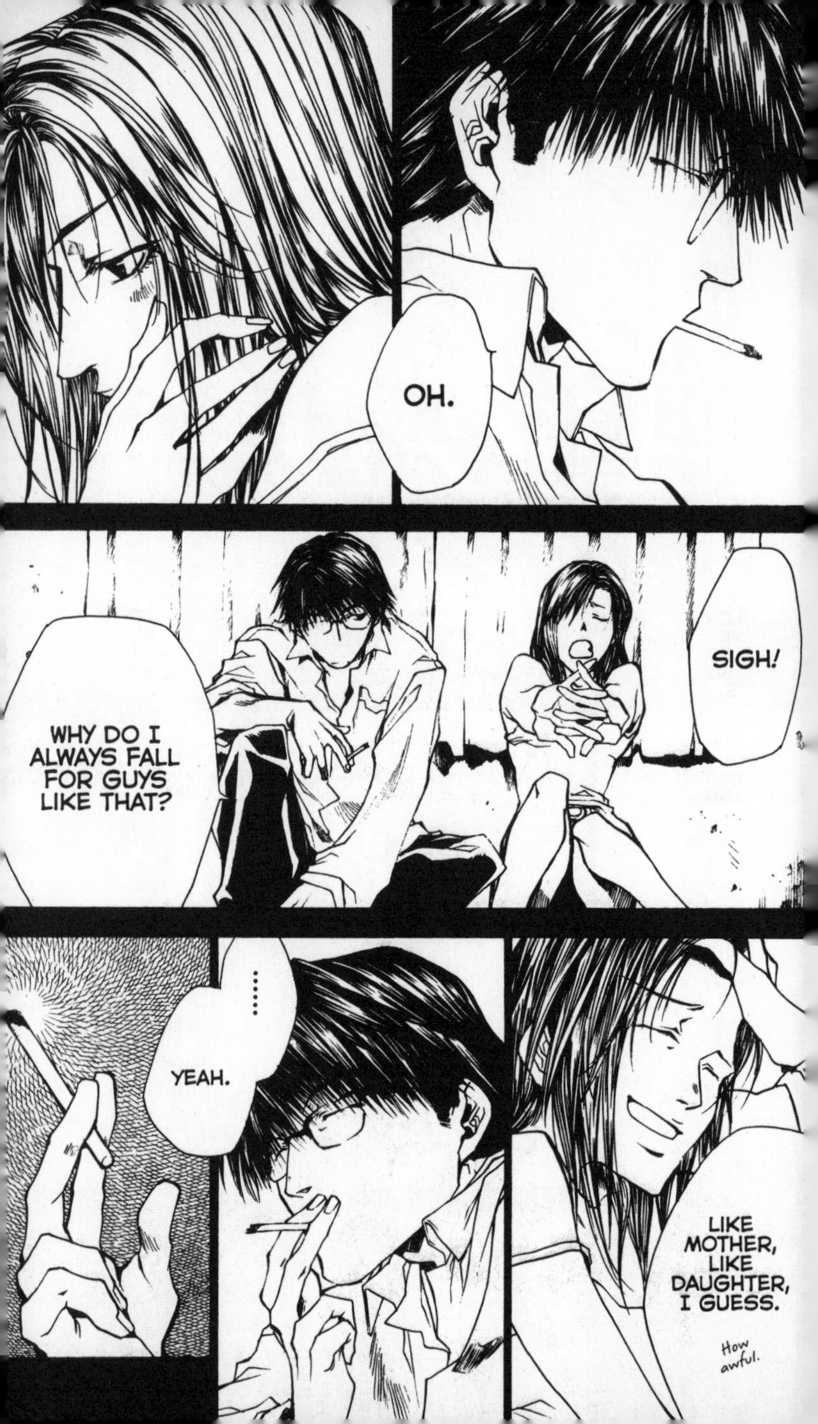
OH.
SIGH!
WHY DO I ALWAYS FALL FOR GUYS LIKE THAT?
LIKE MOTHER, LIKE DAUGHTER, I GUESS.
How awful.
......
YEAH.

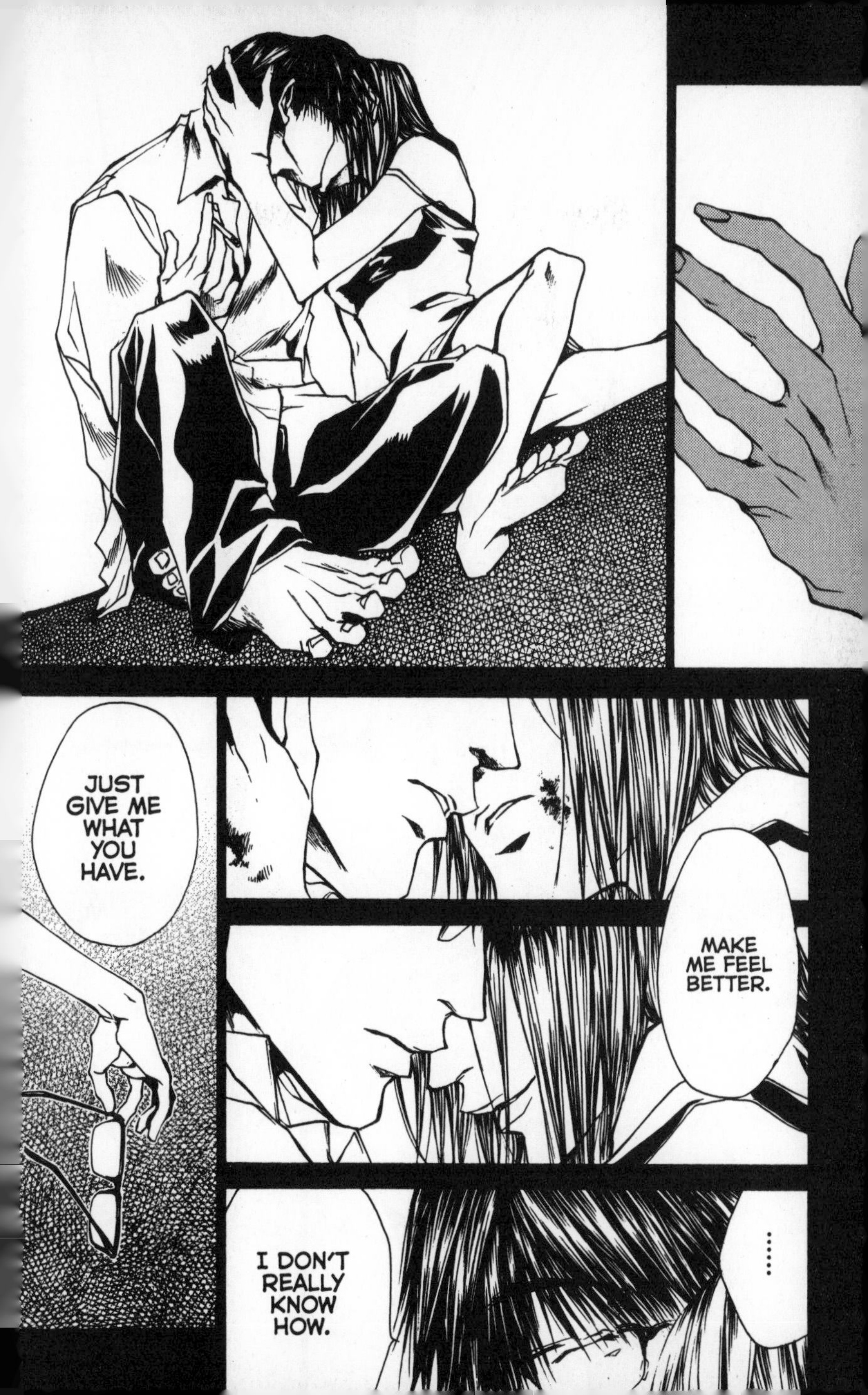
MAKE ME FEEL BETTER.
......
I DON'T REALLY KNOW HOW.
JUST GIVE ME WHAT YOU HAVE.

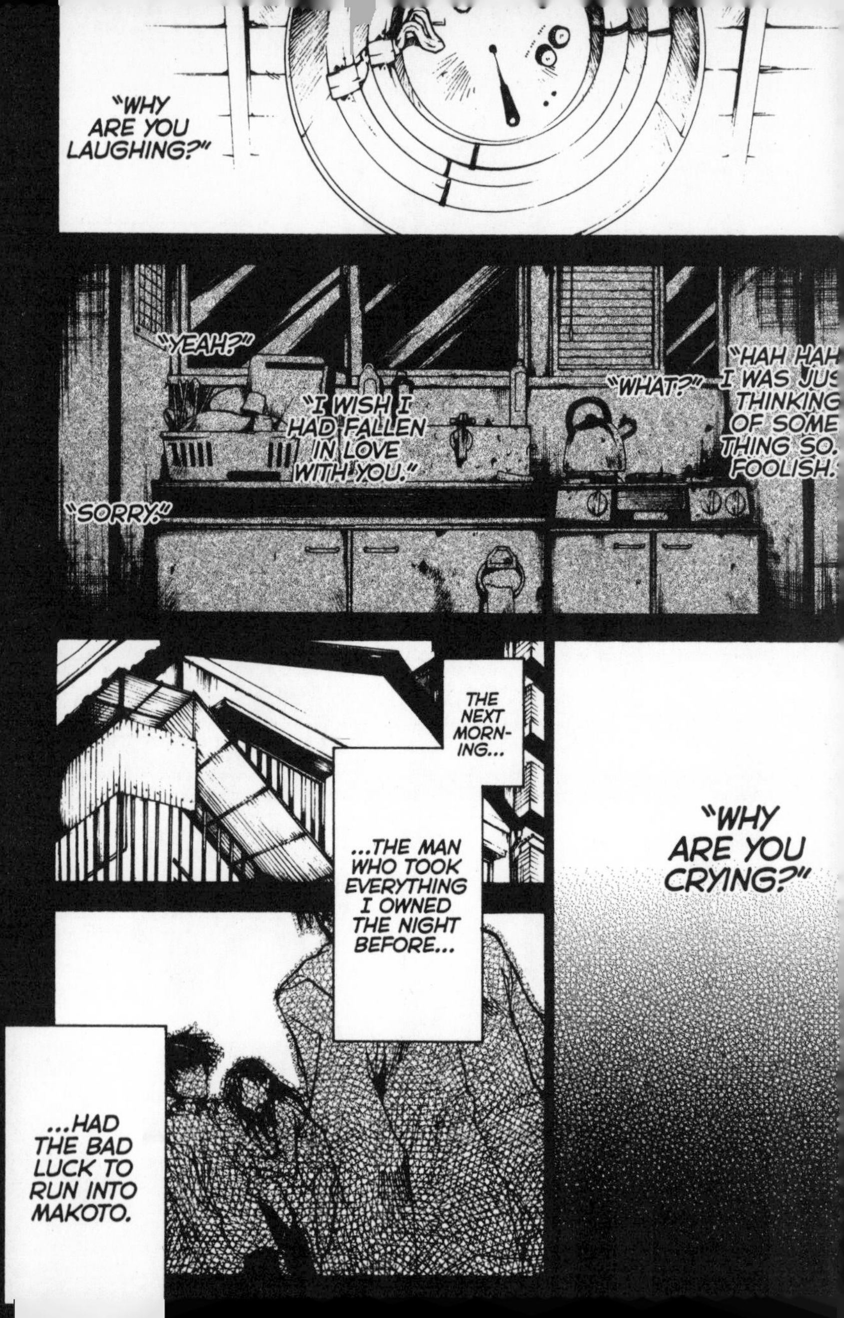
"WHY ARE YOU LAUGHING?"
"HAH HAH I WAS JUS THINKING OF SOME THING SO FOOLISH.
"WHAT?"
"YEAH?"
"I WISH I HAD FALLEN IN LOVE WITH YOU."
"SORRY."
"WHY ARE YOU CRYING?"
THE NEXT MORNING...
...THE MAN WHO TOOK EVERYTHING I OWNED THE NIGHT BEFORE...
...HAD THE BAD LUCK TO RUN INTO MAKOTO.

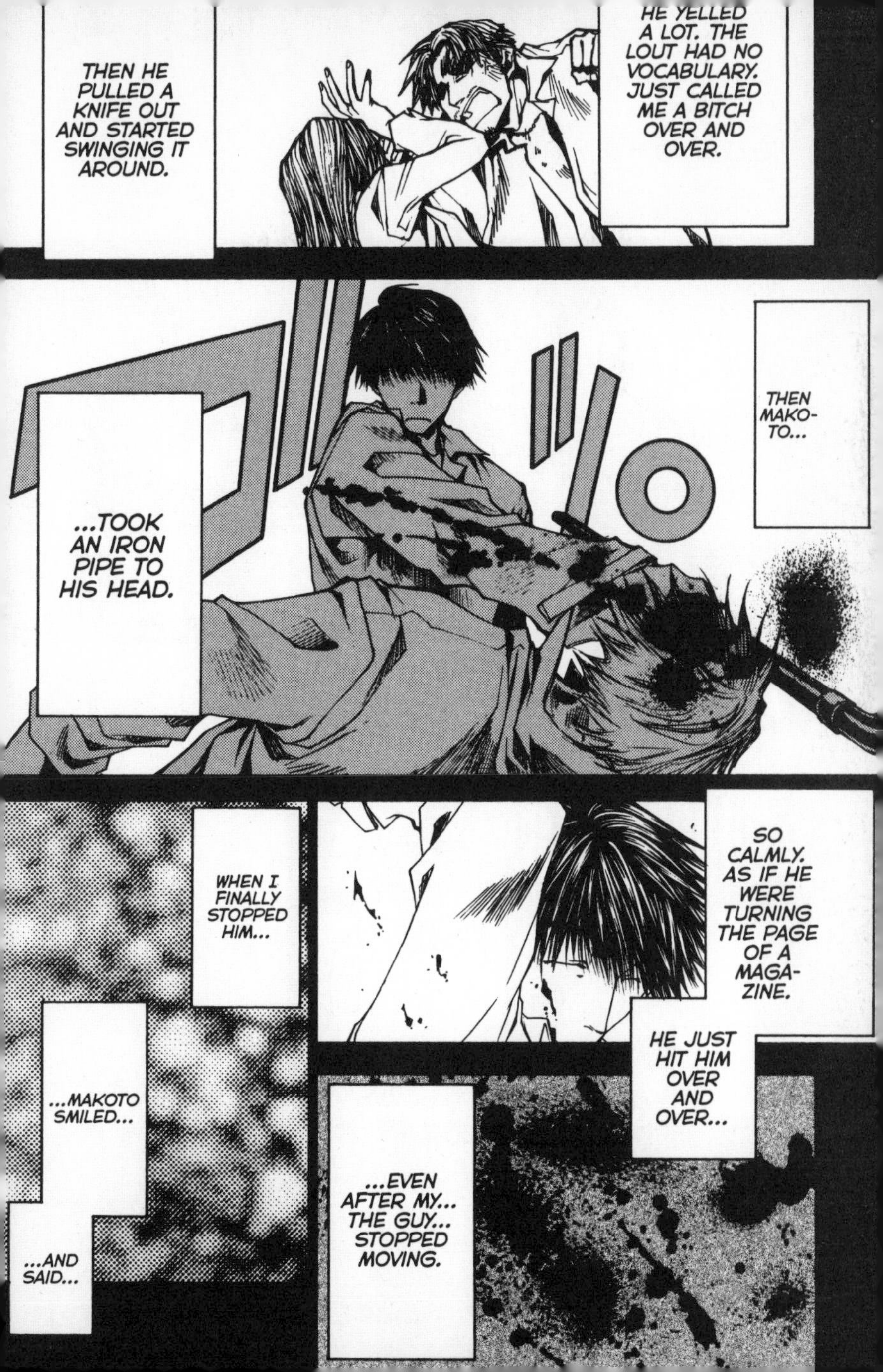
HE YELLED A LOT. THE LOUT HAD NO VOCABULARY. JUST CALLED ME A BITCH OVER AND OVER.
THEN HE PULLED A KNIFE OUT AND STARTED SWINGING IT AROUND.
THEN MAKO-TO...
...TOOK AN IRON PIPE TO HIS HEAD.
SO CALMLY. AS IF HE WERE TURNING THE PAGE OF A MAGA-ZINE.
HE JUST HIT HIM OVER AND OVER...
...EVEN AFTER MY... THE GUY... STOPPED MOVING.
WHEN I FINALLY STOPPED HIM...
...MAKOTO SMILED...
...AND SAID...

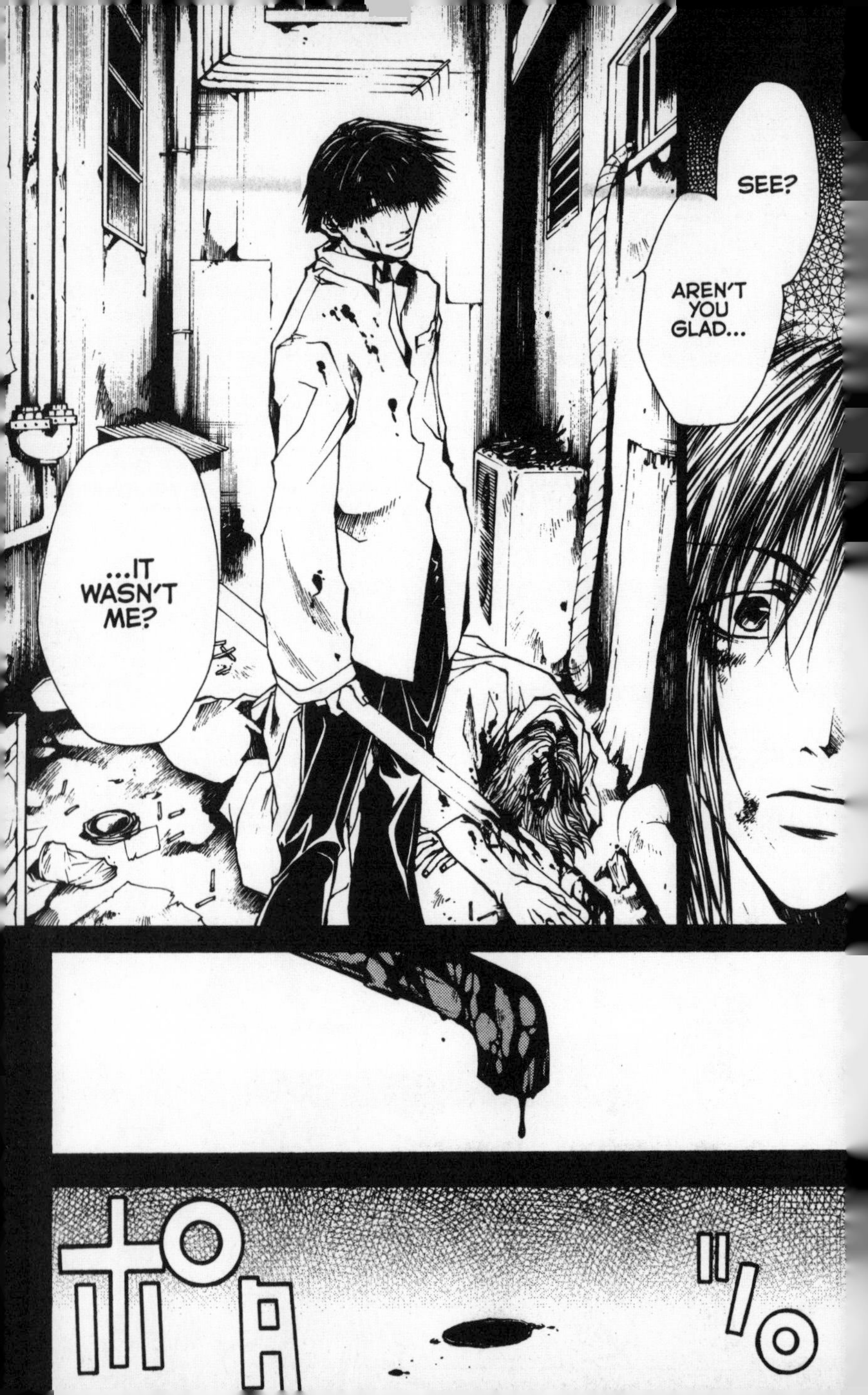
SEE?
AREN'T YOU GLAD...
...IT WASN'T ME?
ポタ

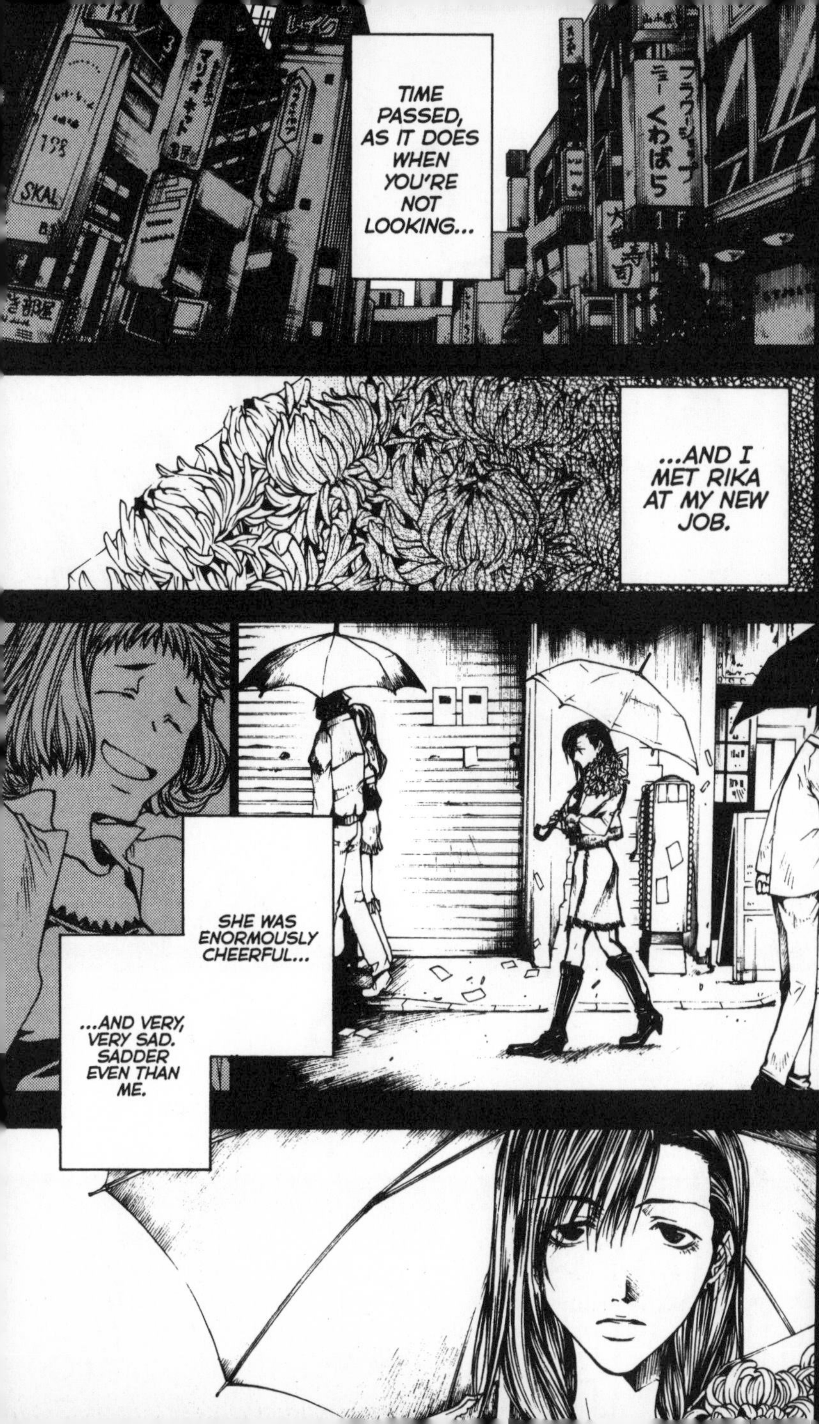

TIME PASSED, AS IT DOES WHEN YOU'RE NOT LOOKING...
...AND I MET RIKA AT MY NEW JOB.
SHE WAS ENORMOUSLY CHEERFUL...
...AND VERY, VERY SAD. SADDER EVEN THAN ME.

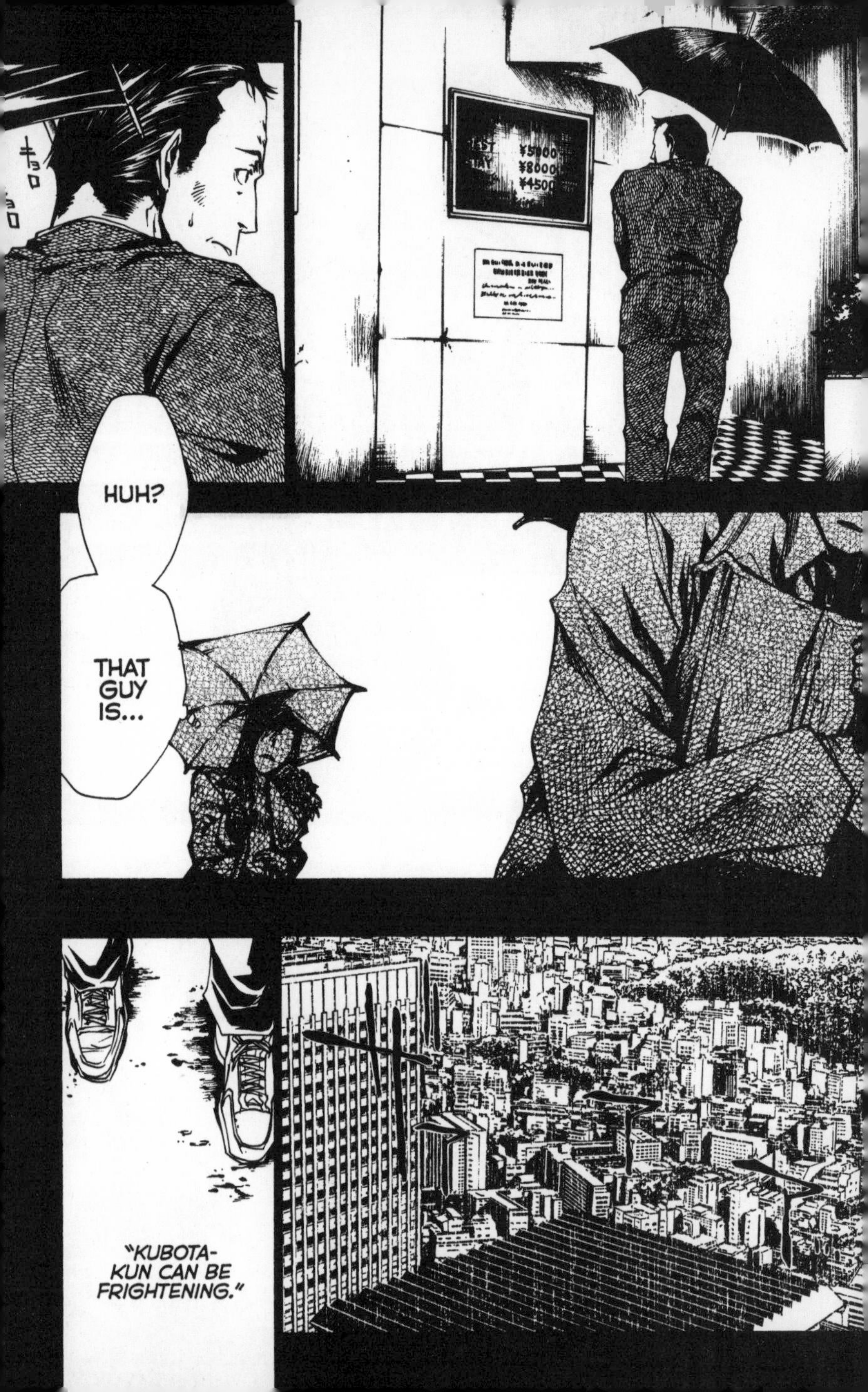
¥5000
¥8000
¥4500
キョロ
HUH?
THAT GUY IS...
"KUBOTA-KUN CAN BE FRIGHTENING."

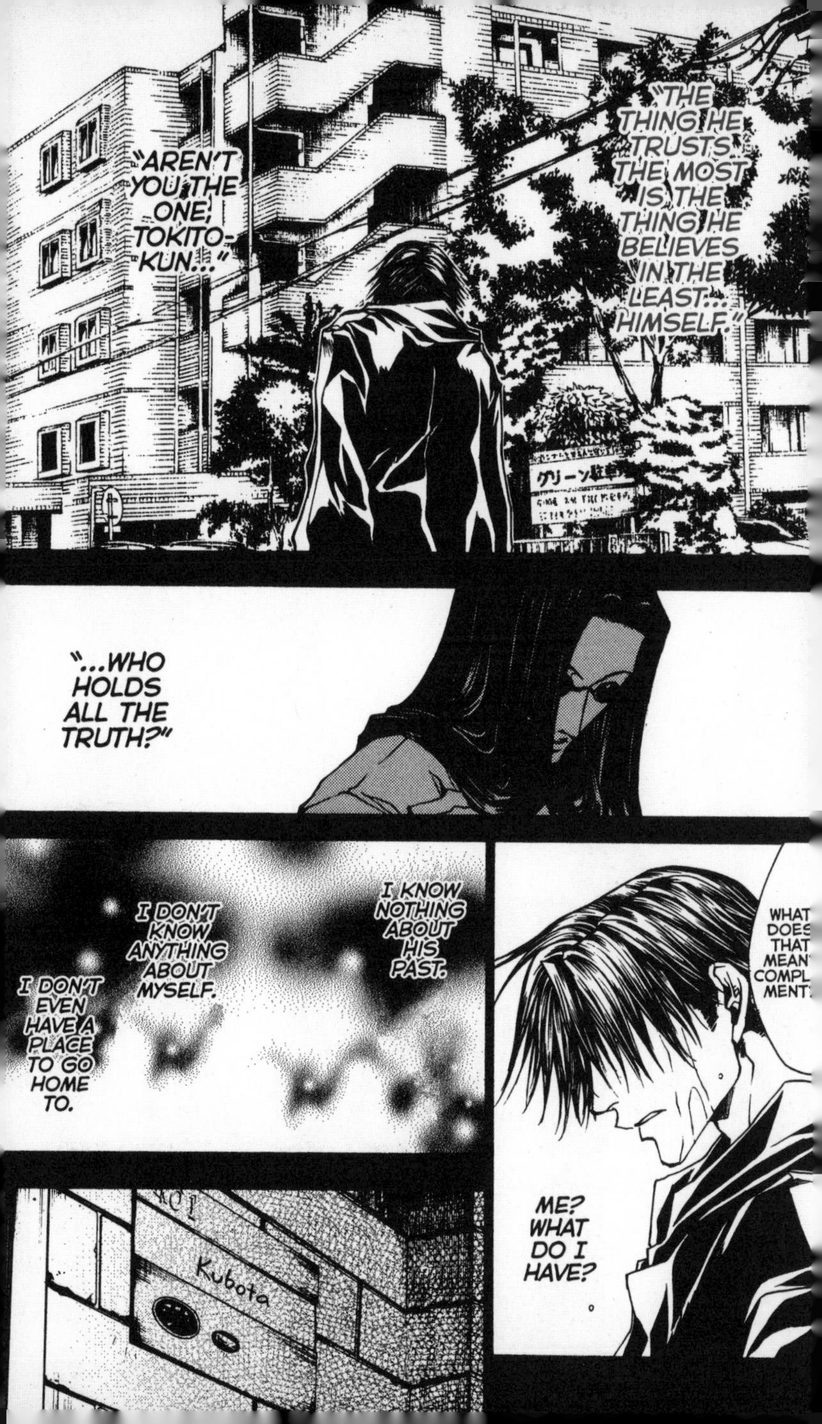

"THE THING HE TRUSTS THE MOST IS THE THING HE BELIEVES IN THE LEAST... HIMSELF."
"AREN'T YOU THE ONE, TOKITO-KUN..."
グリーン駐車
"...WHO HOLDS ALL THE TRUTH?"
WHAT DOES THAT MEAN COMPL MENT
ME? WHAT DO I HAVE?
I KNOW NOTHING ABOUT HIS PAST.
I DON'T KNOW ANYTHING ABOUT MYSELF.
I DON'T EVEN HAVE A PLACE TO GO HOME TO.
Kubota

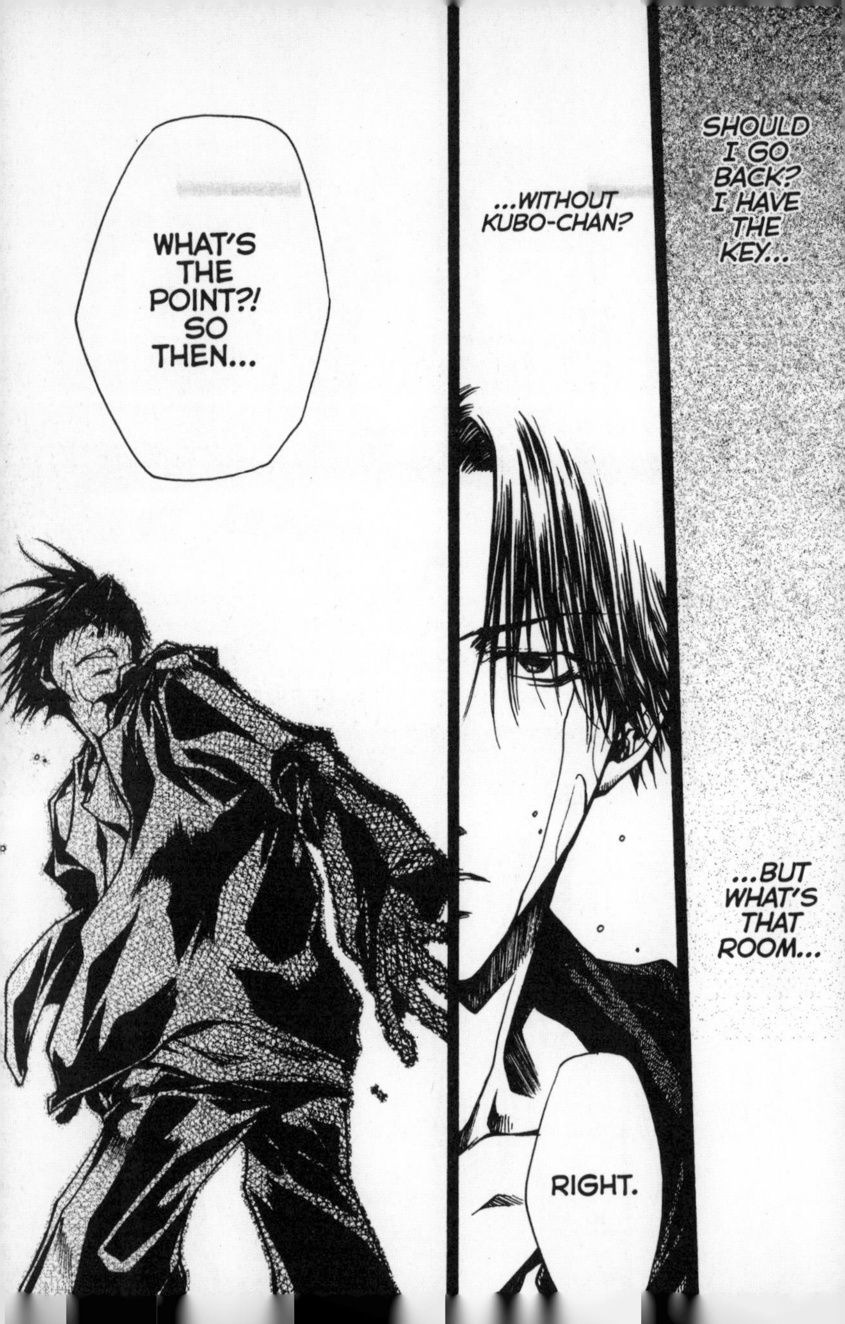
SHOULD I GO BACK? I HAVE THE KEY...
...BUT WHAT'S THAT ROOM...
...WITHOUT KUBO-CHAN?
RIGHT.
WHAT'S THE POINT?! SO THEN...

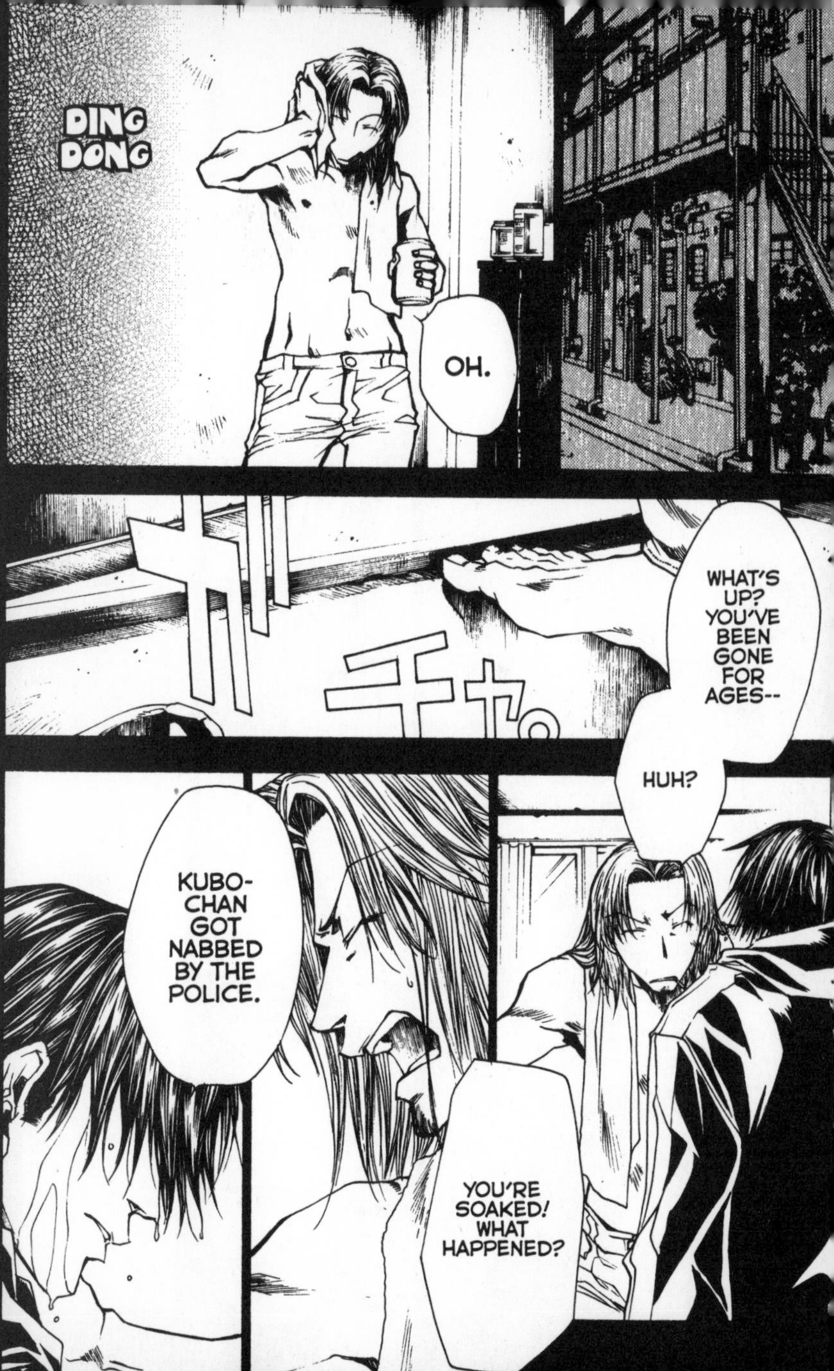
DING DONG
OH.
ガチャ。
WHAT'S UP? YOU'VE BEEN GONE FOR AGES--
HUH?
YOU'RE SOAKED! WHAT HAPPENED?
KUBO-CHAN GOT NABBED BY THE POLICE.

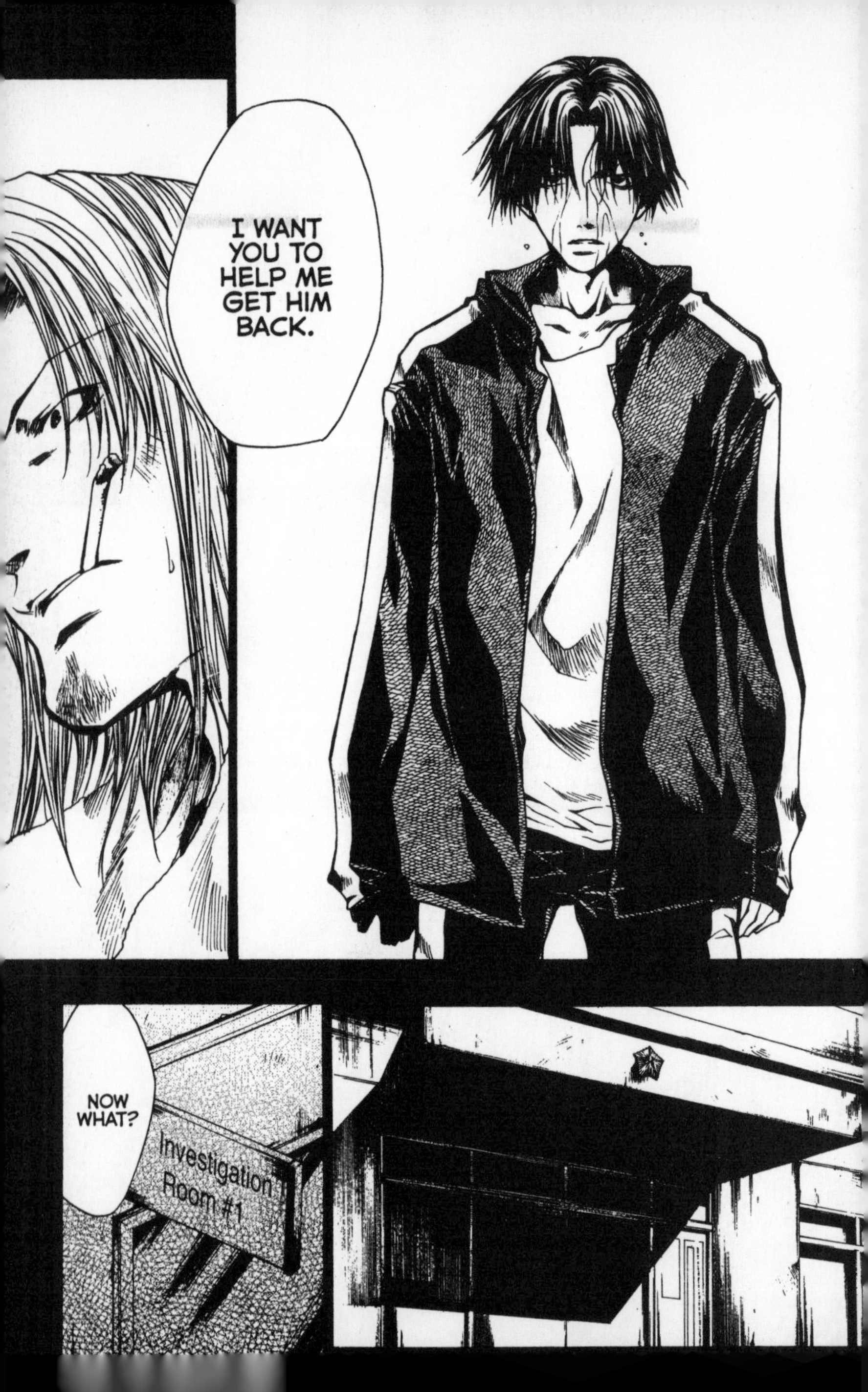
I WANT YOU TO HELP ME GET HIM BACK.
NOW WHAT?
Investigation Room #1

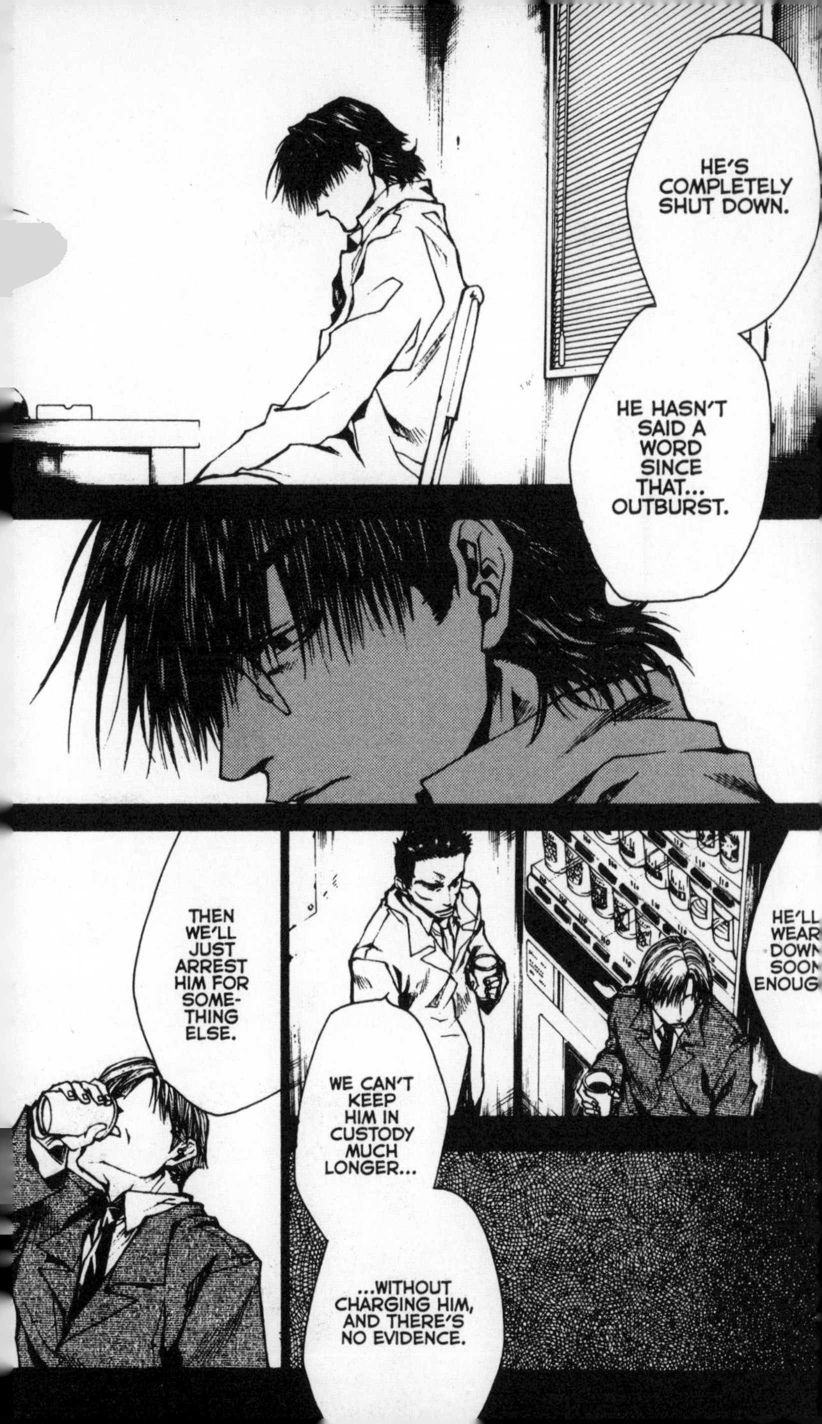
HE'S COMPLETELY SHUT DOWN.
HE HASN'T SAID A WORD SINCE THAT... OUTBURST.
HE'LL WEAR DOWN SOON ENOUG
WE CAN'T KEEP HIM IN CUSTODY MUCH LONGER...
...WITHOUT CHARGING HIM, AND THERE'S NO EVIDENCE.
THEN WE'LL JUST ARREST HIM FOR SOME-THING ELSE.

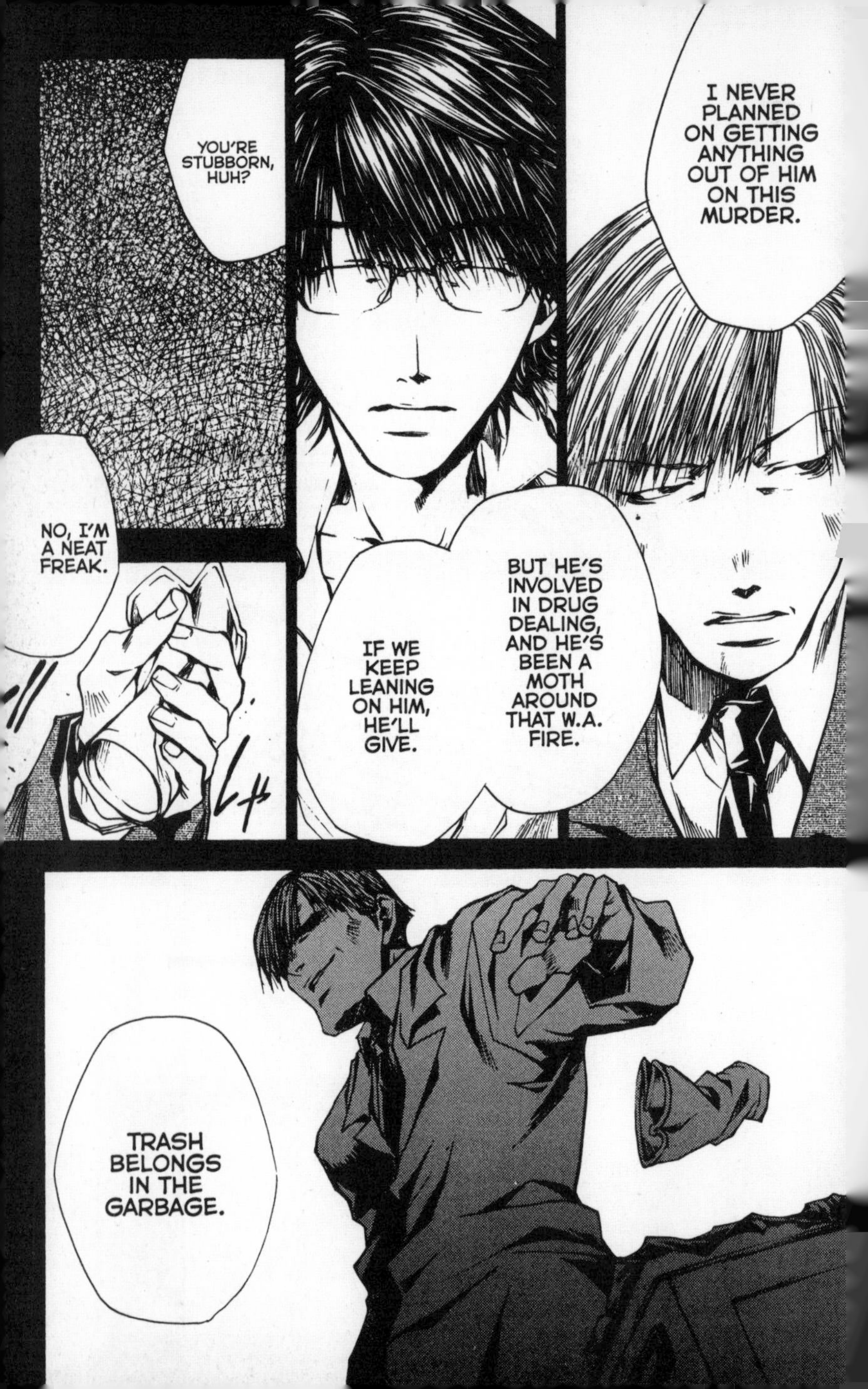
I NEVER PLANNED ON GETTING ANYTHING OUT OF HIM ON THIS MURDER.
BUT HE'S INVOLVED IN DRUG DEALING, AND HE'S BEEN A MOTH AROUND THAT W.A. FIRE.
IF WE KEEP LEANING ON HIM, HE'LL GIVE.
YOU'RE STUBBORN, HUH?
NO, I'M A NEAT FREAK.
TRASH BELONGS IN THE GARBAGE.

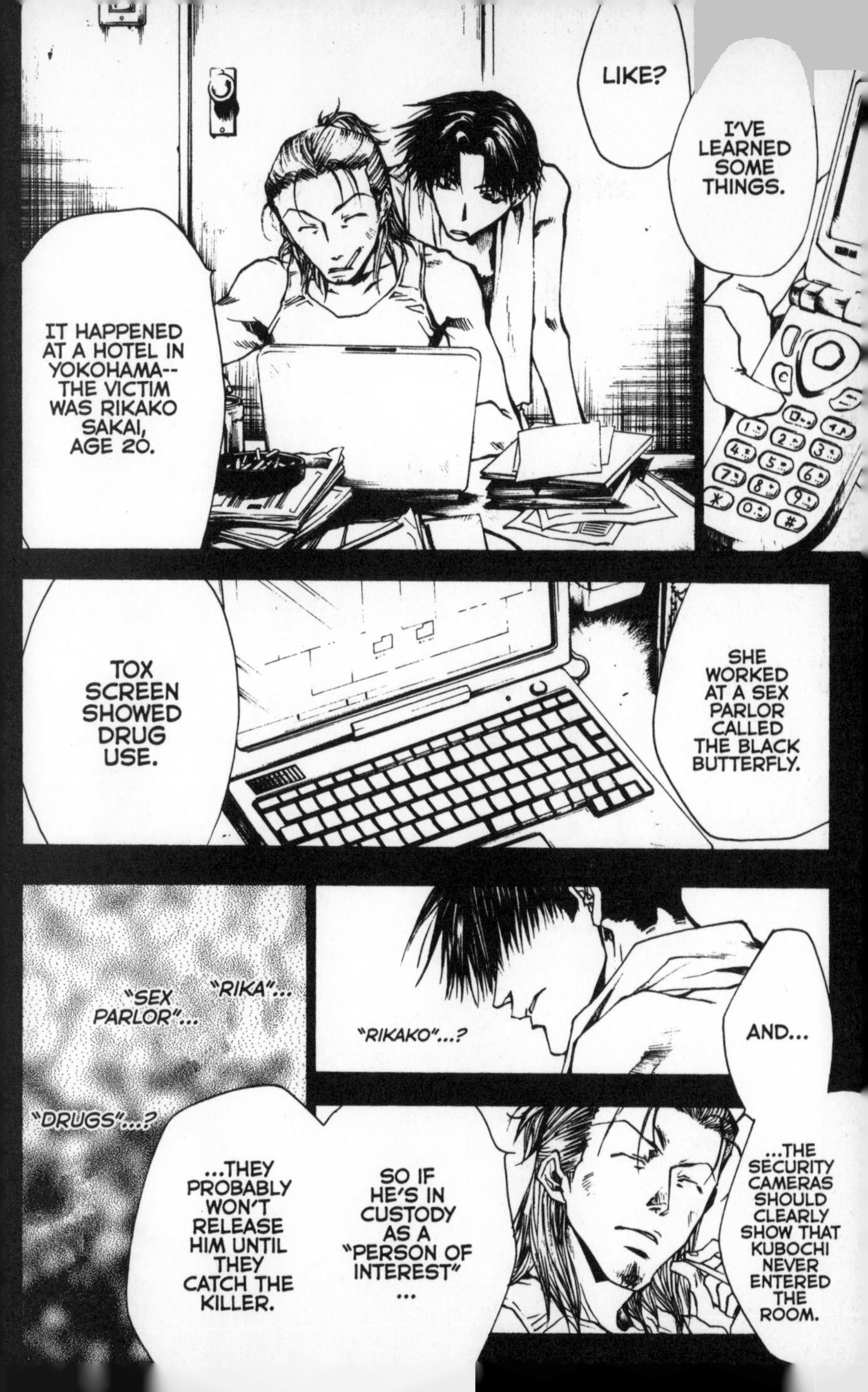
I'VE LEARNED SOME THINGS.
LIKE?
IT HAPPENED AT A HOTEL IN YOKOHAMA-- THE VICTIM WAS RIKAKO SAKAI, AGE 20.
SHE WORKED AT A SEX PARLOR CALLED THE BLACK BUTTERFLY.
TOX SCREEN SHOWED DRUG USE.
AND...
"RIKAKO"...?
...THE SECURITY CAMERAS SHOULD CLEARLY SHOW THAT KUBOCHI NEVER ENTERED THE ROOM.
SO IF HE'S IN CUSTODY AS A "PERSON OF INTEREST" ...
...THEY PROBABLY WON'T RELEASE HIM UNTIL THEY CATCH THE KILLER.
"RIKA"...
"SEX PARLOR"...
"DRUGS"...?

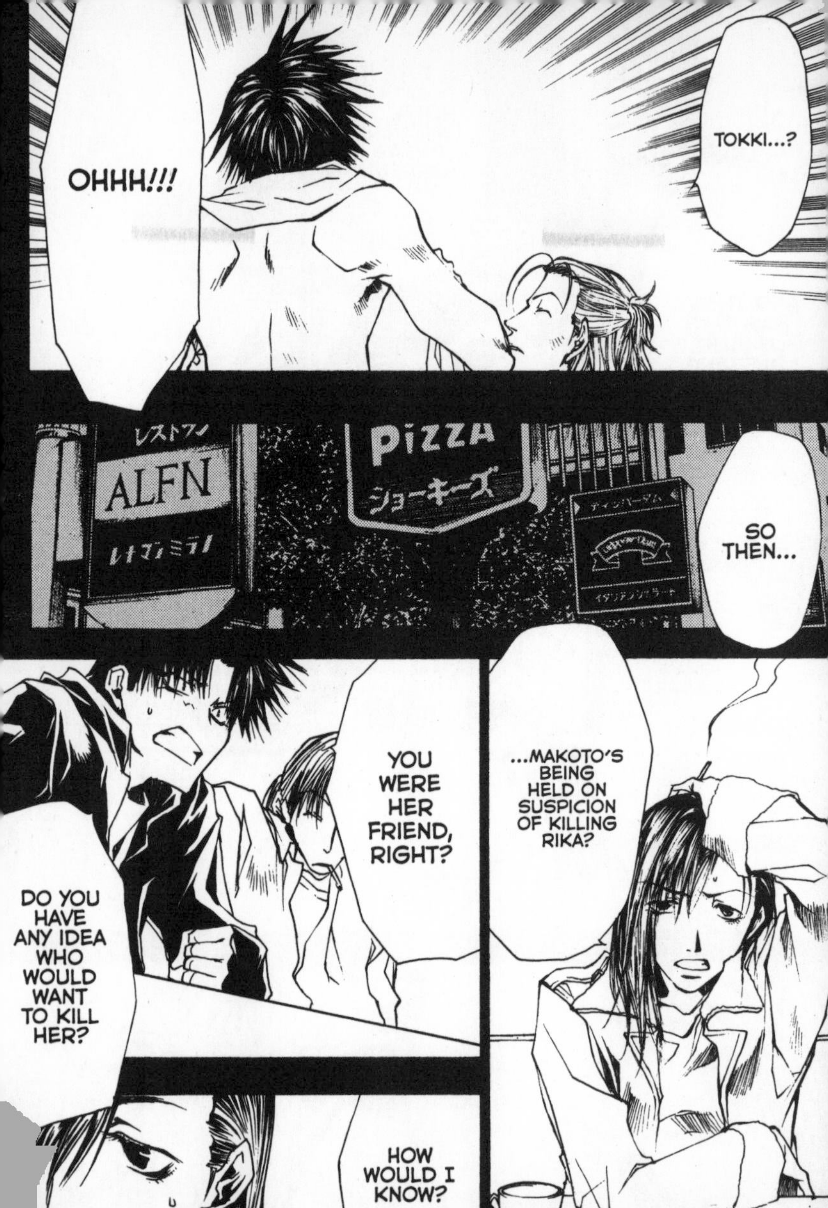
TOKKI...?
OHHH!!!
SO THEN...
ALFN
Pizza
ショーキーズ
...MAKOTO'S BEING HELD ON SUSPICION OF KILLING RIKA?
YOU WERE HER FRIEND, RIGHT?
DO YOU HAVE ANY IDEA WHO WOULD WANT TO KILL HER?
HOW WOULD I KNOW?

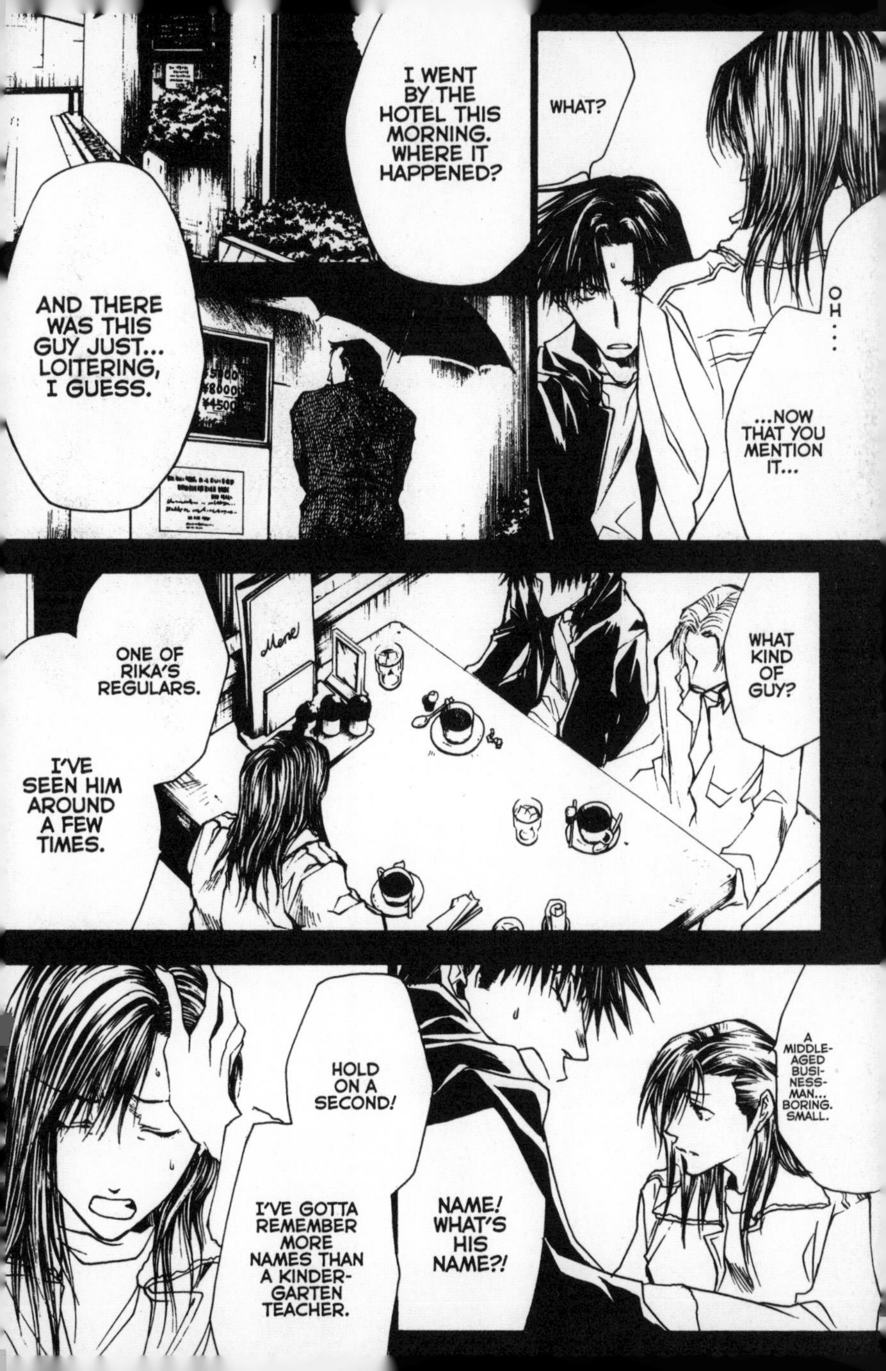
WHAT?
OH...
...NOW THAT YOU MENTION IT...
I WENT BY THE HOTEL THIS MORNING. WHERE IT HAPPENED?
AND THERE WAS THIS GUY JUST... LOITERING, I GUESS.
WHAT KIND OF GUY?
ONE OF RIKA'S REGULARS.
I'VE SEEN HIM AROUND A FEW TIMES.
A MIDDLE-AGED BUSINESSMAN... BORING. SMALL.
HOLD ON A SECOND!
NAME! WHAT'S HIS NAME?!
I'VE GOTTA REMEMBER MORE NAMES THAN A KINDERGARTEN TEACHER.

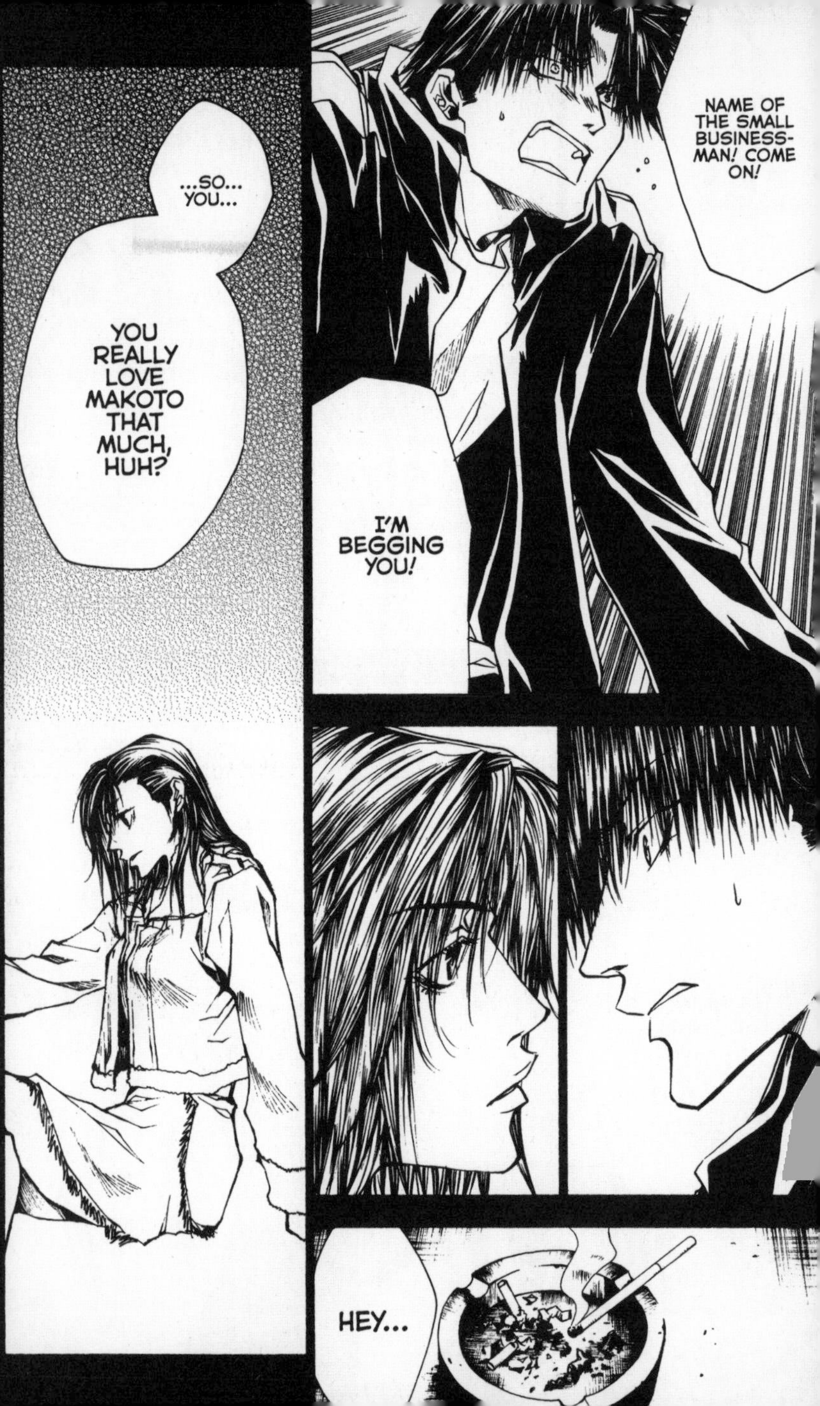
NAME OF THE SMALL BUSINESS-MAN! COME ON!
I'M BEGGING YOU!
HEY...
...SO... YOU...
YOU REALLY LOVE MAKOTO THAT MUCH, HUH?

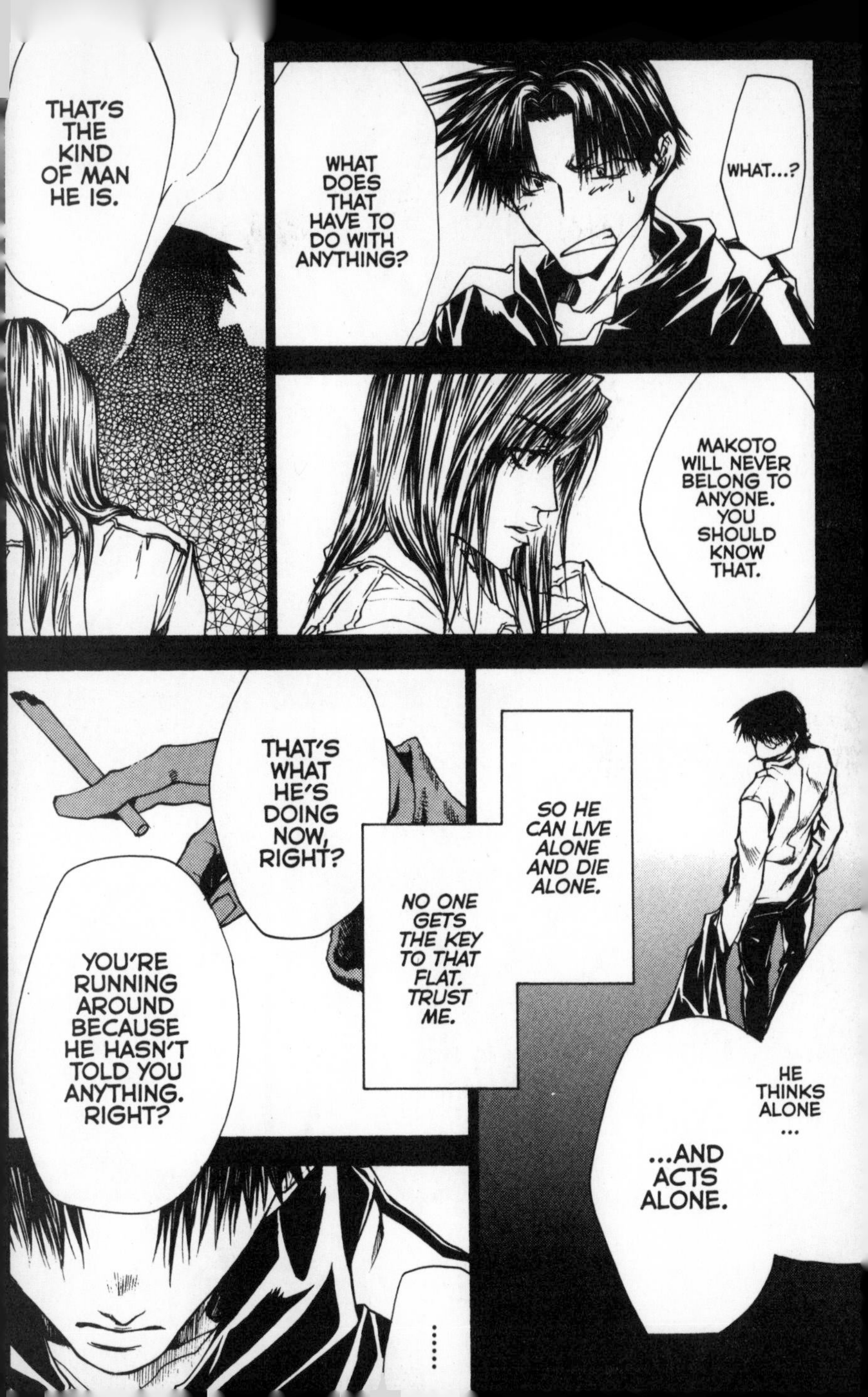
WHAT...?
WHAT DOES THAT HAVE TO DO WITH ANYTHING?
MAKOTO WILL NEVER BELONG TO ANYONE. YOU SHOULD KNOW THAT.
THAT'S THE KIND OF MAN HE IS.
HE THINKS ALONE...
...AND ACTS ALONE.
SO HE CAN LIVE ALONE AND DIE ALONE.
NO ONE GETS THE KEY TO THAT FLAT. TRUST ME.
THAT'S WHAT HE'S DOING NOW, RIGHT?
YOU'RE RUNNING AROUND BECAUSE HE HASN'T TOLD YOU ANYTHING. RIGHT?
......

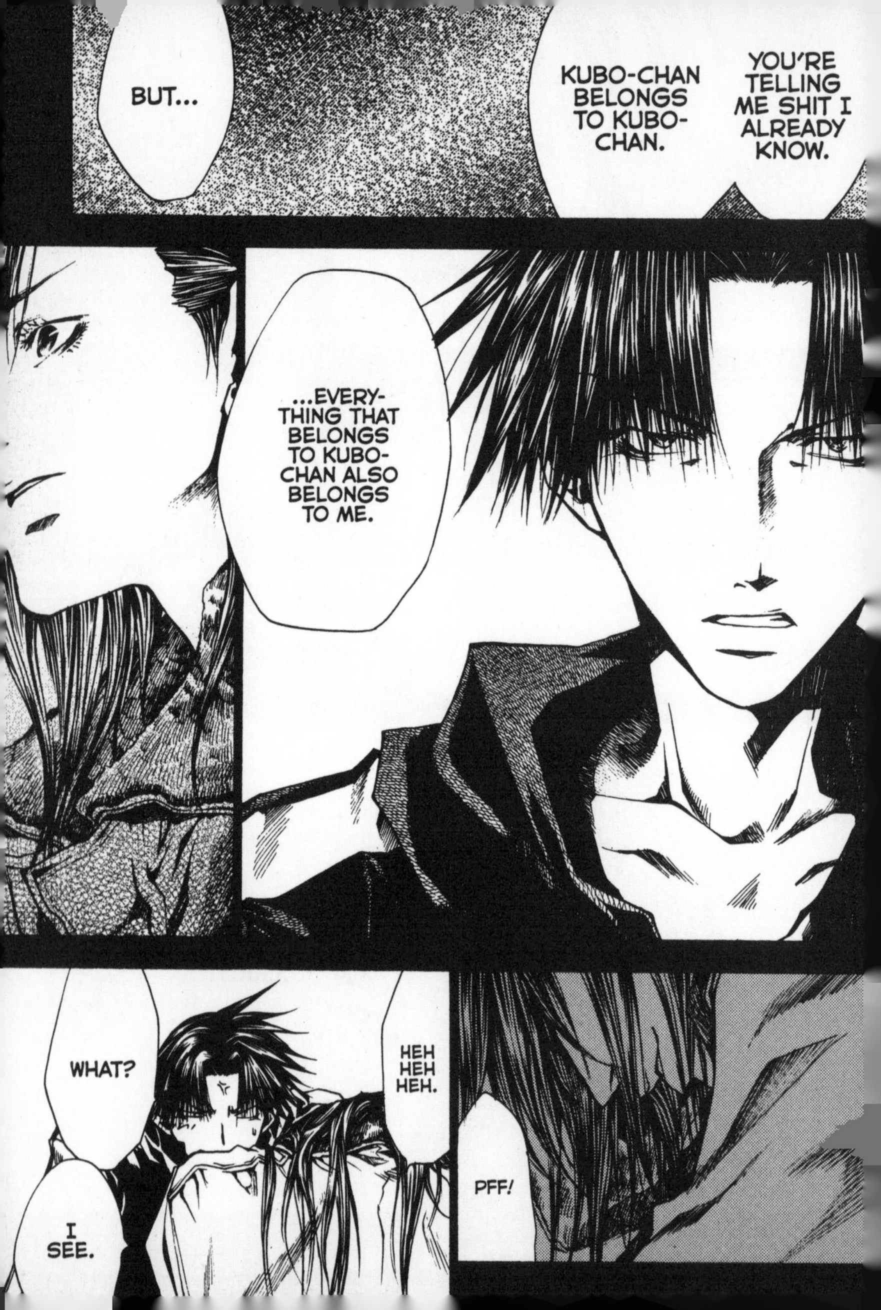
YOU'RE TELLING ME SHIT I ALREADY KNOW.
KUBO-CHAN BELONGS TO KUBO-CHAN.
BUT...
...EVERYTHING THAT BELONGS TO KUBO-CHAN ALSO BELONGS TO ME.
PFF!
HEH HEH HEH.
WHAT?
I SEE.

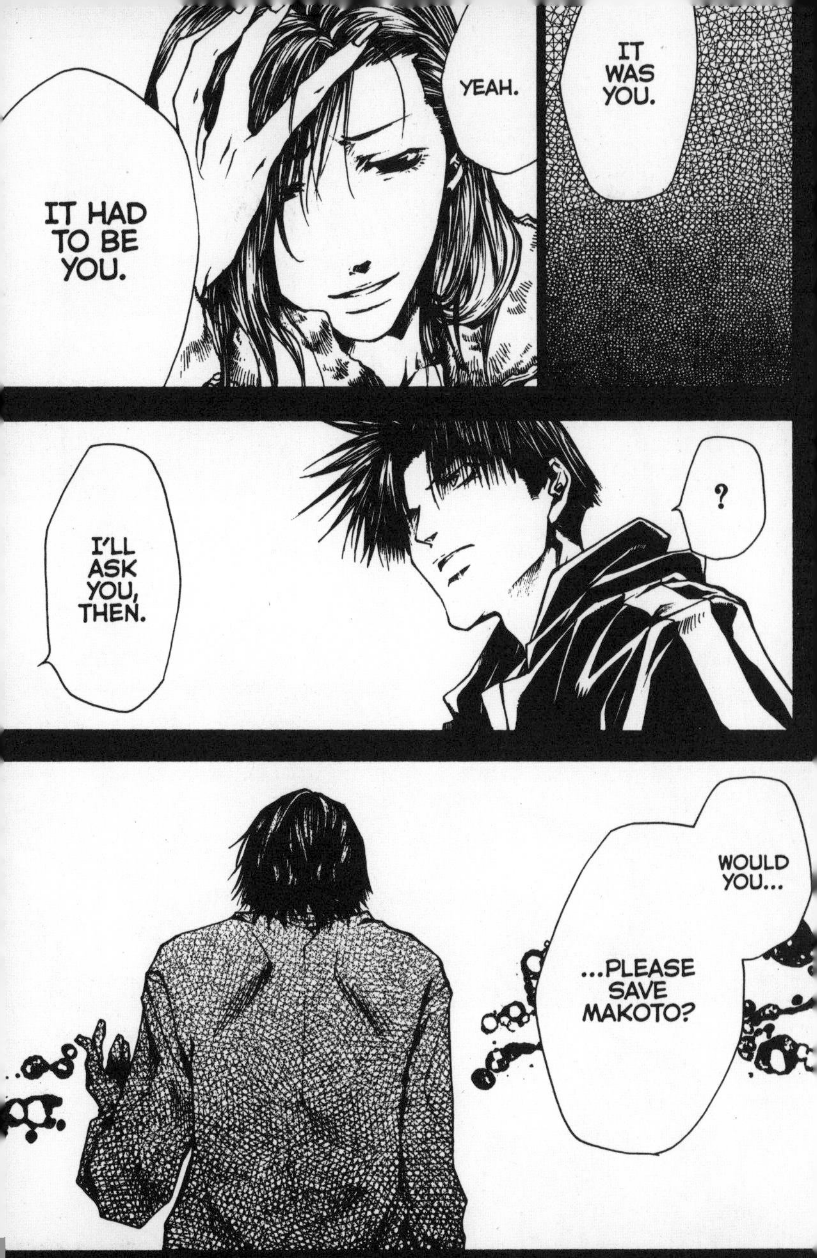
IT WAS YOU.
YEAH.
IT HAD TO BE YOU.
?
I'LL ASK YOU, THEN.
WOULD YOU...
...PLEASE SAVE MAKOTO?

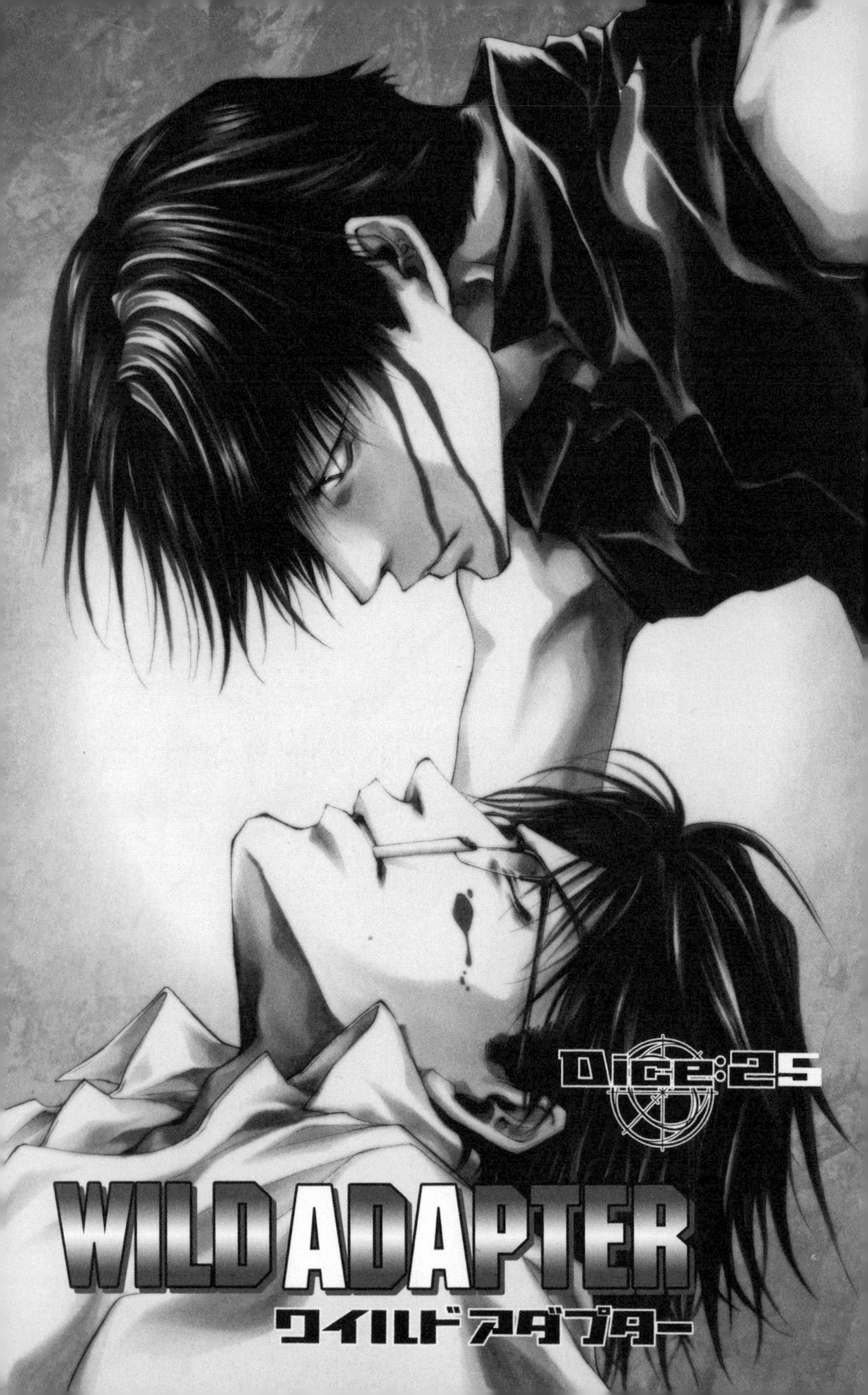
DICE:25
WILD ADAPTER
ワイルドアダプター

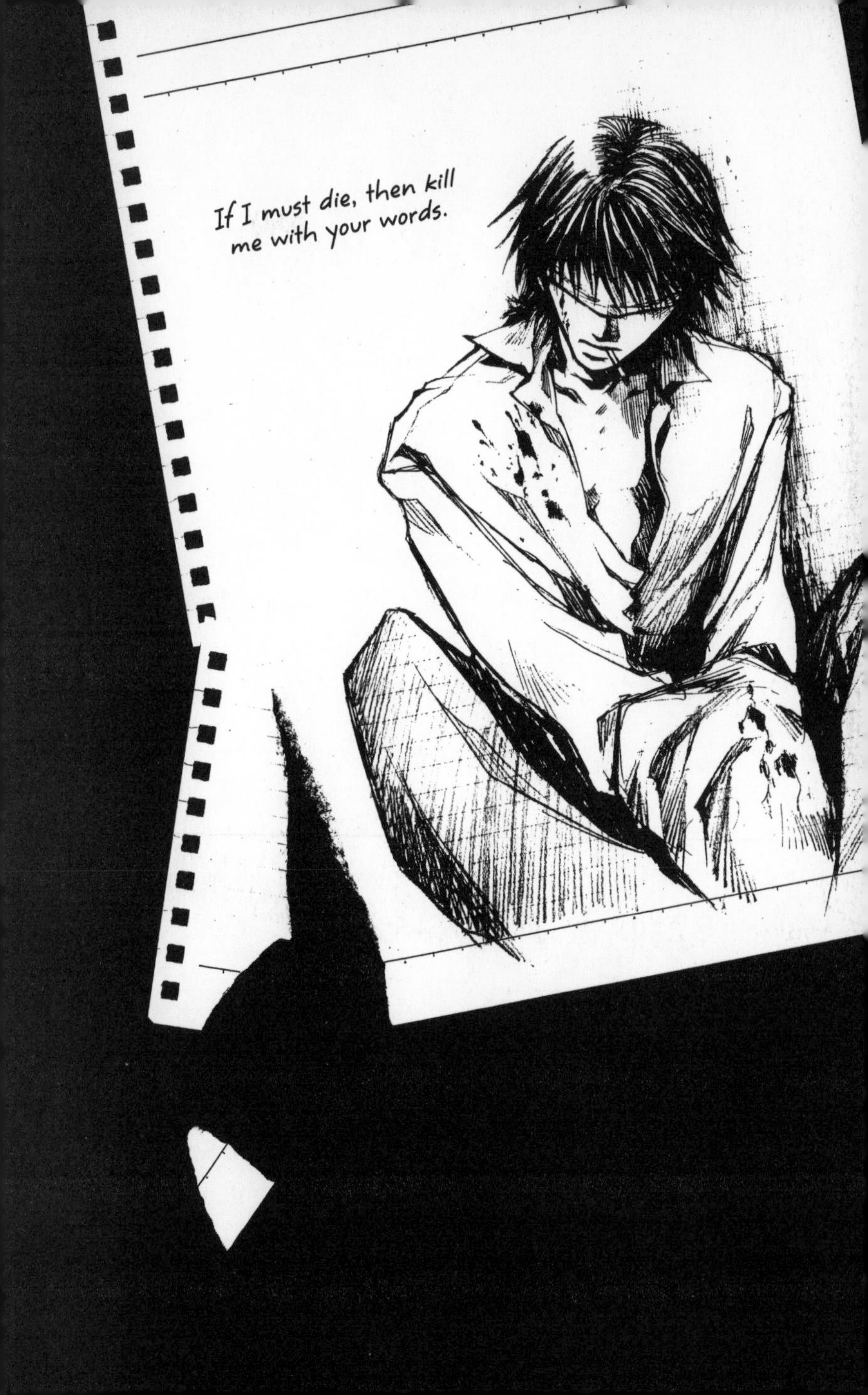
If I must die, then kill me with your words.

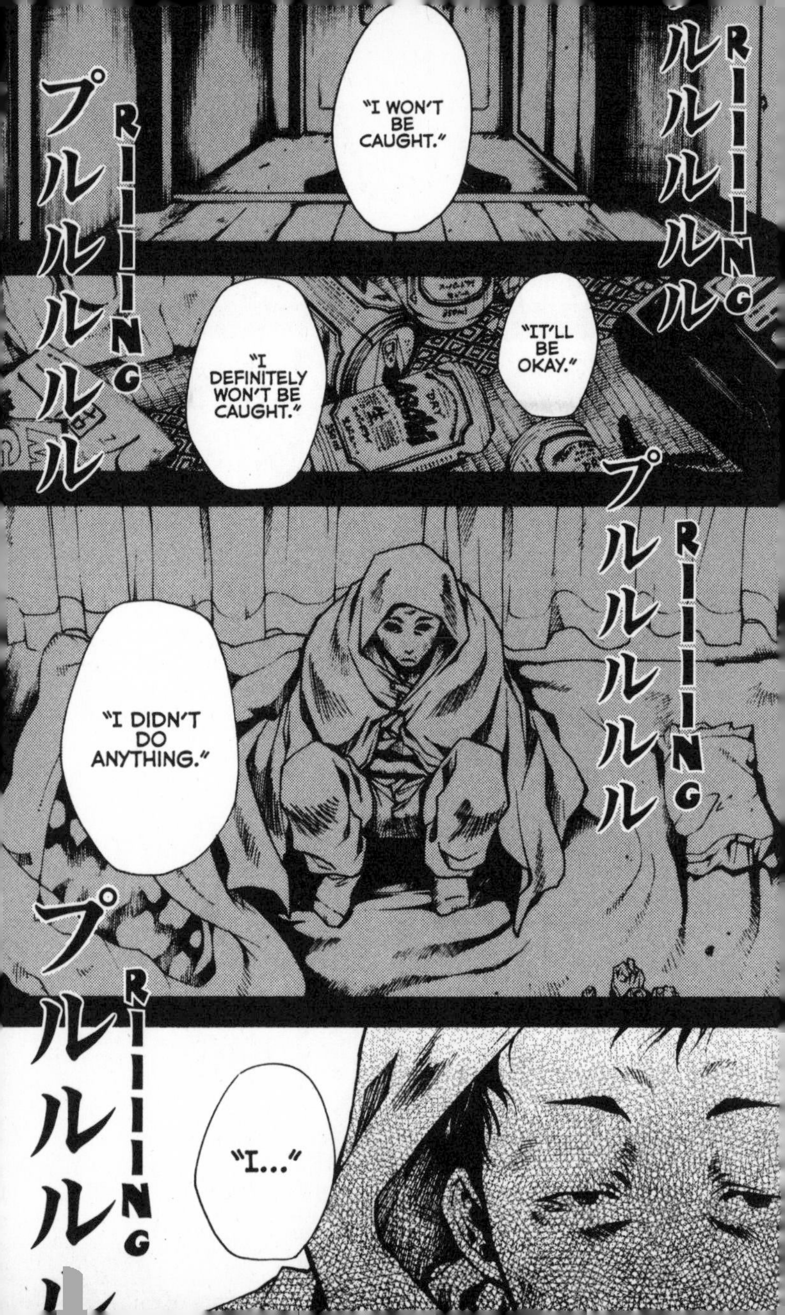

ルルルル
RIIIING
"I WON'T BE CAUGHT."
プルルルル
RIIIING
"IT'LL BE OKAY."
"I DEFINITELY WON'T BE CAUGHT."
プルルルル
RIIIING
"I DIDN'T DO ANYTHING."
プルル
RIIIING
"I..."

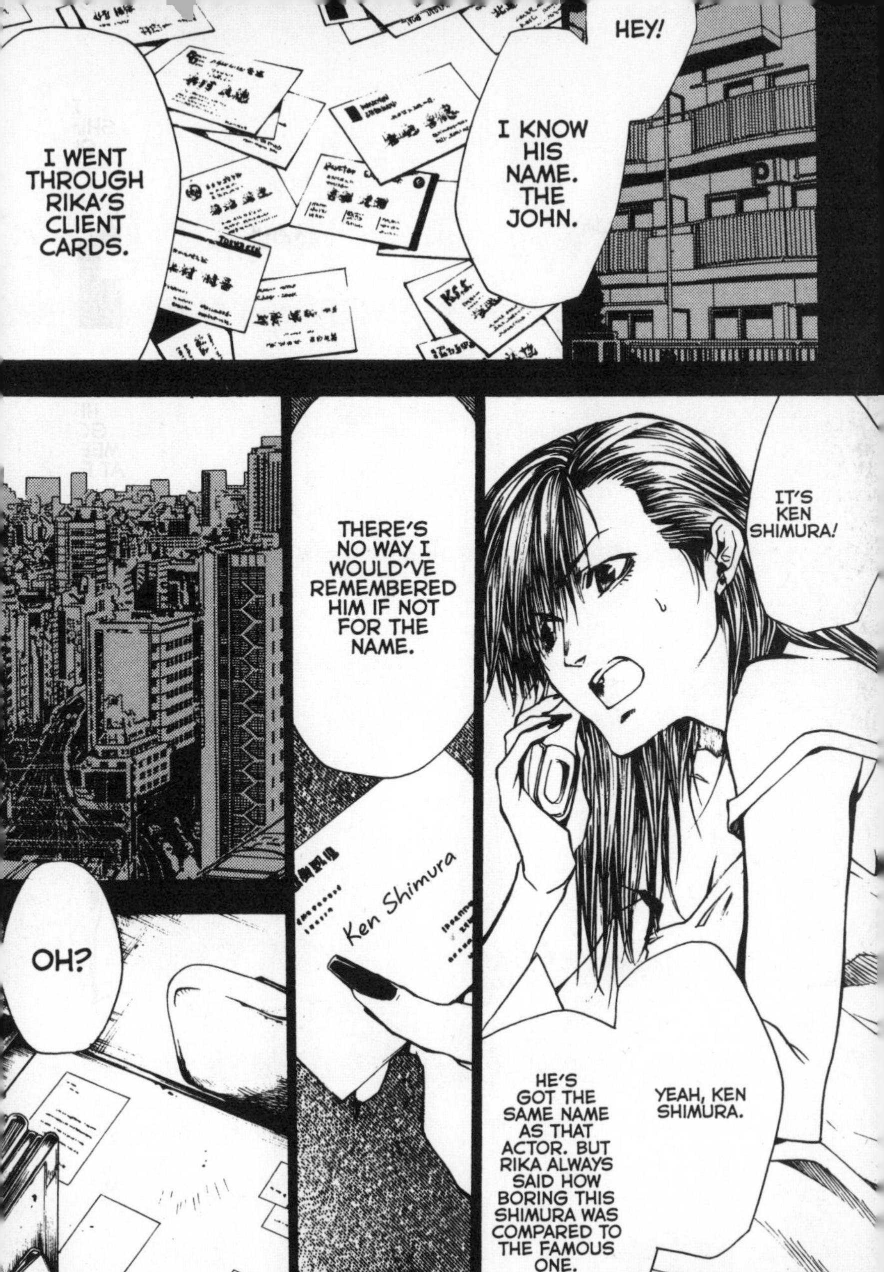
HEY!
I KNOW HIS NAME. THE JOHN.
I WENT THROUGH RIKA'S CLIENT CARDS.
IT'S KEN SHIMURA!
YEAH, KEN SHIMURA.
HE'S GOT THE SAME NAME AS THAT ACTOR. BUT RIKA ALWAYS SAID HOW BORING THIS SHIMURA WAS COMPARED TO THE FAMOUS ONE.
THERE'S NO WAY I WOULD'VE REMEMBERED HIM IF NOT FOR THE NAME.
Ken Shimura
OH?

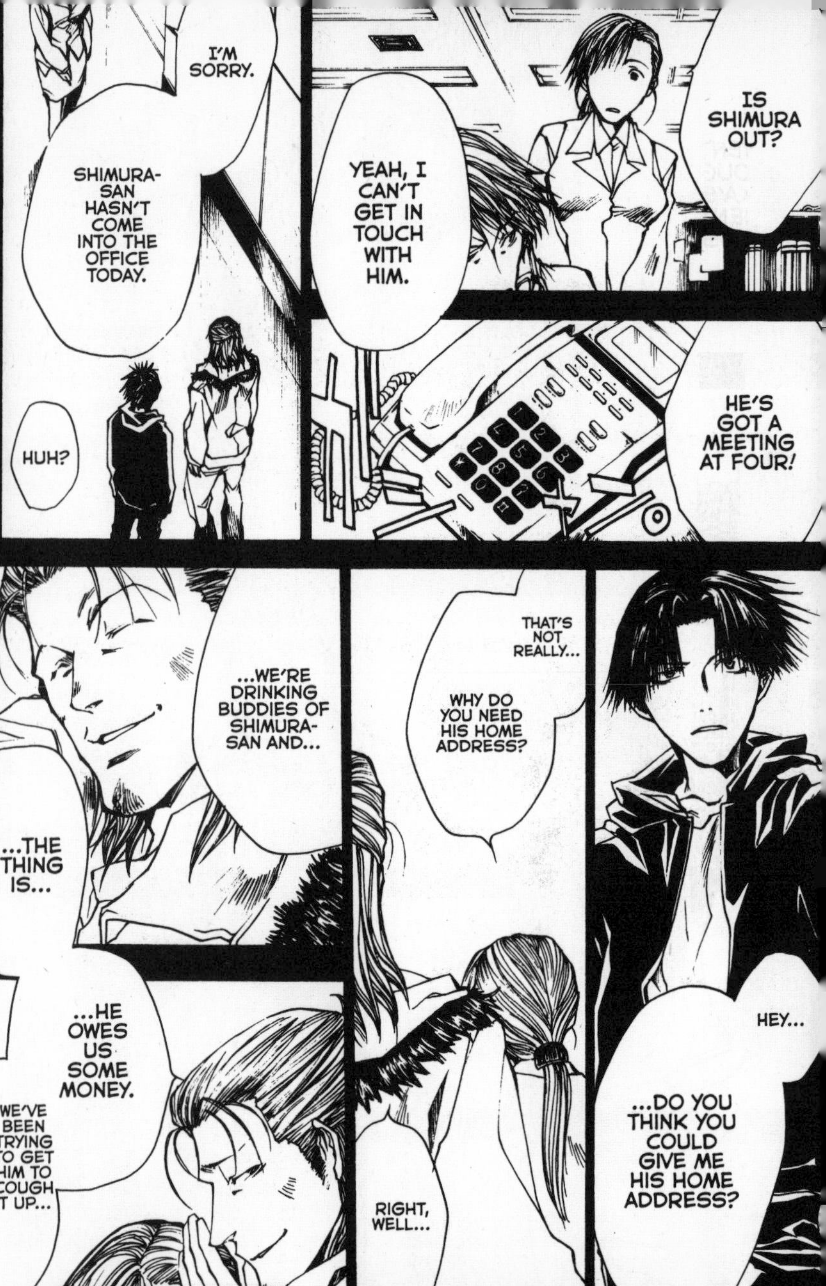
IS SHIMURA OUT?
YEAH, I CAN'T GET IN TOUCH WITH HIM.
HE'S GOT A MEETING AT FOUR!
I'M SORRY.
SHIMURA-SAN HASN'T COME INTO THE OFFICE TODAY.
HUH?
HEY...
...DO YOU THINK YOU COULD GIVE ME HIS HOME ADDRESS?
THAT'S NOT REALLY...
WHY DO YOU NEED HIS HOME ADDRESS?
RIGHT, WELL...
...WE'RE DRINKING BUDDIES OF SHIMURA-SAN AND...
...THE THING IS...
...HE OWES US SOME MONEY.
WE'VE BEEN TRYING TO GET HIM TO COUGH IT UP...

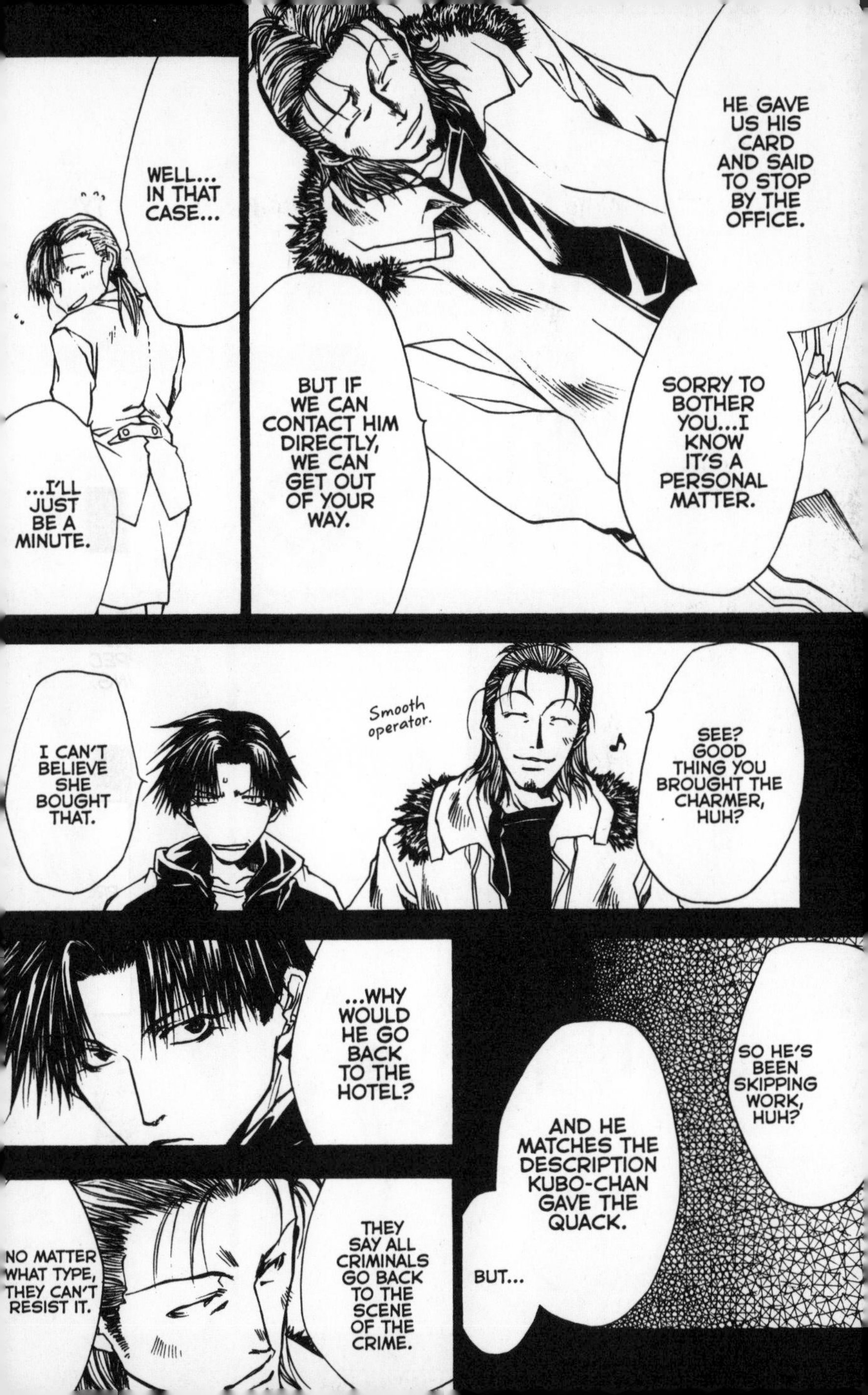
HE GAVE US HIS CARD AND SAID TO STOP BY THE OFFICE.
SORRY TO BOTHER YOU...I KNOW IT'S A PERSONAL MATTER.
BUT IF WE CAN CONTACT HIM DIRECTLY, WE CAN GET OUT OF YOUR WAY.
WELL... IN THAT CASE...
...I'LL JUST BE A MINUTE.
SEE? GOOD THING YOU BROUGHT THE CHARMER, HUH?
Smooth operator.
I CAN'T BELIEVE SHE BOUGHT THAT.
SO HE'S BEEN SKIPPING WORK, HUH?
AND HE MATCHES THE DESCRIPTION KUBO-CHAN GAVE THE QUACK.
BUT...
...WHY WOULD HE GO BACK TO THE HOTEL?
THEY SAY ALL CRIMINALS GO BACK TO THE SCENE OF THE CRIME.
NO MATTER WHAT TYPE, THEY CAN'T RESIST IT.

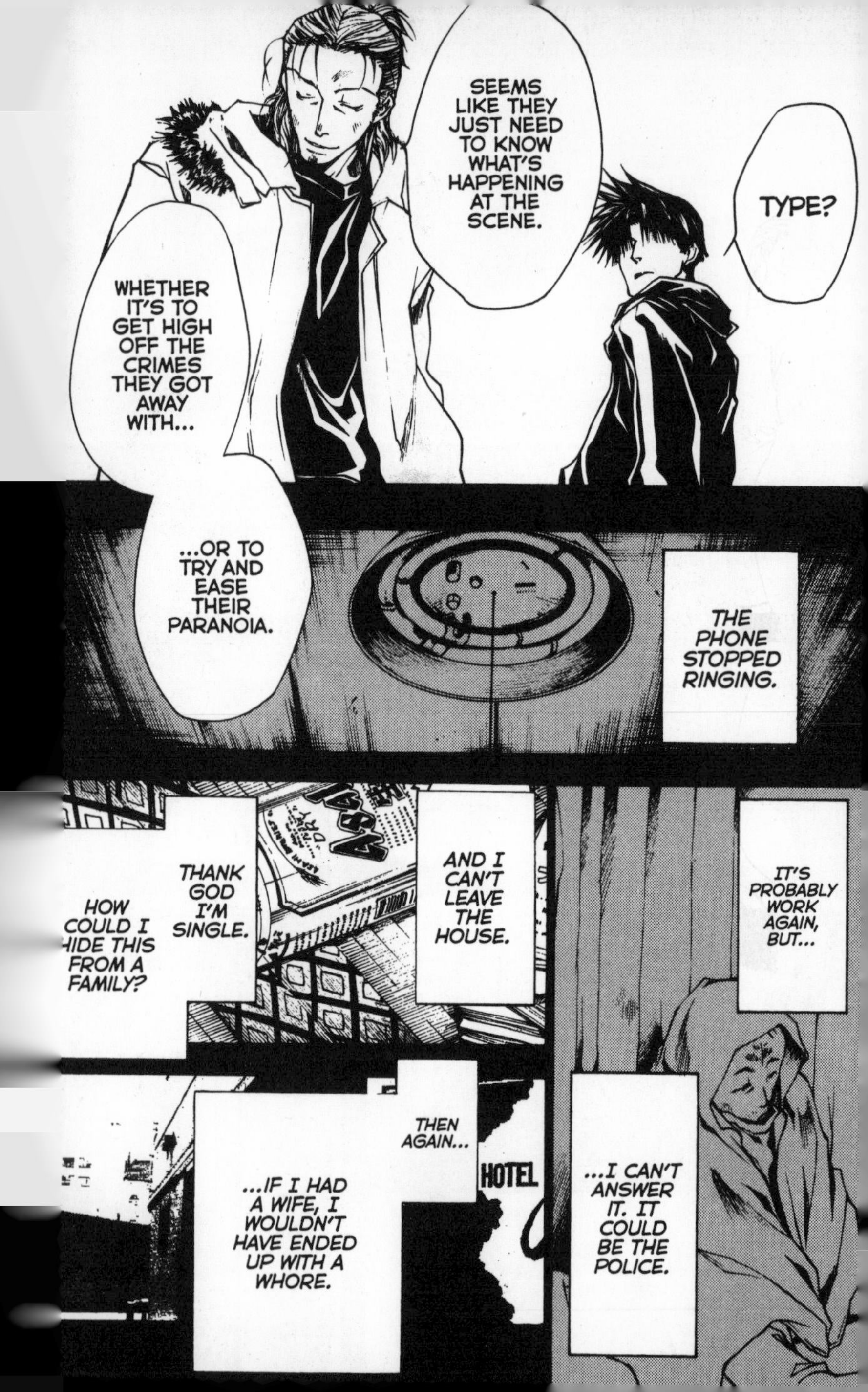
TYPE?
SEEMS LIKE THEY JUST NEED TO KNOW WHAT'S HAPPENING AT THE SCENE.
WHETHER IT'S TO GET HIGH OFF THE CRIMES THEY GOT AWAY WITH...
...OR TO TRY AND EASE THEIR PARANOIA.
THE PHONE STOPPED RINGING.
IT'S PROBABLY WORK AGAIN, BUT...
...I CAN'T ANSWER IT. IT COULD BE THE POLICE.
AND I CAN'T LEAVE THE HOUSE.
THANK GOD I'M SINGLE.
HOW COULD I HIDE THIS FROM A FAMILY?
THEN AGAIN...
HOTEL
...IF I HAD A WIFE, I WOULDN'T HAVE ENDED UP WITH A WHORE.

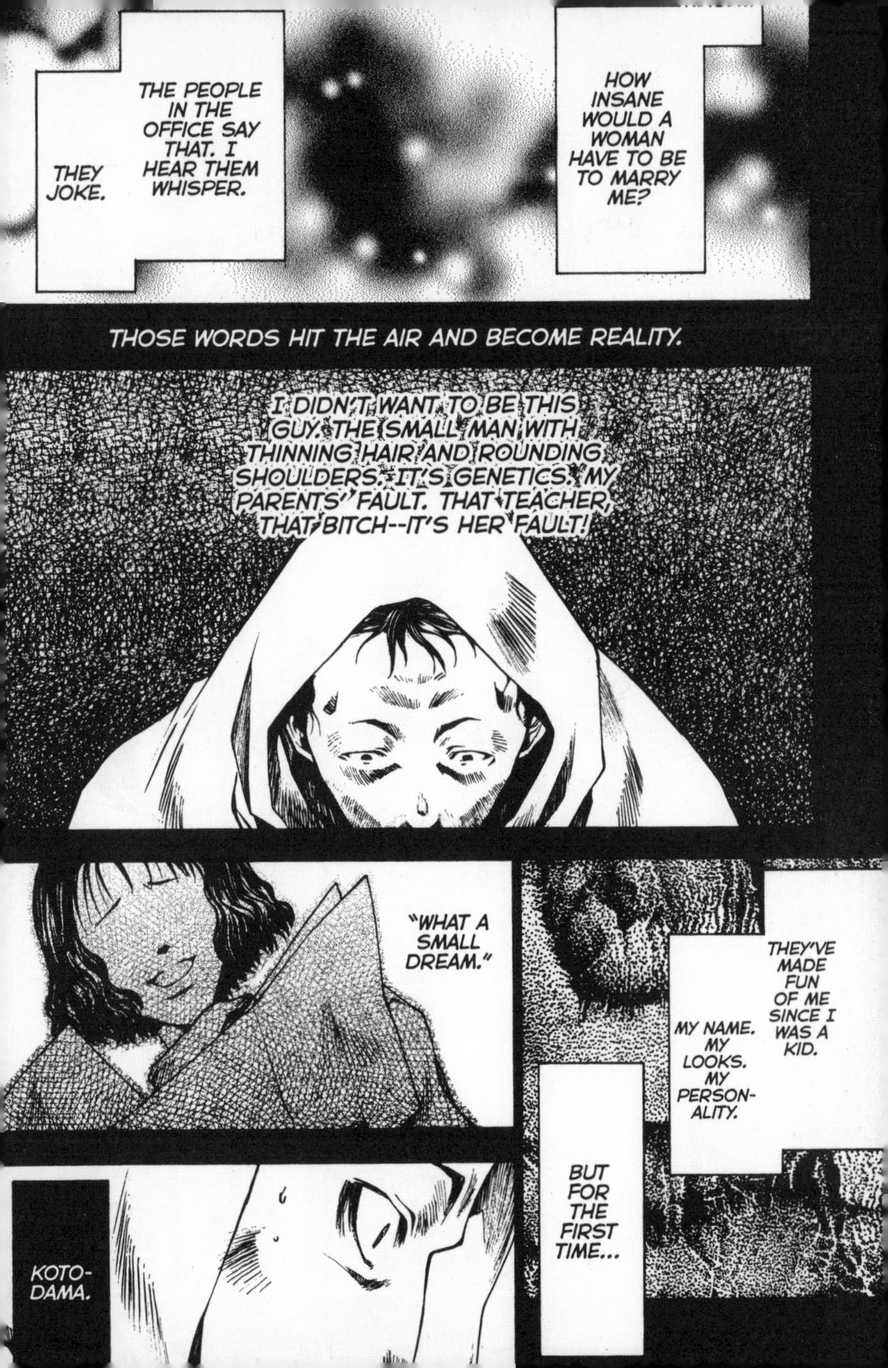
HOW INSANE WOULD A WOMAN HAVE TO BE TO MARRY ME?
THE PEOPLE IN THE OFFICE SAY THAT. I HEAR THEM WHISPER.
THEY JOKE.
THOSE WORDS HIT THE AIR AND BECOME REALITY.
I DIDN'T WANT TO BE THIS GUY. THE SMALL MAN WITH THINNING HAIR AND ROUNDING SHOULDERS. IT'S GENETICS. MY PARENTS' FAULT. THAT TEACHER, THAT BITCH--IT'S HER FAULT!
THEY'VE MADE FUN OF ME SINCE I WAS A KID.
MY NAME. MY LOOKS. MY PERSON-ALITY.
BUT FOR THE FIRST TIME...
"WHAT A SMALL DREAM."
KOTO-DAMA.

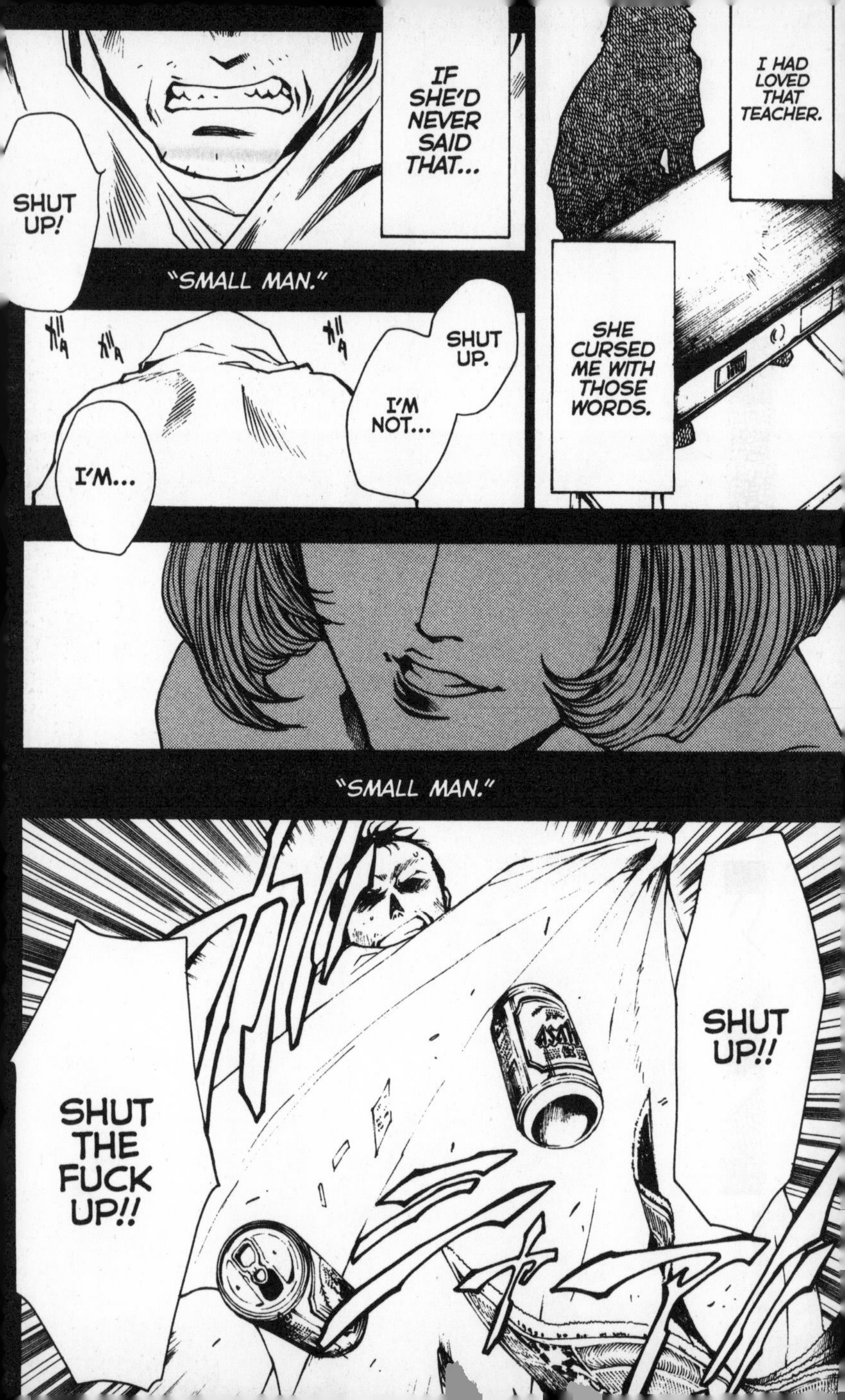
I HAD LOVED THAT TEACHER.
SHE CURSED ME WITH THOSE WORDS.
IF SHE'D NEVER SAID THAT...
SHUT UP!
"SMALL MAN."
SHUT UP.
I'M NOT...
I'M...
"SMALL MAN."
SHUT UP!!
SHUT THE FUCK UP!!

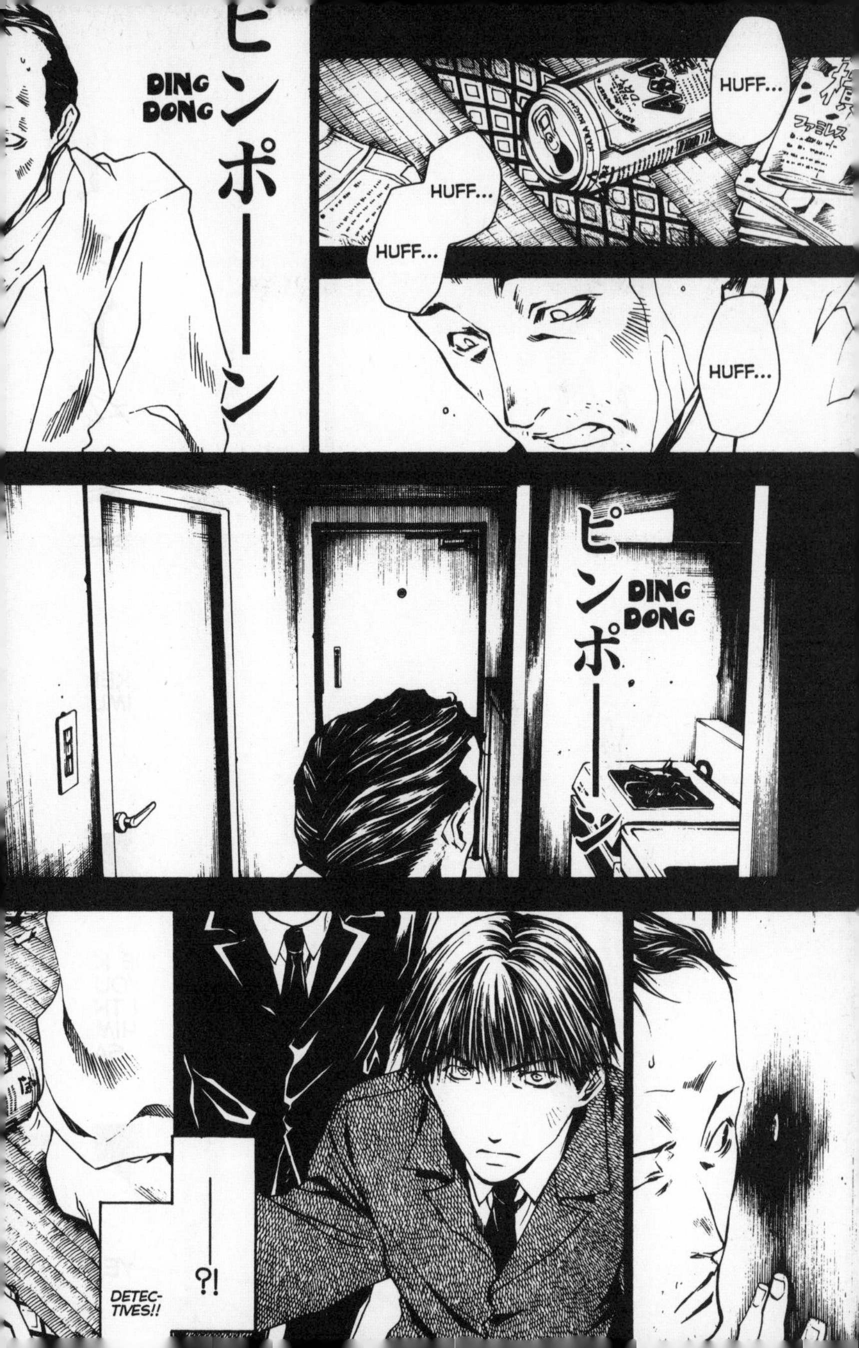
HUFF...
HUFF...
HUFF...
HUFF...
ピンポーン
DING DONG
ピンポーン
DING DONG
—?!
DETECTIVES!!

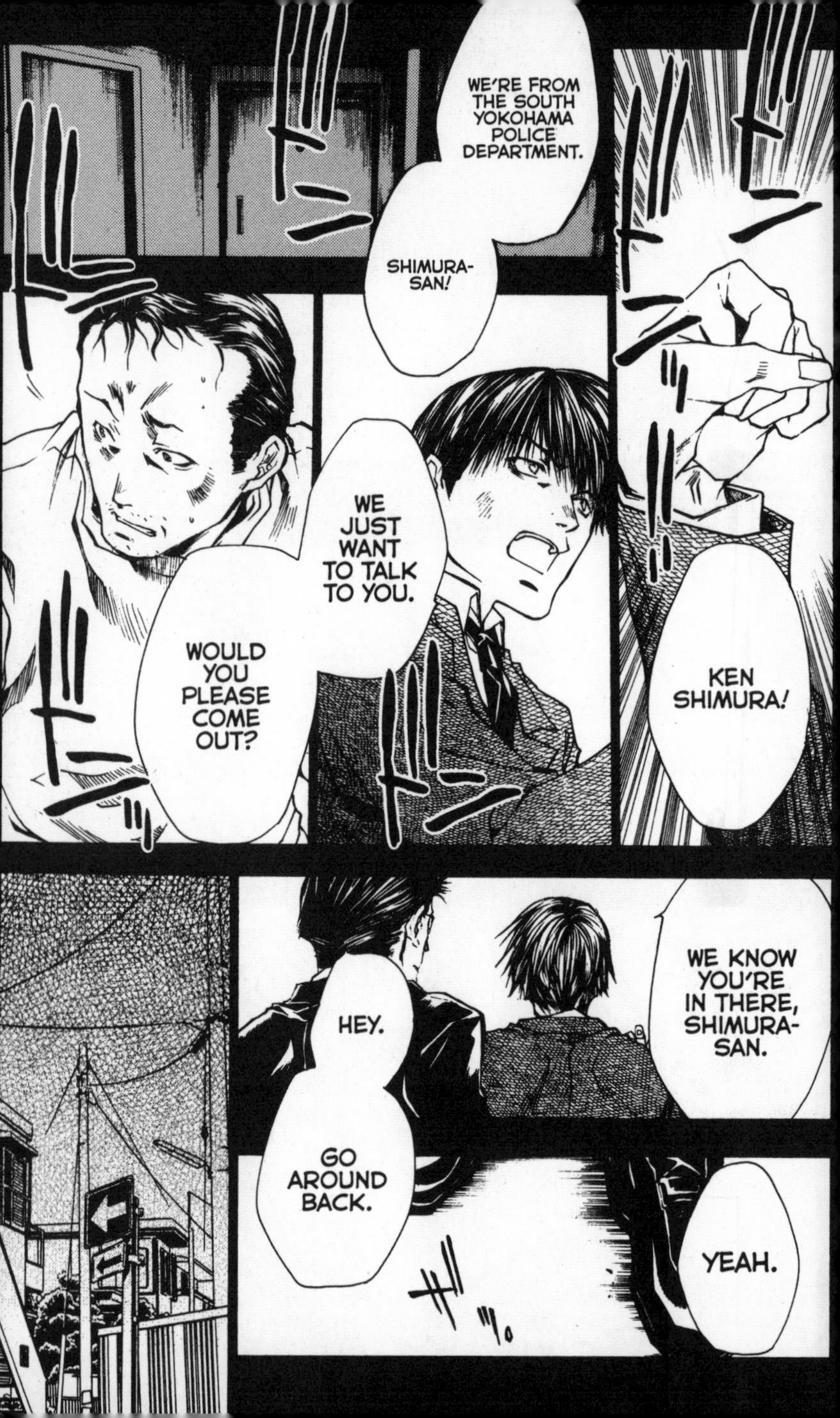
KEN SHIMURA!
WE'RE FROM THE SOUTH YOKOHAMA POLICE DEPARTMENT.
SHIMURA-SAN!
WE JUST WANT TO TALK TO YOU.
WOULD YOU PLEASE COME OUT?
WE KNOW YOU'RE IN THERE, SHIMURA-SAN.
HEY.
GO AROUND BACK.
YEAH.

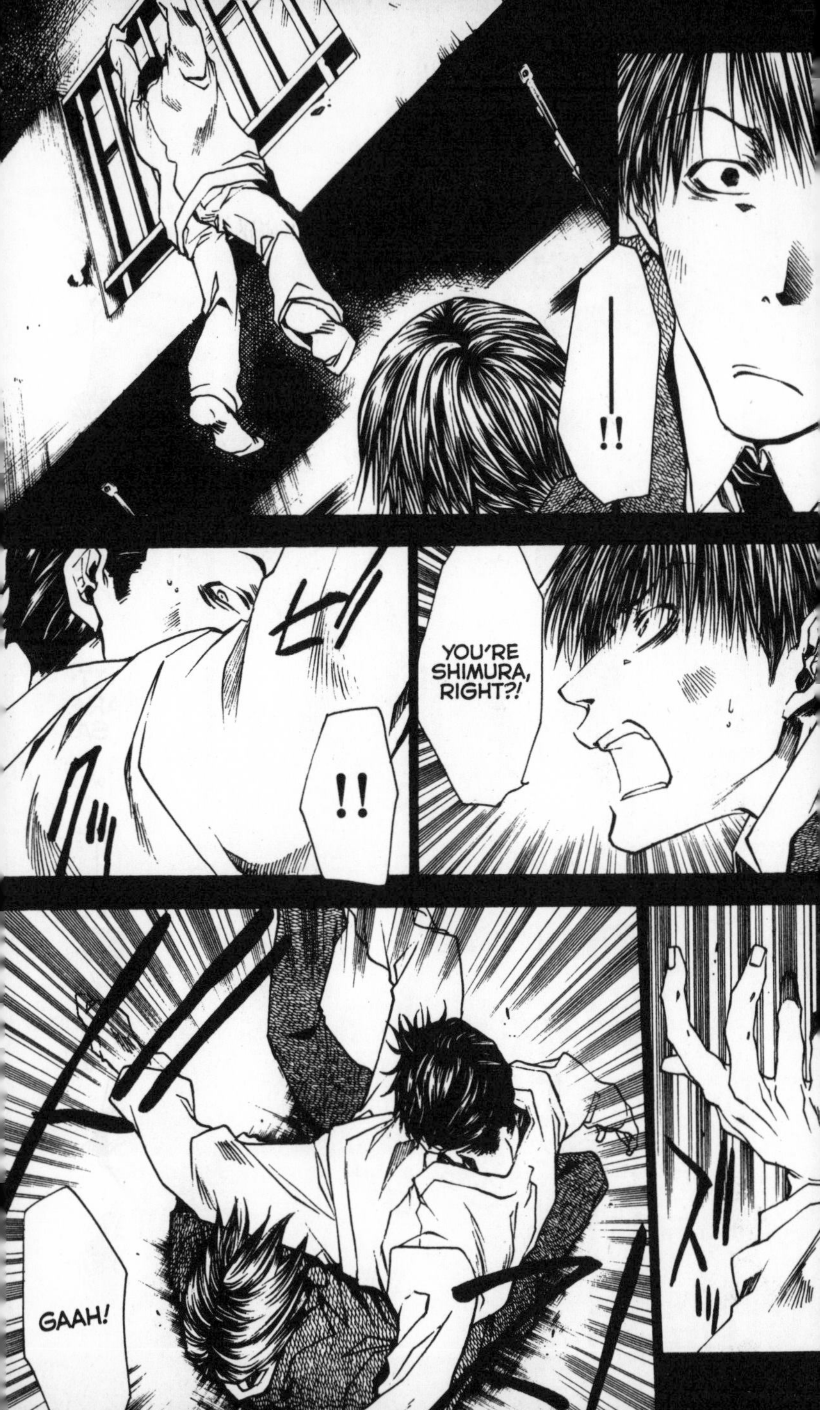
!!
YOU'RE SHIMURA, RIGHT?!
!!
GAAH!

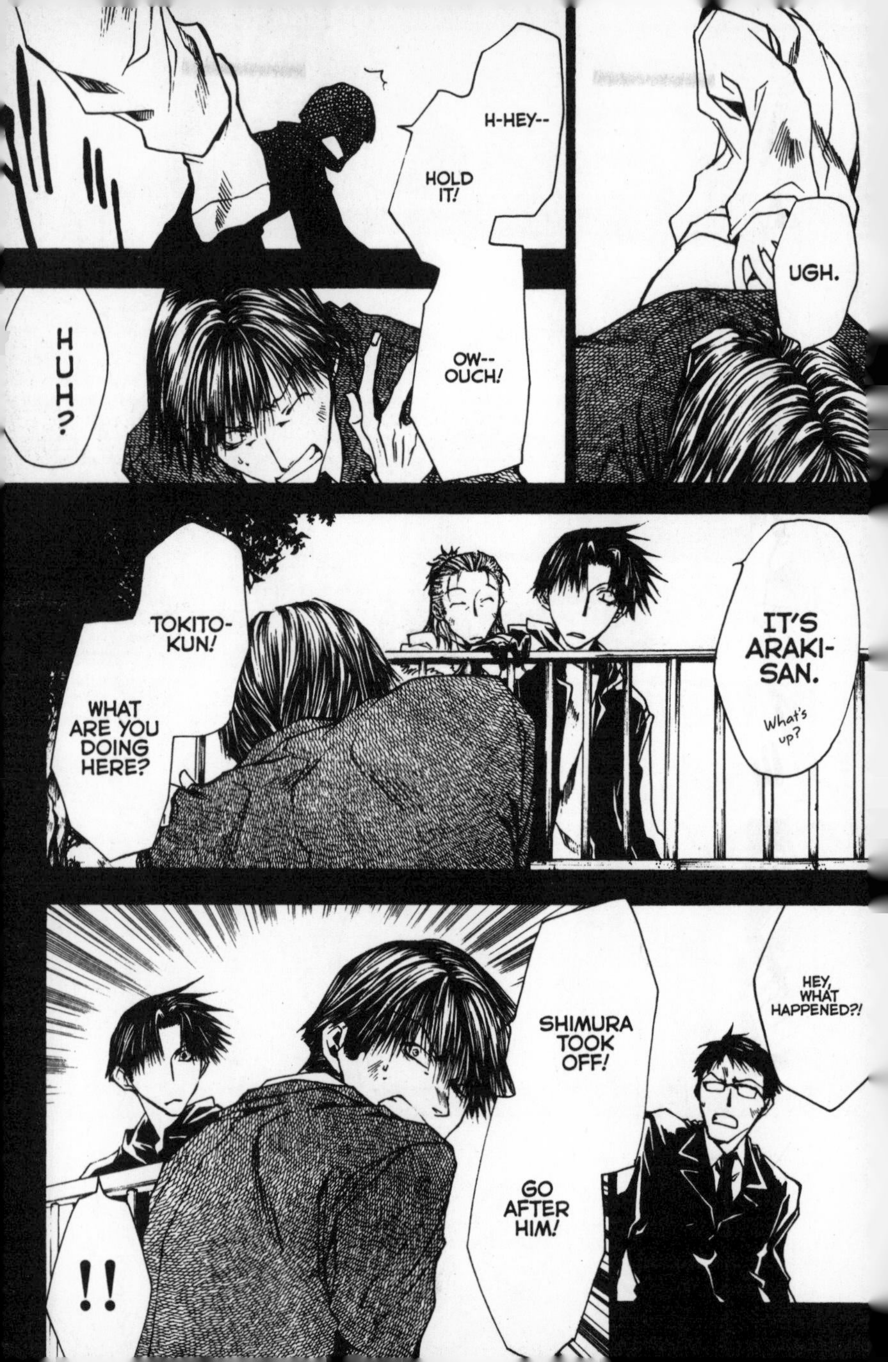
UGH.
H-HEY--
HOLD IT!
OW-- OUCH!
HUH?
IT'S ARAKI-SAN.
What's up?
TOKITO-KUN!
WHAT ARE YOU DOING HERE?
HEY, WHAT HAPPENED?!
SHIMURA TOOK OFF!
GO AFTER HIM!
!!

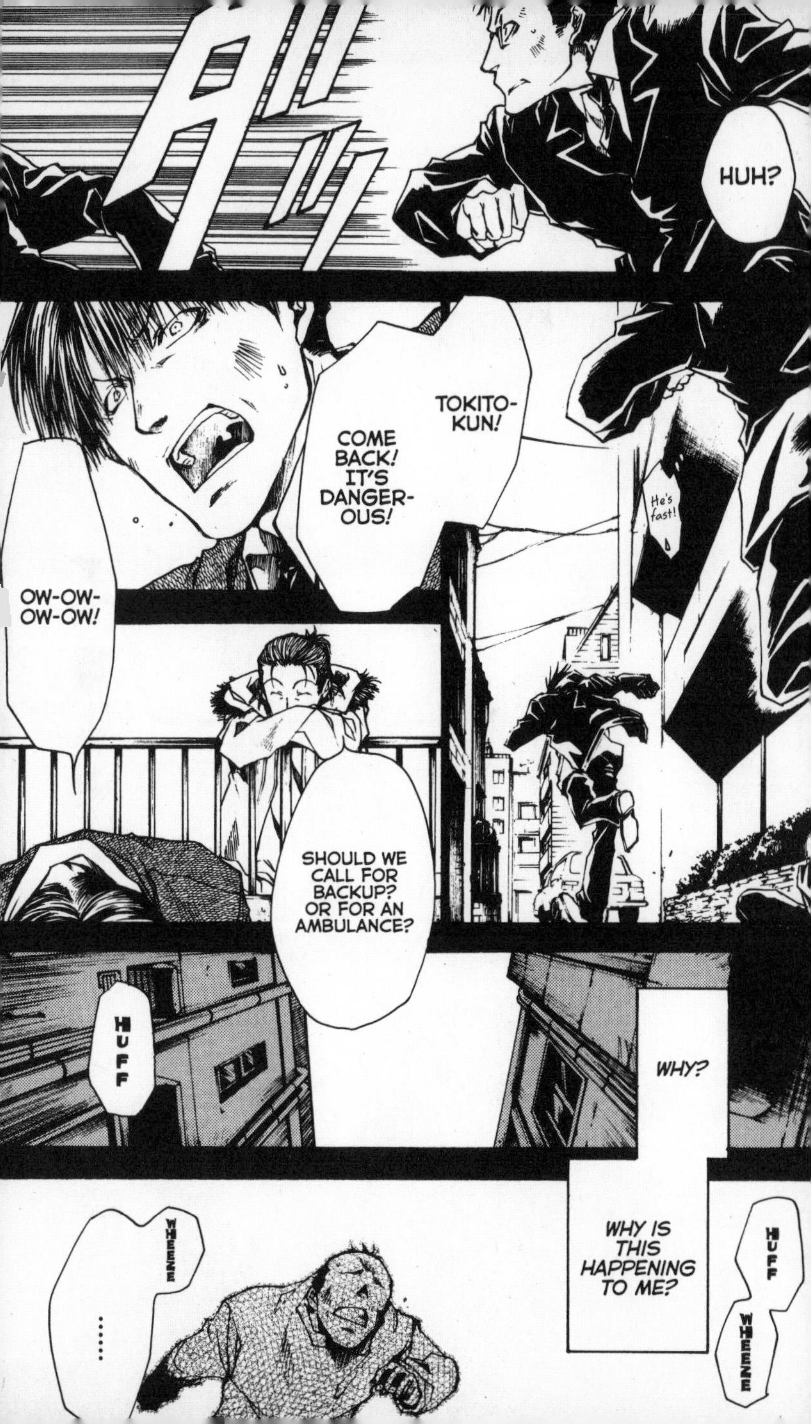
HUH?
He's fast!
TOKITO-KUN!
COME BACK! IT'S DANGER-OUS!
OW-OW-OW-OW!
SHOULD WE CALL FOR BACKUP? OR FOR AN AMBULANCE?
WHY?
HUFF
WHY IS THIS HAPPENING TO ME?
HUFF
WHEEZE
WHEEZE
......

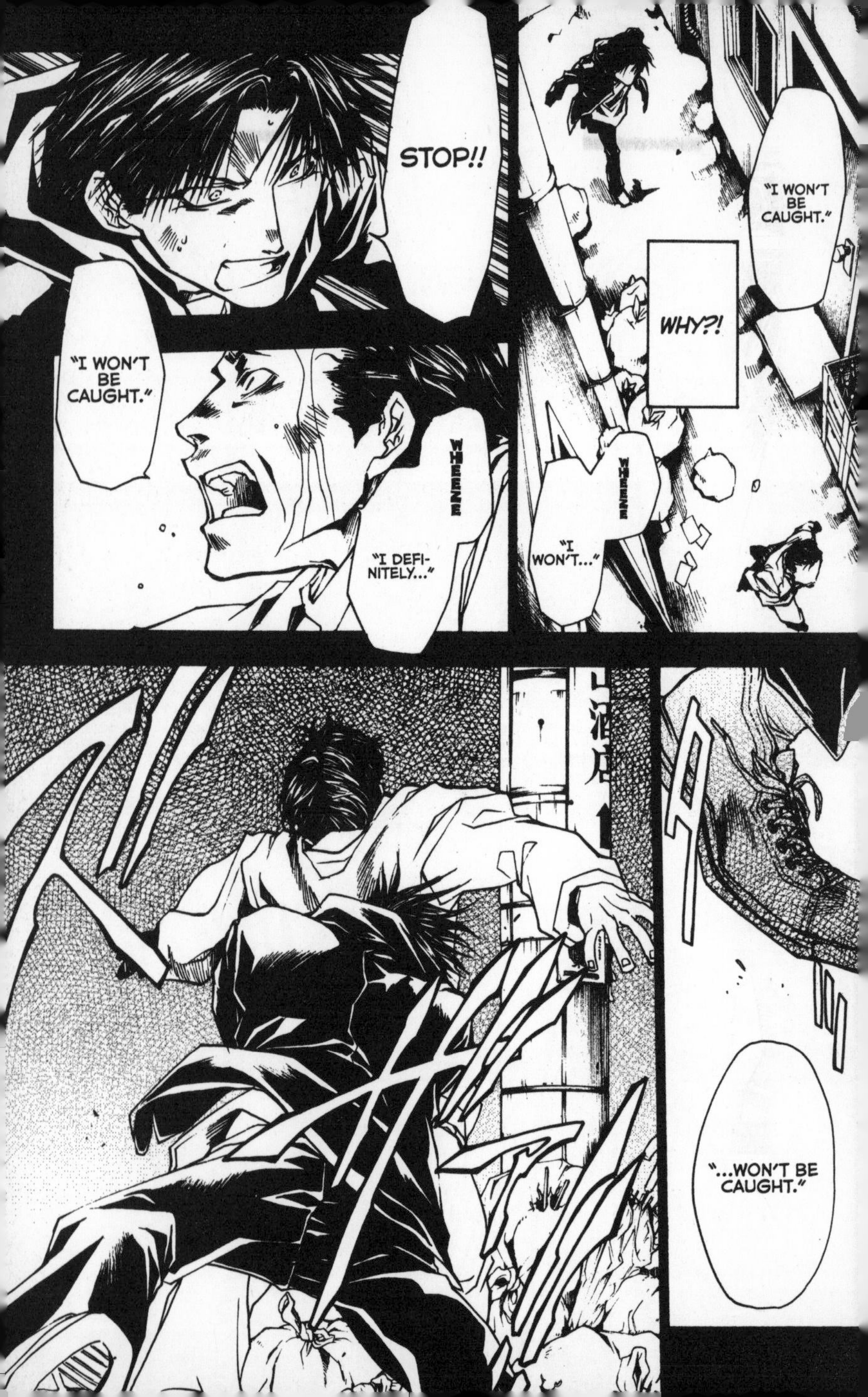
"I WON'T BE CAUGHT."
WHY?!
WHEEZE
"I WON'T..."
STOP!!
WHEEZE
"I DEFINITELY..."
"I WON'T BE CAUGHT."
"...WON'T BE CAUGHT."

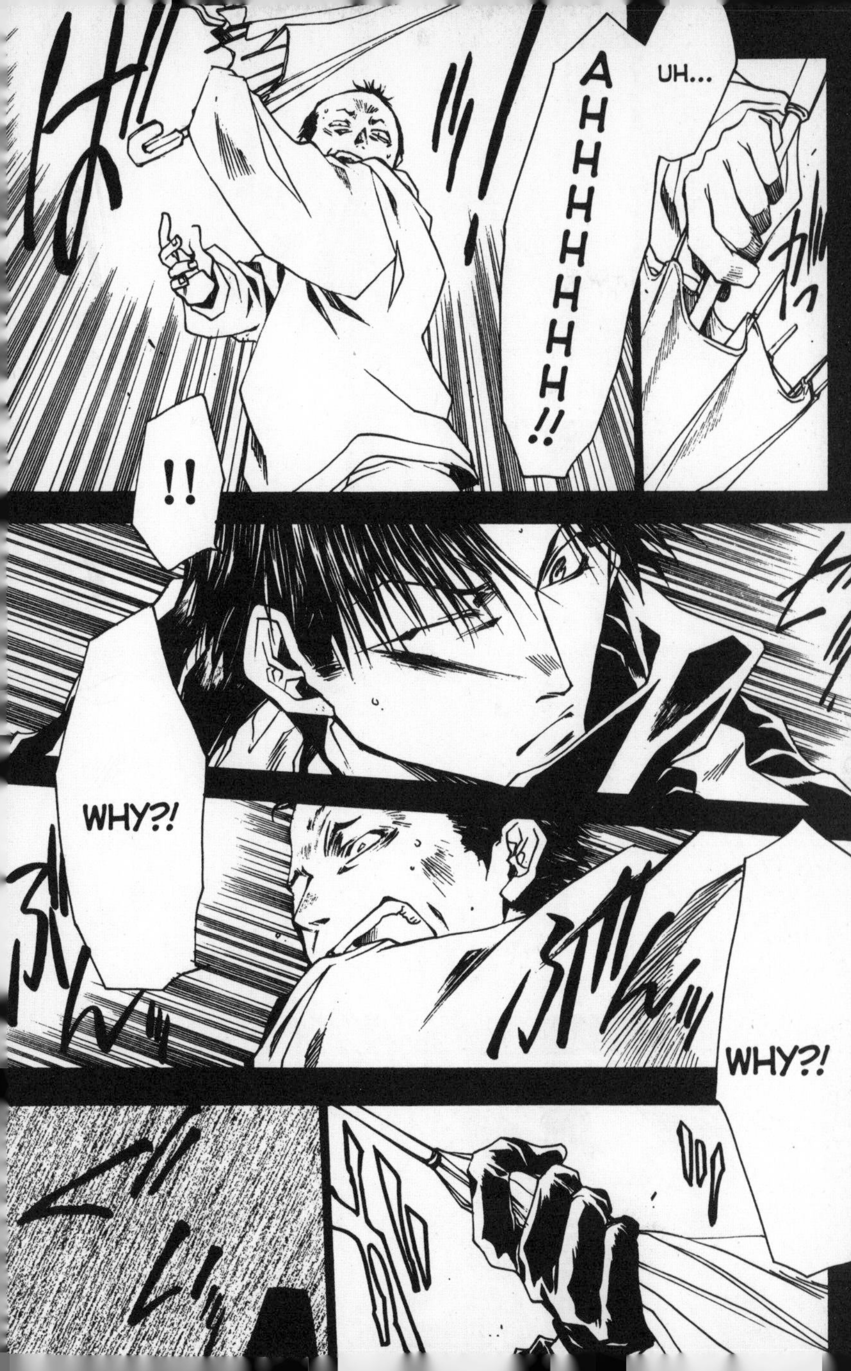
UH...
AHHHHHHHH!!
!!
WHY?!
WHY?!

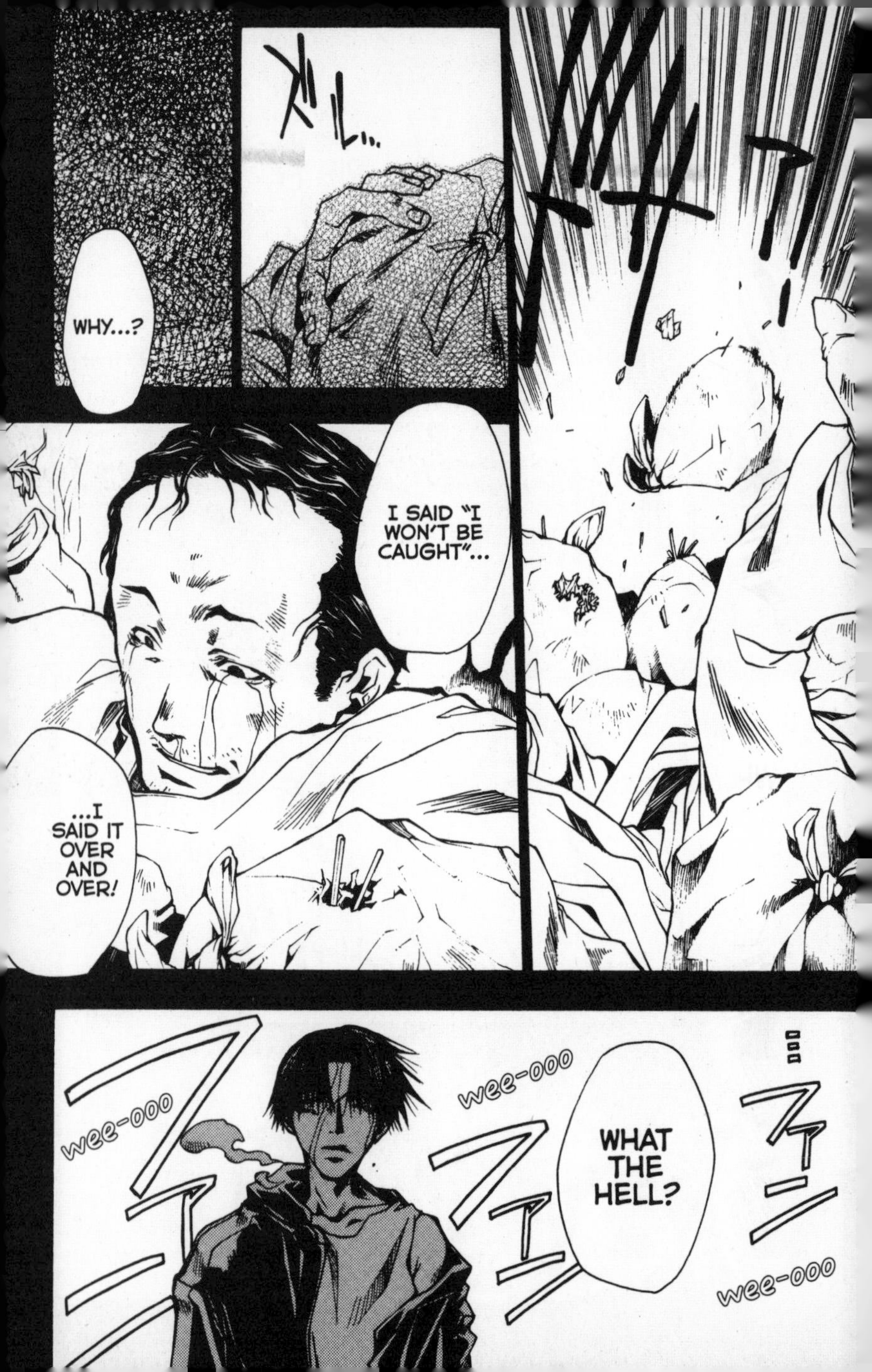
ズル...
WHY...?
I SAID "I WON'T BE CAUGHT"...
...I SAID IT OVER AND OVER!
wee-ooo
WHAT THE HELL?
wee-ooo
wee-ooo
wee-ooo

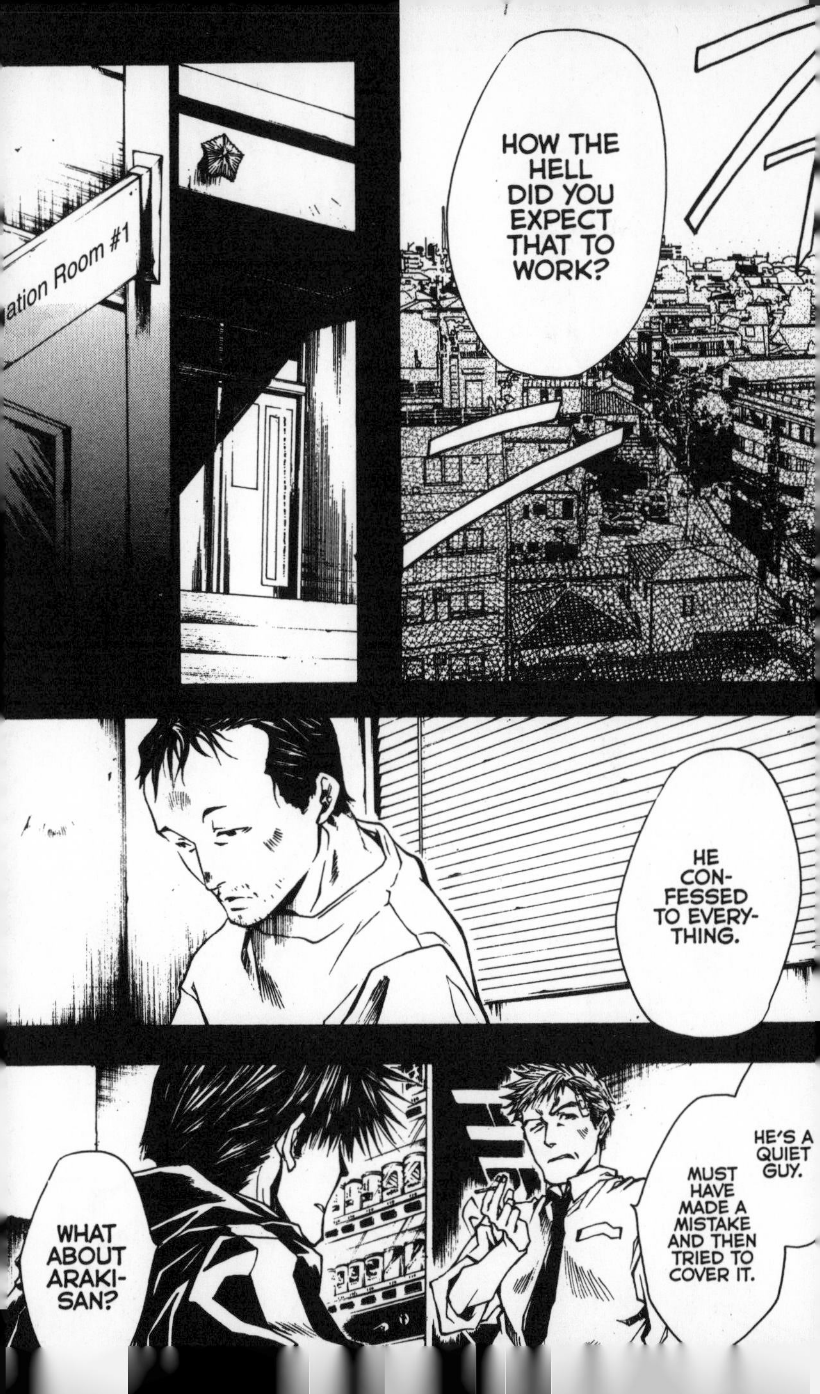

HOW THE HELL DID YOU EXPECT THAT TO WORK?
ation Room #1
HE CON-FESSED TO EVERY-THING.
HE'S A QUIET GUY.
MUST HAVE MADE A MISTAKE AND THEN TRIED TO COVER IT.
WHAT ABOUT ARAKI-SAN?

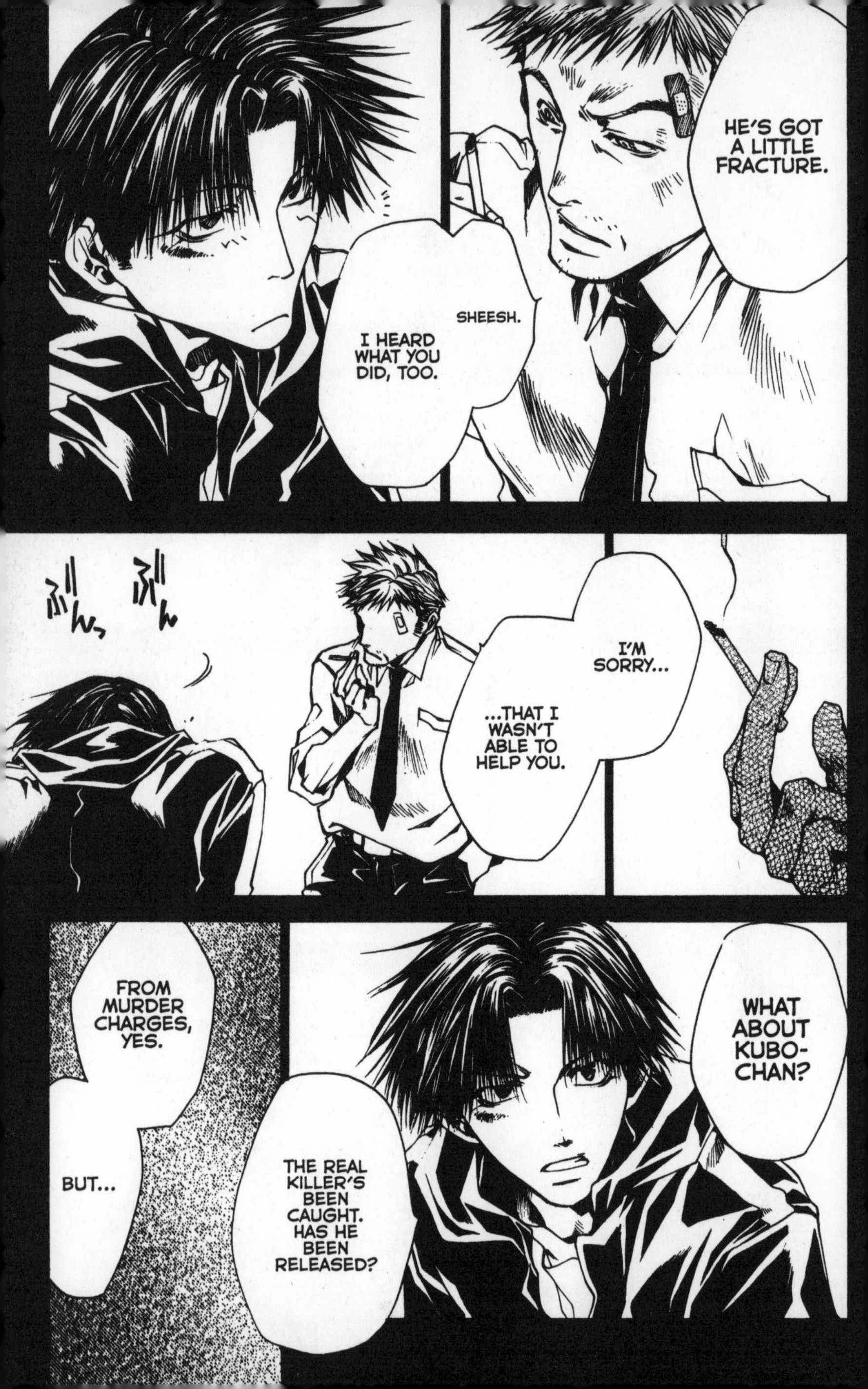
HE'S GOT A LITTLE FRACTURE.
SHEESH.
I HEARD WHAT YOU DID, TOO.
I'M SORRY...
...THAT I WASN'T ABLE TO HELP YOU.
ぶん
ぶんっ
WHAT ABOUT KUBO-CHAN?
THE REAL KILLER'S BEEN CAUGHT. HAS HE BEEN RELEASED?
FROM MURDER CHARGES, YES.
BUT...

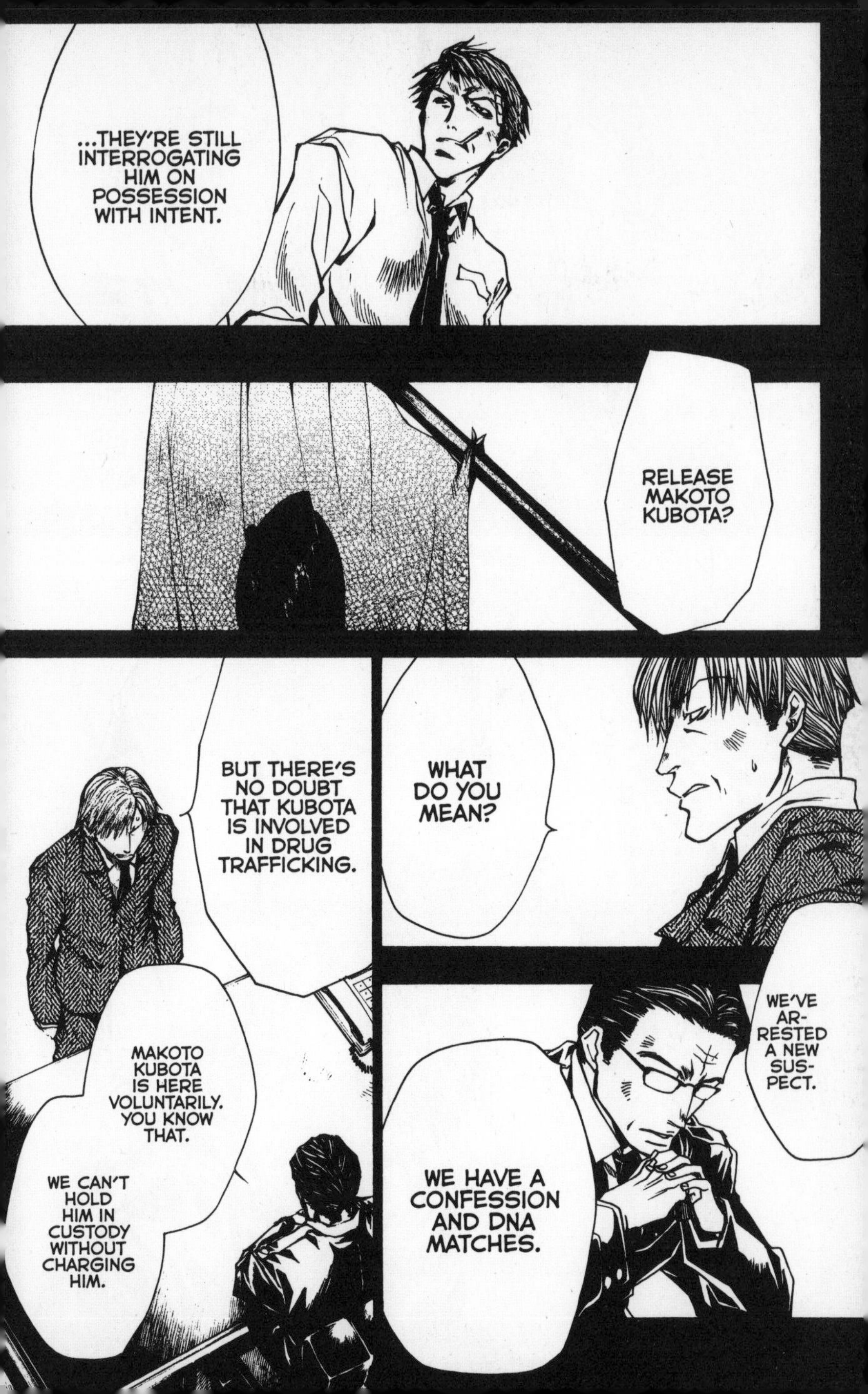
...THEY'RE STILL INTERROGATING HIM ON POSSESSION WITH INTENT.
RELEASE MAKOTO KUBOTA?
WHAT DO YOU MEAN?
WE'VE AR-RESTED A NEW SUS-PECT.
WE HAVE A CONFESSION AND DNA MATCHES.
BUT THERE'S NO DOUBT THAT KUBOTA IS INVOLVED IN DRUG TRAFFICKING.
MAKOTO KUBOTA IS HERE VOLUNTARILY. YOU KNOW THAT.
WE CAN'T HOLD HIM IN CUSTODY WITHOUT CHARGING HIM.

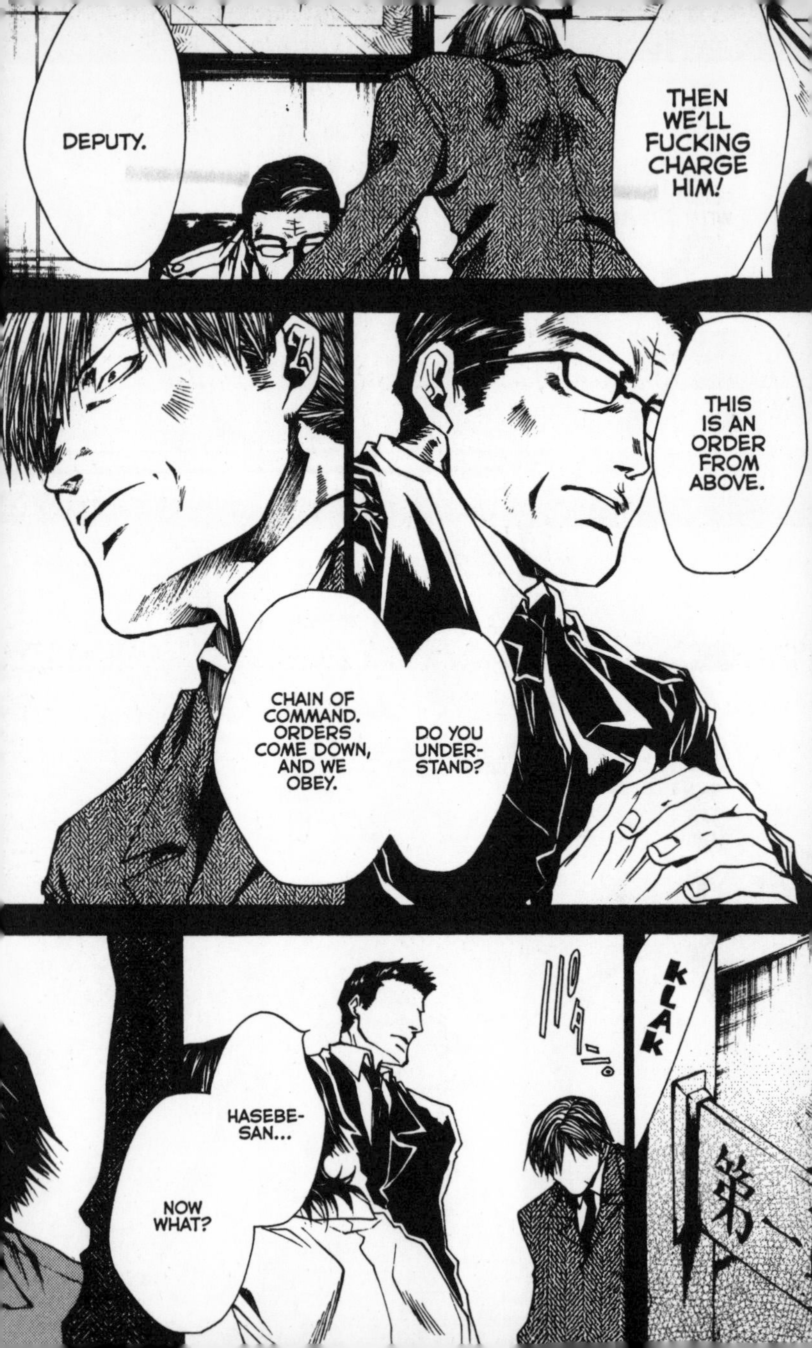
THEN WE'LL FUCKING CHARGE HIM!
DEPUTY.
THIS IS AN ORDER FROM ABOVE.
CHAIN OF COMMAND. ORDERS COME DOWN, AND WE OBEY.
DO YOU UNDER-STAND?
KLAK
第一
HASEBE-SAN...
NOW WHAT?

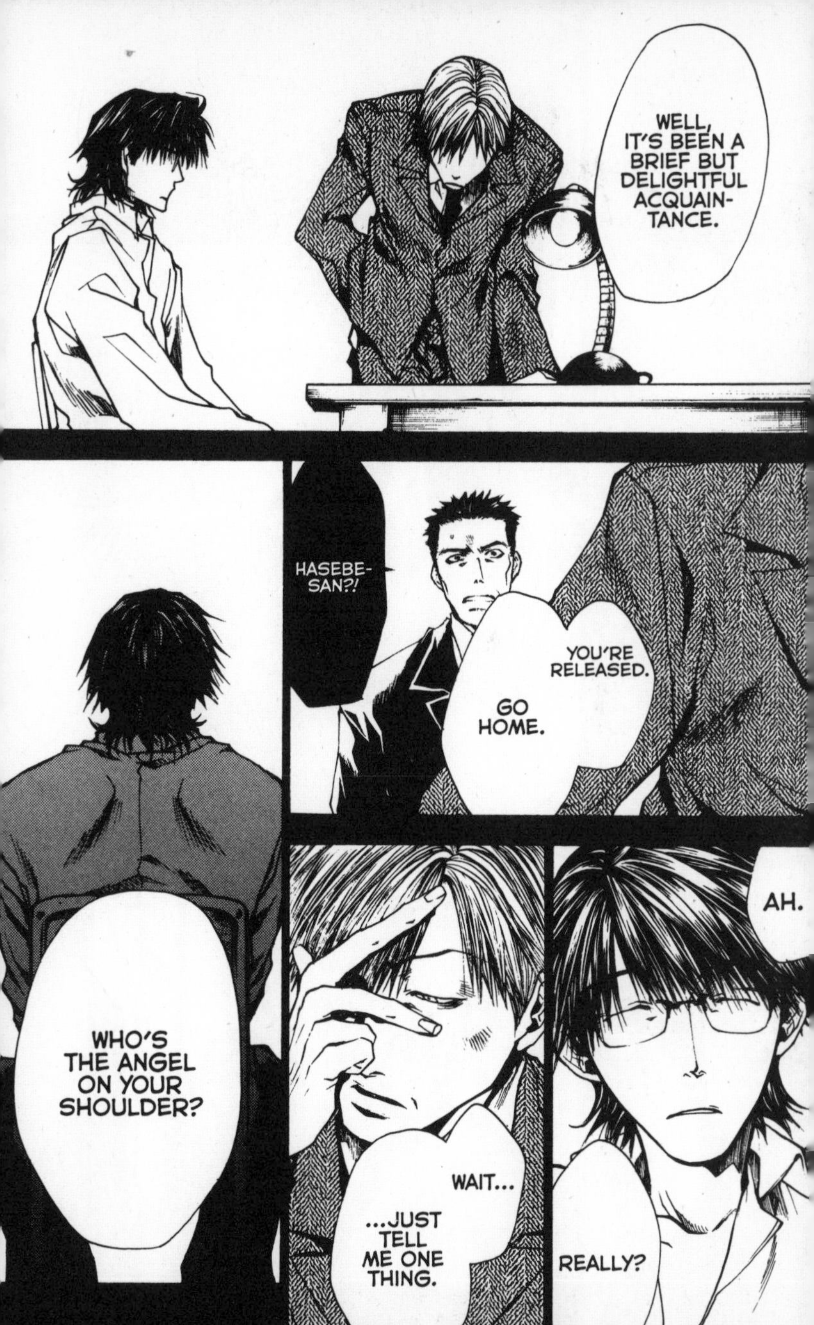
WELL, IT'S BEEN A BRIEF BUT DELIGHTFUL ACQUAINTANCE.
YOU'RE RELEASED.
GO HOME.
HASEBE-SAN?!
AH.
REALLY?
WAIT...
...JUST TELL ME ONE THING.
WHO'S THE ANGEL ON YOUR SHOULDER?

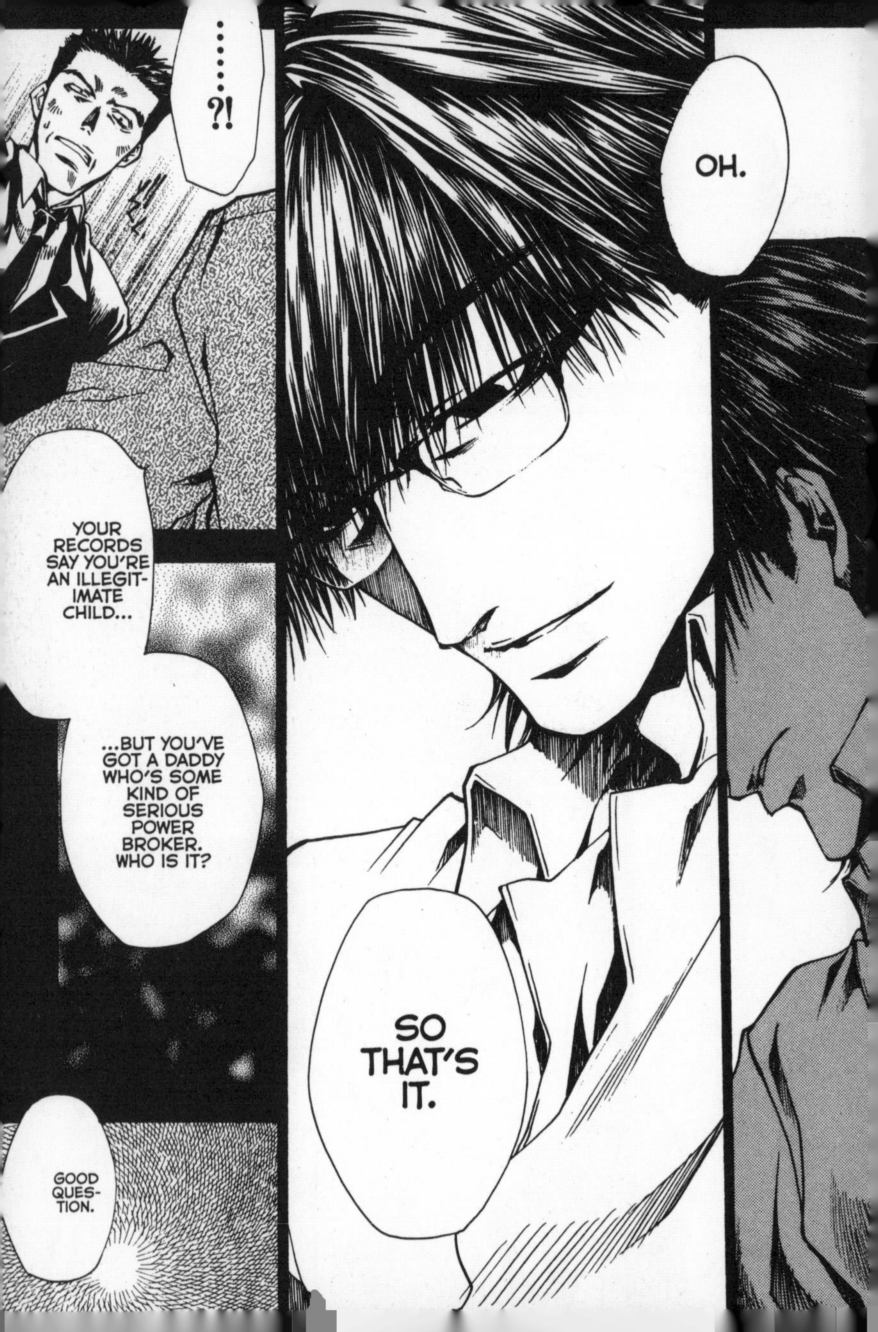
OH.
SO THAT'S IT.
……?!
YOUR RECORDS SAY YOU'RE AN ILLEGIT-IMATE CHILD...
...BUT YOU'VE GOT A DADDY WHO'S SOME KIND OF SERIOUS POWER BROKER. WHO IS IT?
GOOD QUES-TION.

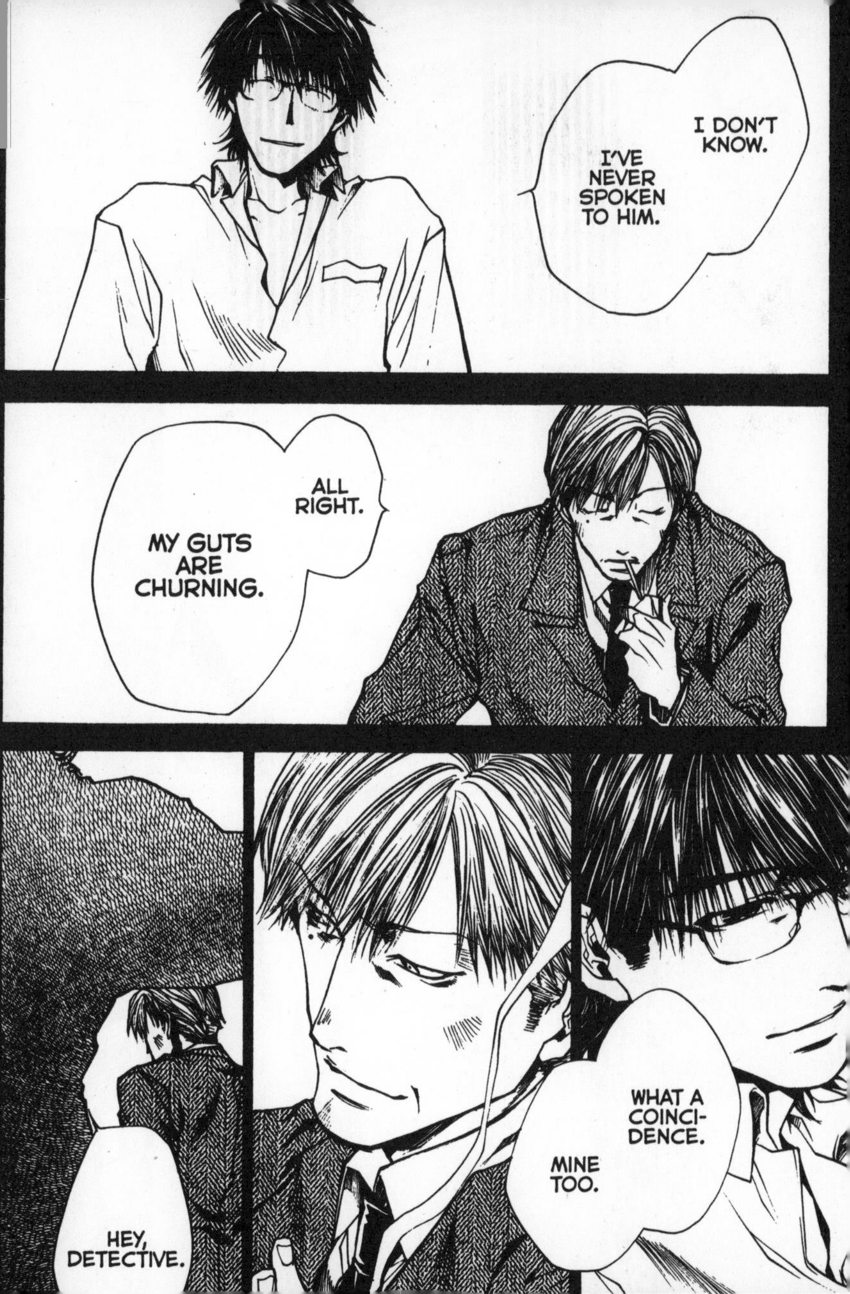
I DON'T KNOW.
I'VE NEVER SPOKEN TO HIM.
ALL RIGHT.
MY GUTS ARE CHURNING.
WHAT A COINCIDENCE.
MINE TOO.
HEY, DETECTIVE.

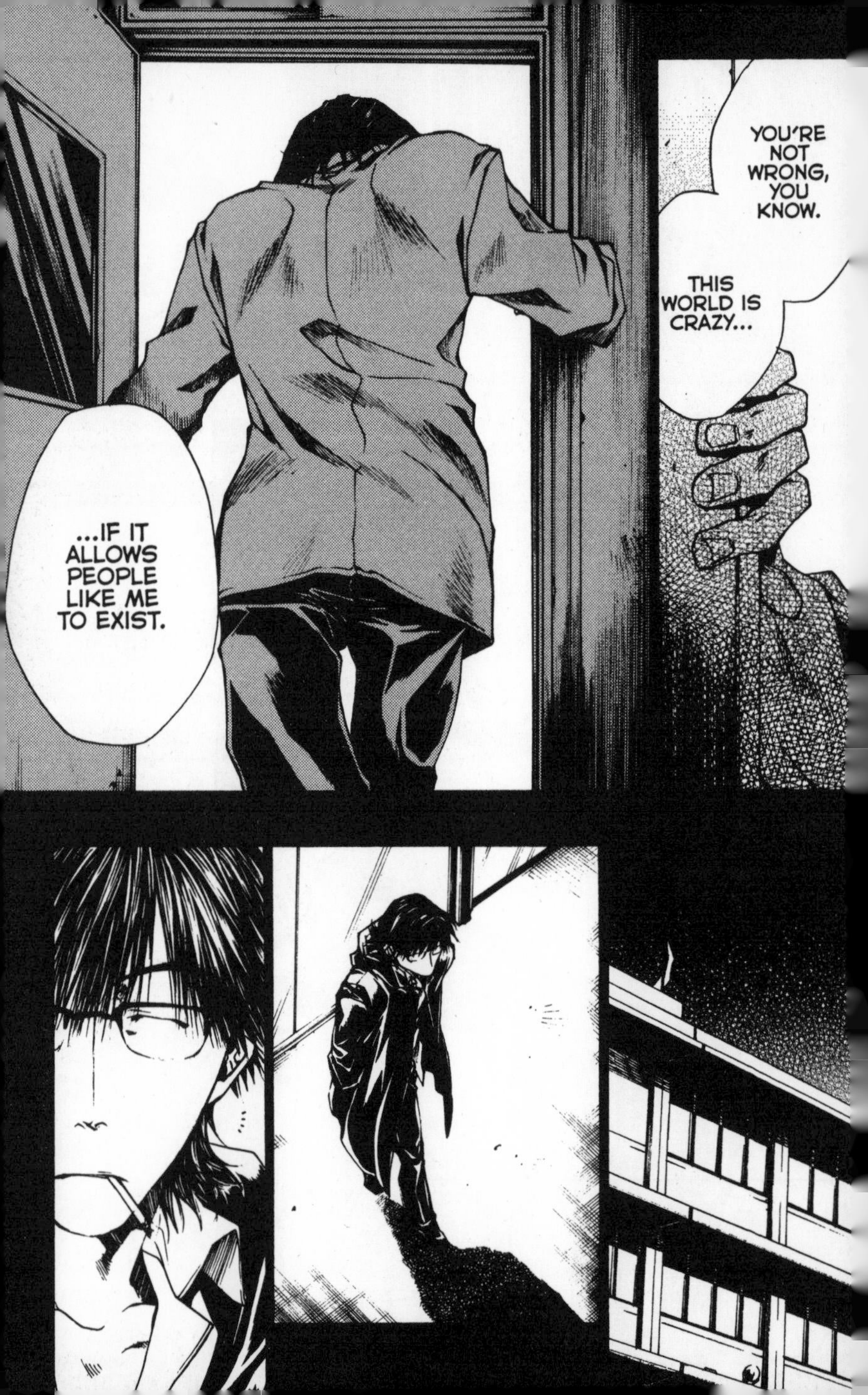
YOU'RE NOT WRONG, YOU KNOW.
THIS WORLD IS CRAZY...
...IF IT ALLOWS PEOPLE LIKE ME TO EXIST.

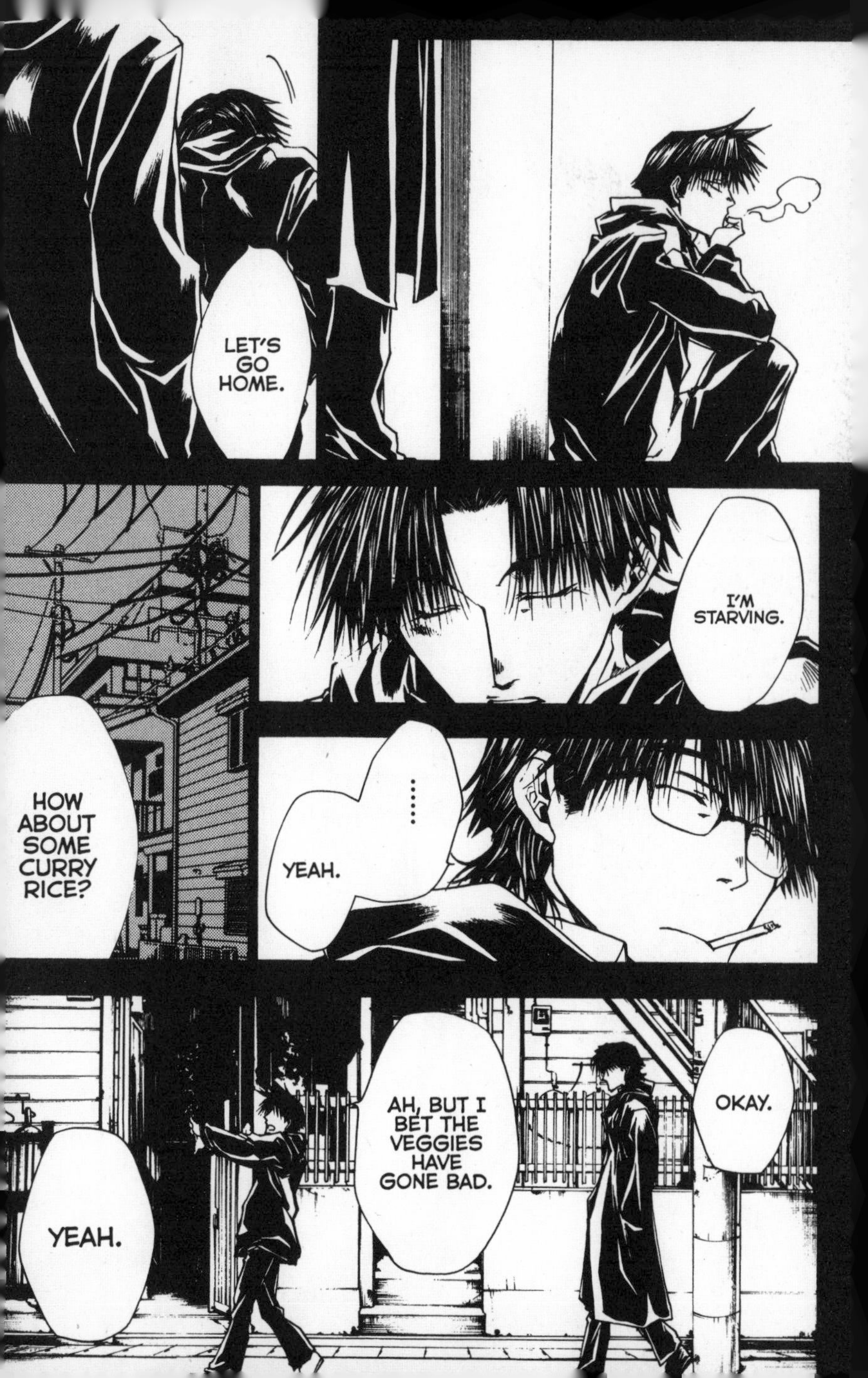
LET'S GO HOME.
I'M STARVING.
......
YEAH.
HOW ABOUT SOME CURRY RICE?
OKAY.
AH, BUT I BET THE VEGGIES HAVE GONE BAD.
YEAH.

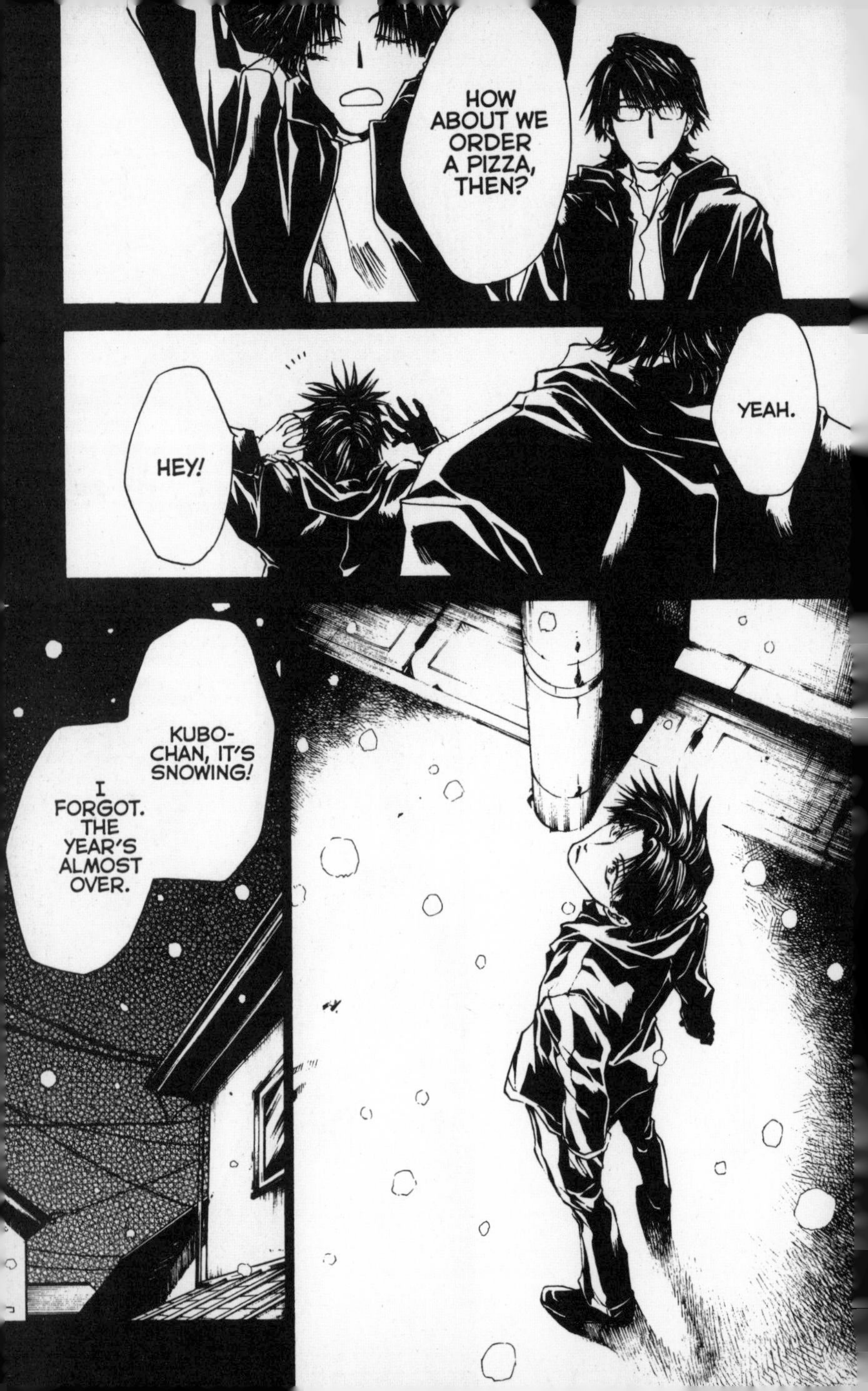
HOW ABOUT WE ORDER A PIZZA, THEN?
YEAH.
HEY!
KUBO-CHAN, IT'S SNOWING!
I FORGOT. THE YEAR'S ALMOST OVER.

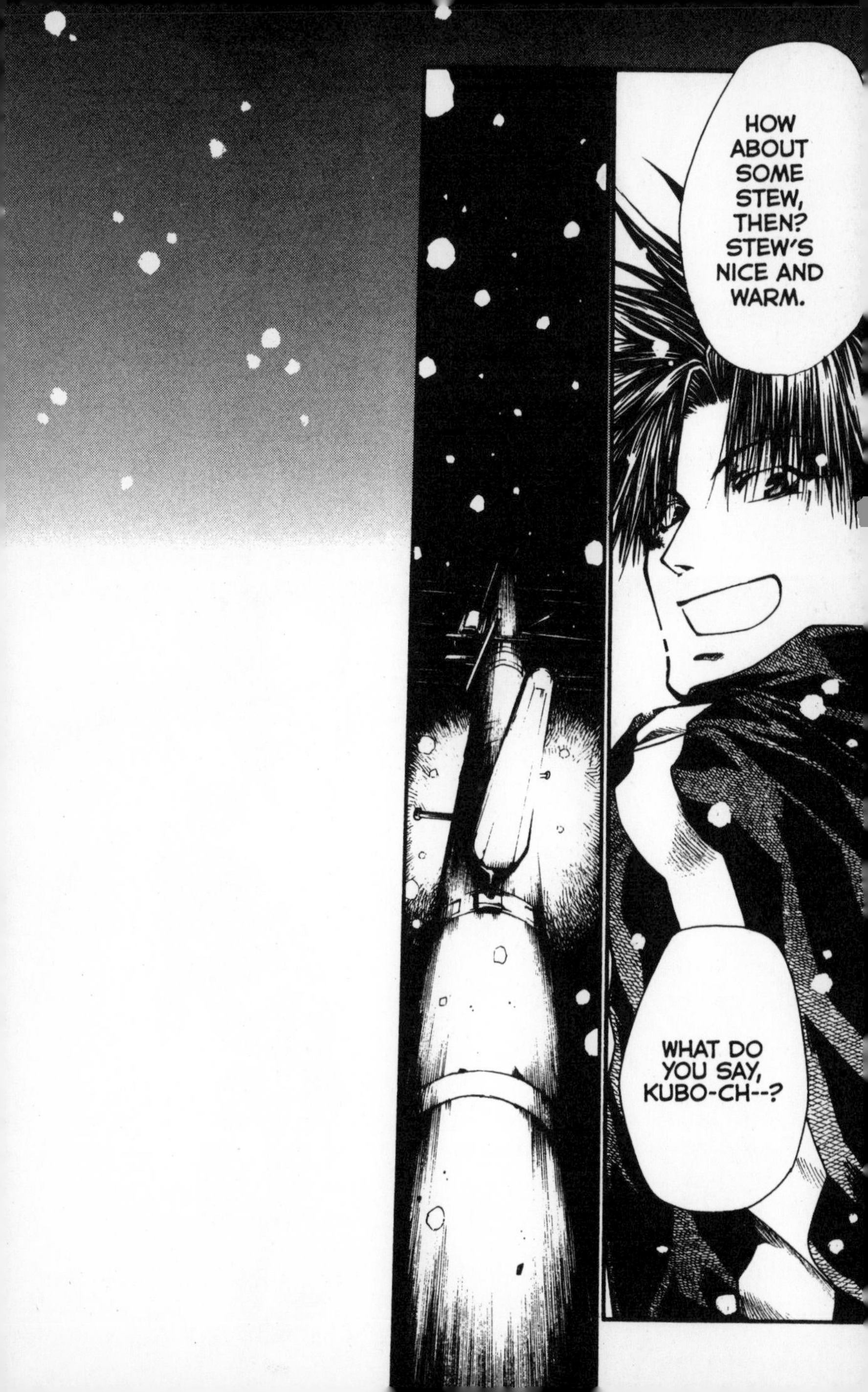
HOW ABOUT SOME STEW, THEN? STEW'S NICE AND WARM.
WHAT DO YOU SAY, KUBO-CH--?

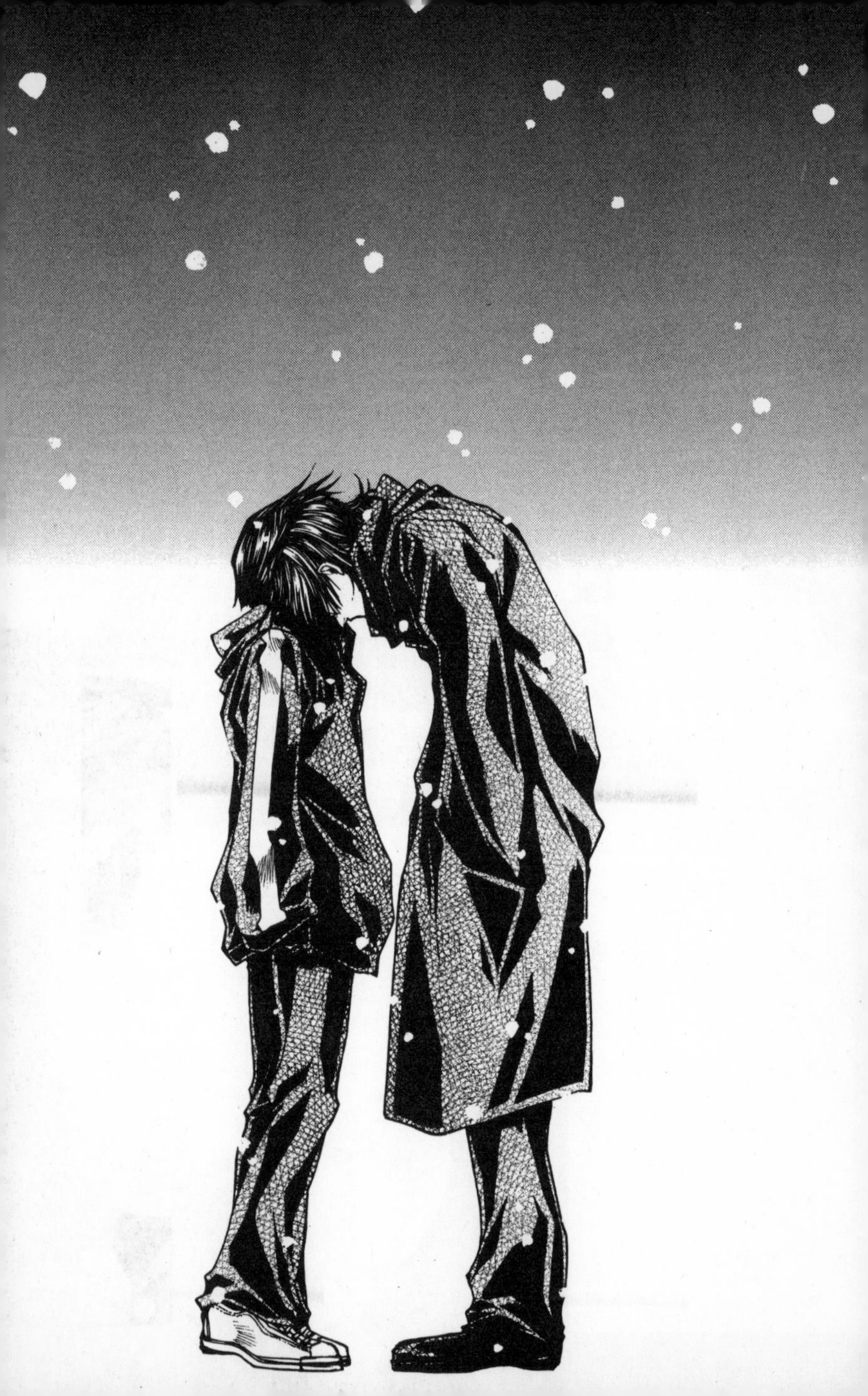

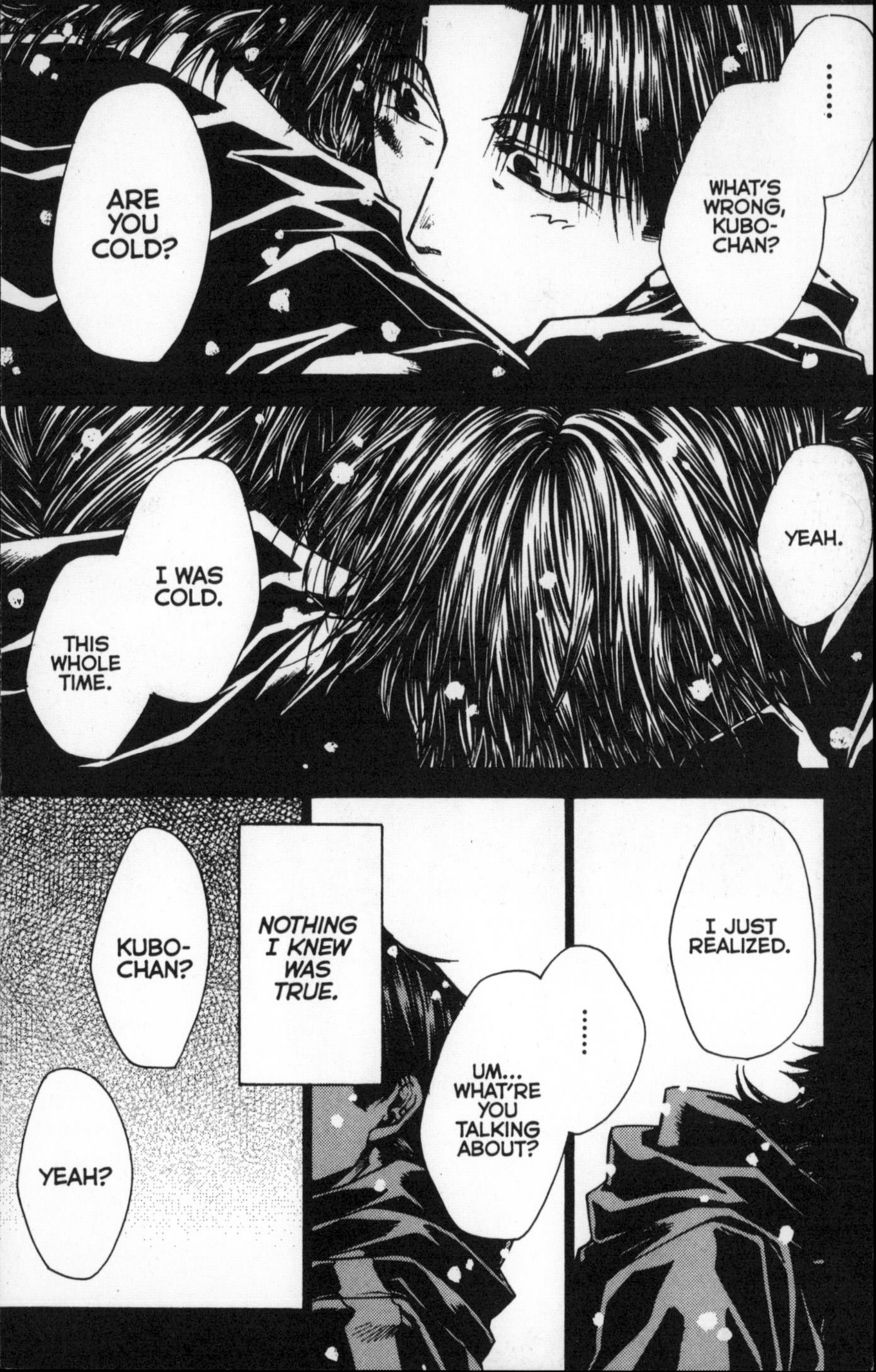
......
WHAT'S WRONG, KUBO-CHAN?
ARE YOU COLD?
YEAH.
I WAS COLD.
THIS WHOLE TIME.
I JUST REALIZED.
......
UM... WHAT'RE YOU TALKING ABOUT?
NOTHING I KNEW WAS TRUE.
KUBO-CHAN?
YEAH?

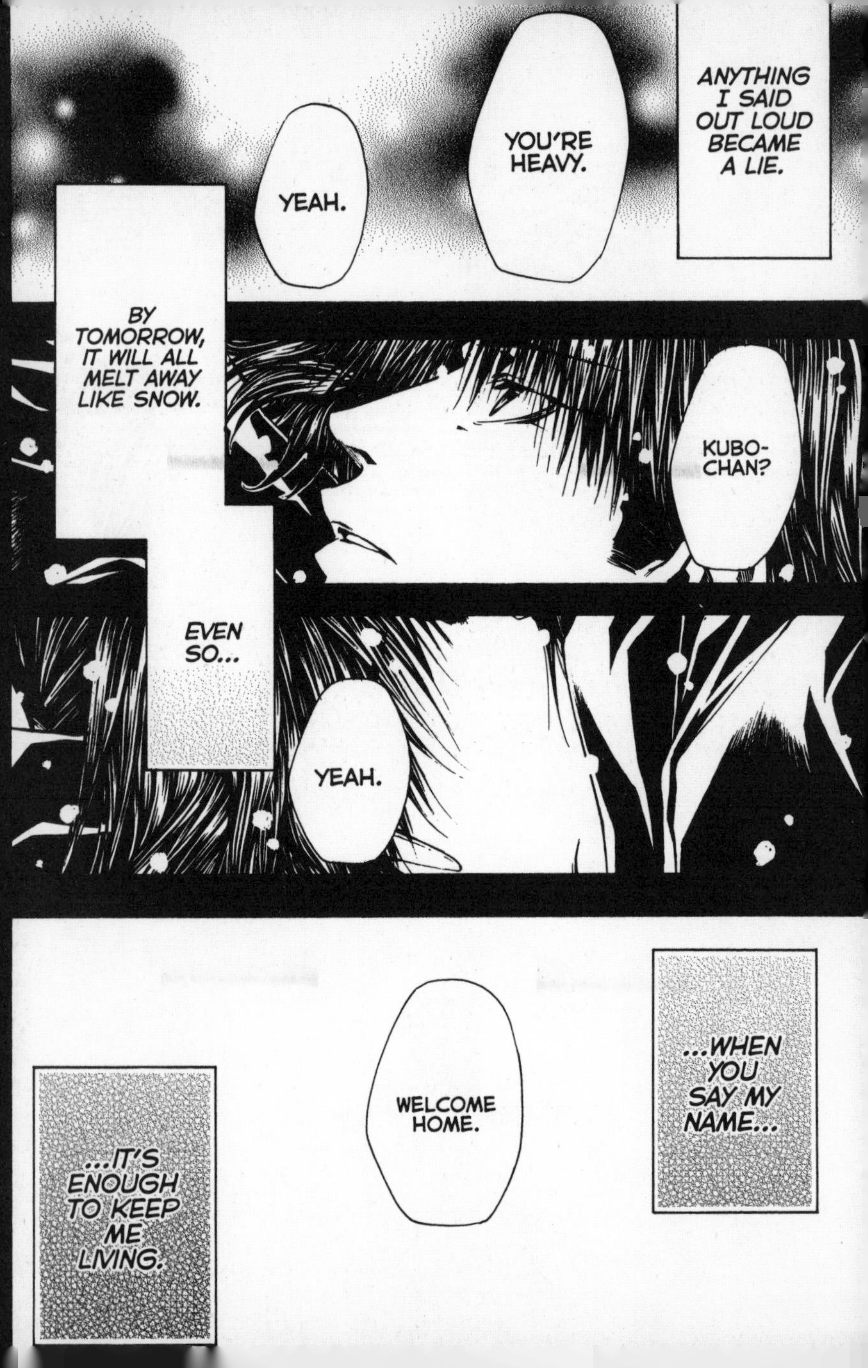
ANYTHING I SAID OUT LOUD BECAME A LIE.
YOU'RE HEAVY.
YEAH.
BY TOMORROW, IT WILL ALL MELT AWAY LIKE SNOW.
KUBO-CHAN?
EVEN SO...
YEAH.
...WHEN YOU SAY MY NAME...
WELCOME HOME.
...IT'S ENOUGH TO KEEP ME LIVING.

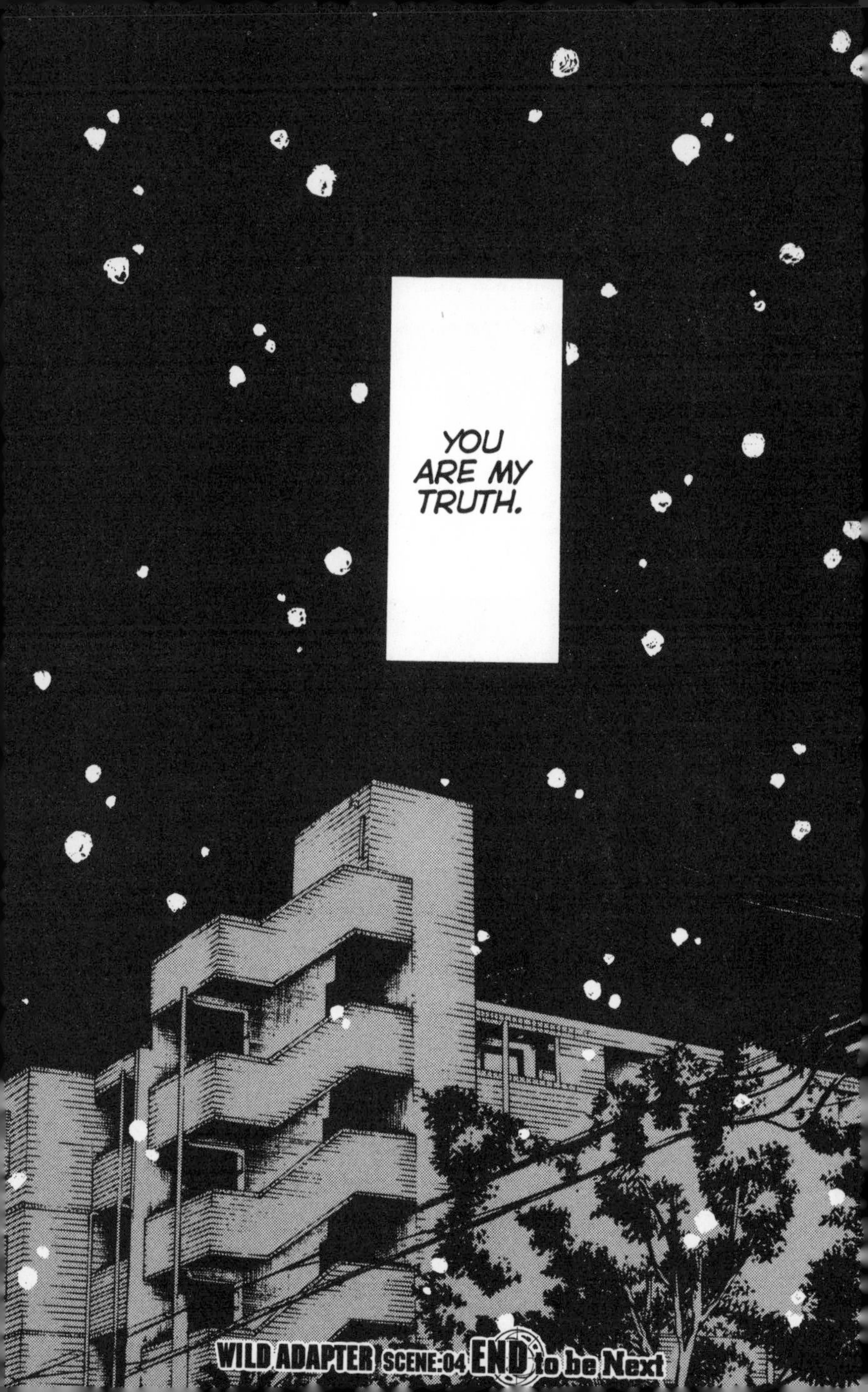
YOU ARE MY TRUTH.
WILD ADAPTER SCENE:04 END to be Next

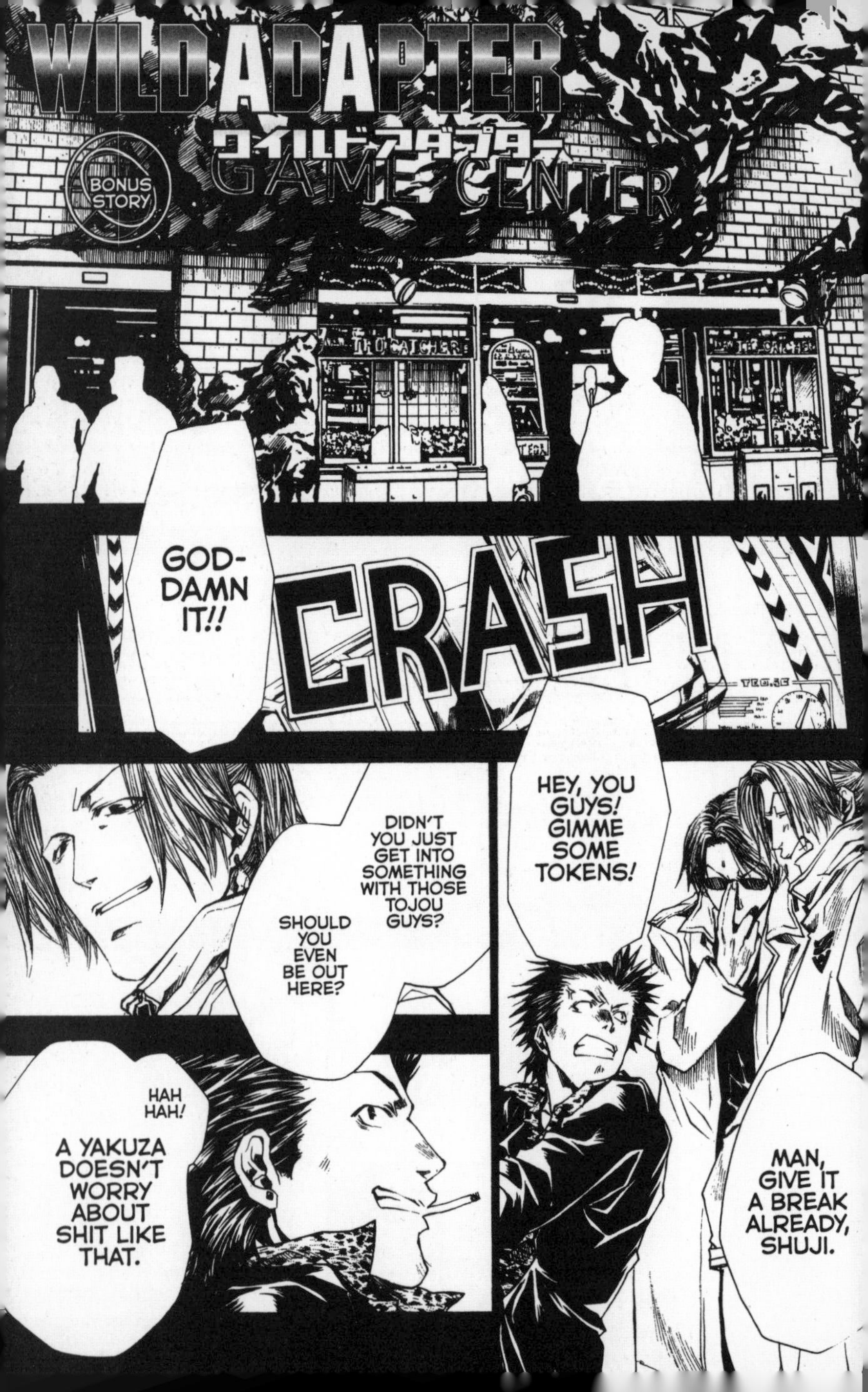
WILD ADAPTER
ワイルドアダプター
BONUS STORY
GAME CENTER
GOD-DAMN IT!!
CRASH
HEY, YOU GUYS! GIMME SOME TOKENS!
MAN, GIVE IT A BREAK ALREADY, SHUJI.
DIDN'T YOU JUST GET INTO SOMETHING WITH THOSE TOJOU GUYS?
SHOULD YOU EVEN BE OUT HERE?
HAH HAH!
A YAKUZA DOESN'T WORRY ABOUT SHIT LIKE THAT.

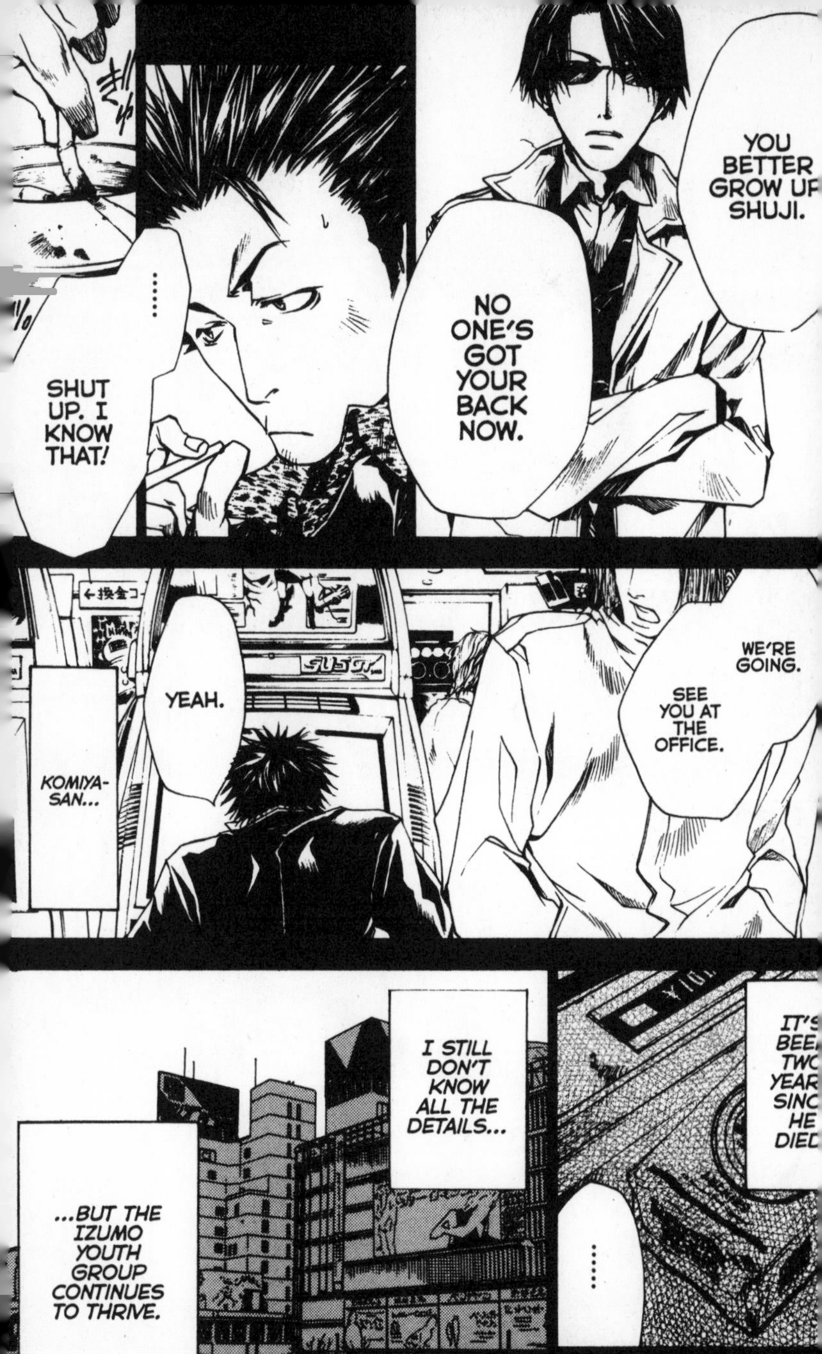
YOU BETTER GROW UP SHUJI.
NO ONE'S GOT YOUR BACK NOW.
......
SHUT UP. I KNOW THAT!
WE'RE GOING.
SEE YOU AT THE OFFICE.
YEAH.
KOMIYA-SAN...
IT'S BEE TWO YEAR SINC HE DIED
......
I STILL DON'T KNOW ALL THE DETAILS...
...BUT THE IZUMO YOUTH GROUP CONTINUES TO THRIVE.

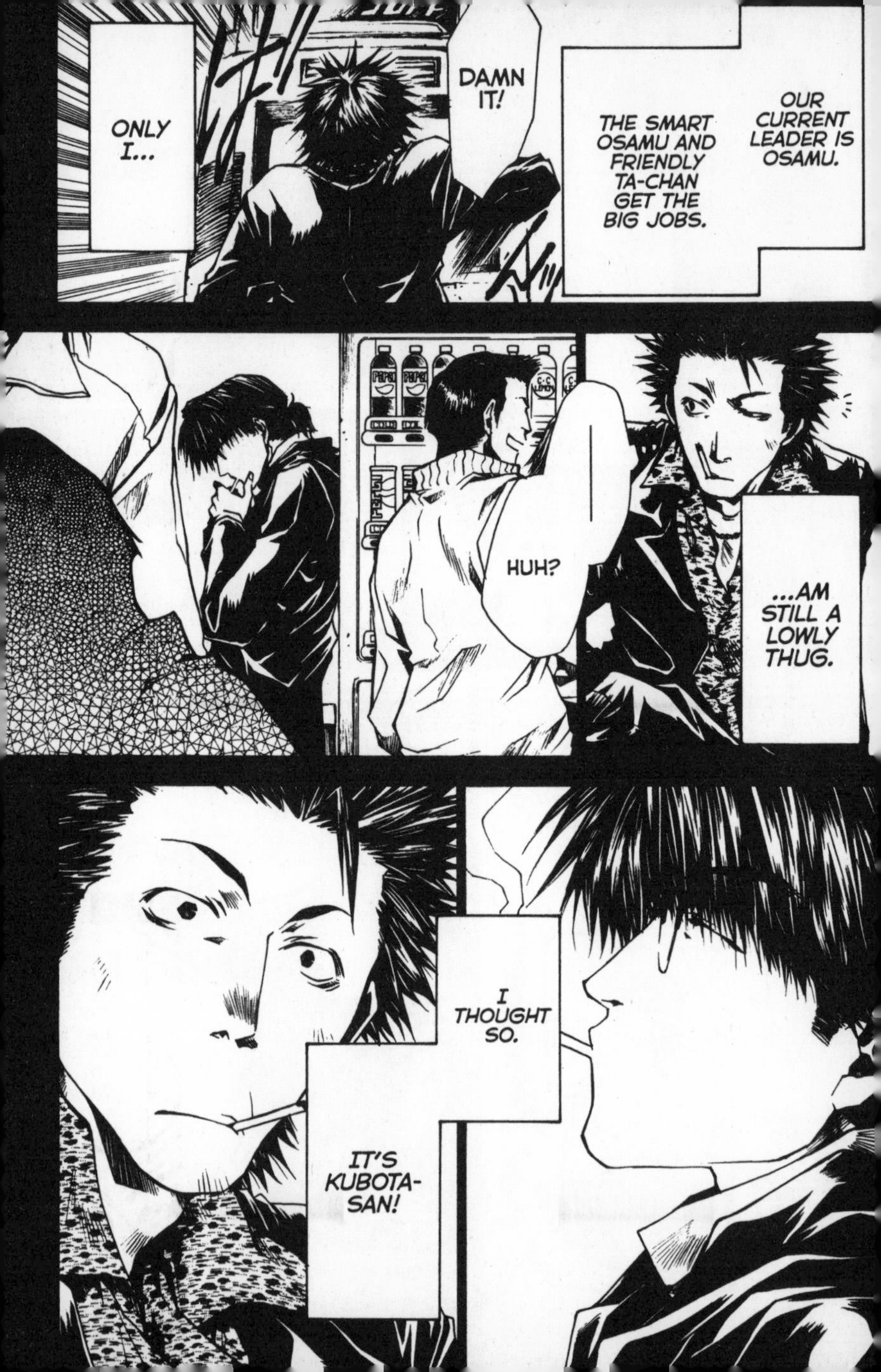
OUR CURRENT LEADER IS OSAMU.
THE SMART OSAMU AND FRIENDLY TA-CHAN GET THE BIG JOBS.
DAMN IT!
ONLY I...
...AM STILL A LOWLY THUG.
HUH?
I THOUGHT SO.
IT'S KUBOTA-SAN!

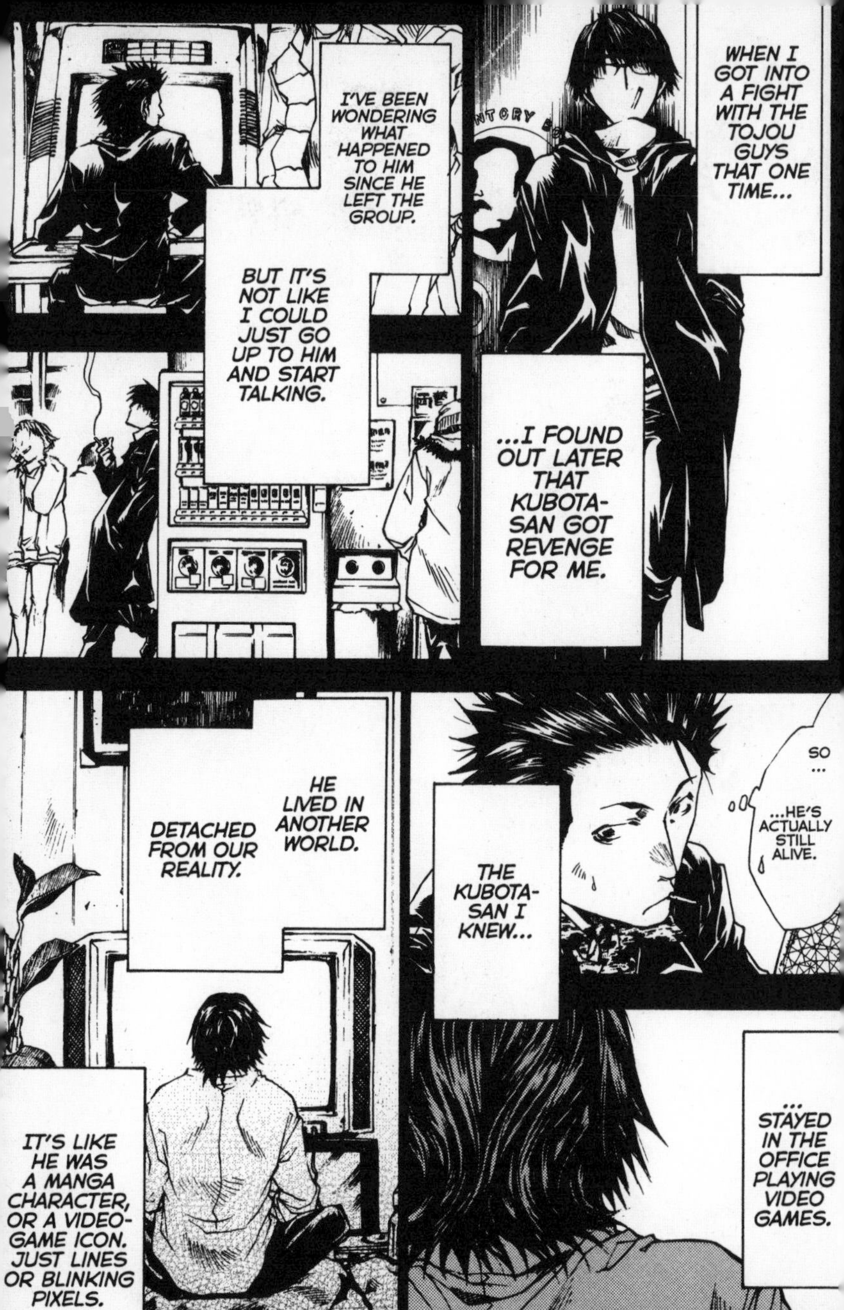
WHEN I GOT INTO A FIGHT WITH THE TOJOU GUYS THAT ONE TIME...
...I FOUND OUT LATER THAT KUBOTA-SAN GOT REVENGE FOR ME.
I'VE BEEN WONDERING WHAT HAPPENED TO HIM SINCE HE LEFT THE GROUP.
BUT IT'S NOT LIKE I COULD JUST GO UP TO HIM AND START TALKING.
SO...
...HE'S ACTUALLY STILL ALIVE.
THE KUBOTA-SAN I KNEW...
...STAYED IN THE OFFICE PLAYING VIDEO GAMES.
HE LIVED IN ANOTHER WORLD.
DETACHED FROM OUR REALITY.
IT'S LIKE HE WAS A MANGA CHARACTER, OR A VIDEO-GAME ICON. JUST LINES OR BLINKING PIXELS.

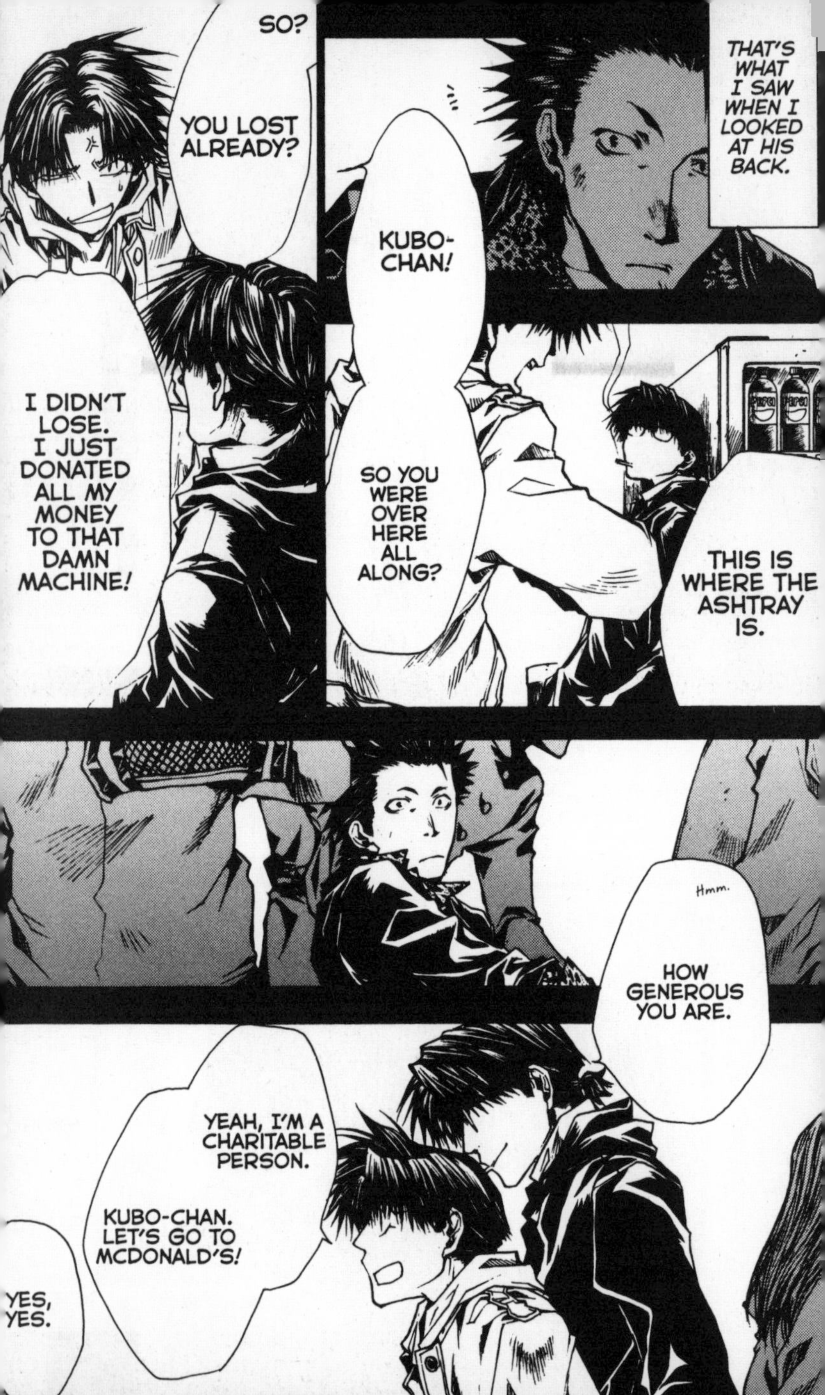
THAT'S WHAT I SAW WHEN I LOOKED AT HIS BACK.
KUBO-CHAN!
SO YOU WERE OVER HERE ALL ALONG?
THIS IS WHERE THE ASHTRAY IS.
SO? YOU LOST ALREADY?
I DIDN'T LOSE. I JUST DONATED ALL MY MONEY TO THAT DAMN MACHINE!
Hmm.
HOW GENEROUS YOU ARE.
YEAH, I'M A CHARITABLE PERSON.
KUBO-CHAN. LET'S GO TO MCDONALD'S!
YES, YES.

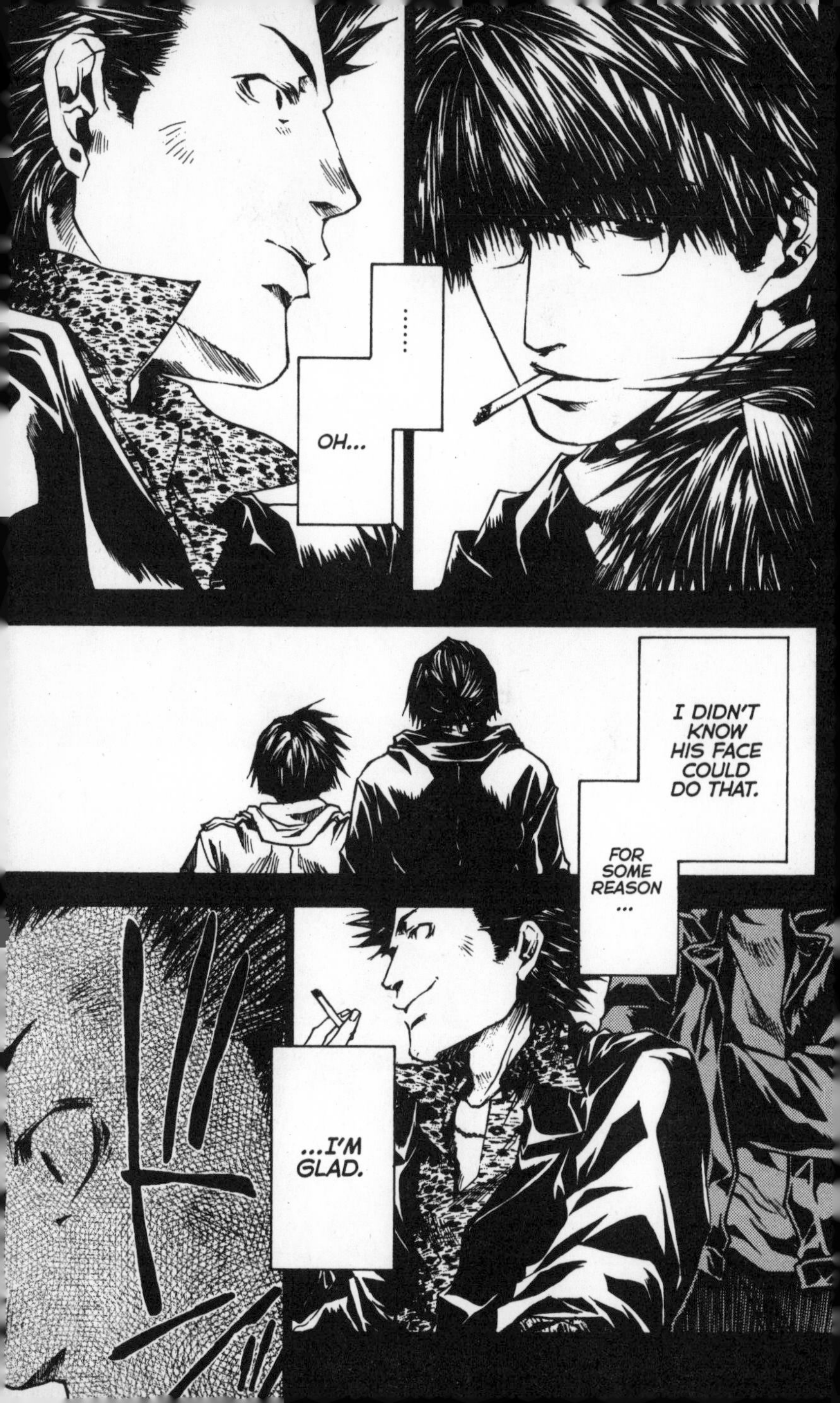
......
OH...
I DIDN'T KNOW HIS FACE COULD DO THAT.
FOR SOME REASON ...
...I'M GLAD.

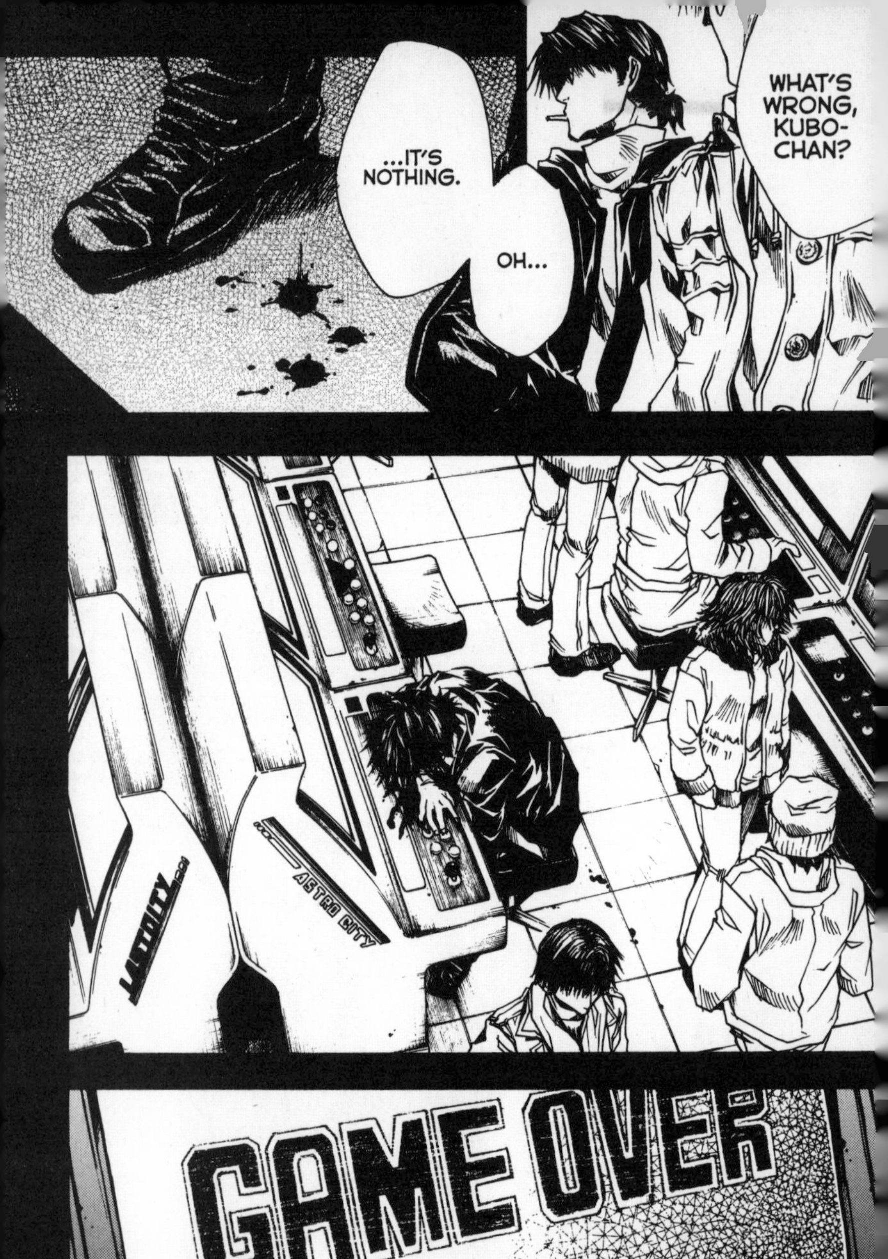
WHAT'S WRONG, KUBO-CHAN?
...IT'S NOTHING.
OH...
ASTRO CITY
GAME OVER

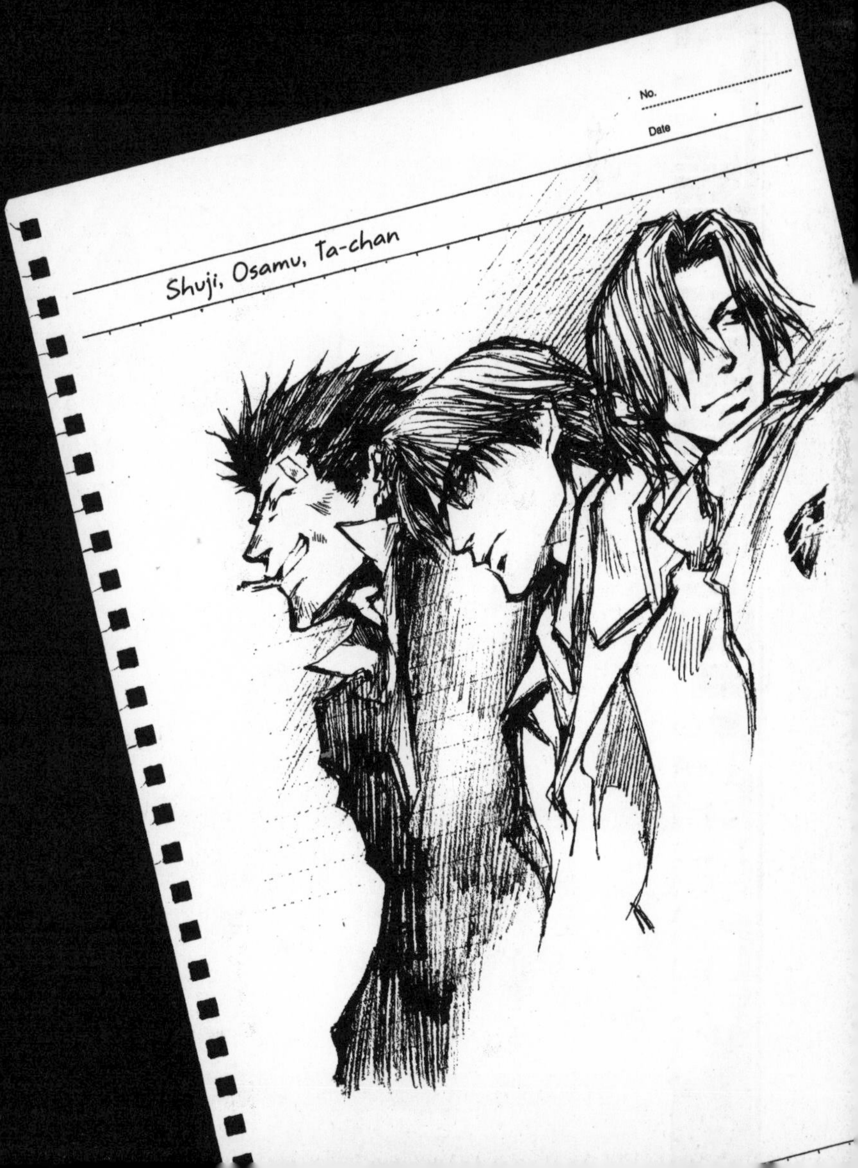
No.
Date
Shuji, Osamu, Ta-chan

ALL STORIES AND PICTURES by

KAZUYA MINEKURA

Assistant

•

KATSUYA SEINO

RIE TAHARA

TAKANO

TOMOMI NISHIYAMA

Total Design

•

HIDEYUKI EBIHARA

Editor

•

KAZUKO OSHIO

Presented by Chara

WILD ADAPTER 04

SCENE:

Do you believe in words?
As soon as you speak it,
words have the power
to make it happen.

ワイルドアダプター— KAZUYA MINEKURA

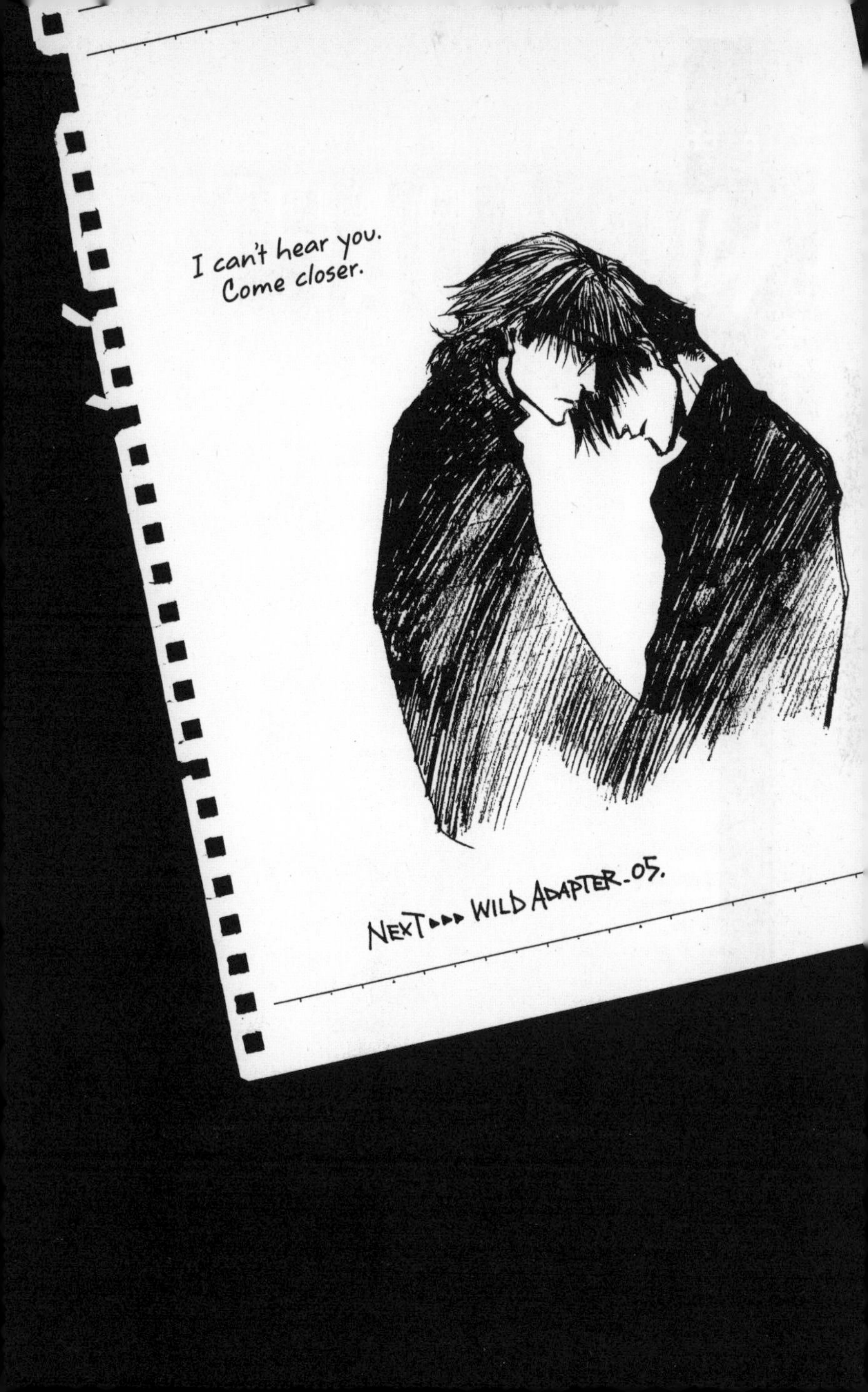
I can't hear you.
Come closer.
NEXT▸▸▸ WILD ADAPTER_05.

In the next volume of

WILD ADAPTER

Pusued by rival yakuza factions and
linked to the mysterious and dangerous
drug "Wild Adapter," the distant
Kubota and prickly Tokito have formed
a relationship where they trust no
one but each other... But just how did
this strange bond come to pass in the
first place? Finally, the missing year
is revealed, and we learn just what
happened after Kubota picked up his
little "stray cat" off the street!